Practical AVR Microcontrollers

Games, Gadgets, and Home Automation with the Microcontroller Used in Arduino

Alan Trevennor

Apress·

Practical AVR Microcontrollers

ISBN-13 (pbk): 978-1-4302-4446-2

ISBN-13 (electronic): 978-1-4302-4447-9

President and Publisher: Paul Manning
Lead Editor: Michelle Lowman
Developmental Editor: Matthew Moodie
Technical Reviewer: Cliff Wootton
Editorial Board: Steve Anglin, Ewan Buckingham, Gary Cornell, Louise Corrigan, Morgan Ertel, Jonathan Gennick, Jonathan Hassell, Robert Hutchinson, Michelle Lowman, James Markham, Matthew Moodie, Jeff Olson, Jeffrey Pepper, Douglas Pundick, Ben Renow-Clarke, Dominic Shakeshaft, Gwenan Spearing, Matt Wade, Tom Welsh
Coordinating Editor: Jill Balzano
Copy Editor: Lori Jacobs
Compositor: SPi Global
Indexer: SPi Global
Artist: SPi Global
Cover Designer: Anna Ishchenko

Distributed to the book trade worldwide by Springer Science + Business Media New York, 233 Spring Street, 6th Floor, New York, NY 10013. Phone 1-800-SPRINGER, fax (201) 348-4505, e-mail orders-ny@springer-sbm.com, or visit www.springeronline.com.

For information on translations, please e-mail rights@apress.com, or visit www.apress.com.

Apress and friends of ED books may be purchased in bulk for academic, corporate, or promotional use. eBook versions and licenses are also available for most titles. For more information, reference our Special Bulk Sales–eBook Licensing web page at www.apress.com/bulk-sales.

Any source code or other supplementary materials referenced by the author in this text is available to readers at www.apress.com. For detailed information about how to locate your book's source code, go to www.apress.com/source-code.

"To Wendy, who made it all possible."

—

Contents at a Glance

Contents

Foreword

The computer-on-a-chip functionality of microcontrollers is nowhere better demonstrated than in the Atmel AVR family. The AVR family offers a huge range of microcontrollers, from very simple devices with limited capabilities to much more complex chips that have numerous built-in features for interconnectivity and interfacing as well as much larger memory capacities—all in a single integrated circuit. Yet, all the AVR family use the same basic execution unit for running programs, which means you can start with the simple members of the AVR family and, when you're ready, graduate to the larger, more complex members without having to relearn how they are programmed.

There are lots of interesting books on AVR microcontrollers around, and like this one, many will tell you how to use your desktop machine as a development platform for making AVR programs. However, most other books focus on AVR programs that flash lights, measure temperatures, make sounds, interface to keypads, and so on. As valuable as those things are (and this book covers many of those areas too) it has always been my hope to find a book that has more of a focus on how to make AVRs actually *do* stuff. I want to make things move or change, to make things *happen* in the real world.

There are books that focus on using microcontrollers to provide the intelligence for robots, which is great, but again, not quite what I had in mind. Maybe I watched too much Thunderbirds and Star Trek as a kid, but it always seemed to me that the potential for microcontrollers goes far beyond merely flashing lights. I always imagined that having some degree of intelligence built into a device that could do useful things, and having that device be able to talk to other intelligent devices—all without human intervention—would result in magic!

Having never found the book I wanted and finding that I now had the space and time to play around with some of my ideas, I set about building a lot of them. Now, I am going to share them in this book.

Even if you don't need or want the gadgets and projects I present here in this book, I'm willing to bet that they will spark some of your own ideas and that you'll be able to use many of the concepts and techniques described here to make your own ideas become realities.

That's one major reason for writing this book, to spread the joy! It has been my key learning in creating this book (and yet more stuff that hasn't made it into this one) that the limitless possibilities of the microcontroller stimulate creativity like you may never have experienced before. Another, bigger, reason is that this is Fun, and that's an intentional capital "F"!

It's also worth saying that there are more and more jobs opening up that involve product and project engineering using embedded microcontrollers: if you look you'll see them going on in every sector; from the automotive industry to the defense industries to the entertainment business, they are all finding a tidal wave of applications for microcontrollers. So, if you're of a mind to seek a career using the technology, nothing you learn from within these pages should be wasted.

Alan Trevennor
North Cornwall
United Kingdom
August 2012.

About the Author

Alan Trevennor Alan originally wanted to work in music radio. However, after getting hooked on digital electronics via a Science of Cambridge MK14 computer kit, Alan Trevennor joined the UK computer industry in 1980 as a hardware engineer, fixing DEC PDP-11 systems.

In the 1980s he wrote hardware-related books about operating systems and Amstrad computers. He progressed to systems engineering and became a key member of DEC's UK Unix support team. He created and taught many training courses and user guides for DEC's Unix-related products, RISC computers, TCP/IP networking, and other subjects. He also contributed technical articles to many magazines.

In the 1990s Alan migrated to being a digital media solutions architect with Compaq and then HP. From then until he left HP in 2009, Alan worked on digital media technical solutions and business consultancies. He worked for customers as diverse as the BBC, Reuters, Allied Domecq Leisure, BT, Music Choice, The National Trust, RBS, Glaxo, Virgin Radio, and Nokia. Coming full circle, he later spent a great deal of time in music radio stations as part of a team working on a joint HP/Nokia project—Visual Radio. During an incredibly varied career Alan has created numerous technical solutions (some using AVR microcontrollers) as well as large amounts of user training materials and documentation.

Alan now lives in Cornwall, UK, with his wife and son. He runs a "hobby" business part time and works full time as a technical author for Microtest, a creator and supplier of advanced medical software—based in Cornwall.

About the Technical Reviewer

Cliff Wootton Cliff Wootton is a former Interactive TV systems architect at BBC News.

The "News Loops" service developed there was nominated for a BAFTA and won a Royal Television Society Award for Technical Innovation. He is an invited speaker on pre-processing for video compression at the Apple WWDC conference. He also taught postgraduate MA students about real-world computing, multimedia, video compression, metadata, and researching the deployment of next-generation interactive TV systems based on open standards.

He is currently working on R&D projects investigating new interactive TV technologies, involved with MPEG standards working groups, writing more books on the topic, and speaking at conferences when not lecturing on multimedia at the University of the Arts in London.

Acknowledgments

This book is the product of so many overlapping things that I hesitate to enumerate them all. However, I also hesitate to water it down to basics with an "everyone who knows me" type of generality. So, let me try to steer a middle course.

Special thanks to Wendy for her patience while life went on hold during the writing of this book, and also for letting me use our home to try out my ideas—and being so encouraging about them. Special thanks also to Laurence for his technically appreciative feedback, ideas, and inputs.

To the team at Apress—thank you. To Michelle Lowman who kicked it all off, to Jill Balzano who had the unenviable job of bringing it all together to a tight timescale. To Matthew Moodie who—as technical editor—contributed so much to the structure and content of the book. To Cliff Wootton who as technical reviewer contributed greatly to making the book more understandable and generously contributed ideas of his own for me to adopt. Also, thanks to Lori Jacobs who—as copy editor—made the text much more readable and understandable by spotting mistakes and inconsistencies; things that I would never have spotted if I'd looked at the text for a million years!

In the more general sense, I need to thank Reece Fitzhardy who—all those years ago—freely gave of his knowledge and time to get me to the point where the TTL data book no longer looked like gibberish to me! I thank Alf-Egil Bogen and Vegard Wollan, originators of the AVR architecture, and Atmel who gave it wings!

I thank the folks at Maplin UK, Sparkfun US, and Aaron and the support team at Pololu who have given me help and information whenever I asked for it.

I thank the many thousands of people—but of course most especially the core team—who created something truly remarkable and revolutionary in the Arduino hardware and software.

Also . . . but I'd better stop there. Sorry if I forgot anyone important!

Introduction

The microcontroller unit (MCU) is the ultimate electronics tinker-toy, and in this book you're going to see how to tinker away with it to your heart's delight! My intended audience for this book is those who like to learn hands-on. Learning by doing and seeing has always been my preferred way to learn: If it's yours too, let's take the ride together. For those who like to understand the "why" first of all, the book also includes some background material that explains why using microcontrollers in everyday situations can be such a powerful concept.

My only assumption is that you have some very basic knowledge of digital electronics. But, if that's *not* you, don't worry! There are some appendixes that will give you the start that you need—and the book's web site (and various references through the text of the book) also point you to some valuable AVR MCU-related online resources.

MCU Basics

I'll start with a summary of the absolute basics, just in case you're new in MCU town, if you're not, feel free to skip to the next section. A microcontroller is truly a "computer on a chip."

For straightforward applications such as making LEDs flash, or driving a simple clock display, it's likely that you would only need just one MCU (Microcontroller Unit) chip. For more complex applications (such as those in some of the project chapters of this book) you often need to add helper chips, but the MCU still does all the brainwork.

There are dozens of different microcontroller types on the market (PIC/PICAXE, Intel, ARM, Philips/NXP, Toshiba, Panasonic, and many more) and they all have strengths and weaknesses.

The AVR[1] family of MCUs from Atmel Corporation has become one of the most available and capable general-purpose MCU product sets—and via platforms like the Arduino (more of which later on) has reached a market prominence in the low-cost MCU world. AVR also compares favorably on cost with other low or mid-range microcontroller families.

Microcontrollers evolved partially from the digital memory chips industry and partly from the simpler microprocessors that they have now largely displaced for new designs. We'll be looking at the evolution of the microcontroller in more detail in the first section of this book.

Every AVR MCU consists of a processor core, some programmable flash memory, and some RAM. It will also have on-chip extras, such as input/output (I/O) ports, timers, serial communications ports, analog to digital convertors, and maybe even a USB port.

All chips in the AVR range have the basic processor core and memory, but as you go up the range of products they include more and more of the extras (and bigger and bigger on-chip memory capacities). Using the simplest of AVR MCU chips (a small eight-pin device costing no more than a dollar; see the photo) you can easily make an LED flasher or other simple circuits.

---

[1] Weirdly, nobody at Atmel wants to tell what the initials AVR stand for. In fact, the guys who invented AVR, Alf Egil Bogen and Vegard Wollan, tease anyone who asks the question! Was it a combination of their initials? No, they say. They even made a teasing video. Search for "The Story of AVR" on youtube to see it.

I mentioned Arduino previously. Arduino is a packaged MCU system that uses an AVR chip at its heart but provides extra facilities such as bringing all the I/O pins of the MCU out to convenient connectors, providing voltage regulation, and so on. We now live in a world where a majority of people are used to using a computer at a high level, using a Windows, Mac, or Linux machine. However, the essential aim of Arduino is to make it easy for non-techs and beginners to try out low-level computing and computer programming for the first time. Low-level computing may use essentially the same technology as your desktop machine, but it's a very different beast.

Arduino is a superb platform, and the software development environment that comes with it is also excellent. However, an Arduino board will cost you between three and four times as much as just an AVR chip, and very few individual projects use all the features of an Arduino board.

So, in many projects it can be beneficial to use just a stand-alone AVR chip with a minimum of external components, and that will be our concentration in this book. As a subsidiary benefit, you will also be more likely to gain a deeper understanding of the AVR from using it outside a packaged hardware environment such as Arduino.

About Our MCU Setup

For many readers, this book will contain a lot of new stuff. To make it easier to assimilate, I have elected to use the Arduino software development environment throughout the book. Arduino's development software (which is 100% free for anyone to download and use) runs on Windows, Linux, and Mac OS X: For the most part, the Arduino software looks and feels the same on them all. So, using Arduino's development environment has the added benefit that you won't be skipping great chunks of the book that don't apply to the machine you are using. Arduino's programming language is very easy to use—another benefit if you're new to all this.

Since this is not primarily a book about programming, we will only be going beneath the covers of the Arduino software when we really have to; that won't be very often, but it will be fully explained when we do. So, although we'll be using the Arduino software, there won't be an Arduino board in sight! We'll use a low-cost AVR programmer board and AVR chips—often we'll be using just the AVR chip on its own.

Note Atmel has an excellent (and free) development package of its own, "AVR Studio," which lets you program in the C language, or in AVR native assembler.[2] But at the time of writing it's only available on Windows PCs (XP or later)—inexplicably, there is no Mac or Linux version. So, we don't use it in this book.

---

[2]Assembly language programming is a very low level way of programming, requiring far more knowledge of the intricate details of the chip you are programming and its characteristics. Assembly language programs can often run a little faster on a given processor, but they take very much longer to write and debug than higher-level programming methods like the ones we use in this book.

Putting AVRs to Work

While an AVR is a single-chip computer, it doesn't have anything approaching the capability of your desktop machine—which costs many tens of times more. Therefore, it makes sense to use the greater capabilities, resources, and power of your desktop computer to create the software that an AVR needs and then to download that software into the AVR chip. The following diagram overviews how this works.

On your desktop machine, you install an AVR development environment (all free) which lets you create and compile your AVR software. An AVR programmer (several available) simply connects via USB to your desktop and uses a technique called in-system programming (ISP) to connect to your AVR chip and upload the software you have created into it. I'll go into much more detail and provide a shopping list in Chapter 2.

Note   In this book we'll be using your AVR plugged into a specially set up breadboard (see Appendix C for a basic tutorial on breadboards). However, in other approaches the AVR could be plugged into a circuit board or even a full-scale AVR programmer product.

So, the preceding diagram represents the development environment we will be using throughout this book. It's important to understand that because the AVR family uses erasable and reusable on-chip memory, you can reprogram AVR chips tens of thousands of times if you need to, which means you can keep modifying your program until it's exactly how you want it. Once you have your software exactly right, your AVR chip can be detached forever from the programmer and can go off to have a life of its own in a dedicated application.

In this book we'll be looking at practical examples of how to use useful project elements (such as motors, solenoids, and sensors of various kinds) and software concepts. Then, we'll be making a set of project applications for AVR chips. After you've seen the descriptions and built some of these project applications for yourself, I'm willing to bet that your own application ideas will come thick and fast. It seems that AVRs (and MCUs in general) have that effect on creative minds!

Book Structure

This book is split into two major sections, each of which is further subdivided into smaller sections.

Part 1: Basics

Part 1 deals with the background and the basics. You may already know a lot of this stuff, or you may just be itching to get started with the practical side of things, so feel free to skip any sections that lie outside your area of interest or experience.

We all learn in different ways, and a lot of the stuff in this section is intended for those people who learn better by first understanding "why" things are valuable and "why" one way of doing things is better than another. If you're a "how" learner, you'll probably want to just skim through some bits of Part 1 which deal with history and theory and get onto the more practical sections. If you're going to do that, though, please be sure not to skip the section on setting up your development environment; we'll all need to look at that!

All through Part 1, we will be gently introducing programming, showing you how to program the AVR with some minimal programs that are fully explained so that if you've never programmed before, you'll get the introduction you need.

Part 2: The Projects

Part 2 of this book is all about specific projects using AVRs. These are projects you can build or adapt to your own needs. This section of the book covers a mix of digital electronics, a little lightweight "making" for the controlled mechanisms, software details, and, of course, lots about AVR microcontroller applications.

For each project we'll look at the design of the hardware and any mechanisms needed, discussing any trade-offs and possible adaptations or alternative uses for it. We'll overview the software for the project, detailing any tricky parts of it. The fully commented software will all be available for download from the book's web site: http://www.apress.com/9781430244462.

Photographs and diagrams are used to give you as much detail as possible on each project as built, so that you can build one for yourself if you want to or adapt it to your own needs when you make your own version of it.

Following is a list of the projects:

- Chapter 8: "Good Evening, Mr. Bond: Your Secret Panel." Shows how to build a sliding panel mechanism and control it with an AVR. What's behind the panel? Well, wait and see, but I bet you'll soon have your own ideas about what you want behind *your* secret panel, and what secret way you want to be able to open it!

- Chapter 9: "Crazy Beams—Exercise Your Pet!" Cats (and dogs too) are fascinated by moving beams of light, and they get great exercise chasing them around the room. This project gives them all the beams they could ever want to chase, and it never gets tired of playing the game with them!

- Chapter 10: "WordDune: How Much Do You Really See?" We all like to think we could find a needle in a sand dune. Can you find words in a sea of letters? It starts easy, but it gets harder as it goes on.

- Chapter 11: "The Lighting Waterfall: Light the Way—Ever So Prettily!" Don't just "plip" those lights on in that long thin walkway, let's do it with some style!

- Chapter 12: "Moving to Mesmerize":

  - Moiré wheel: Put a light behind a spinning wheel and watch the magic!

  - Animation projector: Flashing LEDs can make shadow magic.

  - Duck shooting game: All the fun of the fair!

- Chapter 13: "Smart Home Enablers." We examine just why the "home of the future" has been so very long in arriving! We look at some get-started foundational projects and ideas that can help make yours a "smarter home."

Appendixes

Finally, we have a number of reference appendixes. These are intended for those "wazzat?" moments, when you encounter an unfamiliar term, technique, or concept. To save time and confusion, readers who are completely new to a subject area might want to read one or more of these before starting on the projects.

- Appendix A: Common Components: Some basics about resistors, capacitors, diodes, LEDs, and integrated circuits (chips).

- Appendix B: "A Digital Electronics Primer." New to the world of digital electronics? Never fear, this appendix is just for you. It won't make you into an overnight digital wizard, but it should give you just enough to get started.

- Appendix C: "Breadboards." What are they, what are they for, how do you use them and why are they so darn useful?

- Appendix D: "Serial Communications." Often puzzling to newcomers, serial communications is a must-understand technology for realizing the full benefits of connected MCU projects.

Where Do We Go from Here?

It's essential that you read Chapter 2 in order to set up your AVR development system. However, after that, if you feel that you already know enough it's not essential that you following any particular reading order: if one subject area appeals to you most, by all means go there first if you feel you already have the knowledge (or are happy to refer back to previously skipped sections).

Make maximum use of the detailed keyword index if you come across the unfamiliar—and don't forget the appendixes, which are there for your reference.

Coming Up Next

Part 1: Chapter 1: "A Brief History of Microcontrollers"—the computer industry takes a RISC.

The Basics

CHAPTER 1

■ ■ ■

A Brief History of Microcontrollers

Although it's not essential that you understand how microcontrollers developed to the point where they are today, it's an interesting story, which can help you understand where an AVR microcontroller fits into the overall hierarchy of information technology (IT) and electronics products. More important, by having such an understanding you can make better choices and decisions about when and where to use a microcontroller, in preference to other alternatives.

If you open up a CD player or a VCR from the 1980s (perhaps you have one in the attic, or in your garage, I know I do!) you will find that they are absolutely stuffed with circuit boards, and that each circuit board is densely populated with integrated circuits (chips) and components that made the thing work.

By contrast, open up a DVD player made in the last few years and you are likely to find quite a lot of empty space, and just one quite small circuit board that contains perhaps two or three quite large chips and a handful of other components. Yet, it's probable that the modern device offers far better quality and robustness. It will certainly offer massively more product features and options than its 1980s predecessor.

This transformation is due to two main factors:

- The increasing miniaturization of electronics and components, which has enabled more and more circuitry to be put onto single chips, reducing the chip count needed for any given function.

  The transistors in the first family of logic chips (launched in the early 1970s) each measured about 10 microns[1] across. Just to give you some idea of scale, a human hair averages about 100 microns in width. At the time of writing this, in 2012, the size of transistors on current generation chips can be as small as 22 nanometers. That's just 22 billionths of a meter! That gives you some idea of the pace of miniaturization that has gone on inside integrated circuits since the 1970s.

- The progressive transition from implementing device functions in hardware to implementing them in software running on microcontrollers.

Let's start with a quick timeline before getting into the whys and wherefores of microcontrollers and AVR.

---

[1]A micron (now more often called a micro-meter) is one millionth part of a meter, or about 0.0000394 inches.

A Microcontroller Timeline

Until the mid-1980s most electronic products were still built using extremely intricate and clever combinatory logic[2] circuits, implemented with an awful lot of chips! Starting in the early 1980s, a minority of manufacturers started to build in microprocessors to their products in order to reduce chip count, which brought down manufacturing costs and thus reduced end-user prices.

The earliest 8-bit microprocessors such as the Intel 8080 or the Zilog Z80 first appeared toward the late 1970s and were a significant advance on what had gone before. Engineers and designers soon realized that once you put a microprocessor into a device, you could not only make it do much more, but you could also update it much more cheaply if defects or flaws in the original design came to light. Many product defects could now be addressed by using semiskilled labor to plug in a replacement firmware ROM (read-only memory) (this was in the days before programmable flash memory) rather than having to use skilled labor to expensively rework or replace thousands of complete circuit boards. As the 1980s wore on, more and more products had a microprocessor at their core.

Even though microprocessors were a huge improvement on what they replaced, they weren't a complete magic bullet for bringing down costs and complexity of product design. The problem was that, to make a microprocessor do anything useful, it had to be surrounded by a large number of additional chips for input output (I/O) and it usually needed other support chips too–such as real-time clock chips and address decoders.

By the 1990s, improved silicon processing and chip manufacturing techniques resulted in the ability to put ever more circuitry on one chip. One of the ways this was used was to augment the microprocessor chip with additional functions and features that had previously been implemented by separate external chips. To differentiate these new super-micro chips from their simpler forebears, these came to be called microcontrollers. Some examples of functions that moved from being external chips to being part of the microcontroller are

- Serial ports to enable the subsystem to talk to a desktop computer or other RS232 port-equipped devices.

- Timers to enable the microcontroller to have an accurate time reference on chip and to carry out events at accurate preset intervals. These timers also enabled microcontrollers to generate music and sounds, since interval accuracy could be assured.

- Serial digital channels to enable microcontrollers to chat with one another, over just two linking wires.

- Analog to digital convertors allowing a microcontroller system to sense analog signals and store or process them as digital data.

- Digital to analog convertors that allowed microcontrollers to interface with external devices like motors that need a continuously variable voltage.

- Input ports for sensing on/off states of things in the outside world.

- Output ports for switching on/off things in the outside world.

---

[2]Combinatory logic circuits use individual chips in combination to provide each function. For example, in a microcontroller project that controls ten motors for an industrial process, we would use a software counter for each motor to count how many times it had turned. In the combinatory logic implementation of the same thing, there would have to be an actual counter chip for each motor sensor. So, in a microcontroller approach to this function, a whole board full of counter chips could be replaced by perhaps 20 lines of software. This would reduce cost, power consumption, heat generation, and size. Furthermore, if the design were updated, in the combinatory approach, rewiring and very likely redesigning of the board would be needed. In the microcontroller approach a simple software update would attain the same result.

Once microcontrollers started to be designed into consumer goods and control systems during the 1990s, the already impressive electronic miniaturizations of the previous two decades took another big jump, in terms of both size reductions and the ability to sport more options and features than ever before.

By the first decade of the 2000s, nobody would seriously consider designing anything other than the very simplest consumer electrical device without the use of some kind of microcontroller. They are everywhere; they get more capable and more complex as time goes on. As a technical person, unless you understand microcontrollers at some level, you will be at a considerable disadvantage compared to those who do.

Why Microcontrollers?

The ubiquity of microcontrollers is the main reason you should know something about them. However, it's also very satisfying to use and design with microcontrollers. You can get things running very quickly that previously would have taken very much longer to complete. You can also have a considerable amount of fun in the process, and what's life without a little fun? The AVR family of microcontrollers is a wide ranging and cost-effective way to implement your projects. The ever-growing popularity of AVRs means that there is an enormous and very active online support community to help you out if you get stuck. It also means that there is a massive amount of free AVR software available that makes your projects far easier and faster to complete.

Why Should You Learn About Microcontrollers?

To answer this question simply: Because they are fun! The fascination of what you can do and what you can make with them is never ending. It has been rightly said that the computer is the ultimate tinker toy: you can use it an infinite number of ways to enhance your job, your learning, your hobby, or your social life. The value of microcontrollers is that they allow you to extend the benefits of computing into the real world.

You probably already own quite a few microcontrollers without knowing it. They are embedded in most of the appliances and devices around you.[3] Anyone who wants a real understanding of how modern products work–from cars to mobile phones to toys–needs to have at least a rudimentary understanding of microcontrollers.

What Can You Do with a Microcontroller?

Okay, well here's the heart of the matter. Desktop computers (PCs and Macs) are excellent–they are truly a wonder of the age. In concert with the Internet, the desktop computer you buy from the store can do just about anything you want with digital information.

The desktop computer is essentially a resource-rich computer for reliably processing and storing information in a networked world. It can do many things at once (e.g., check your e-mails, and do virus checking while you are browsing the news online) because it is running a complex operating system that is capable of multitasking on a scale that is *truly* (to use that overused word accurately for a change) awesome[4]—what we see on the screen is only the tip of the iceberg of the work going on inside the machine.

Having said that, a modern desktop computer has a central processor running at something around an unimaginable 3 billion cycles per second, and many processors have a multicore architecture, meaning that they are capable of executing two, or even four, sets of instructions streams at this speed, simultaneously! Your modern desktop machine is likely to have a hard drive inside offering at the very least 500 gigabytes (that's

---

[3]Thus, you will often find microcontrollers referred to as embedded computers, and the software they run is often generically called embedded software.

[4]Did you know, for example, that both Linux and Windows update their time clock and the statistics for all the running tasks and certain other internal data at least 100 times . . . per second?

500,000,000,000 bytes) of storage, and it probably has a RAM (random-access memory) of 2 gigabytes or more. So, in computing terms, it is a resource-rich machine. Alan Turing himself could not have wished for more.

Want to edit a video? No problem. Find out who your great, great, great, great, great grandfather was? Yes, can do! Want to send an e-mail to the other side of the world in just a few minutes? Yes of course, tell you what, let's make it one minute! Want to index your family photo collection? Shazam! It's done. Want to play hi-def movies? Let's do it!

The reason desktop machines have evolved into these monstrous–and comparatively expensive–computers is that they are general-purpose machines. The capabilities of even a low-end desktop machine are now so high that you could use it for any of the previously mentioned information management tasks without any problem, but in its default state it's actually quite poor at interfacing with the real world.

But: Do you want to be notified when your freezer fails? Want to intelligently control the speed of a fast running motor? Want to implement a control system for deriving electricity from the rainwater running down from your roof gutters? Hmmm, no, that's a bit trickier–your out-of-the-box desktop computer can't do that without adding on quite a lot of extras.

The dirty little secret about modern desktop machines is that most of them barely ever break into a canter. Graphical compilation (compressing and encoding videos, 3D game compiling, etc.) are among the most demanding tasks that a desktop PC can be set to do, and comparatively few of them are ever used for these things. Playing full-screen video is probably the most challenging thing that most desktops are asked to do, and almost any modern machine can do that and still have processing power to spare. So, it's fairly clear that much more mundane computing tasks really don't need that huge amount of processing power.

The desktop computer in your house (statistically you are likely to have more than one, by the way) is the de facto "home hub" for IT in your house. But, as we saw, there are "real world" tasks that are actually beyond this general-purpose behemoth. It's very good at processing information, but in its default state it's useless at interfacing with other devices in the real world. Enter microcontrollers.

On paper, a microcontroller looks like a very poor relation to that desktop machine of yours. It will have a processor that runs at only small a fraction (perhaps a 300th) of the one on your desktop, and it's unlikely to have more than a fraction of the memory capacity. It doesn't have inbuilt support for interfacing to hard drives and you can't just plug it in to the Internet.

On the other hand, you can get a midrange microcontroller chip for the price of a Skinny Latte and you can build a complete microcontroller system for rather less than the price of a business lunch. The microcontroller will have inputs and outputs suitable for use with real-world devices, and with a little effort, it can talk to your desktop's serial or USB ports.

So, here's how it pans out:

- Use your desktop computer for general-purpose big-world stuff, Internet, e-mail, downloading and playing video, word processing, printing stuff, instant messaging, social networking, building photo libraries, editing photos, and . . . you get the picture. The standard USB and serial ports on your desktop machine can also be used to talk to external microcontroller systems, to allow it access to real-world data, and to be the brain that controls real-world stuff like heaters and motors and lights.

- Use a microcontroller as a single-purpose stand-alone computer that performs a particular small-world task, like controlling some lights, measuring the temperature, and passing the results on to your desktop machine. Microcontroller systems can take orders from your desktop machine, "Switch that heater on, Put that light out." But a microcontroller system doesn't have to be connected to a desktop machine; it can happily work as a complete single-purpose, simple, but still intelligent, stand-alone computer.

In summary: The desktop computer is built, sold, and operated as a general-purpose computer. It is intended to find and manipulate any digital information, in any way you want. A microcontroller is a much simpler, scaled-down computer that is far cheaper than a desktop machine but is suitable to be programmed to do just one task very well.

A microcontroller system can be the interface to real-world devices (freezers, temperature sensors, fans, heaters, lights) for a desktop machine,[5] or it can just be used built into a stand-alone system. Such applications are often called Smart Appliances because, thanks to the fact that they are software controlled, they can allow an appliance to exhibit a limited range of adaptive behaviors. Modern cars usually feature several microcontrollers embedded in their various systems.

In this book we look at a variety of microcontroller-based projects. Some are interfacing projects that benefit from connection to a desktop computer, while others are stand-alone, independent systems.

Why AVR?

There are, in fact, a large number of different (and software-incompatible) microcontroller families on the market, of which AVR is one. Probably the market leader in this field is the PIC (Programmable Intelligent Computer[6]). PIC was gradually developed as an upgrade to a previous generation of microprocessors by General Instruments in the early 1980s. The product line was inherited by Microchip Technologies–the commercial successors to GI–which by the mid-1990s had added additional refinements such as on-chip user-writable program memory.

PIC chips offer excellent value and there is a lot of support software and hardware available for them–they deserve their success. However, PIC chips are not especially clock efficient. That is, a PIC chip driven at a certain clock rate will not achieve as much useful work as other microcontrollers, due to certain inefficiencies inherent in the PIC architecture.[7] The PIC was not originally designed around a RISC methodology (see the following section)–whereas the AVR family of microcontrollers has a more recent design and is RISC to the core.[8] To answer the preceding question, "Why AVR?," I am a fan of AVR because it is fast, well designed, easy to use, well supported, and cheap to buy.

Some History: The Computer Industry Takes a RISC

To understand what RISC (Reduced Instruction Set Computer) really means, and how today's computing benefits from it, we need to look briefly at how computer processors developed in the 1970s and 1980s and how computers were used back then.

Early electronic computers offered the programmer very few machine instructions. Adding or subtracting two numbers, moving a value from one storage register to another, loading and saving registers to main memory–and that was about it. The people who programmed these pioneering machines in the late 1940s and into the 1950s were working in pure machine code: They had to learn the binary values for each instruction that the machine understood and construct great slews of binary codes for the processor to execute. No screens, no hard drives or floppy drives, everything keyed in on a large bank of switches and lights. Very hard work!

However, as technology advanced into the 1960s and 1970s, increased machine capabilities made it possible for higher-level programming languages to appear. These languages were implemented by compilers: a compiler is a program that converts human-readable programs–written in languages like FORTRAN, BASIC, or C—into

---

[5] If you look closely at any USB accessories you may have for your desktop computer you may be able to see that they do in fact have a microcontroller at their heart. Many toys, novelties, and domestic appliances are similarly built around a microcontroller. If you have a USB memory stick or pen drive, you will find it almost certainly has a microcontroller inside.

[6] Originally it stood for Peripheral Interface Controller.

[7] Some of these have been addressed in more recent PIC chips, but some still remain.

[8] Various tests have concluded that if an AVR and a PIC are clocked at the same speed and set to do an identical task, the AVR will be around four times faster than the PIC. I have never tried this, but I have observed notable speed differences in strong favor of the AVR.

actual machine instructions. The advent of compilers (and their increasing importance and scope during the period 1960-1980) meant that human programmers gradually became insulated from the need to know intricate details of the computer processors for which they were creating software.

CISC: The Computer Industry Gets a Complex!

By the early 1980s, huge improvements in semiconductor manufacture made it possible to implement ever more complex computer processors, and there was a kind of a gold rush. Each major manufacturer of the time (IBM, Sperry, ICL, Boroughs, DEC, etc.) vied to give successive generations of processors ever more complex and comprehensive instruction sets. The theory was that if you implemented commonly used functions such as string searches or list processing as a single machine instruction, then your machine would out perform its competition. Equally important, if your processor achieved more useful work with each instruction, you needed fewer instructions for any given program task, and the program size would be smaller. Minimizing program size was a very important consideration in 1980, when a computer that had 512 kilobytes of RAM (half a megabyte) was a top-of-the-range machine!

This gold rush went on until the mid-1980s with processors getting faster, but more complex, with each passing year. By the mid-1980s, a processor like Digital Equipment Corp.'s VAX boasted an instruction set totaling about 160 instructions, further subdivided into more than 400 variants.

By the 1980s, almost nobody was programming large computers in machine language any more. Almost all software was being written in high-level languages like C, PASCAL, BASIC, and FORTRAN. A very lucrative software industry had grown up writing compilers.

A compiler is not an easy or cheap piece of software to create. A compiler has two major headline functions. The first function (the front end) is to examine the source code written by a human programmer and make sure it obeys the rules of the high-level language; then, if all is well, it will convert the steps of that code into a number of generic "tokens." The second function (the back end) is to take that set of generic tokens and convert it into a stream of machine code. Obviously, the back end must produce a machine code stream that is specific to the instruction set of the target machine: the machine on which the executable version of the program is to be run.[9]

The KISS Principle Reasserts Itself

You've doubtless heard of the "Keep It Simple Stupid" (KISS) principle - a way of saying that a back-to-basics approach to things can often be a revelation. Well, the computer industry had its own KISS moment back in the mid-1980s.

A study came out of Stanford University in California from a team headed by Professor John L. Hennessy. This study was the result of work that had taken several years to complete. The team had analyzed–in exhaustive detail–the machine code streams produced by a wide a range of compiler products. The results pointed to a somewhat shocking conclusion: one that changed the whole field of processor design. The study found that 90 % of compiler-generated software used only about 10 % of the available instructions on any given processor type. So, it seemed that all the effort that processor designers had put into designing ever more ambitious instruction sets was wasted; most of the software running on these computers actually wasn't using their more sophisticated features!

When Hennessy's team sought the reasons for this underuse of instruction sets, they found that the main underlying cause wasn't a technical one at all–it was a commercial one.

Team members realized that the market had evolved in such a way that most compilers were being created by independent companies, not by the computer manufacturers themselves. These compiler companies were achieving economies of scale by creating their products in such a way that they could be used on many ranges

---

[9]There are quite a few other intermediate steps performed by a compiler; these are only the major ones.

of computers. Thus, a compiler vendor might have a FORTRAN compiler which worked on IBM, ICL, DEC, Intel, and Unisys machines. That compiler would have a common front-end section, and a manufacturer-specific back-end section.

Given the cost and complexity of developing compilers for all these platforms, the back-end sections tended to use only the simpler instructions of the computers concerned, and not the more complex, unique, ones. It simply wasn't worth the compiler vendor's time and effort to optimize the back-end part of the compiler per computer architecture. This then was the main reason most of the software analyzed by the Stanford study used only 10 % of the available instruction sets. Additionally, during the later 1980s RAM memory sizes in computers grew much larger; in 1988 even a desktop machine would have 8 or perhaps 16 megabytes of RAM installed. That meant that the need to keep program sizes to the absolute minimum was easing, further reducing the need to use complex, machine-specific, instructions.

Professor Hennessy's Stanford team reflected that, through the 1980s, improvements in speed and device density in the underlying silicon technology had been used to enable more complex processor architectures and larger and ever more complex instructions sets. However, the team's detailed analyses of numerous software programs conclusively showed that, in fact, very few programs made use of these advanced features. They characterized the state-of-the-art machines of the mid-1980s as CISC (Complex Instruction Set–pronounced "SISK") computers.

They posed a new question: given the great increases in capacity and speed of semiconductors, if processors had stayed very simple, with small, elegant instruction sets, how much faster would they be running now? They imagined a stripped-down processor along these lines, and they called it a RISC computer.

They showed that if you designed a machine with a uniform instruction set, in which each instruction had the same format, and in which there were only very simple conditional branch instructions,[10] then you could dedicate more chip space to features that would enhance execution speed, such as a subsystem to prefetch instructions from memory into the processor "pipeline," meaning that the processor was continuously busy, rather than spending an appreciable percentage of its time waiting for its next instruction to be fetched. In an ideal RISC design, the processor completes one machine instruction for each and every clock cycle–something CISC processors could never do. In other words, the goal of a RISC processor design is that if its clock speed is, for example, 20 MHz, then it will be able to execute 20 million instructions per second.

RISC Goes Primetime

The work done by the Hennessy team was so influential that, within only a few years, it changed the course of computer technology. The R2000 from MIPS Computer (released in late 1985) was the first commercially available microprocessor to implement the RISC principles. It took a couple of years, but eventually, when the R2000 was implemented in Unix systems from DEC and Silicon Graphics (SGI), among others, its performance left equivalent CISC-based machines for dead.

The R2000 was swiftly followed by the R3000 and successive generations of RISC processors from MIPS and many others. The RISC processors outperformed their CISC predecessors for almost all mainstream applications.

Since that time, all new mainstream processor designs have used most of the ideas embodied in the RISC philosophy. By 1990, CISC designs were either starting to fade away or–as with the Intel range used in personal computers–being updated to include as much RISC-ness as possible, while still retaining historical compatibility. In other cases, companies brought out new RISC architectures to replace eclipsed CISC architectures; for example, DEC's Alpha RISC architecture replaced its older VAX range of CISC processors and Apple and Sun Microsystems traveled a similar route in changing their base hardware platforms. The blazing performance of MIPS Computer products meant that they showed up in a new class of products: game consoles. Crack open an old PlayStation or a Nintendo 64 and you'll find a MIPS chip in there doing the graphics chores.

---

[10] Such an instruction might be "branch if zero"—meaning if the result of the last instruction was zero then do "this," or if it was not zero then do "that."

Wraps Off AVR

In 1996 the semiconductor company, Atmel, released a new product called AVR (by the way, Atmel says that the initials AVR don't stand for anything in particular). The AVR is a microcontroller chip designed, from the ground up, around the RISC principles whose history and provenance we discussed in the previous section.

This innovative product used, for the first time on a microcontroller, flash memory, meaning that it could easily be reprogrammed with new software while in situ[11] on its application board. AVR also included innovations around the amount of I/O capability it had on-chip–it featured more than was usual at the time.

It was around this time that it started to become essential to differentiate between microprocessors (a processor on a chip) and microcontrollers (a potentially complete computer, with processor, memory, and I/O subsystem on a chip).

After the first 8-bit AVR microcontroller was released by Atmel in 1996, there was a steady stream of new AVRs to follow, each faster and more capable than the last. This eventually included a family of 32-bit AVR processors for use in very demanding applications such as engine management systems.

The AVR family has several primary characteristics:

- It is a common family of processors with code compatibility across the range because the processors all use the same RISC processor core.

- The range of code-compatible chips allows the designer to find the right trade-off between features and cost. All AVR chips have the microprocessor core, but each chip in the range features a different set of peripheral ports and devices, with differing amounts of flash and RAM memory. This range of products allows the designer to select the chip which offers exactly the right amount of capability, and price point, for the job in hand. This is very important when designing commercial products: for several reasons, the number and cost of components are often a key decider of the success or failure of a consumer product.

- AVR espouses RISC design principles and makes very good use of each clock cycle, allowing it to outperform older architectures running at the same clock speed. Of course, since not all microcontroller uses are time-critical, this is less of a consideration in some applications than others, and speed of execution is not the only thing to be considered in designing a microcontroller application. Nevertheless, where speed is an issue–or likely to become an issue–AVR is a very good choice.

---

[11]The first microprocessors had no on-chip program memory; they needed external ROM chips to hold their programs. The second generation of microcontrollers offered updatable program memory, but it was implemented using EEPROM (Electrically Erasable Programmable Read Only Memory), which required that the chip be removed from circuit and put into an infrared light box which caused the light-sensitive cells on the memory portion of the chip to be reset. Once erased, the memory could be reprogrammed. Flash memory—used on third-generation microcontrollers onward—behaves very much like a RAM and is thus far easier to use and reuse: with careful design the flash memory can be updated in place (i.e., without physically removing the microcontroller from the application circuit).

Summary

The application of the RISC philosophy to computers in general enabled a big step up in computer performance, and when used in the AVR family, it made it possible to offer a highly performing processor core that could be common throughout the extensive AVR product range.

The advent of the microcontroller truly revolutionized the consumer electronics field, and many others (such as the automotive field). The availability of microcontrollers also facilitated the creation of whole new industries and classes of devices–such as GPS (global positioning system) receivers and MP3 players.

So, now that you know why you should be interested in microcontrollers, and why AVRs are such a good entryway into this fascinating subject—it's time to start getting our hands dirty with some practical work!

Coming Up Next

Building our AVR test bed and development system. Putting together the basic tools and equipment we need to get going.

CHAPTER 2

Building Our AVR Test Bed

We're going to call it our AVR test bed but really, it's a lot of things rolled into one. It provides a means of trying out the project ideas in this book, it provides a way to upload your software into your AVR chip, and it gives you a place to try out your own ideas, based on this book's projects, or the completely new ones you're bound to have before long.

In this chapter we'll look at the details of the test bed, tell you what you need to get to build it, and give you detailed instructions on how to build and test it. Testing a test bed, now, there's a challenge!

Test Bed Details

The AVR test bed is really our development system—testing is only part of what it does for us. The test bed is to be built around a prototyping breadboard: if you're new to the idea of a breadboard, read through Appendix C which gives you an initial walk through what a breadboard is and what it can do for you.

The main purposes of the test bed are

- To provide an easy to use and fully functional AVR programmer that is compatible with the Arduino software suite.

- To host the AVR processor and provide permanent wiring to interface it to the AVR programmer.

- To provide a logic level (not RS-232) serial interface that allows your AVR projects to talk back to your desktop machine without having the need to use a conventional serial port.

- To provide a suitable power supply for AVR projects.

Using this rig, you can create and debug your AVR programs and get to a final configuration of the hardware for your project. Once you have a final working version of the hardware and software for your project and have installed your software into the AVR chip, your computer and the AVR are disconnected. You build permanent project board and that particular AVR goes off to operate completely separately, forever. In other words, once the desktop computer has served its purpose as a development and programming platform, your AVR project is completely independent.

Test Bed Ingredients

It's likely that you will already have many of the tools, and maybe even some of the parts, you need to build your test bed. For the rest, the pieces you need to get are all widely available; in most locales you can get them from reasonably local stores, but if not, you can get any of them from multiple sources on the Internet.

A Desktop Computer

Preferably this will be a machine that is exclusively yours, or one that you can use whenever you are able to work on your projects. The beauty of this requirement is that it does *not* need to be a fast machine; provided it still works reliably, an old "chuggabox" will do. As compared to modern office applications, the demands that the Arduino software puts on a machine are not all that heavy. The file sets involved are all small by today's standards, the software sets to install are not big, and the central processing unit (CPU) demands are comparatively light, so an old system might be perfectly suitable.

Although you don't need the latest and greatest hardware, you should make sure that the system you use is up to date on all required operating system updates and security enhancements before you begin using the machine. Some of the features a development system requires may be missing from a machine with outdated system software. On an Apple machine you will need to be using an up-to-date Mac OS X installation. For Windows, you will need to be on at least Windows XP with Service Pack 3, or an up-to-date installation of Vista or Windows 7. Linux versions are less critical; however, your installed kernel version should not be more than a couple of years old.

■ **Tip**   Use the command line `uname -v` to see the build date of your currently in-use Linux kernel.

The machine you use must have a spare USB port (USB2 for preference, but in most cases I think USB1 will work too): any machine made post-millennium should have this. To work well, the system you use should have 1 gigabyte (GB) of RAM memory or more (especially if you are running Windows). If you're a patient person, you can get away with less, but don't expect anything to happen quickly. Using an old machine has the advantage that your main desktop can be used concurrently for other things (or by other people) while you are doing AVR stuff. I used to use my main desktop for AVR work, but now I use an old laptop with a 15-inch screen, 1 GB of memory, and a 1.7 gigahertz (Ghz) processor, which works perfectly well. You'll need a maximum 300 megabytes of free disk space to install everything required.

If you don't have a suitable old machine of your own, you're likely to find someone on your local Freecycle group offering an obsolete machine for free: find your nearest Freecycle group by visiting www.freecycle.org/ which lists the huge number of Freecycles sites around the world. Failing that, Internet auction sites such as eBay and Craigslist, for example, are usually awash with old machines selling for minimal prices (but be sure to check you are buying a known working machine; also precheck the shipping and packing charges of a "cheap" purchase before bidding or buying).

Finally, if you are reusing or buying an older machine to be your development machine it's always worth looking for, or asking for, the installation disks that originally came with it. Reinstalling any system from scratch is a sure way to get it back to its maximum possible performance. All computer systems get slower as they get older–nothing to do with the hardware, it's just that various aspects of the operating system–such as file system performance–degrade as more software is installed and removed and more files accumulate on the hard drive. I have always found Windows systems to be especially prone to this syndrome.

If you *are* planning to reinstall the operating system on your development machine, make absolutely sure before you begin that you have any special driver installation kits you may need (e.g., check to see if the system has a graphics card or a network card in it which needs its own special driver installing). Also, make sure you have a way to reinstall your security software (virus protection software): an unprotected machine that has been installed from an old version of an operating system kit is very vulnerable. A wise precaution is to take a complete *image* backup[1] (don't just save all the files) of the hard drive before you begin the reinstallation. That way, if something goes wrong, you at least have the option of putting the system back as it was. Products like Ghost and TrueImage for Windows, SuperDuper or Retrospect for Mac OS, and Clonezilla or PartImage for Linux will all perform image backups to an attached USB hard drive.

Allow a realistic amount of time for a reinstallation. The reinstallation from the original installation disc may not take more than an hour, but the subsequent cycle of automated patches and updates required to get your system up to the latest revision can go on for many hours . . . or even days!

Summary List of Other Parts

In the following section, I detail each of the things that you'll need to build your test bed, but to begin, here is a summary list of the other major pieces apart from a desktop computer:

- An AVR programmer.

- An in-system programming (ISP) connector breakout board from Sparkfun–and some 0.1" header pins to solder onto it. We'll be looking at ISP in more detail in the section "About In-System Programming."

- A breadboard to build up your circuits upon (see appendix A for basic information about breadboards, and see the section "Breadboard" for specifics in this application).

- A power supply providing an output of +5 volts DC. This power supply should be capable of providing at least 1 amp at its output. It's possible you may already have a suitable unit left over from some old piece of equipment.

- A TTL level serial port USB dongle (see the section "TTL Level Serial Port"). If your AVR programmer has such a port already, as the Pololu AVR programmer does, then it's not essential that you get one. You might like to get one of these anyway if you plan to build permanent versions of any of the projects in this book. You probably won't want to use your test bed to communicate with your permanent projects forever.

- An inline fuse holder and a suitable quick-blow glass fuse (see more details later in this chapter in the section "A +5V-Regulated Supply").

- The Arduino software installation kit, which you can download from www.arduino.org. Get the latest available version for your chosen platform (Mac, Linux, Windows). The examples in this book all use Arduino version 1.0.

- At least one ATmega328 (a 28-pin device), but you'll probably want to buy two or three because it's likely you'll want to build up more than one project at a time; also, if you're experimenting with electronics there always comes a time when you make a mistake and need a spare.

Figure 2-1 shows the basic test bed. As you can see, the AVR chip is placed onto a breadboard. At the top left of the picture, the AVR breakout board allows the programmer to connect to the board. The other end of the AVR programmer connects to your computer via a USB cable: in this picture, the programmer cable is not yet connected.

---

[1]If you are unfamiliar with the concept of an image backup, Wikipedia can tell you what you need to know. Look at the Wikipedia entry for "Disk Image."

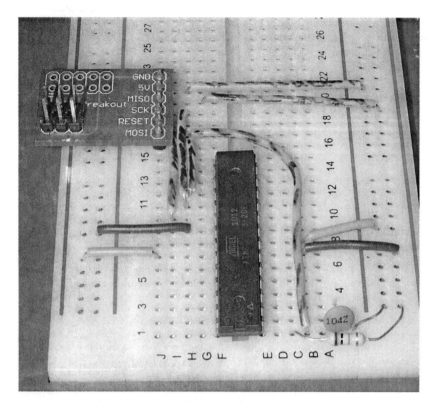

Figure 2-1. *Basic test bed*

The "Piece Parts" section lists each of the required items: you'll see why you need each one, what it does for you, where you might buy it, and how you can install it.

Toolkit: Required Items

As in any endeavor, it's essential to have the right tools to do a good job. In addition to the tools found in most homes (general-purpose screwdrivers, pliers, a set of standard-size twist drills and perhaps an electric drill, hammers, etc.), the following list includes the minimum specialist toolkit I would recommend for the electronic projects in this book:

- *A soldering iron with interchangeable tip*: You will need one fine tip for small-scale electronics work and one larger tip for things like soldering larger power supply leads, and so on. A medium-size tip may possibly be usable for both purposes, but it will often make soldering tasks harder and more error-prone than they need to be. The soldering iron should be an electric type, with a heating element of between 20 and 40 watts. Gas-powered soldering irons are great for many general tasks, but they are harder to use successfully for this kind of work.

- Don't forget you'll need solder too. Lead-free solder (the healthiest kind to use) is available in reels and tubes from all electronics hobby stores.

- *A pair of fine long-nosed (sometimes called needle-nosed) pliers*: What you're looking for is something that makes it easy to pick up a thin sewing needle. If your pliers can do that, then they are the right ones for the job.

- *A pair of small wire cutters*: These need to be small enough for the tip of their cutting points to get into fairly small spaces but beefy enough to be able to cut through a bobby pin (also called a hair-grip) without making your hand hurt.

- *A small blade-headed electrical screwdriver (as shown in* Figure 2-2*) and a small cross-headed (a.k.a. Phillips head) screwdriver*: The electrical screwdrivers are usually insulated all the way up the shank with a plastic handle (often having a neon lamp embedded inside the handle–as in the illustration that follows,–allowing it to be used as an AC voltage indicator, as per instructions that will come with it).

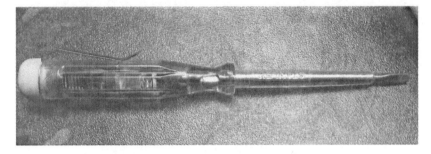

Figure 2-2. *Small screwdriver*

- *A general-purpose digital voltmeter (DVM)—also sold as a "digital multimeter"*: Almost any modern DVM will be suitable for our purposes. It should be capable of measuring the following quantities:

  - DC volts from 0 to 600.

  - AC volts from 0 to 600.

  - Resistance from 0 ohms to 20 megohms.

  - Amps from 0 to 10 amps.

- It would be useful for it to have a continuity test facility, whereby it bleeps if there is direct contact between two tested points. I think any DVM now on sale should meet these needs.

- A craft knife of some sort, preferably with safety features such as a retractable blade.

- Some 1/2" (12mm)- or 1" (25mm)-wide electrical tape.

- A set of miniature twist drills in sizes less than found in most DIY (do-It-Yourself) drill kits. These are usually sold as "mini HSS drill" sets. You will need sizes from 1/8" (about 3mm) downwards. Such kits are usually quite cheap and are readily available from online sources like Amazon, model-making shops, and larger DIY outlets.

- *A "bits box" containing various sizes of small nuts, bolts, and self-tapping screws*: You can usually buy a mixed bits box at your local hardware store or electronics shop. Many people keep a bits box, so there may be something suitable in your house already.

Toolkit: Optional Items

As well as the preceding items, which you will definitely need, a number of other items may be useful to you, though they are not essential for every reader.

- A *"helping hands" work holder* (see Figure 2-3): These come in various shapes and sizes, they are sold by electronics hobby stores, handicrafts stores and various other outlets. Essentially, these are stands with a number of alligator clips mounted on arms. Apart from the base (usually quite a heavy thing to provide stability) everything else can be adjusted to almost any position you want. This allows you to hold your circuit board or project in just the right position for you do some soldering or make various adjustments to it; some (like the one in Figure 2-3) come with extra refinements like a soldering iron holder and a magnifying glass with an integral light. This gives superb close-up visibility of the job under way.

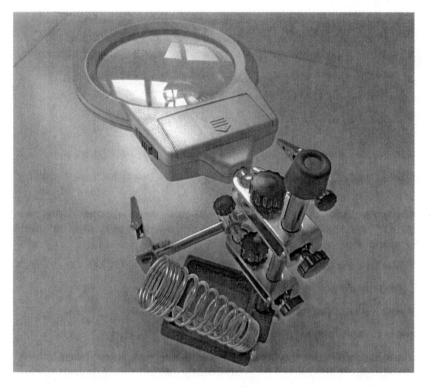

Figure 2-3. *Helping hands (image courtesy of Jinhua Top Optical Instrument Co. Ltd.)*

- A *logic probe*: This is a handy little device that can tell you whether the probed point in a circuit is at logic high, logic low, or pulsing between the two. Handy sometimes, even though not essential equipment.

- *Component grab bags*: Most electronics outlets do bags of LEDs, resistors and capacitors, and other components. Each bag contains a selection of one type of component. It's usually a lot cheaper to get these than to buy the same components individually. You may not have a use for so many components immediately, but it's very handy to have a few spare components around when you are experimenting and trying out new ideas.

Piece Parts

In the following sections we look at each of the piece parts of the test bed in more detail.

Breadboard

Remember, Appendix A provides an introduction to electronics, and Appendix C provides an introduction to breadboards.

The breadboard is the indispensable foundation for the test bed. It allows you to plug in components and make interconnections between them, without soldering. It's also reusable. When you have finished developing, proving, or understanding a circuit, you can just unplug everything and start again, using it for something new and completely different!

Because no soldering is involved, you can make circuit wiring changes very quickly without risk to components of overheating through repeated exposure to heat. However, it's unlikely that you would ever want to put a circuit into long-term use while it was still on a breadboard (though it has been done). Breadboards are superb for on-the-fly designing and for getting your projects working right, but they are not space efficient.

Usually, once a project is working, you transfer it to a smaller, permanent board–either a solder strip board or a printed circuit board that you might design with some piece of free software like Fritzing or Eagle. Look in the appendixes for additional information.

The breadboard I used for my test bed rig is a fairly standard layout with 64 rows of pins, columns labeled A through J, and power rails at each side. Some breadboards have slightly fewer rows, but this does not matter for our purposes here: the majority of standard-size (as opposed to miniature) breadboards have the same number of columns.

Breadboards need jumper wires, but few breadboards come with a supply of them, so you'll need to make or buy some. If you want to make your own breadboard jumpers you'll need some 22 or 23 AWG (0.65mm diameter) insulated, solid core, not stranded, wire. This can be bought from any hobby electronics outlet. Though it's not essential, you may want to get several different colors, since this makes jumpers easier to differentiate in more complex setups. If you're making your own jumpers, you'll probably want to buy about ten feet (about three meters) of each color.

Many people prefer to buy ready-made jumpers which are widely available in boxed kits (look for "Breadboard jumper kit"), providing various colors in various lengths.

A +5-Volt Regulated Supply

If you've been doing any kind of electronics previously, you may be lucky enough to have your own lab-grade power supply (such as the one shown in Figure 2-4), in which case, you're all set.

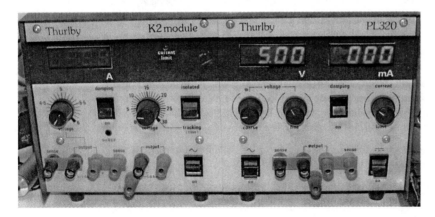

Figure 2-4. *Lab grade power supply*

Such a power supply will provide you with an adjustable, overload-protected power source. Often these kinds of power supplies have multiple outputs (as in Figure 2-4) so that you can get, for example, +5 volts for the logic circuits and also a separate +12-volt output for motors, relays, and so on.

However, lab supplies can be pretty expensive (though, as ever, look for bargains in online auctions), but there are *much* cheaper alternatives: maybe something you already have will work?

Look around your home for "wall-wart" AC to DC power adaptors left over from a now defunct phone, PDA, MP3 player, or similar devices. If you're home is anything like mine, you'll have some orphaned adaptors tucked away somewhere. You're looking for one that gives an output of +5 volts DC, with *at least* 1 amp current. If you find one with 2 or even 3 amps output capability, that's even better.

If you're going the wall-wart route, you will need to add an inline fuse to the positive (+) lead to protect yourself and your circuitry. Your usual electronics supplier should be able to supply you a spring-loaded inline fuse holder that will hold a variety of small fuse sizes. You will need one that can hold 1-inch or 1.25-inch fuses (in metric, the closest standard size is 20mm, which is fine).

Example suitable fuse holders are

- Digi-Key F1468-ND (United States).

- Maplin PC78 (UK).

Also, of course, you will need some fuses to put into this holder. These days such fuses are almost always supplied in boxes of ten. There are two main flavors of fuse, slow-blow (sometimes called time-delay) fuses and quick-blow fuses. We need to use the quick-blow type. You need a 1.25" (or 20mm) quick-blow fuse rated at 1.25 amps. Some of the later projects have additional power requirements and thus will require additional power and fusing, but I will detail those in the descriptions of those particular projects. However, you might like to get a couple of fuse holders and keep one for later.

So, back to the power supply: in my junk box I found an old Compaq iPAQ PDA (personal digital assistant) power supply/charger (see Figure 2-5). This offers +5 volts DC output at 2 amps. So, I prepared it for use with my test bed rig by doing the following:

1. I cut off the device-specific output plug.

■ **Caution** When you cut off the output plug, take care that there is no remaining charge in the power supply unit (PSU). Make sure the device has been unplugged for at least five minutes, and if possible, when you cut the wires, cut them one at a time. Also, *always* use cutters with insulated handles whenever dealing with electrics of any kind. Always be mindful that most electronic circuits store some level of charge for some minutes after they are switched off or disconnected.

---

2. I used my DVM to identify which was the positive lead and which the negative (in the case of this PSU, as in many others, the two wires look the same, or have only minute differences). To identify the positive lead, set your DVM to its 20-volt DC range then connect the positive probe (red) to one wire and the negative (black) wire to the other:

    a. If your DVM reads a negative voltage (e.g., "–5.1") then the positive lead is the one you've got connected to the black probe.

    b. If your DVM reads a positive voltage (e.g.,"5.1") then the positive lead is the one you've got connected to the red probe.

3. I installed my inline fuse holder in the positive lead (see the following illustration).

4. I made neat solder ends on the output leads.

Figure 2-5. *A repurposed 5 volt supply*

and voilà! A high-quality +5V power supply for free (well, almost for free).

If you don't have a suitable supply already hanging around to reuse, then you should be able to get one cheaply from your usual electronics supplier. Many larger DIY stores (e.g., Home Depot in the United States, B&Q in the UK, or your local equivalent) carry suitable products. Online auction sites offer a large number of suitable new products, and there are always bargains to be had from people trying to sell off their surplus used PSUs from lost or discarded gadgets.

Do make sure that any device you buy

- Is being sold as a working unit, not something in an unknown condition.

- Has an output of +5 volts DC (NOT AC).

- Has a *regulated*[2] output to ensure maximum smoothness of the voltage level.

- Can supply +5 volts at one amp (often written as "1@" or "1.0@"), or more.

- Has an output wire that you can cut into and replace the ending. Integrated supplies that form a cradle for some other device are not usually so easily adapted to a new use.

And don't forget to buy the fuse holder (previously discussed) and a pack of correctly rated fuses too.

Depending on the thickness of the wires on the output of your power supply, you may need to solder some 22 AWG tails on them; these will more easily plug into the power rails on your test bed breadboard (see Figure 2-6) making a secure power connection.

---

[2]Try to avoid PSUs that only offer only "rectified" output, since the output voltage may not be smooth enough for logic chip applications. You need a supply with a "regulated" output, which gives a far more stable supply. PSU manufacturers usually state on the product label if the output is regulated, or they may use the phrase "For ITE Equipment." If neither of these appear on the label, then it's best to assume that the product concerned is not right for this usage.

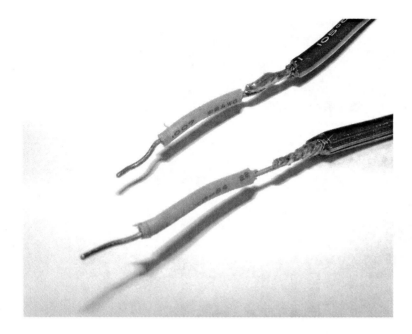

Figure 2-6. *Power supply leads with breadboard-friendly tails added*

Don't forget to put some tape (or some shrink-wrap sleeve, if you have any) around the solder joints to prevent any nasty accidents resulting from them shorting out to one another, or to other things.

The power from your +5V supply feeds onto the breadboard at the far end from the AVR chip (shown in Figure 2-7). (Positive goes to the red, negative to the black.)

Figure 2-7. *PSU attach points*

Finally, we need to bridge and combine the various break points in the power rail around the breadboard. As you can see in Figure 2-8 we do this by adding linking jumpers between the power rails on each side (the vertical jumpers in this photo). We also add jumpers (the horizontal jumpers in the photo) to make sure both rails on both sides of the breadboard are energized. All this happens half way along the breadboard, around position 32-34.

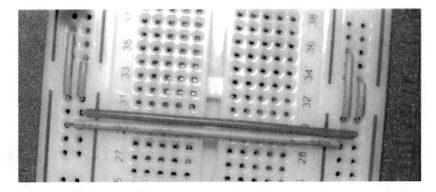

Figure 2-8. *Bridging and linking the power supply rails*

Now, plug in your power supply to the wall socket. Connect your DVM (still on its 20V DC range) to a couple of points on the breadboard, one +5V and one ground and make sure you are getting around about 5 volts. If you have any problem setting up the power supply

- Check to see if the fuse in your fuse holder is blown. If it is, look for a mistake in your wiring on the breadboard, you should only have positive joined to positive and negative to negative. With the power supply disconnected (and no components plugged onto the breadboard) using the continuity test (beeper) facility of your DVM to see if there is any connection between the positive and negative around the breadboard.

- If your wiring is fine, make sure a good fuse is installed in the holder and attach your DVM to the PSU outputs (be careful not to short them together) and make sure that you still have +5 volts (give or take 0.2 volts) coming out of it.

- If the PSU has its own separate mains fuse (some have an integral AC-side fuse), check that it is okay.

- If you can, try a different power supply.

The AVR Chip

To maintain simplicity and familiarity we're going to use the ATmega328 AVR MCU chip throughout this book (or the low-power version ATmega328pu is also okay). You can buy the ATmega328 from many electronics suppliers, for example

- www.sparkfun.com/products/9061 (United States).

- www.coolcomponents.co.uk/catalog/product_info.php?products_id=272 (UK).

- Various international eBay vendors.

We are using the ATmega328 because it's an easily obtainable and capable device with lots of useful features and I/O, and it has 32 kilobytes of program memory as well as RAM and flash memory for software to use. It's also fully qualified to work with the Arduino software development environment that I use throughout this book.

Once you get confident enough to branch out on your own a bit, you might want, for a few simpler projects, to try using an AVR ATTINY85 instead. The TINY85 is also widely available

- www.sparkfun.com/products/9378 (United States).

- www.rapidonline.com (use order code 73-5122) (UK).

- Various eBay vendors.

The TINY85 has only 8 Kbytes of program memory, and 512 bytes of internal RAM, so it has its limitations. However, it can do more than you might at first think.

Our concentration is going to be on the ATmega328 and you'll see how it fits onto the test bed rig in just a little while.

AVR ISP Programmer

There are two ways to install the software you create into your AVR chip.

- Parallel programming.

- Serial programming.

The process of installing your software into the chip is usually called uploading, and we say that we are programming the chip.

Programming in Parallel

Parallel programming is a technique in which the programmer connects with all the pins of the AVR processor and treats it almost as if it were just a memory chip that it was writing data into. The programmer drives the whole process and the AVR processor remains inert until the programmer is disconnected. Parallel programming is done by multifunction programmer boards, mainly the ones offered by Atmel such as the STK500. The STK500 offers all kinds of facilities for interrogating, diagnosing, and probing a large variety of AVR microcontrollers. It also offers a number of useful development system capabilities; for example, it has a bank of LEDs and a bank of push buttons. It also has a full RS-232 port that can interface directly to a desktop machine. Additionally, the STK500 has a number of other facilities that can be very useful in hardware and software development.

The main downside to using parallel programming is that–in most cases–you have to unplug the AVR chip from your circuit, plug it into a programmer board, program it, remove it from the programmer and then move it back to your circuit every time you want to update the code! All that (especially when you are developing or debugging your code) gets to be a real chore very quickly and is very prone to mishaps such as bending chip pins or plugging chips in wrongly, resulting in damage to the chips.

So, the STK 500 is an excellent product and you can buy it from many of the same sources as you would buy AVR chips, but it is not a cheap product and–although I considered using it as the test bed platform for this book—I have taken the view that it's very much overkill and anyway it's not especially suitable for our purposes. I just want you to program the AVR as cheaply and effectively as possible using a desktop machine. So, you will be using the other principal AVR programming method.

About In-System Programming

In-system programming (ISP) is the means by which you can upload your developed code into your AVR microcontroller while your AVR is still installed in its application circuit. A special interface allows an ISP device (a much simpler beast than the parallel programmer) to send blocks of data to the AVR, and the AVR programs the uploaded code into *itself* a little at a time. This method is slower than parallel programming, but the kit to do it is quite a lot cheaper and it does actually work out faster, because you're not swapping the chip from your application circuit to your programmer all the time. The ISP route is a lot faster and more practical for development work.

The setup we're using allows you to use ISP to upload software into the AVR chip, in situ, on the breadboard. You can update your software without removing your MCU chip from the board. It gets reprogrammed where it sits.

The next diagram gives you the general idea of the set of signals needed to implement ISP.

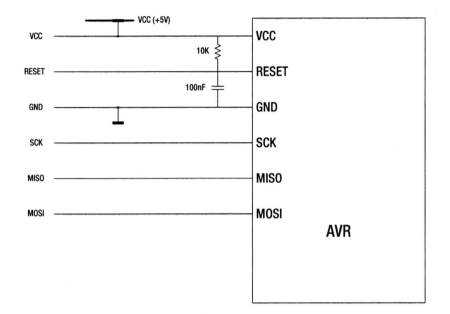

Figure 2-9. *AVR ISP hook-up signals*

You'll find more details about this hook-up a little later in this section, but as you can see, it uses just four signals (plus VCC and ground) from the programmer to the AVR chip to allow programming.

- MOSI.

- SCK.

- RESET.

- MISO.

- VDD (+5 volts).

- Ground.

Using the first four of these signals in a particular protocol, ISP allows the programmer to upload data into the MCU's program memory. The protocol consists of holding the RESET pin active (i.e. to a logic low), and then essentially using the serial clock (SCK) and memory serial in (MOSI) and memory serial out (MISO) as a serial port to upload new contents into an internal buffer. The AVR itself then writes the uploaded data into its own flash memory. There is a little more to it than this, but that's basically how it works. See the data sheet of any ISP capable AVR chip for full details.

All AVR microcontrollers, from the small 8-pin chips to the high-end 40-pin devices, have these four signals and all of them can be programmed in this way. With this basic setup you can hook your ISP programmer up to any AVR. This makes it easy to provide an ISP connection on all your projects so that you can update the firmware in them whenever you need to.

You may already have used ISP without realizing it, because Arduino boards incorporate an ISP programmer. However, that means that every time you buy an Arduino board you're buying yet another programmer, buried somewhere there in the Arduino board. Our approach in this book is a little different.

Atmel itself has offered several ISP programmers for AVR, the main current one is called (not unreasonably) the AVRISP MKII programmer (usually abbreviated to AVRISP2). Atmel's original product has been widely copied and cloned (I guess Atmel doesn't mind, as long as it sells more microcontroller chips) which means there are a huge number of programmers around which are called AVRISP2 programmers: this class of programmer is very often abbreviated in configuration files and documentation to "AVRISP2." As there are so many, I have only been able to test or try a handful.

The original Atmel programmer works, of course, flawlessly but is often offered at more than twice the price of some of the other products that do the same job. I tried three cheap imported AVRISP2 clones. Two of these three worked fine, one seemed to have some problems; it failed to program correctly on about 30% of the attempts.

Then, I found the Pololu programmer . . .

I have elected, for this book, to recommend the Pololu USB AVR programmer.[3] It simply connects to your desktop via any available USB port and you can use it with any mainstream desktop machine (Mac or PC, Windows XP or later, Mac OS X, or Linux). The Pololu programmer (which comes ready to use, it's not a kit like some other programmers) is comparatively cheap when compared to Atmel's own AVRISP2 programmer and works in just the same way, being compatible in every way. It offers an extra logic level serial port that can be very useful.[4] Figure 2-10 (courtesy of Pololu) shows the programmer (front and back view).

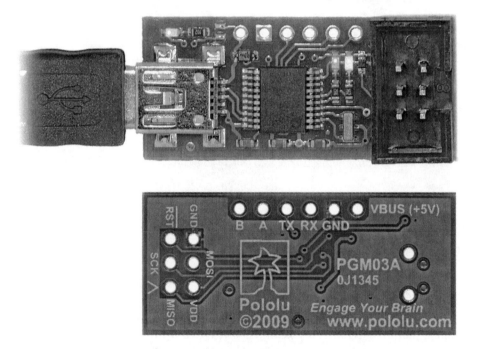

Figure 2-10. *Pololu USB/AVR programmer (courtesy of Pololu)*

As you could infer from the signal names in the photo, the six-way ISP cable that comes from the programmer to your circuit (your test bed rig) carries the six signals needed for ISP.

I need to stress here that if, for any reason, you want to use a *different* AVRISP2 compatible programmer, or an Atmel original, that is fine, it won't make much difference except in relatively unimportant areas–which I will point out as we go through the rest of the book.

---

[3]In the interests of transparency, I have no financial, personal, or business connection with Pololu, other than as a satisfied customer.

[4]Although the mainstream functions of the Pololu programmer can all be used on a Mac, Mac OS X system users may have to download additional, unsupported software to use the TTL level serial port. See the Mac-specific sections of the product description at www.pololu.com/catalog/product/1300.

As Figure 2-10 shows, as well as having the six-way ribbon cable to provide the ISP signals, the Pololu programmer board also offers some additional signals. These are as follows:

- *B & A*: These are extra logic level signals that you can manipulate via the modem signals of the serial port (RTS, DTR, etc.). These signals give you additional I/O lines that you can use to control something from the desktop. They seem like they would one day be useful, though I haven't yet found a use as yet.

- *TX & RX*: These are the logic level serial port transmit and receive lines. These are suitable for direct connection to the serial of the AVR chip. See the section "TTL Serial Port."

- *GND (Ground)*: This gives access to the ground plane of the board, and by extension the ground plane of the desktop. It is a requirement that the desktop machine, programmer, and test bed grounds be connected to one another prior to any other connections being made. If the grounds are not common, damage might occur to either or both of them. Usually this is not a problem because the ground link between the two devices is made through the ground wire contained in the ribbon cable and the USB cable. So, although this is something always to bear in mind, it's not usually an issue.

- *VBus (+5V)*: This gives access to the +5V supply that the programmer gets via its USB cable. In very limited circumstances you could use this to power your project, but only if your project required a very small amount of current (<100ma). This is different from the +5V supply you need to provide to your test bed breadboard–as previously detailed.

Figure 2-11 shows the programmer connected up: the mini-USB cable going off to the desktop at the left hand, and the ribbon cable going off to the test bed at the right. The programmer is supplied as an unboxed but otherwise ready-to-use board. Along with it you will get the six-way ISP ribbon cable and a USB (form A plug to mini plug) cable.

Figure 2-11. *Pololu programmer connected*

Although the programmer is perfectly usable as delivered, I wanted to put it in a box. Call me a worrier if you will, but having a bare PCB (printed circuit board) flapping around on a work surface that also contains lots of other electronic bits and pieces just seems like tempting fate to me. I'll cover the boxing exercise in the next section.

Once you have obtained your programmer (and boxed it–if you are going to; remember, it's not 100% necessary, just precautionary) you'll need to install it. The programmer's home page (www.pololu.com/catalog/product/1300) links to a list of resources, among which is an excellent user manual which includes detailed installation and configuration instructions for each of the supported platforms. Also there is an installation kit for Windows (XP, Vista, and 7). Linux and Mac systems do not need an installation kit; just follow the configuration instructions in the Pololu documentation.

Boxing the Programmer

This section describes how I boxed the programmer. This step is optional: if you are happy with your programmer as delivered, please skip this section.

I got a small semitransparent blue plastic project box and built the programmer into it. The style of box looks pretty classy, but the main reason for using it is that I can still see the LED indicators on the programmer board, which is sometimes essential to be able to know what's going on.

To continue to have access to the additional connections offered by the programmer (see Figure 2-10) I extended the various Pololu board connections out to a small-size screw connector block on the outside of the box. Following is the process I used, accompanied by illustrations of each step.

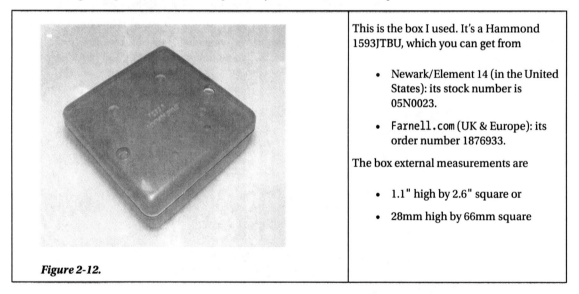

Figure 2-12.

This is the box I used. It's a Hammond 1593JTBU, which you can get from

- Newark/Element 14 (in the United States): its stock number is 05N0023.

- Farnell.com (UK & Europe): its order number 1876933.

The box external measurements are

- 1.1" high by 2.6" square or

- 28mm high by 66mm square

Figure 2-13.

This photo shows the innards of the box. It has lots of mounting points (and comes with two self-tapping screws for these mounting points) so that if your programmer board has fixing holes in it you could probably find a way to mount it on one or more of these points. Measure carefully though; there is not much height to play with in this particular box, so you may need a taller one.

The Pololu programmer has no mounting holes. Originally, I thought I would drill some very small holes in the base of the box, thread a thin cable tie around the underside of the box, and lash the programmer into the base of the box with that the cable.

But then, a stroke of luck . . .

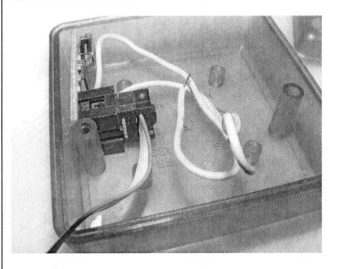

Figure 2-14.

It turns out that the Pololu programmer (shown here with TX and RX wires already attached) slots in exactly and tightly between the box edge and one of the screw pillars.

So, now, it's just a matter of drilling a hole in the box side, large enough for the mini-USB plug to pass through snugly.

I mark the approximate center of the programmer's USB socket (the box being semitransparent, I can easily see where that is). I then take the programmer out and put it out of the way.

I put the box into something to hold it steady (use a clamp or a vise) and I drill a 0.3" ho le (8mm) at the marked point.

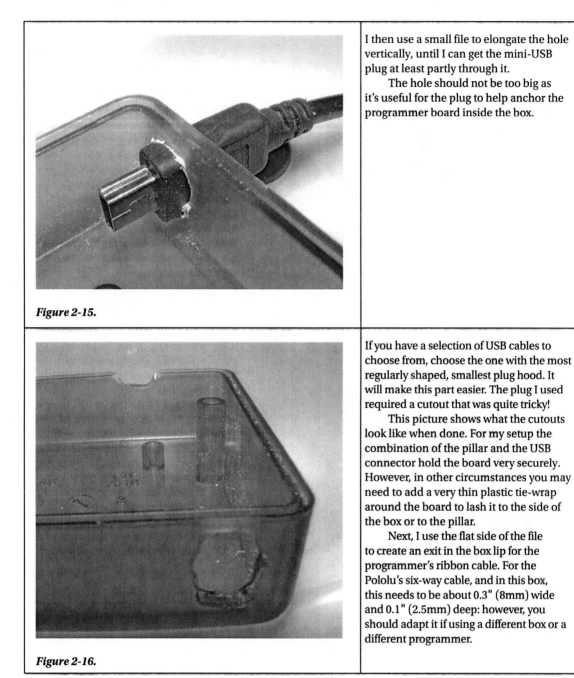

Figure 2-15.

I then use a small file to elongate the hole vertically, until I can get the mini-USB plug at least partly through it.

The hole should not be too big as it's useful for the plug to help anchor the programmer board inside the box.

Figure 2-16.

If you have a selection of USB cables to choose from, choose the one with the most regularly shaped, smallest plug hood. It will make this part easier. The plug I used required a cutout that was quite tricky!

This picture shows what the cutouts look like when done. For my setup the combination of the pillar and the USB connector hold the board very securely. However, in other circumstances you may need to add a very thin plastic tie-wrap around the board to lash it to the side of the box or to the pillar.

Next, I use the flat side of the file to create an exit in the box lip for the programmer's ribbon cable. For the Pololu's six-way cable, and in this box, this needs to be about 0.3" (8mm) wide and 0.1" (2.5mm) deep: however, you should adapt it if using a different box or a different programmer.

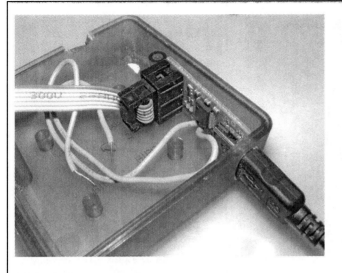

Figure 2-17.

The essential thing for the ribbon cable cutout is that, with the lid on, the cable is not overly loose, but also it's not unduly compressed by the box lid, which would eventually cause problems–even it didn't do so immediately.

I elected to put a tiny bit of tape around the ribbon cable at this point, to provide extra cushioning for the cable, but also because the cable felt a little too loose through the opening.

Figure 2-18.

Next, I took a five-way section of small-size screw terminal and, marking the fixing points, drilled two holes large enough to fit some tiny nuts and bolts to hold the terminal onto the side of the case, at a height that would allow a cable exit underneath it.

I drilled a 1/4" (6.5mm) hole under the screw terminals, large enough to comfortably get five small wires through. I then fixed the screw terminal in place.

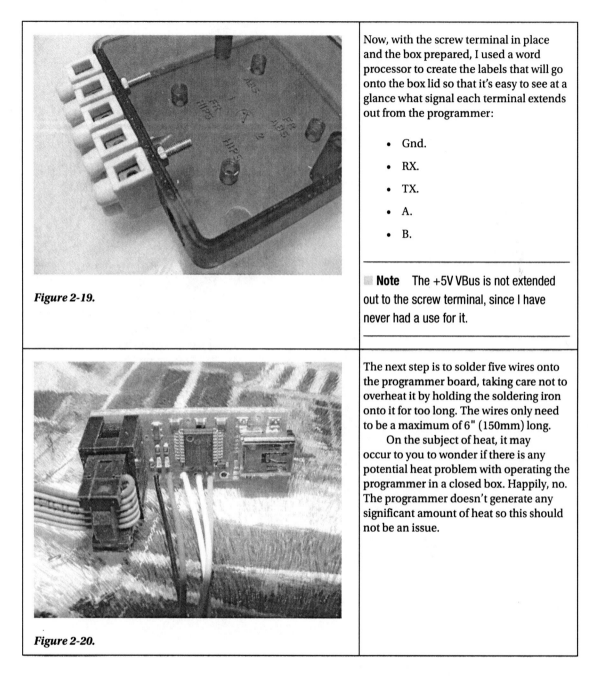

Figure 2-19.

Figure 2-20.

Now, with the screw terminal in place and the box prepared, I used a word processor to create the labels that will go onto the box lid so that it's easy to see at a glance what signal each terminal extends out from the programmer:

- Gnd.

- RX.

- TX.

- A.

- B.

■ **Note** The +5V VBus is not extended out to the screw terminal, since I have never had a use for it.

The next step is to solder five wires onto the programmer board, taking care not to overheat it by holding the soldering iron onto it for too long. The wires only need to be a maximum of 6" (150mm) long.

On the subject of heat, it may occur to you to wonder if there is any potential heat problem with operating the programmer in a closed box. Happily, no. The programmer doesn't generate any significant amount of heat so this should not be an issue.

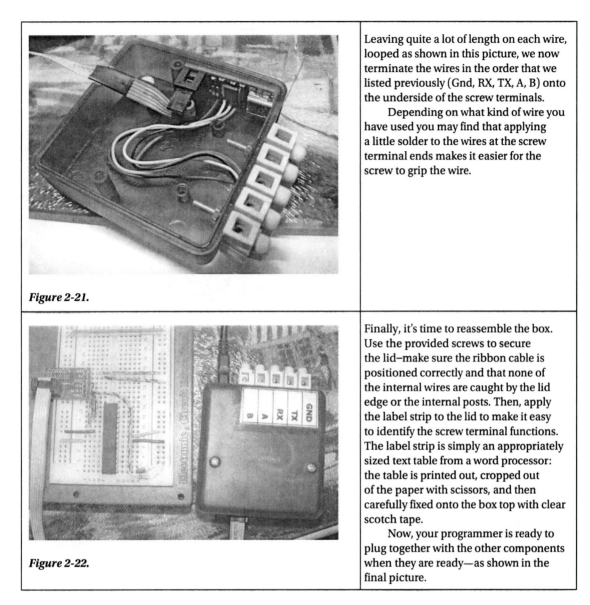

Figure 2-21.

Leaving quite a lot of length on each wire, looped as shown in this picture, we now terminate the wires in the order that we listed previously (Gnd, RX, TX, A, B) onto the underside of the screw terminals.

Depending on what kind of wire you have used you may find that applying a little solder to the wires at the screw terminal ends makes it easier for the screw to grip the wire.

Figure 2-22.

Finally, it's time to reassemble the box. Use the provided screws to secure the lid—make sure the ribbon cable is positioned correctly and that none of the internal wires are caught by the lid edge or the internal posts. Then, apply the label strip to the lid to make it easy to identify the screw terminal functions. The label strip is simply an appropriately sized text table from a word processor: the table is printed out, cropped out of the paper with scissors, and then carefully fixed onto the box top with clear scotch tape.

Now, your programmer is ready to plug together with the other components when they are ready—as shown in the final picture.

Other Programmers

The numerous USB-attached ISP programmers are not the only option for programming your AVR. If you're on an extremely tight budget, or using a computer with no USB ports, you can get a serial port programmer for about $10 (delivered cost)–though it will be delivered as a kit you have to make up. An example of such a product is

www.adafruit.com/index.php?main_page=product_info&cPath=16&products_id=26

This handy little device also uses the ISP programming method, but it uses your computer's serial port rather than USB–so it will probably be quite a lot slower–but, using the information available online and in this book, you should be able to figure out how to make it work with the Arduino development environment.

AVR ISP Programming Adaptor and Pin Headers

The ISP connector that comes as standard with all programmers features two closely parallel rows of pins (either ten pins, or six pins, as in our Pololu example). If our test bed was a PCB then accommodating this connector footprint would not be an issue, but as we know, it's a breadboard. As Appendix A explains, it's a feature of breadboards that all closely spaced connections are connected in some way.

This means that we need to convert the footprint of the six-way (or perhaps ten-way if you are using a different AVR ISP programmer) ribbon cable connector to a row of parallel pins suitable to plug into a breadboard.

Luckily, the Sparkfun people have seen this need and created the "AVR Programming Adaptor" (see Figure 2-23). This is a little PCB that allows the plug from the programmer to be easily connected to the project breadboard. As you can see from the initial photo of the adaptor, the board effectively converts the six-way or ten-way ribbon cable connector from your ISP programmer to a single row of pins carrying the required ISP signals (MOSI, MISO, RESET, etc.).

Figure 2-23. *Sparkfun AVR programming adaptor*

At the time of this writing, this adaptor is only available from Sparkfun (or its resellers around the world):

www.sparkfun.com/products/8508

Many of Sparkfun's various distributors around the world also seem to stock it too. Click on the "distributors" tab on Sparkfun's home page to find your local outlet of Sparkfun products.

The pin headers can be obtained from most electronics suppliers, for example

- www.sparkfun.com/products/117 (United States).
- Maplin JW59P (UK).
- Your local electronic components supplier.

The AVR Programming Adaptor comes as just a PCB; so, we need to solder some pins from a pin header (like the one shown in Figure 2-24) onto this board.

Figure 2-24. *Header pin strip*

Assembling the Programming Adaptor

We need to solder some header pins into the adaptor board. We're going to use some sections from a pin header, in conjunction with the Sparkfun AVR Programming Adaptor board, as shown in Figure 2-25.

Figure 2-25. *Adding header pins*

You'll find that with most pin headers, you can break off the number of pins you require quite easily by hand: the plastic housing has snapping points between each pin position–but if you find this difficult you can use some small cutters to make the breaks, though this can leave the pins a little loose in the plastic.

1. Start by breaking off two lots of three pins (*or* two lots of five pins if you have a ten-way ISP ribbon cable if you're using a programmer with a ten-way cable). Then, also break off one lot of six pins.

2. Put the six-pin strip on the AVR breakout board's underside, beneath the "Gnd, 5V, MISO, SCK" labels. The longer length of the pins should be positioned straight down from the underside of the board.

3. Now, solder the short ends of the pins which are poking through the PCB topside, as in Figure 2-25.

4. Next, put your two three-pin groups into the top side of the board (or into the five-pin groups above if you have a ten-way cable from your programmer), and solder on the underside. Make sure there are no sneaky solder bridges shorting together any of the soldered pins; remove any bridges you find. Figure 2-25 shows how the board looks when the pins have been connected as described (in this case, for a six-pin cable).

5. Now, plug the completed breakout board assembly into your breadboard at row 16–as shown in Figure 2-26.

Figure 2-26. *The completed breakout board in place on the test bed breadboard*

▓ **Note**   Only the six pins on the edge of the board actually plug into the breadboard. The other set of pins *only* connects to the programmer's ribbon cable plug.

6.   Next, plug the ribbon cable from the programmer into the adaptor board. Note that the red wire side of the plug faces toward the pin names on the board (MOSI, RESET, etc.).

7.   Finally, you need to connect the breakout board to the microcontroller chip using some breadboard jumpers that you will leave always connected. The jumpers need to implement the connections shown back in Figure 2-9. As you can see, the idea is to wire the ISP signals to the chip pins which have the same names. That's what we do in the next diagram–Figure 2-27.

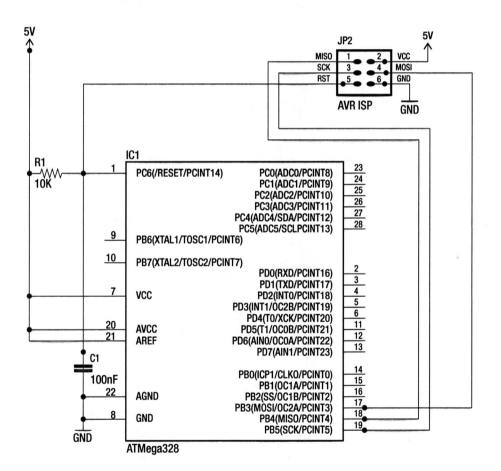

Figure 2-27. *Test bed: permanent connections to AVR breakout*

Figure 2-27 uses the AVR's native pin names, not their Arduino names: we'll investigate the difference between native and Arduino pin names in the next chapter. Notice that we need R1 and C1 to ensure that the reset is properly asserted at power on.

Figure 2-27 shows a photo of the completed breadboard setup: from the breakout board, permanent jumper wires connect to the AVR chip. These permanent jumper wires are cut to size and striped using a Sharpie pen. This is intended to make it easy to differentiate them from the temporary per-project wires we shall attach. The resistor and capacitor permanently connected to pin 1 of the chip form the reset circuit.

The unstriped jumper wires bring five volts DC and ground connections to the ATmega328 AVR chip. On this AVR chip, pins 7 and 20 connect to +5V, and pins 8 and 22 connect to ground. The little dot on the chip (at bottom right Figure 2-28) shows which is pin 1: the pins then number from 1 to 28 around the chip in an anticlockwise direction.

Figure 2-28. *Permanent jumper between AVR chip and breakout*

Our PSU feeds +5 volts of power onto the far end of the breadboard–as we saw earlier.

One of the best aspects of ISP programming is that when the programmer is not active, it goes into an electrically inert state that doesn't ordinarily interfere with anything else. This means that you don't need to unplug the programmer from the breadboard if you don't want to. I usually leave mine connected all the time and it hasn't caused a problem as yet.

There's one additional clarification to make about the signals on the ISP cable: we saw earlier that the Pololu programmer board has a "+5V VBUS" connection, via which it is possible to draw a small amount of power, derived from the USB port to which the programmer is connected. The AVR programmer adaptor also has a connector which is marked "+5V" on the adaptor board,[5] but it is not the same thing.

The +5V connection on the adaptor is there to allow the programmer to sense whether the AVR circuit to which it is connected is actually on-power. If the programmer does not "see" something in the region of +5V coming *in* from the AVR circuit to which it is connected, it will not even attempt to carry out programming. Thus, you should always make sure that your test bed rig is powered by your own +5V supply before attempting to carry out any programming. Your test rig will *not* be able to obtain useful amounts of power from the programmer via this line.

Test Bed Software—Installation and Setup

There's little point in detailing the installation and setup instructions for the programmer here because you may be using a different programmer from mine, but in any case all the programmers I have tried out come with setup instructions (either on paper in the box with them, or via a web site link). The recommended Pololu programmer is very well supported with an extensive downloadable user manual that details installation for all supported platforms. There's also a section on troubleshooting and alternate configurations and uses. The web pages for the product provide a lot of additional material that may be of interest once you get into using the programmer.

Once you have your programmer installed, you will find that although it physically interfaces via USB, it looks to your operating system like one or more additional serial ports (these are virtual serial ports). In the case of the Pololu programmer (and others) there will actually be two new serial —one for the programmer and one for the extra logic level serial port that it also provides.

During the installation of the programmer you may see messages which tell you the name of the new virtual ports that are being created (e.g., on Linux and Mac OS X these will be something like /dev/ttyACM0, while on Windows it will be COM3 or something similar. It's not essential, but it's a good idea to make a note of these port names or numbers for later reference.

Once your programmer is installed, it's time to move on to the software development environment setup.

Choosing the Software: Why Arduino?

As well as the ones to be described, there are a number of commercially available AVR software creation packages, some offering programming languages such as BASIC. However, our main candidates for this book's software development environment were the two main free packages for AVR:

- Atmel's AVRStudio is a free package that gives you the full range of C and assembly language programming functions, including detailed access to the darker, seldom-used, functional corners of the AVR chip. However, at present, AVRStudio runs only on Windows PCs; there is no Mac or Linux version. For this reason we won't be using it in this book. If you *are* using a Windows PC, you may want to download it to try out, here's the URL (uniform resource locator):

    ```
    http://www.atmel.com/microsite/avr_studio_5/default.aspx
    ```

---

[5]The issue here is really with Sparkfun's labeling of this pin. It should more properly be marked as "VDD" or "VDD-Sense." Within the Pololu documentation this pin is always called VDD.

- Arduino, also a completely free package, offers a development environment which uses a language called Processing. This is syntactically similar to the C language, but it simplifies code creation by hiding some of the more detailed aspects of C or those particular to operating system and environment. Arduino also simplifies the use of I/O pins on the AVR chip, making it exceptionally easy to use. The Arduino software development environment is very capable, well documented, and easy to use, and it's available for all three major desktop environments: these are the main reasons we use it throughout this book.

AVRStudio and the Arduino software *can* coexist on a single Windows PC quite happily without any problem–just don't try to use them simultaneously.

Both AVRStudio and Arduino feature an interactive development environment (IDE). Both packages include the WinAVR C compiler, their main use of which is to take your source code and to compile a machine code version of it. They write into an uploadable hexadecimal format file (see Wikipedia's "Intel Hex" page). Then, they both use a program called AVRDude (formerly known as AVRprog) to do the actual upload of this hex file, via the programmer, into your MCU chip. As it's such a useful utility with so many options, you'll be looking at AVRDude in a lot more detail in the next chapter.

Of course, most of the components described previously also do additional things, but this is the essence of how both these packages work.

To obtain the Arduino software, go to the Arduino home page at www.arduino.org and get the latest available version. You should also get the installation guide appropriate to your desktop type (Mac, Linux, or Windows) from that same site. I won't review the installation procedure here, because the platform-specific install guides that accompany the kit download are very extensive and take you through the process step by step. They provide information about what to do if things don't go smoothly, but they usually do. I've never yet had a problem installing an Arduino software kit.

Once installed, you need to make some customizations to allow the Arduino software to use your Pololu test bed programmer: if you have elected to use a different programmer, the vendor should be able to tell you how to do the equivalent of this customization. If you have used an AVRISP2 (or a clone product) then you should not need to do anything extra.

For the Pololu programmer we need to modify two files:

- `boards.txt`
- `programmers.txt`

These files will be found under the installation location of the Arduino software, in file system locations as follows:

- On Windows it's the following, where xxx is the Arduino version number). Under the installation location you will find a folder called `hardware` and under that will be another folder called `Arduino` and inside that will be the two files noted above:

  `C:\Program Files\Arduino-xxx`

- On Linux and on Mac OS X you'll find the base folder for Arduino at the following location. Under the installation location you will find a folder called `hardware` and under that will be another folder called `Arduino` and inside that will be the two files we need to edit:

  `/usr/share/Arduino`

As specified by Pololu at www.pololu.com/docs/0J17/3 you need to use a text editor (just a plain text editor such as Notepad on Windows, or gedit or vi on Linux or Mac) to modify `programmers.txt` and `boards.txt`; you should make sure to save a copy of the original files (e.g., copy boards.txt to original_boards.txt) in case you make any mistakes in editing.

Add the following three lines to the end of programmers.txt. This enables the Arduino to know about the AVRISP2 programmer and compatible programmers–such as the Pololu board and many others.

```
avrispv2.name=AVR ISP v2
avrispv2.communication=serial
avrispv2.protocol=avrispv2
```

Next, add the following lines at the bottom of the boards.txt file.[6] You can download ready-made versions of these files–with these additions already made–from the Pololu link quoted above.

```
############################################################
orangutan48.name=Pololu Baby Orangutan B-48 via Programmer
orangutan48.upload.using=avrispv2
orangutan48.upload.maximum_size=4096
orangutan48.build.mcu=atmega48
orangutan48.build.f_cpu=20000000L
orangutan48.build.core=arduino
############################################################
orangutan168.name=Pololu Orangutan or 3pi robot w/ ATmega168 via Programmer
orangutan168.upload.using=avrispv2
orangutan168.upload.maximum_size=16384
orangutan168.build.mcu=atmega168
orangutan168.build.f_cpu=1000000L
orangutan168.build.core=arduino
############################################################
orangutan328p.name=Pololu Orangutan or 3pi robot w/ ATmega328p via Programmer
orangutan328p.upload.using=avrispv2
orangutan328p.upload.maximum_size=32768
orangutan328p.build.mcu=atmega328p
orangutan328p.build.f_cpu=1000000L
orangutan328p.build.core=arduino
############################################################
```

Adding these lines adds three AVR chip definitions to the Arduino infrastructure: these are for ATmega48, ATmega168, and ATmega328 chips, respectively.

Note that each processor type has a build.f_cpu parameter; this specifies the clock speed at which the chip is running. For a newly bought ATmega328 (or ATmega328p or ATmega328pu) that has never previously been programmed, be sure that this line says:

- 1000000L (that's a one followed by six zeroes and an L)as shown, and *not*
- 20000000L (that's a two followed by seven zeroes and an L).

Although it can operate at up to 20 MHz, as shipped by Atmel, your AVR chip will be set to operate at its own internal clock speed of just 1 MHz. You can change this–and will do so in the next chapter, where I will explain what's going on at that stage.

---

[6]Are you curious about why the name "Orangutan" appears in all this? Well, the whole reason Pololu produces an AVR programmer is because its Orang-utan robotics controller uses an ATMEGA168 chip.

■ **Note** Although you are not advised to use anything other than the quoted AVR chips, if you do find that you own a variant of the ATmega328P (e.g., the ultra-low power version) or are using some other AVR than an ATmega168 or 328, you may need to make additions or modifications to AVRDude's configuration file. You can find more information about this area in the next chapter.

Once these file modifications have been made, you will need to close and then restart the Arduino IDE (if it was already running).

Test Bed Testing

Now, you have built your development system hardware, installed the Pololu programmer, installed and set up the Arduino environment, and it's time to move on to the most exciting part, actually putting it to work.

Start up the Arduino software according to the instructions you saw at the end of the Arduino installation. When Arduino has started up, click File ➤ New to create a new sketch (yes, Arduino's name for projects is "sketches").

In the white code space that appears within the Arduino window, type the following program code:

```
// Comments start with a "//"
#define THE_LED  8
// The above sets THE_LED to mean Arduino digital pin 8 (pin 14 on the chip - see Chapter 3)
void setup()
{
  pinMode(THE_LED, OUTPUT);
}

void loop()
{
  if (digitalRead(THE_LED)==low)
  {
    digitalWrite(THE_LED, high);
  }
  else
  {
    digitalWrite(THE_LED, low);
  }
  delay(4000);
}
```

You don't need to understand the detail of this code at this point (this is something else you'll look at in the next chapter); however, what this code should do is to slowly pulse pin 14 of the AVR chip low-high-low-high. Make sure you type the code exactly as shown, with all capital letters precisely in the places shown and all punctuation marks (especially the semicolons) in place. Be sure get the bracket types correct, don't confuse normal round brackets with curly brackets–although we use them both in programming, they mean different things and are not interchangeable.

When you have entered this code, your Arduino window should look pretty much like Figure 2-28:

When you are sure you have entered the code correctly click the verify button on the Arduino interface: This has a ✓ symbol on it (see top of Figure 2-29). This will compile the program but does not yet load it into your AVR chip. If all is well, you should see the "Done compiling" message and some text that tells you how big the compiled binary sketch is. However, if you have made a mistake in typing the program, you will see an error message in red, indicating the nature of the error. This message will usually give you enough information—especially in a small program like this one—to realize where the problem is.

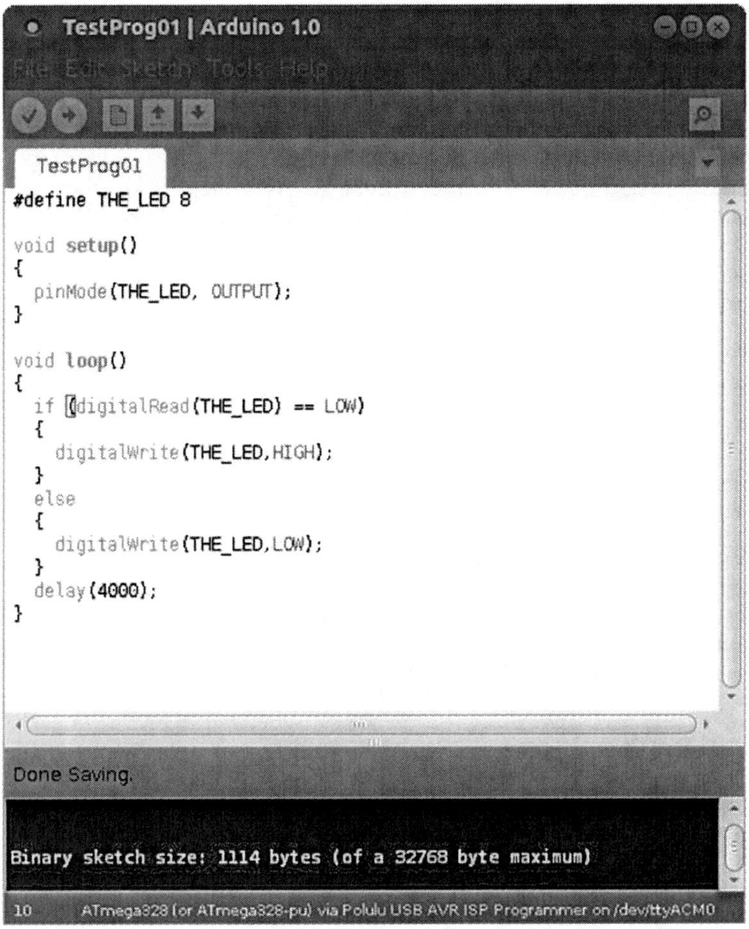

```
TestProg01 | Arduino 1.0

TestProg01

#define THE_LED 8

void setup()
{
  pinMode(THE_LED, OUTPUT);
}

void loop()
{
  if (digitalRead(THE_LED) == LOW)
  {
    digitalWrite(THE_LED,HIGH);
  }
  else
  {
    digitalWrite(THE_LED,LOW);
  }
  delay(4000);
}

Done Saving.

Binary sketch size: 1114 bytes (of a 32768 byte maximum)

10    ATmega328 (or ATmega328-pu) via Polulu USB AVR ISP Programmer on /dev/ttyACM0
```

Figure 2-29. First test program

When you have located and fixed any errors and can successfully process the file, save the sketch (project) by clicking File ➤ Save As… and then save the sketch as TestProg01 or some equivalent name that you will remember for use in the next chapter.

Now, having compiled the program without errors, we can upload the program into your AVR chip! From the Tools menu choose Board and from the list of possible boards choose the programmer whose details and processor type you entered in the previous stage of the installation. In the case of the recommended programmer you'd select Pololu Orangutan… 328p.

Next, from the Tools menu choose Serial Port and select the serial port to which your Pololu programmer is attached. These selections only need to be made once; they will be maintained for all your subsequent Arduino sessions unless you change them again or upgrade the Arduino software.

Now, the magic moment! When you press the ➜ button on the Arduino interface, you tell it to upload your code into the AVR via the programmer. The first time through, this may take a minute or so, but you should see the LEDs on the programmer flash rapidly when programming takes place. When programming completes, the programmer goes to sleep again, and your program starts to run inside the AVR chip!

To verify the programming has worked, connect a DVM with ground probe to pin 8 of the chip, and the positive probe to pin 14. You should see the voltage change between somewhere close to zero and something close to 5 volts about every four seconds?

Congratulations! You've programmed your first AVR.

Oh no! It didn't work? Try the following:

- *With power off the test bed*: Check that you have your AVR chip installed the right way round. See Figure 2-28 which shows the dot on top of the chip indicating pin 1 at bottom right in the photo.

- *With power on*: Look at the LEDs on the programmer board itself. Refer to the documentation for your programmer as to what these mean. A steadily flashing light usually means a problem. Fast flashing lights are good; they indicate programming activity.

- *With power on*: Double-check that your power supply is delivering 5 volts to your breadboard–and that both the +5V and ground from your power supply are being continued all the way along the power rails of the breadboard. Remember that many breadboards have one or more breaks in their power supply rails up and down the breadboard: these breaks will need jumpers installing to continue the power bus–as Figure 2-30 (see also Figure 2-8).

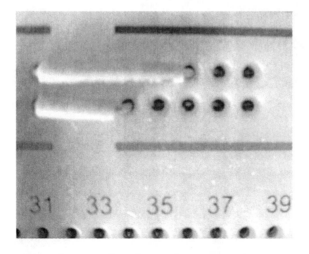

Figure 2-30. Breadboard power bus continuation jumpers

- *Check power connections*: Make sure you have made the power connections to pins 7, 8, 21, and 21 of the AVR chip as depicted in the circuit diagram of Figure 2-28 and use your DVM (carefully) to check these pins to see that your chip is getting power. If it's not, check the inline fuse you fitted to the power supply. If it's blown, you've probably made a mistake in your wiring somewhere. For example check that you haven't used a column of holes on the breadboard for two different purposes. Check Appendix A for breadboard details if you need to.

- *With power off*: Check and double-check the connections between your AVR chip and the AVR breakout board against the diagram in Figure 2-28 make especially sure that you have made the connections as shown between ground and VCC – without these, the programmer will not be able to detect that the AVR is there.

- *Upload your code again*: If there is any possibility that your AVR chip has been used before (i.e., it is known to be not new) then it is possible that it had been previously set by some other usage to run at a different speed than the default 1 MHz we put in the boards.txt file. Try editing the speed parameter to 8000000L (that's eight with six zeroes and an L, meaning 8 MHz) and then restart the Arduino program and try uploading your code again.

- *Double-check the programmer board*: If, after checking thoroughly, you think your test bed is all correct, then it's possible that the problem is more with your programmer board. Refer to the supplier's web site for additional troubleshooting tools or techniques, and for any possible required driver or software updates.

- *If all else fails, don't be downhearted*: The next chapter contains some useful tips on using the AVRDude program which will give you extra testing methods to try to determine the problem.

TTL Level Serial Port

We saw previously that many AVRISP programmers offer a TTL level[7] serial port. But what does this mean and why is it useful? As you probably know (especially if you've read Appendix B), the serial port on a desktop computer uses a system that, ultimately, dates back to the 1960s, called RS-232. This system (which forms the basis for the later serial communication standard CCIT V24) requires the translation of normal computer logical levels (+5 volts for high and <1 volt for low) to greater voltages. Chips that do this voltage level translation, such as the famous MAX232 series from Maxim semiconductor, translate a logic low into a +12-volt level and a logic high into a –12V logic voltage. Those same chips also feature receivers that turn the received +12 volts and –12 volts signals back into standard logic levels at the receiving end.

The purpose of this voltage translation is mainly to allow long cable runs for serial cables. If computer cabling is run alongside mains cables and other sources of electrical noise (as it often is in the industrial settings where serial communication was first used), then quite a lot of interference can be induced onto them. By changing the voltage range of the signals from about 4.2 volts to about 24 volts, RS-232 greatly reduces the serial data's vulnerability to corruption during transit across long cables. RS-232 has a lot of value when long cables are involved; however, long serial cables are now more or less a thing of the past, most communication between

---

[7]TTL stands for Transistor-Transistor Logic—a family of logic chips first launched by Texas Instruments in the mid-1960s. These use a standardized system of two voltages to represent binary values 0 and 1—also called low and high. Consequently, electronics that use the same voltage levels are often referred to as using TTL levels (shorthand). Many of the original TTL format devices are still made, albeit using far more modern electronics to implement the same functions. Check out the 74HC000 for just one example; it has exactly the same pin-out as the 7400 chip, which was launched in 1966.

systems and peripherals now happens over newer and faster interconnects such as Ethernet over Cat5/Cat6 cables or Wi-Fi, and we also use shorter-haul connections such as USB or FireWire where previously we might have used serial.

However, serial data communication is still a very handy way for MCU-based systems to talk to one another and to larger machines. It's cheap, easy to use, and well understood. Better still, many MCU chips are equipped with a TTL logic level serial port, so, in theory, no extra chips are needed on the project to allow it to exchange messages with the outside world. I add "in theory" because, if the machine you want to talk to only has an RS-232 serial port, then you can't directly connect. You'd have to add an RS-232 level translator chip to your project to connect with it.

Please *don't* ever try connecting an RS-232 port to a TTL level port: It's a really good way to damage the devices at both ends of the connection–perhaps irreparably.

For our purposes we only need short cable runs (perhaps three feet –or 900mm) between our MCU and our desktop machine: Using TTL signaling levels over such a short distance should pose no problems, in most circumstances. Fewer and fewer desktop machines now feature a serial port, and even on those that do, the port will be using RS-232. So, how do we get a TTL level serial port on a desktop machine? As ever, technology comes to the rescue here. You can buy, very cheaply from some Asia-Pac vendors, a USB dongle for your desktop machine that offers the following functionality:

- The hardware (inside the USB plug) to implement a new virtual serial port such as COM4 (Windows) or /dev/ttyUSB0 (Mac and Linux). This pretends to be a real serial port, which means you can talk to it through a terminal emulator such as Hyperterm (bundled with every version of Windows since forever–though not with Windows 7) and Minicom or Screen on a Linux system or Terminal.app on a Mac.

- TTL data send and receive wires that you CAN safely connect directly to your AVR's equivalents (TX to RX in each case) as in Figure 2-31.

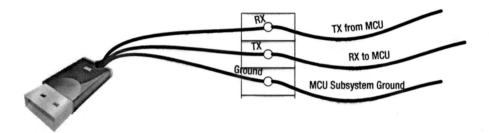

Figure 2-31. *TTL level serial dongle to MCU connections*

The USB plug (electronics inside) plugs into an unused USB port on your desktop machine. The ground connection is common between the dongle and the MCU board (and should always be made first). Then, the dongle's transmit (TX) line goes to the MCU's receive (RX) line, and vice versa.

Of course, because your operating system sees the device as a standard serial port, in addition to communicating using typed commands in a terminal emulator, you can also create software on the desktop side (e.g., with the Arduino IDE) to talk to your AVR project.

We'll be making regular use of the TTL level serial connection in the "Projects" section of this book.

Summary

In this chapter you have looked at the various materials and methods needed to construct our "test bed rig." You looked at the various parts needed and we saw how to put them together to make what you need. You've seen how you can use the test bed rig to program a simple program into the AVR and how to make sure it works. You've also looked in detail at how an AVR gets programmed and finally at how you can use the TTL serial channel provided by the programmer to simply allow your AVR application to talk to your desktop computer.

If you're new to this whole field you may well have found this section heavy going–there is a lot to take in here. However, the good thing is, you're still here and still reading. So take a breather and then let's continue with some more steps into MCU-land!

Coming Up Next

Arduino and the Naked AVR: we find out how to use a bare AVR with software meant for an Arduino.

CHAPTER 3

▧ ▧ ▧

Arduino and the Naked AVR

In the introduction we looked at the trade-offs involved in using just AVR chips for projects as opposed to a packaged AVR-centric system such as Arduino.

The essential logic is this: MCU (MicroController Unit) chips are available very cheaply and so it's viable to use them, in even the simplest of projects, to add functionality and flexibility you could never get from a non-MCU approach.

Packaged systems intentionally abstract the core hardware; the stated aim of many of them is to attract people with more interest in creativity than electronics. They do this by abstracting the core computing function as a black box. This highly laudable intent has worked! There are now many thousands of people using Arduino and similar systems who would never have previously thought of themselves as electronics enthusiasts or programmers. The people who put together Arduino, in particular, should be lauded from the rooftops; they found a way to bridge the creative and technical worlds in a way that I believe to be radical and truly new. In the same way that we now hear famous physicists saying they were hooked into science via watching the Apollo Moon landings as kids, I think we'll hear the designers of future technological wonders say that, for them, it all started with an Arduino!

Using a packaged system for simple projects can be overkill, and the costs of that overkill can mount up if you're doing lots of small projects. Looking at published projects that use an Arduino Duemilanove and a protoshield to do time control of one solitary room light, you do have to wonder if, for those who err more toward the technical side, the packaged approach can be taken too far!

This book contends that, for those who already have some electronics knowledge, and those who are willing to learn, it's possible to get the best of both worlds: we can reap the benefits of a packaged approach to software but be able to build projects with hardware that is suited exactly to the purpose and that we understand more fully. The electronics knowledge required is not very heavy and the appendices of this book are intended to get you started in various areas that may be partly or completely new to you.

In the last chapter we saw how to put together a test bed rig that we can use for developing and testing projects. In this chapter we look at some detailed differences between implementing circuits with and without an MCU. Then, we look at some basic things you need to know about AVR chips. Finally, we look in detail at how the various elements of the Arduino IDE and that test bed rig function together.

Comparing Approaches

There are few projects for which you could use an AVR alone. Figure 3-1 probably represents a minimal configuration.

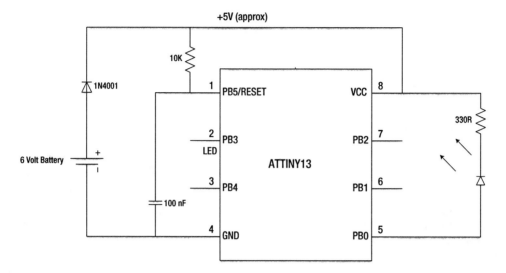

Figure 3-1. *A minimal LED flasher circuit using an AVR*

Figure 3-1 shows an AVR circuit that could flash an LED. There's no need to build this circuit, but let's just run through its important points.

- The circuit is powered from a 6-volt battery; and because of the 1n4001 diode this is dropped to about 5.4 volts. This is okay because most (but not all) AVRs can operate from supply voltages between 1.8 volts and 5.5 volts. Always check the data sheet for your device for the power supply voltage limits (maximum and minimum).

- The AVR depicted is an entry-level ATTINY13 device which comes in a small eight-pin DIP (Dual Inline Package) as shown in Figure 3-2.

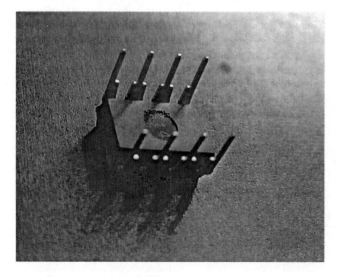

Figure 3-2. *An eight-pin DIP device*

- Hanging off pin 5 (PB0) we have the LED, which is protected by a 330 Ohm current limiting resistor (330R). This resistor protects the LED and the AVR's PB0 pin from pulling too much current (amperage). Most ordinary LEDs need between 15 milliamps (0.015 of one amp[1]) and 20 ma to light up properly but not be damaged by excessive current. Happily, the ATTINY13's PB0 and PB1 port pins can each handle this same amount of current. So, this resistor is used to limit the flow through the LED to a comfortable amount for both the LED and the AVR.

- We have a 10 K Ohm (10,000 ohms) resistor and a 100 nf (100 nanoFarads) capacitor connected to the reset pin (pin 1). These ensure that the AVR is reset properly when the circuit powers up.

And that's it! Just seven small components (including the battery) required to make an LED flasher.

Pre-MCUs you'd automatically reach for some kind of timer chip to do this job. Let's compare the approach just discussed with using a single-purpose device such as a 555 timer chip (if you're unfamiliar with this chip, take a look at http://www.555-timer-circuits.com/):

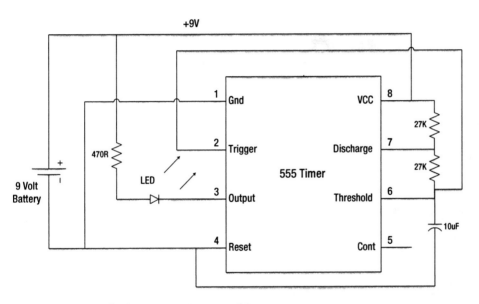

Figure 3-3. *A LED flasher circuit using a 555 chip*

You will see that this circuit shown in Figure 3-2 also uses seven small components (including the +9 V battery) to flash an LED on and off at a speed determined by the components connected to pins 6 and 7.

Could this 555-based circuit do more for us than just flash an LED on and off? Well, you could add another LED/resistor pair connected to the output the opposite way around: you would then get two LEDs that flash in strict alternation (one on while the other is off, but never on together and both can only flash at the same rate):

---

[1]You can work out these equivalences by using Ohm's law (there's a great Wikipedia page on that). Also, did you know you can also just type "20 milliamps in amps" or "100 millivolts in volts" or "3 volts divided by 150 ohms" into Google to get answers to these kinds of conversions?

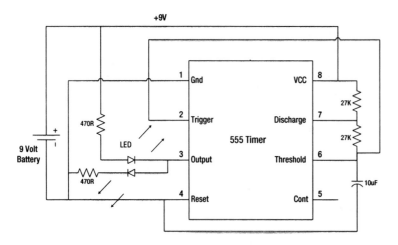

Figure 3-4. *A dual-LED flasher circuit using a 555 chip*

In Figure 3-4, we have added that additional LED. Now, as well as pulling current through the first LED when the 555 chip's output (pin 3) is low, it also pushes current from the output through the second LED when it is high. You could add a variable resistance to augment the 27 K fixed resistors, which would allow you to vary the flash rate or duty cycle of both LEDs. But after that you're pretty much at the limit of what this simple circuit could do.

AVR Pulls Ahead

The AVR circuit, on the other hand, is capable of doing a lot more. For example, it too can run two LEDs, as in Figure 3-5 in which we've connected an additional LED, this time to pin 6 (PB1) of the AVR.

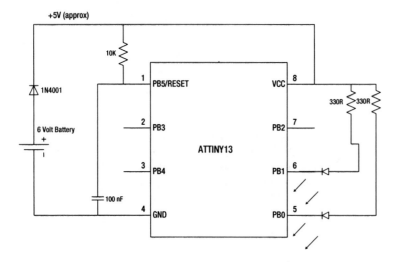

Figure 3-5. *A dual LED flasher circuit using an AVR*

These two LEDs could, easily, be made to flash completely independently of each other at different rates and even at different intensities. Since (on the ATTINY13 and many other AVRs) these particular AVR pins can source or sink 20 ma of current, we could repeat the trick we did with the 555 circuit and add two more LEDs in opposite polarity.

Figure 3-5 shows how a push-pull AVR version of the circuit would look: there are two additional LEDs. When the output ports are set by software to a logic LOW level, the two top LEDs will turn on, when the output ports are set to HIGH the bottom two will turn on. Like the 555 output pin, the AVRs pins are sinking (pulling) current when LOW, but sourcing current (pushing) when HIGH.

So, now if we were to create the software to make it do so, our AVR could flash two pairs of LEDs on and off at whatever rate we wanted it to and in whatever combination we wanted it to, in an almost infinite variation. We can change what it does and how it does it, without having to modify the hardware *ever* again, which could never be the case with the 555 equivalent. But, there's more.

Go AVR!

You may notice that in the four-LED version of the AVR circuit (see Figure 3-6), there are still three pins of the AVR that have no connection. These are pins 2, 3, and 7 (PB3, PB4, and PB2, respectively). On this particular AVR chip these port pins are not capable of driving or sinking more than 10 ma: However, if we added an additional 50-cent driver chip (e.g., a ULN2803), these pins between them could control at least three more LEDs—meaning that this AVR could control seven LEDs. You'll be using the ULN2803 in several projects later in this book for just such a purpose.

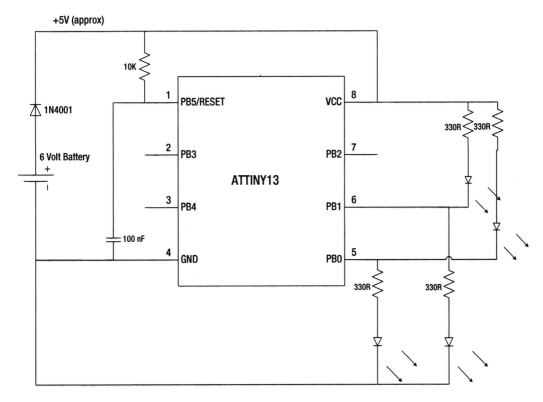

Figure 3-6. *A quadruple LED flasher circuit using an AVR*

If you didn't need any additional LEDs you could use those spare port pins for something else. On the AVR, as on most microcontrollers, any port pin can be configured by software to be either an input or an output. So, if you configure the unused pin 3 (PB4) to be an input, you can use it to sense the state of a switch—SW1: Figure 3-7 has this feature added.

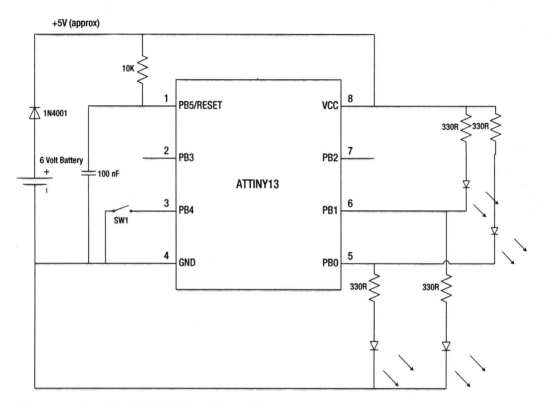

Figure 3-7. *A quadruple LED flasher, with switch input*

Now, the software you put into your AVR is able to sense the state of the switch (when the switch is closed, the PB4 pin will read LOW; when the switch is open, it will read HIGH[2]). That means that the software can alter the circuit's behavior depending on the state of the switch. For example, it might flash the LEDs at one speed when the switch port reads HIGH and at a different speed when it reads LOW. We could go even further and connect a switch to all three unused port pins and implement a whole hatful of different LED flash rates or LED intensity changes, according to the switch settings—but I guess you get the idea.

So our little eight-pin AVR circuit offers some fairly surprising capabilities especially when considering its low component count and low cost.

However, we have so far ignored the elephant in the room. The AVR would need programming and would need some software to be written for it—and the 555 timer would not. So, if you were simply making a project to flash one or two LEDs on and off, the AVR probably provides more capability and possibility than you would need. Although the amount of hardware is about the same, it would take additional effort to write software and upload it into the AVR; however, no such extra effort is needed with the 555 timer approach, where you just calculate the value of the components you need to set the required flash rate and duration and you're done!

---

[2]In many logic circuits you would need a pull-up resistor on a logic circuit input pin to make the input tend toward the HIGH level when a switch was open. However, AVR ports have an internal pull-up resistor on them which can be activated to preclude the need for an external resistor.

But, if the goal of your project was rather more complex, if you needed to make multiple LEDs flash independently and at different rates at different times, or in direct response to changes of input, then it would—no question—be better to use an AVR. It's a fact of life that few project requirements are as simple as the one depicted in this scenario. As the projects you attempt get more complicated, the MCU becomes an ever more obvious choice for implementing it. Eventually, climbing the ladder of complexity, you reach a point where the MCU becomes the only serious choice.

Now that you have a feel for the basic trade-offs and advantages that can be had from using an MCU approach, even for a simple requirement, I hope that you agree that the MCU approach to projects is a good one and provides a palette of possibilities whose end you might never reach.

Putting All the Pieces in Place

In this book you will use the Arduino software development environment, but in a slightly different way than if you were using Arduino hardware. So, before you dive deeper into some of the building blocks, it's perhaps a good idea to zoom out and look at what the pieces are and—in broad-brush detail—how they fit together.

Figure 3-8 shows the pieces of the Arduino programming setup I use in this book. A block diagram of a 100 % Arduino environment would look much the same except that the AVR programmer and AVR chip would all be packaged into a single box called Arduino hardware, representing a product such as an Arduino Uno or Duemilanove board.

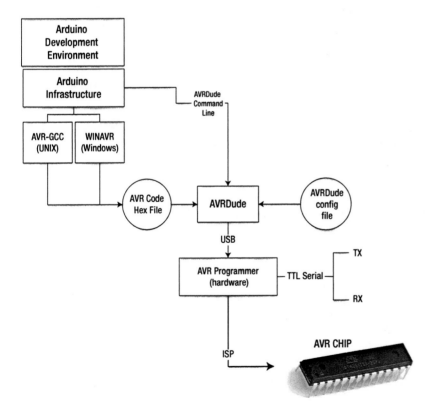

Figure 3-8. *AVR MCU development system: block diagram*

The Arduino IDE

Starting from top left, we have the Arduino IDE. This is a desktop computer application that gives us a place to enter our program code and to exercise various levels of control over the tool chain. For example, we can initiate a compile (Arduino calls it a Verify) operation on our code which attempts to build an AVR executable version of the program we have entered—and tells us of any problems with what we have written. From here we can tell Arduino to begin uploading our completed code to our selected AVR device and do a whole load of other things. For example,

- We can select which type of AVR programmer we want to use.

- We can print out our program code.

- We can have Arduino autoformat our code to "beautify" it with proper indents to make it easier to read.

- We can create a code archive—and many other useful things.

Arduino infrastructure software

Underneath the IDE, in Figure 3-8, there is a layer of what I have called Arduino infrastructure software. This contains things like task management facilities, file management routines, and autoupdate modules. One of the main tasks in this layer is to take the code that we entered, which is in a very simplified C-like language, and to surround it with a full jacket of C language constructs that a C or C++ compiler can use—including make files to control things like the AVR processor for which the code is being built, code optimization levels, and so on.

C Compilers

Underneath the infrastructure are the C compilers. These are all based on the GNU C/C++ compiler, but there are special variants of them for Unix (Linux and Mac) environments and a distinct variant called WINAVR for Windows systems. The compiler takes the code produced by Arduino and compiles it into a body of machine code which implements our programming, and which is customized for the AVR chip type we are using. It also links in some standard library code modules, plus any additional libraries our code may need to use.

Hex File

The result of the compilation and linking process task goes into a hex file on the hard drive. This hex file is essentially a text file, and all it contains is a long slew of hexadecimal numbers that represents the finished code that has to be uploaded to the AVR chip.

Errors

Any errors from the previous processes show up in the Arduino IDE window in the bottom section—usually in red text. These messages are generally quite detailed and numerous: if or when you have to analyze such a message stream, the important thing is to scroll back to the first ones; the latter ones are very often just further errors resulting from the first one or two.

AVRDude, the AVR Programmer, and the AVR Chip

When the compilation has successfully completed, and the hex file has been created (a fresh hex file won't be created if the process fails), the Arduino infrastructure issues a command sequence to AVRDude (more on that soon) to upload the contents of the hex file[3] to the AVR chip via the hardware. In an Arduino board, the programmer and the AVR chip are all on the Arduino. In our case we are using a separate USB programmer connected via ISP to our AVR chip, which will be on the test bed rig we built in Chapter 2.

The AVR Type

There are a few things to note about the infrastructure depicted in Figure 3-8. First, the Arduino suite, the compiler/linker level, *and* AVRDude all have to agree about which type of AVR will be the target for the software that is being developed. In theory, this is taken care of from the top level down. The Arduino's boards.txt and programmers.txt files between them contain all the known possibilities, and the choices made inside the IDE, in regard to which board to use, ripple down through the other components depicted in Figure 3-8.

However, because they were crafted by different teams in different places at different times, for different purposes each of the depicted functional blocks has *its own* separate list of AVR chips that it knows about, and these are pretty extensive but not exhaustive. For example, I bought an ATmega328PU (which is the micropower version of the ATmega328) and neither Arduino nor AVRDude had ever heard of it. We'll look at dealing with such an issue later in the section "AVRDude: Getting Started."

We'll look in some detail at AVRDude in the next section, but what about the compilers and Arduino? How do we find out what AVR chips they know about? You can make the avr-gcc compiler list all the AVRs it knows about using the following command:

```
avr-gcc --target-help | more
```

You'll find avr-gcc in the bin subfolder of wherever you installed WinAVR on your Windows system (typically it gets installed on the top level of your C:\ drive. On Linux/Mac it's usually installed in /usr/bin. In most cases you should just be able to type the command as just shown, since the installations add these folders to the users search path on both Unix and Windows systems.

Arduino's Configuration Files:

Arduino lists all the boards specified in boards.txt in its Tools menu: for Arduino, boards.txt is a crucial file. As you saw, we edited it in Chapter 2 to introduce a new programmer to Arduino. Let's now look a little closer at the entries in boards.txt.

boards.txt can be found

- On Mac and Linux systems in /usr/share/Arduino/hardware/Arduino.

- On Windows systems: Wherever you elected to install Arduino (e.g., C:\Program Files\Arduino-1.0): then Hardware\Arduino.

If you look at the contents of boards.txt you will see it is split into a number of entries each one separated from the next by a line of ###### characters. Each entry specifies a target MCU board.

---

[3]If you're interested to see the contents of this hex file, you'll find it in a build. subdirectory under /tmp on Linux and Mac and under the \Documents and Settings\<USER>\Local Settings\Temp folder on Windows. You should be able to use the more command to view it on Unix, or the Type command to view it on Windows, or just use a text editor to view it.

Let's anatomize the main items in one of these entries so that we can see what kind of material is specified in this file. We'll begin with the standard entry for an Arduino Duemilanove. Here's what it contains at the time of this writing.

```
atmega328.name = Arduino Duemilanove w/ ATmega328

atmega328.upload.protocol = arduino
atmega328.upload.maximum_size = 30720
atmega328.upload.speed = 57600

atmega328.bootloader.low_fuses = 0xFF
atmega328.bootloader.high_fuses = 0xDA
atmega328.bootloader.extended_fuses = 0x05
atmega328.bootloader.path = atmega
atmega328.bootloader.file = ATmegaBOOT_168_atmega328.hex
atmega328.bootloader.unlock_bits = 0x3F
atmega328.bootloader.lock_bits = 0x0F

atmega328.build.mcu = atmega328p
atmega328.build.f_cpu = 16000000 L
atmega328.build.core = arduino
atmega328.build.variant = standard
##########################################################################################
```

The first line is the name we want to use for the board; this is what appears on the Tools➤Boards list inside the Arduino IDE. Here, it's Arduino Duemilanove w/ ATmega328.

The second line specifies the communications and command protocol that the programmer expects the host computer to use when sending it instructions or data. Being the major AVR platform, Arduino has a dedicated protocol. Other possibilities include STK500 (Atmel's development system) and AVRISP2—which is the one we will be using with our USB connected programmer.

The next line (atmega328.upload.maximum_size) specifies the largest amount of program code memory that the AVR plugged into this board can accommodate—in this case it's 30,720 bytes.[4] If this was an earlier Arduino board using an ATmega168 this number would be halved, because the '168 offered only half as much memory as the '328.

Next is the upload speed. Programmer boards always need to limit the speed that data are uploaded. The AVR chip uses its master clock to synchronize the reprogramming of its memory with new data. If uploads happen too fast, the AVR cannot keep up, and the upload will fail. This setting allows the speed to be capped.

We'll be looking at the subject of fuses in the section "The AVR and Its Fuses." Essentially, in this context, an AVR fuse is a switch that can be programmed to turn various features of the MCU on or off (e.g., power fail detection can be enabled or disabled via a fuse). The next four parameters specify things (such as fuse settings) to do with the bootloader module for this AVR processor. A bootloader is a program that, if required, permanently resides in the MCU memory: for certain kinds of programming, the bootloader provides intelligence inside the AVR that cooperates with the programmer to update the MCUs main program. However, I plan to use ISP programming in this book and ISP programming does not use or require a bootloader.

The next item of interest is atmega328.build.mcu which is a crucial one for us. It is from this entry that Arduino learns what AVR chip is plugged into this programmer board. In this case it is the standard ATmega328p AVR chip that comes installed on an Arduino Duemilanove board. Remember that chip name. You shall see it again when you look at AVRDude's configuration file later in the "AVRDude's Configuration File" section.

_____

[4] This is not the full 32768 bytes of program memory that the ATmega28 offers because about 2,000 bytes are reserved for use with the bootloader that this style of programming requires—see main text.

Next up is the definition of the AVR chip's clock speed. `atmega328.build.f_cpu` specifies in Hz the clock speed of the AVR; in this case it's 16 million Hz (16 MHz), which is the speed at which the MCU in this Arduino runs. It's important for a number of reasons that this number is correct. Many of the standard Arduino facilities, such as the serial communication, the `delay` (`Some_Number_of_Milliseconds`) function, and many others use this number to adapt the speed of their operations, so if it is wrong, all the elements in your project or program that make use of precise timing will be wrong too.

Finally, `atmega328.build.core` specifies what core software should be used to build your application code around. We will always use Arduino for this, but in other contexts you will see things like `avrnetio` instead.

Do you remember that we added an entry to `boards.txt` back in Chapter 2? This was to make the Pololu AVRISP programmer known to Arduino. Let's look through the entry that we created there.

```
orangutan328p.name = Pololu USB AVR Programmer
orangutan328p.upload.using = avrispv2
orangutan328p.upload.maximum_size = 32768
orangutan328p.build.mcu = atmega328p
orangutan328p.build.f_cpu = 1000000 L
orangutan328p.build.core = arduino
orangutan328.build.variant = standard
```

- As before, we begin the board specification with a name. This really is *just* a name; we could call this board `Shiney McFloopy` if we really wanted to!

- Then, we see that instead of a protocol (which would imply the use of a bootloader) we have `upload.using` specified as `avrisp2`.

- Next is the memory size, in this case the full 32,768 bytes of program memory are available because ISP programming does not require a bootloader.

- The MCU type is as the same as before.

- The `f_cpu` specification here is of interest. It's set down to one million Hertz (1 MHz rather than the 16 MHz which was specified for the Arduino entry). This is because, when a brand-new unprogrammed AVR chip arrives, it will be factory set to run at 1 MHz, even though it's capable of a lot more. We'll look at the logic of this in the next section of this chapter, "AVR Out of the Box."

- Because we still want to use the Arduino software core, that specification stays the same as it would be for a "real" Arduino.

- Finally we specify the build variant as "standard."

If you want to go deeper into the parameters specified in `boards.txt`, you'll need to get a copy of the full data sheet for your AVR (in this case an ATmega328) from the Atmel web site and read up on things like fuses and the many different internal elements of the MCU. Ideally, the foregoing gives you enough familiarity with the `boards.txt` file to make any small changes that your projects may require.

Always remember that when you make any change to `boards.txt` (or `programmers.txt`), they won't show up in the Arduino graphical user interface (GUI) until you exit and then restart it. Arduino reads `boards.txt` and `programmers.txt` just once, at its start-up time.

On the subject of `programmers.txt` we made some additions to that in Chapter 2 as well, so let's review that. Here's what we added there:

```
avrispv2.name = AVR ISP v2
avrispv2.communication = serial
avrispv2.protocol = avrispv2
```

These are simple enough;

- We added a programmer called AVR ISP v2, as in the boards.txt case, this name is just a name, nothing more.

- The communication media is serial; this is important, programming happens very differently when a parallel programmer (such as some modes of the STK500) is used.

- Finally, we name the protocol that will be used over the serial programming link, and that is our old friend avrisp2.

So, now let's move on to look at some AVR basics.

AVR Out of the Box

Here are some basic facts that you should know about AVR chips:

- All AVR chips have a built-in clock oscillator. This is *not* to be confused with a time-of-day type of clock! This clock sets the AVR chip's internal rate of operations and therefore controls how much work it can do in a given time. People often call the clock speed of a processor its heartbeat. The faster the clock oscillator, the faster the AVR processor runs. As shipped, most AVRs have an internal clock rate of 8 MHz (8 million cycles per second); but, for compatibility reasons, the chips are shipped with this clock rate stepped down to a far slower 1 MHz rate. One million clock pulses per second may still sound like a lot, but for an electronics device, it's really pretty slow. The majority of currently available AVR chips have a maximum clock rate of 20 MHz, so if you used your AVR at 1 MHz, you'd be seriously underusing your chip and it would do far less useful work than you'd probably be hoping for.

In order to make an AVR run faster than its default 1 MHz speed, you can do one of two things:

- You can fit an external crystal (at, say, 16 MHz) and some capacitors to the chip across its "Xtal1" and "Xtal2" pins. You'd then need to program the AVR to use the frequency of the external crystal as its clock source. Shortly, we'll look at the details of doing this.

- You can simply turn off the CKDIV8 function of the chip, which will take the clock speed up to a much more useful 8 MHz. This approach has attractions because you don't have to bother fitting additional components to your project, saving time, space, and cost. It does, however, mean that your AVR is still running at less than half its possible maximum speed. Depending on the project in which you want to include your AVR, this may or may not be a problem (see section "Using an External Crystal").

- A brand-new AVR chip has a completely blank program and flash memory. Out of the box, it will do the sum total of not much, until you program it.

- AVRs can run on quite low supply voltages. Although we are going to use +5 volts with the test bed rig, when you come to deploy your projects, the possibility exists of running them on batteries: any supply voltage between 1.8 volts and 5.5 volts is fine for the AVRs we will use in this book—and, in fact, the majority of eight-bit AVR processors can run on this voltage range (but always check the data sheet for the exact device you have in front of you—there are *many* variants.).

Of course, you need to take into account whether the other elements of your projects (motors, LEDs, displays, Solenoids, etc.) will be okay running on batteries too. Also, you'll have to remain aware that if you develop the hardware side of your project to use +5 volts but then make a permanent version of it that runs on 3 volts (e.g., 2 x AA batteries) you'll need to recalculate the value of things like current limiting resistors. For example, at +5 V a 270R resistor will limit the current flow through an LED to about 18 milliamps (since 5 ÷ 270 = 0.01851): however, on a +3 V supply, that same resistor will limit the current to only 11 milliamps and the LED will be much less bright. So you'd have to reduce the resistor to something around 175R. These are the kinds of considerations that you need to take into account when taking advantage of the wide supply voltage capabilities of an AVR.

Using an External Crystal

Using an external crystal to drive the AVR at a faster speed than is available from its internal oscillator is simply a matter of adding a suitable crystal and some capacitors across its Xtal1 and Xtal2 pins. For example, suppose that we wanted the ATmega328 on our AVR test bed to run at 16 MHz. We would connect the crystal and capacitors as shown in Figure 3-9: In Figure 3-9 we see these components connected across the Xtal pins of the (partially shown) ATmega328.

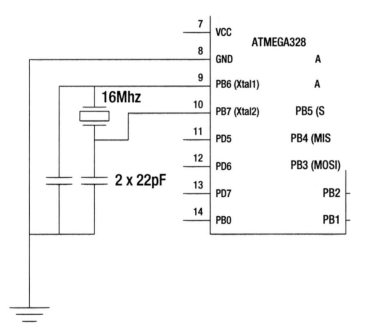

Figure 3-9. *Connecting a 16 MHz crystal to an ATMEGA328 AVR*

As you can see, the crystal is connected across pins 9 and 10. A ceramic disc capacitor goes from each of these pins to ground. This is how this arrangement looks when it's been added to the test bed breadboard.

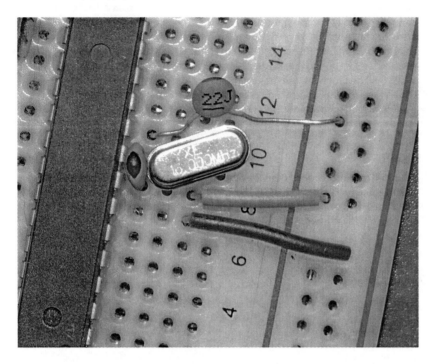

Figure 3-10. *Crystal and caps installed on the test bed rig*

The enclosing can for this crystal is a long thin one, which means it has to be mounted between the pins diagonally. Although not so common, crystals can be obtained in other packages that offer pins at the same spacings as the MCU chip, which makes the mounting more convenient.

As you can see, adding the crystal and capacitors does increase the permanent clutter on the test bed. My personal preference (and you will, I am sure, develop your own opinion about this) is to use an external crystal only when a project really demands the extra speed. In most of my projects, I have found that using the internal 8 MHz clock gives enough speed for what needs to be done, but the choice is, of course, entirely yours. Whether or not you use a 16 MHz or an 8 MHz clock is not a big deal because we specify the MCU clock speed in the setup (see the previous `boards.txt` and `programmers.txt` discussion). The software components of the Arduino development environment take care of any clock speed–related adjustments for us during program compilation and upload.

When you use an external crystal with your AVR, you need to reprogram the appropriate AVR fuses to make the AVR use the crystal as its clock source. Before you look at exactly how to do that though, you need to look at this whole topic of AVR fuses.

The AVR and Its Fuses

Certain crucial aspects of an AVR's operation can be modified by programmable fuses. These are essentially switches that turn things on or off within the AVR processor. Each AVR has one or more fuse bytes in which each bit represents a fuse. You can alter any or all of these fuses from the AVRDude program, which you will look at in the next section. First, let's look in detail at the fuses for just one type of AVR MCU, our trusty ATmega328.

■ **Warning**   Be **very** careful! When changing fuses on your AVR chip it is quite easy to make your AVR unusable by misprogramming a fuse byte. Check and double-check before you make fuse changes. You can, for example, unintentionally set lock bits which prevent your AVR from ever being reprogrammed again.

The ATMEGA328 AVR has three fuse bytes.

- The Fuse Low Byte (called FLB in the AVR data sheets, AVRDude calls this lFuse).

- The Fuse High Byte (called FHB in the AVR data sheets, AVRDude calls this hFuse).

- The Extended Fuse Byte (EFB in the AVR data sheets, AVRDude calls this eFuse).

■ **Important**   A "programmed" (or active) bit in an AVR fuse will read as "0" and an unprogrammed (inactive) bit will read as a "1." This is the opposite way round to most logic systems—and therefore something to bear in mind when reading the following descriptions.

Fuse Low Byte

The FLB contains the items of most interest in our projects context. By and large, because we have elected to use the Arduino software development environment, we are sheltered from many of the more intricate details of the AVR architecture. However, the FLB contains some items which are still useful to know about.

The general format of the FLB is:

FuseName	CKDIV8	CKOUT	SUT1	SUT0	CKSEL3	CKSEL2	CKSEL1	CKSEL0
Bit #	7	6	5	4	3	2	1	0

The following details the items of interest in this fuse byte.

Bit	Name	Details
7	CKDIV8	If this bit is 0 then the AVR's master clock (the built in 8 MHz clock) will be divided by 8. If this bit is 1, then the clock will be used as is. Factory default = 0 (feature on)
6	CKOUT	If this bit is 0 then the ATmega328 pin 14 (PortB0) will become an output of the MCU's master clock. This allows you to synchronize external circuits to the MCU's internal clock if you need to. Factory default value = 1 (feature off).
5 & 4	SUT1 and SUT0	These two bits allow you to set the start-up time delay for the MCU. This is a way to allow external circuitry to get ready before the MCU starts operation, and also to allow time for a power supply to stabilize. The default value (10 - binary) specifies that 6 clock cycles will elapse before MCU operation begins. See the AVR datasheet for full details.

(*continued*)

Bit	Name	Details
3-0	CKSEL3-0	These bits allow you to provide a code that tells the MCU what clock source to use. There are three sets of possibilities:

  - The MCU's own internal clock (see CKDIV8 at bit 7).

  - An external crystal and appropriate capacitors.

  - An oscillator. You can also get a four-terminal device called an oscillator: this class of device includes a complete crystal/amplifier combination in one package and provides a steady frequency, logical level, output without the need for additional capacitors. An oscillator package needs to be fed with power (thus the need for four connections) and tends to be more expensive than the crystal + caps approach.

So, the settings of CKSEL3-1 provide for a number of clock types and start-delay options.

If we're using the MCU's internal 8 MHz clock oscillator, we set these bits to 0010 (i.e., only CKSEL1 is set to "1"; the rest are "0").

When using an external crystal we leave CK0 as a "1." If we're using an external crystal and capacitors (see above) to provide 12 MHz or above, we usually set CKSEL3-CKSEL1 to 011. If using a slower crystal we could use a variety of different values (see the device's data sheet for the detailed possibilities)

We'll see how programming fuses works out in practice in the section "AVRDude."

High Fuse Byte

Now let's look at the hFuse values for the ATmega328. The general format of hFuse byte is

FuseName	RSTDISBL	DWEN	SPIEN	WDTON	EESAVE	BOOTSZ1	BOOTSZ0	BOOTRST
Bit #	7	6	5	4	3	2	1	0

The following details the items of interest in this fuse byte.

Bit	Name	Details
7	RSTDISBL	If programmed to "0" disables the external reset pin, which becomes just another I/O pin. Factory default value = "1" (Reset pin is enabled).
6	DWEN	This enables the use of an external debugger device. This is most useful when using Atmel's AVRStudio, which we are not. Factory default = "1" (disabled).
5	SPIEN	Serial programming enabled. This bit allows you to use serial programming using ISP techniques. If you set this bit incorrectly your AVR will no longer allow ISP programming—so be careful! Factory default value = "0" (SPI enabled).

(continued)

Bit	Name	Details
4	WDTON	Watchdog timer on. The AVR has a hardware-implemented watchdog timer. A watchdog timer is essentially a counter that has been loaded with a certain value. Without any software intervention, this counter counts down toward zero. If it ever reaches zero it causes a hardware reset of the MCU, which will completely restart its program. The idea is that the software application program running inside the MCU periodically reloads the watchdog timer to stop it from ever reaching zero: if the application program crashes or the processor malfunctions, it will stop recharging the watchdog counter which will at some stage fairly soon (typically a few milliseconds) reach zero and cause a restart—thus restoring sanity and normal service. This scheme works very well for some kinds of applications, but not all types require it. So, the default value is "1" disabling the WDTON. Factory default = "1" (WatchdogTimer = disabled).
3	EESAVE	If this bit is programmed the EEPROM contents will remain unchanged when the chip is commanded to do a chip erase. Factory default "1" (EEPROM contents will be erased when chip erase is commanded).
2 - 1	BootSZ1 & BootSZ0	Selects the bootloader program size. We don't use a bootloader in our approach. Factory default = 00.
0	BOOTRST	Selects that the MCU jumps to a reset vector when powered up. This allows you to make special arrangements for what piece of code gets executed first at power up. We don't use this. Factory default = "1" (feature disabled).

Extended Fuses

The extended fuse register only uses the lower three bits. These specify a code for "brown-out" (a.k.a. power fail) detection level. The ATmega328—and indeed most AVR chips—have a special feature whereby, when their supply voltage drops below a certain level (programmed in the extended fuse register) they can jump to a preset address in memory to execute some emergency power fail and shutdown routines. The general idea is that there will be enough time to do some tidying up before the power fails fully.

This kind of feature is most useful when running on batteries, since battery power gradually ebbs away and the MCU would have time to do whatever it needed to do (stop all motors, turn off all lights, etc.). However, if a project or application is running from mains power, as most of ours do, then this feature is not of much use, since failures will almost always be sudden and fast. So, we don't use this feature—it is disabled which, luckily, is the default setting anyway!

Note   In the section "AVRDude," you'll look at programming fuses and find out how to calculate what values you need to use when changing fuse values (and what tools are available to make that tedious task easier).

While device signatures are not fuses (i.e., you can't change them), they are fundamental to identifying and thus being able to correctly configure an AVR MCU, so this seems like a good time to introduce the topic.

Each AVR device type has a specific three-byte signature code. This code differs even among devices that are functionally the same. For example, the ATmega328 device signature is 1E-95-14, whereas the functionally identical but lower power consumption version of the same MCU, the ATmega328p, returns a signature of 1E-95-0 F. This means that taking all the low power, lower voltage, higher clock rate variants of the AVR family of device into account, there are a large number of possible device signatures that can be returned. Most of the software and utility programs that we use through this book come preconfigured to recognize only the most common device signatures. For example, we might want to use an uncommon variant of an MCU, such as an ultra-low-power consumption version if we were making a project for battery powered operation. In that case, we'd have to add some definitions to the configuration files. We'll see how to do this in the section "AVRDude."

Although this concludes our look through AVR fuses and signatures, there is more detailed information contained in the freely downloadable data sheets for AVR chips, like the ATmega328 and its companions. See the www.atmel.com downloads page.

AVRDude

If you're using a packaged system such as Arduino you will find that it will hide most of the low-level details of the actual programming of your AVR chip. However, if you want to get closer to the "naked" AVR (i.e., one not embedded in a packaged system such as Arduino), it is crucial to know a little about a piece of free software called AVRDude. Because it's so central to AVR usage it's already been mentioned quite a lot, but in this section I explore it rather more fully.

AVRDude started out life being called AVRProg and initially it only ran on Linux systems. However, when it was renamed it was also ported to Windows and Mac OS X. If you look around the Internet you will find lots of other programs mentioned that do the same things as AVRDude (PonyProg, UISP, AVRFuses, etc.) but you'll also soon realize that none of those are regularly updated to take into account new devices (the last UISP update, for example, seems to have been in 2005) or they have other limitations, such as they only run on Windows or only on Mac OS X. For these reasons, we concentrate in this book on AVRDude, which is still being regularly updated and maintained and is available for all three major desktop types. It's not the easiest thing in the world to use, but you'll soon get used to using the subset of functions you need.

When you install your Arduino software you'll also install AVRDude. That's because it comes as part of the Arduino software suite. In fact, AVRDude underlies *all* the currently available programming environments for AVR, this includes Arduino, WinAVR, Eclipse, AVR Studio, . . . they all use AVRDude as the means for actually uploading the user's programs into the AVR chip.

In this section we're going to look at AVRDude and play around with some of the useful low-level functions it provides. Luckily, although it can get very complex for more esoteric usages, most mainstream uses of AVRDude are not overly hard to understand.

When you installed the Arduino IDE in the previous chapter, you installed AVRDude as well. Here's where you'll find it:

- On a Linux system: It will be at /usr/share/Arduino/hardware/AVRDude—which in fact is usually a link to /usr/bin/AVRDude (though your setup could vary).

- On a Windows system it will be under the location where you installed Arduino: if you can't remember where it was installed, just right-click the Arduino desktop link (or start menu link) that you normally use to start the Arduino IDE and inspect its properties. One of those should show you where it is installed. Under the install folder you'll find a succession of subfolders and then AVRDude:

    hardware\tools\avr\bin\AVRDude.exe

AVRDude is a command-line tool. At the time of writing you have to type commands for it into a terminal window. There have been GUI front ends written for AVRDude in the past, but as discussed earlier you can't rely on these being up to date, so I think for our limited purposes, it's probably best to stick to the latest version of the command line program.

The Trouble with AVRDude's Terminal Mode

Normally, you run AVRDude to do something, it does that something, and then it exits. However, AVRDude does have a terminal mode into which you can enter using the -t option. This keeps AVRDude running and you can type one command after another to it, finally exiting back to your normal command prompt. However, quite a lot of USB attached programmers won't work with terminal mode, although this seems not to be highlighted in many places. If you try to use such programmers in AVRDude's terminal mode, you will get time-outs and other errors.

The problem is that, when in terminal mode, AVRDude expects the AVR programmer to remain in programming mode for the whole time terminal mode is effective. The firmware of quite a few programmers (including the Pololu AVR programmer, and I believe some of the AVRISP programmer versions) deliberately only stay in programming mode for a very short time. Many things can render an AVR chip unusable ("brick it" in microcontroller parlance) such as unintentionally changing fuse values or other crucial details. So, as a protection mechanism, the firmware in many programmers will quietly exit programming mode if the computer has not sent any programming commands for a couple of seconds.

While this offers great protection for the AVR against accidents, it does mean that AVRDude's terminal mode is more or less useless when such programmers are in the picture. It's no big deal because all the functions of AVRDude can be accessed via AVRDude's single command mode, which sets the programmer board into programming mode when required but then exits, so nothing is really lost. It's just something you need to be aware of.

To avoid confusion in this area we shall forget about AVRDude's terminal mode and only use it in single command mode in this book.

AVRDude: Getting Started

To get started with AVRDude you need to know two things. First, you need to know to what serial port your AVR programmer is connected. Ideally, you made a note of this during the installation of your programmer's software if you're on Windows. On a Linux system, use the command

```
dmesg | grep tty
```

Which should give you an output that looks something like the following:

```
[    0.000000] console [tty0] enabled
[    0.303806] serial8250: ttyS0 at I/O 0x3f8 (irq = 4) is a 16550A
[    0.392571] serial8250: ttyS1 at I/O 0x2f8 (irq = 3) is a 16550A
[    0.482509] 00:08: ttyS0 at I/O 0x3f8 (irq = 4) is a 16550A
[    0.524803] 00:09: ttyS1 at I/O 0x2f8 (irq = 3) is a 16550A
[   19.988367] cdc_acm 1-2:1.0: ttyACM0: USB ACM device
[   19.993007] cdc_acm 1-2:1.2: ttyACM1: USB ACM device
```

From which it's fairly obvious that, on this system, /dev/ttyACM0 and /dev/ttyACM1 are the serial ports provided by the USB AVR programmer. The lower number (0) will be the primary programmer port and the higher number (1) the additional TTL level serial port.

On a Mac system, open up the system profiler and look under USB devices to see the port name(s) being used.

On a Windows system, you need to start the Device Manager (accessible via the Control Panel application, usually under computer management or system maintenance—depending on your Windows version) and look under the Ports heading.

The second thing you need to know is AVRDude's name for the MCU chip you're using. You can find this out by making AVRDude print out the list of AVR chips that it knows about. Try this command line (make sure you get the uppercase and lowercase letters correct if you're on a Unix system):

```
avrdude -p NoneSuch -c avrisp2 -P /dev/ttyACM0
```

Change the device name to be the one you are using on your system—on Windows you will use a COM port number something like COM2: rather than /dev/???. Except in screen logs, I'll represent this as {YOUR_COM_PORT} from now on.

Since there is not an AVR part number code called NoneSuch (and never will be!), AVRDude chokes on this command (we'll come back to the whole fraught issue of part numbers shortly). However, AVRDude helpfully puts out a list of all the AVR parts it *does* know about, and the codes it uses for them—which should look something like this...

```
avrdude: AVR Part "NoneSuch" not found.

Valid parts are:
  t10   = ATtiny10        [/etc./avrdude.conf:15636]
  t8    = ATtiny9         [/etc./avrdude.conf:15596]
  t5    = ATtiny5         [/etc./avrdude.conf:15556]
  t4    = ATtiny4         [/etc./avrdude.conf:15516]
  ucr2 = 32UC3A0512       [/etc./avrdude.conf:15495]
  x128a4 = ATXMEGA128A4     [/etc./avrdude.conf:15397]
  x64a4 = ATXMEGA64A4       [/etc./avrdude.conf:15300]
...
  t2313 = ATtiny2313      [/etc./avrdude.conf:8928]
  m328  = ATMEGA328       [/etc./avrdude.conf:8736]
  m328p = ATMEGA328P      [/etc./avrdude.conf:8546]
  t88   = attiny88        [/etc./avrdude.conf:8360]
  m168  = ATMEGA168       [/etc./avrdude.conf:8172]
  m88   = ATMEGA88        [/etc./avrdude.conf:7986]
...
  t15   = ATtiny15        [/etc./avrdude.conf:1265]
  t13   = ATtiny13        [/etc./avrdude.conf:1092]
  t12   = ATtiny12        [/etc./avrdude.conf:959]
  t11   = ATtiny11        [/etc./avrdude.conf:895]
```

In this case I was using an ATmega328P, and you can see that AVRDude's part code for that is m328p. So, that means I can use the modified version of the command line:

```
avrdude -p m328p -c avrisp2 -P {YOUR_COM_PORT}
```

This invokes AVRDude. Reading from left to right we have:

-p introduces the AVR part number code—as we saw previously. Note that this is a lowercase p.

-c introduces the type of programmer that is in use: here we use avrisp2, which is what AVRDude sees our USB-connected ISP programmers as.

-P (that's uppercase P) introduces the operating system's name for the communications port to which the programmer is connected.

- On this Ubuntu system it was /dev/ttyACM0.

- On a Mac OS X system it's "/dev/USB:tty???? (where ??? is some number).

On Windows it will be something like COM2. The output we get in response to this command is pretty simple:

```
avrdude: AVR device initialized and ready to accept instructions

Reading | ################################################## | 100 % 0.00s

avrdude: Device signature=0x1e950f
```

```
avrdude: safemode: Fuses OK
```

```
avrdude done.  Thank you.
```

AVRDude makes contact with the AVR chip and then reads from it: it retrieves the device-type signature—which in this case is 0x1e950f. As discussed in the previous section, AVR device types have a unique six-character signature code—and the 0x1e950f shown in this example is the code for an ATmega328P.

Because we have not commanded any actions that would require writing to the AVR, the programmer stays in "safe" mode (which essentially means read-only). Finally, the program checks the AVR's fuses (see section "The AVR and Its Fuses") which it pronounces okay. It then politely exits.

■ **It Failed? Tech Tip** Sometimes, just sometimes, if you are using a brand-new virgin AVR chip, it's possible that you will get a time-out error, or nonsensical results when you use AVRDude commands. This happens because—as we saw earlier—an out-of-the-box AVR only operates at a clock speed of 1 MHz and the programmer is not waiting long enough for its responses. If you get this kind of problem, try adding the option -B3 to your command lines to slow down communication with your chip. Unless you have a genuinely faulty AVR, or some kind of ISP wiring problem, that should fix the problem. For example,

```
avrdude -p m328p -B3 -c avrisp2 -P {YOUR_COM_PORT}
```

AVRDude's Configuration File

The first of the options we saw previously was the -p option which lets you specify which kind of AVR device you want AVRDude to operate upon. Because there are so many AVR devices and so many variants of each, AVRDude currently only knows about the mainstream AVR devices: for many AVR MCU subtypes you have to provide it with the information about the device. This is not as much work as perhaps it sounds, but it does involve editing AVRDude's configuration file; so, let's look at what that is, and where it lives.

All of AVRDude's detailed knowledge of AVR chips and programmers comes from its configuration file which is called avrdude.conf. Where does this file live?

- On Linux and Mac OS X systems you will usually find it in /etc. (and you'll need superuser privileges to edit it).

- On an Arduino-installation on Windows you will find it under the installation folder (see the section "AVRDude: Getting Started" on AVRDude.exe installation location) under hardware\tools\avr\etc.

Because avrdude.conf is a text file we can edit it with our favorite plain text editor (gedit, Notepad, emacs, etc.). But *before* that, make a copy of the file just in case you introduce any unintentional problems with your edits. Also, when you have done editing the file and come to save the revised version of it, make very sure that you save it as a plain text file, not in a word processor–specific format (such as an MSWord .docx file). AVRDude can only read a conf file in plain text format. The plain text editors mentioned previously will save in this format.

When you have opened the file and had browsed down it you will quickly realize that, after a few pages of preliminaries, what you're seeing is a repeating list of programmer types (yes, our AVRISP2 programmer type is there) and then a list of AVR MCUs in which each list entry provides the details of an AVR device.

Each new entry begins with a heading like the following:

```
#------------------------------------------------------------
# ATtiny2313
#------------------------------------------------------------
```

The usual case is that you want to add an additional entry that will make AVRDude recognize the signature of a faster version or a lower-power consumption version of an existing device.

Suppose we wanted to make AVRDude recognize the lower-power consumption version of an ATmega328p (which is called the ATmega328pu). Without editing AVRDude's config file, if we type the command

```
avrdude -p m328pu -c avrisp2 -P {YOUR_COM_PORT}
```

we get back an error message like the one below and a long list of AVRDude's known part numbers.

```
AVRDUDE: AVR part 'm328pu' part not found
```

So, to make our ATmega328pu known to AVRDude, we add a new entry to avrdude.conf in the following way. We first locate the existing entry for the ATmega328p which begins as follows:

```
#------------------------------------------------------------
# ATmega328P
#------------------------------------------------------------

part
    id                     = "m328p";
    desc                   = "ATMEGA328P";
    has_debugwire          = yes;
    flash_instr            = 0xB6, 0x01, 0x11;
    eeprom_instr           = 0xBD, 0xF2, 0xBD, 0xE1, 0xBB, 0xCF, 0xB4, 0x00,
                             0xBE, 0x01, 0xB6, 0x01, 0xBC, 0x00, 0xBB, 0xBF,
                             0x99, 0xF9, 0xBB, 0xAF;
    stk500_devcode         = 0x86;
    # avr910_devcode       = 0x;
    Signature              = 0x1e 0x95 0x14;
    Pagel                  = 0xd7;
    bs2                    = 0xc2;
    chip_erase_delay       = 9000;
```

As you can see, this specifies the expected signature byte values 1E-95-0 F. The ATmega328pu version of the chip is more or less identical, except it returns the signature code 1E-95-14. So all we really have to do is copy the entire existing entry for ATmega328p and paste it into a new entry at the end of the file. Then, we modify the device ID, the Description, and the signature for the new entry, so that they look like the following (changed bits in **bold**):

```
#------------------------------------------------------------
# ATmega328PU
#------------------------------------------------------------

part
    id                     = "m328pu";
    desc                   = "ATMEGA328pu";
    has_debugwire          = yes;
    flash_instr            = 0xB6, 0x01, 0x11;
    eeprom_instr           = 0xBD, 0xF2, 0xBD, 0xE1, 0xBB, 0xCF, 0xB4, 0x00,
                             0xBE, 0x01, 0xB6, 0x01, 0xBC, 0x00, 0xBB, 0xBF,
                             0x99, 0xF9, 0xBB, 0xAF;
    stk500_devcode         = 0x86;
    # avr910_devcode       = 0x;
    Signature              = 0x1e 0x95 0x14;
    Pagel                  = 0xd7;
    bs2                    = 0xc2;
```

The remainder of the copied entry stays unchanged. Then, we just save the file back into place.[5]

Now, if we use the command:

```
avrdude -p m328pu -c avrisp2 -P {YOUR_COM_PORT}
```

We get back the expected response with the correct signature.

```
avrdude: AVR device initialized and ready to accept instructions

Reading | ################################################## | 100 % 0.00s

avrdude: Device signature=0x1e9514

avrdude: safemode: Fuses OK

avrdude done.  Thank you.
```

Some points that arise from this description include the following:

- If (or more likely when) you come to upgrade AVRDude (either individually, or as part of an Arduino upgrade) your avrdude.conf file will be replaced with a new one. This will mean that your modifications will be overwritten. It's therefore a really good idea to

    - Make sure your modifications to the file are always added to the bottom of the file.

    - Make sure you keep an additional copy of the file somewhere else so that you can append your customized entries to any new file that an upgrade creates.

- If, after editing the conf file your AVR variant is still not recognized by AVRDude, you should start by double-checking the new entry you made for errors (e.g., look for missing quote marks or ";" terminators on the end of lines). Make sure that you haven't run two lines together when they should be separate, and so on.

    Another possibility is that you have multiple instances of AVRDude installed on your system and the one you are using is looking at a different config file from the one you edited. For example, AVRStudio, WINAVR, and Arduino all come with a copy of AVRDude, so if you have more than one copy installed it's just possible that the AVRDude you are running is looking at a conf file you have not modified. The way to deal with this is to provide AVRDude with a definite location for the conf file (using the –C in uppercase option) on the command line. Add it to the command we used above, as follows:

    ```
    avrdude -p m328pu -C {YOUR CONFIG} -c avrisp2 -P {YOUR_COM_PORT}
    ```

    This ensures that the conf file being used is the one you intend.

- If you use AVRDude frequently, you can save yourself some typing by specifying stuff like your programmer type in a file called {$HOME}/.avrdudeRC where HOME represents your default login directory on Unix or $HOMEPATH on Windows. Refer to the AVRDude manpage on Unix or the AVRDude user manual (supplied with AVRDude as a PDF file on Windows) for more details about the .avrdudeRC file and its possible contents.

Adding a device variant, then, is fairly straightforward.

The more complex case occurs when you want to introduce a completely new AVR chip to AVRDude. Fortunately, the AVRDude maintainer or user community has usually done this work for you, so it's just a matter of downloading the latest version of AVRDude to get the latest config file. However, if this does not solve your

---

[5]Remember that on Unix systems you'll need to have logged in as root or used "sudo" to acquire extra level privileges to alter this file. On Windows this is less of a problem, but you may need to upgrade your login privileges on some Vista and Win 7 systems, depending on how they have been configured.

problem, you get to build an entry for the new AVR. You will need a copy of the full data sheet for the AVR device and you'll need to go through each individual item in the file and find the appropriate value for it in the data sheet of your new device. I've never had to do this, but I imagine it takes a while! If you ever *do* need to do this, be sure to send a copy of the new entry to the AVRDude maintainer (see the latest contact e-mail at `http://www.nongnu.org/AVRDude/`) so that others can be spared having to repeat the task.

AVRDude Examples

A few examples should help make clear how useful AVRDude can be. In these examples I am going to use an ATmega328p and (since this was done on Linux) `/dev/ttyACM0` as my AVR programmer port. Clearly, if you're going to try these out for yourself, you should put your own specifics in place of these two items—for example, `COM2` or whatever COM port you are using on a Windows system.

■ **Important**   Remember that a "programmed" (or active) bit in an AVR fuse will read as "0" and an unprogrammed (inactive) bit will read as a "1." This is the opposite way round to most logic systems—and therefore something to bear in mind when reading the following descriptions.

We'll begin by programming some fuses. In this regard you will definitely find the fuse value byte calculator enormously useful.

`http://www.engbedded.com/fusecalc`

You tell it what AVR you are using, or get as close as you can; for example, it does not list an ATmega328pu, so use an ATmega328. Then, tick the boxes to indicate the options and value you want. It will then give you the byte value that you can need to program into the selected fuse byte. It will even give you the command line options to AVRDude that you should use!

Let's start gently: assuming you are using your brand-new ATmega328p chip we'll clear the CKDIV8 bit in `lfuse`. First, let's see the current values:

```
avrdude -p m328p -c avrisp2 -P /dev/ttyACM0 -U lfuse:r:myLfuse.txt:h
```

This command runs AVRDude and commands it to access the lower fuse byte, to read it, and to put the value it reads into a file called `myLfuse.txt`[6] in hexadecimal byte format. When we examine the contents of the file (using a text editor, or the `cat` command on Unix or the `Type` command on Windows) it is found to contain 0x62. Now, here's the really brilliant thing about the fusecalc tool linked above: once you have read the fuse value as just described, you can enter the value you obtained into the appropriate text box (lower fuse byte in this case) and it will decode it for you, which lets you see what the current fuse settings actually mean. Very useful! When we do that, we see that the hexadecimal value 62 means (among other things) that the CKDIV8 bit is set in this MCU. In other words, it's only running at 1 MHz, which is a waste.

So, using fusecalc again, we clear that bit, and it tells us to program `lfuse` as hexadecimal value E2. So, now we do that:

```
avrdude -p m328p -c avrisp2 -P /dev/ttyACM0 -U lfuse:w:0xE2:m
```

Then, if we repeat the `fuse-read` command, we get to see that the value has indeed changed to 0xE2 and our MCU is now running at a much better 8 MHz. If we are using this AVR from Arduino, we need to go to our

---

[6]If you want to output to your terminal window instead of a file, use - as the file name on Unix systems, or use `CON` (short for CONsole) on a Windows system. For example,

UNIX: `AVRDude -p m328p -c avrisp2 -P /dev/ttyACM0 -U lfuse:r:-:h`
Windows: `AVRDude -p m328p -c avrisp2 -P COM2 -U lfuse:r:CON:h`

boards.txt file and change the clock speed in there. If we're using the board definition we added in Chapter 2, it means that we change from

orangutan328p.build.f_cpu = 1000000 L

to

orangutan328p.build.f_cpu = 8000000 L

Then we use Arduino to reupload whatever code was running in the AVR previously (e.g., the basic LED flasher program). This time, Arduino will cause the code to be compiled taking into account the clock speed change. The timed events (such as time delays governing LED flash rates) will be working exactly as before, but the rest of the code will be running eight times as fast.

It's sometimes interesting to see what the AVR's memory contains: the following command will make AVRDude dump out the contents of your AVR's program memory to the screen (Unix first, then Windows):

```
avrdude -p m328p -c avrisp2 -P /dev/ttyACM0 -U flash:r:-:h
avrdude -p m328p -c avrisp2 -P COM2 -U flash:r:CON:h
```

If your AVR only contains the basic LED flasher (which doesn't contain any text strings) then you won't see anything much, just a big long screed of hex numbers, which is not very exciting. For more excitement, let's modify the basic LED flasher program you used in Chapter 2 in the Arduino programming screen. We will add the following line just immediately before the line that says void setup():

Static String myString = "If you can read this you are looking into the AVR flash memory";

Then, use Arduino to recompile and re-upload the program into the AVR.

Now, try this command (Unix then Windows):

```
avrdude -p m328p -c avrisp2 -P /dev/ttyACM0 -U flash:r:-:r
avrdude -p m328p -c avrisp2 -P COM2 -U flash:r:CON:r
```

This does the same as before, except that it outputs the data from the flash memory as raw data (the final r in the command). Of course, your terminal window won't make much sense of most of this raw data, because it's not text, it is AVR machine code and some of it will translate into "beep" characters, so expect your machine to bleep for a few seconds. However when you get to the block of text that we inserted in the Arduino program, it should faithfully reproduce it among all the strange symbols and beeping.

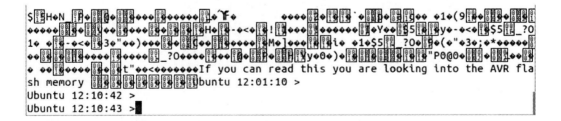

We can list out the contents of the EEPROM memory inside the MCU as well, using the command (Unix then Windows)

```
avrdude -p m328p -c avrisp2 -P /dev/ttyACM0 -U eeprom:r:-:h
avrdude -p m328p -c avrisp2 -P COM2 -U eeprom:r:CON:h
```

On a new chip this is fairly boring, because we just get a screen full of 0xFF which is the empty initial state that the EEPROM memory of the MCU is shipped with.[7] But, we can use an Arduino sketch to fill the EEPROM with something a little bit more interesting. The sketch illustrated in Figure 3-11 will fill each of the first 255 bytes of the EEPROM with its own address (e.g., the EEPROM byte with address 008 gets the value 08 written into it).

```
#include <EEPROM.h>;

void setup()
{
/*
   This runs once at startup. It writes each of the first
   255 EEPROM byte's address into itself, if it has not
   already been done. */
for (int thisAddr = 0; thisAddr <=255; thisAddr ++)
  {
    if (EEPROM.read(thisAddr) != thisAddr)
    {
      EEPROM.write(thisAddr,thisAddr);
    }
  }
}

void loop()
{
// Do nothing.....
}
```

Figure 3-11. CounterFill_EEPROM sketch

The program in Figure 3-11 only writes the value into the EEPROM byte if the location has not already been programmed. Since it is a characteristic of EEPROM memory that you can only change its contents a relatively low (a few thousand) number of times, it's very important to make sure that *any* code you create which writes into EEPROM does not do so unnecessarily. EEPROM is only meant to written into occasionally during the lifetime of your AVR chip. It's all too easy to accidentally create code that gets stuck in a loop writing to an EEPROM location over and over: with the speed of these processors, you can use up all the EEPROM lifetime in just a few moments, meaning that the EEPROM (or at least the "used up" locations within it) are now useless.

---

[7]In some cases it may show you no data at all, from which you are supposed to conclude that there is nothing but blank space in the memory.

Having uploaded this sketch and given it a few moments to run, we return to AVRDude and run the eeprom list command again (Unix then Windows):

```
avrdude -p m328p -c avrisp2 -P /dev/ttyACM0 -U eeprom:r:-:h
avrdude -p m328p -c avrisp2 -P COM2 -U eeprom:r:CON:h
```

and this time, we see the counter values that we just wrote into the EEPROM memory with our sketch (see Figure 3-12)!

```
avrdude: writing output file "<stdout>"
0x0,0x1,0x2,0x3,0x4,0x5,0x6,0x7,0x8,0x9,0xa,0xb,0xc,0xd,0xe,0xf,0x10,0x11,0x12,0
x13,0x14,0x15,0x16,0x17,0x18,0x19,0x1a,0x1b,0x1c,0x1d,0x1e,0x1f,0x20,0x21,0x22,0
x23,0x24,0x25,0x26,0x27,0x28,0x29,0x2a,0x2b,0x2c,0x2d,0x2e,0x2f,0x30,0x31,0x32,0
x33,0x34,0x35,0x36,0x37,0x38,0x39,0x3a,0x3b,0x3c,0x3d,0x3e,0x3f,0x40,0x41,0x42,0
x43,0x44,0x45,0x46,0x47,0x48,0x49,0x4a,0x4b,0x4c,0x4d,0x4e,0x4f,0x50,0x51,0x52,0
x53,0x54,0x55,0x56,0x57,0x58,0x59,0x5a,0x5b,0x5c,0x5d,0x5e,0x5f,0x60,0x61,0x62,0
x63,0x64,0x65,0x66,0x67,0x68,0x69,0x6a,0x6b,0x6c,0x6d,0x6e,0x6f,0x70,0x71,0x72,0
x73,0x74,0x75,0x76,0x77,0x78,0x79,0x7a,0x7b,0x7c,0x7d,0x7e,0x7f,0x80,0x81,0x82,0
x83,0x84,0x85,0x86,0x87,0x88,0x89,0x8a,0x8b,0x8c,0x8d,0x8e,0x8f,0x90,0x91,0x92,0
x93,0x94,0x95,0x96,0x97,0x98,0x99,0x9a,0x9b,0x9c,0x9d,0x9e,0x9f,0xa0,0xa1,0xa2,0
xa3,0xa4,0xa5,0xa6,0xa7,0xa8,0xa9,0xaa,0xab,0xac,0xad,0xae,0xaf,0xb0,0xb1,0xb2,0
xb3,0xb4,0xb5,0xb6,0xb7,0xb8,0xb9,0xba,0xbb,0xbc,0xbd,0xbe,0xbf,0xc0,0xc1,0xc2,0
xc3,0xc4,0xc5,0xc6,0xc7,0xc8,0xc9,0xca,0xcb,0xcc,0xcd,0xce,0xcf,0xd0,0xd1,0xd2,0
xd3,0xd4,0xd5,0xd6,0xd7,0xd8,0xd9,0xda,0xdb,0xdc,0xdd,0xde,0xdf,0xe0,0xe1,0xe2,0
xe3,0xe4,0xe5,0xe6,0xe7,0xe8,0xe9,0xea,0xeb,0xec,0xed,0xee,0xef,0xf0,0xf1,0xf2,0
xf3,0xf4,0xf5,0xf6,0xf7,0xf8,0xf9,0xfa,0xfb,0xfc,0xfd,0xfe,0xff,0xff,0xff,0xff,0
xff,0xff,0xff,0xff,0xff,0xff,0xff,0xff,0xff,0xff,0xff,0xff,0xff,0xff,0xff,0xff,0
xff,0xff,0xff,0xff,0xff,0xff,0xff,0xff,0xff,0xff,0xff,0xff,0xff,0xff,0xff,0xff,0
xff,0xff,0xff,0xff,0xff,0xff,0xff,0xff,0xff,0xff,0xff,0xff,0xff,0xff,0xff,0xff,0
xff,0xff,0xff,0xff,0xff,0xff,0xff,0xff,0xff,0xff,0xff,0xff,0xff,0xff,0xff,0xff,0
xff,0xff,0xff,0xff,0xff,0xff,0xff,0xff,0xff,0xff,0xff,0xff,0xff,0xff,0xff,0xff,0
```

Figure 3-12. *EEPROM memory dump with first 256 locations filled*

Making AVR Use the External Crystal Clock

Earlier in this chapter we looked at how we add an external 16 MHz crystal to the AVR chip on the test bed breadboard. It's time to see how we set the fuses to make the AVR use that crystal, rather than its own internal clock. Again, we first use AVRDude to read the lower fuse byte.

```
avrdude -p m328p -c avrisp2 -P /dev/ttyACM0 -U lfuse:r:myLfuse.txt:h
```

When we examine the contents of myLfuse.txt, it shows us that the current value of that byte is 0x62 (or perhaps 0xE2, if you have worked through the previous example). By using fusecalc we select the external full-swing crystal (which is what an external crystal and capacitors running at greater than 12 MHz gives us) with a 16 K clock (unfortunately, fusecalc deals in kilohertz (KHz), but 16,000 times 1,000 = 16 million!) and 4.1 ms power rise time. With these settings—and with CKDIV8 not ticked, we learn that the lfuse value to program is 0xe7 (binary 1110 0111). We use the following command to program that fuse byte into our AVR (this is the LINUX version of the command, you should know the Windows version by now!):

```
avrdude -p m328p -c avrisp2 -P /dev/ttyACM0 -U lfuse:w:0xe7:m
```

Again, we verify that the fuse has been programmed by reading it back (Unix then Windows):

```
avrdude -p m328p -c avrisp2 -P /dev/ttyACM0 -U lfuse:r:-:h
```

```
avrdude -p m328p -c avrisp2 -P COM5 -U lfuse:r:CON:h
```

Though in fact, as you may have noticed, there's no real need to do that, because AVRDude verifies that the programming has been completed by reading the values back to us straight after the programming. If there had been any problem in writing the fuse byte, AVRDude would have issued a verification error message.

Now, if we are using this AVR from Arduino, we once more need to go to our boards.txt file and change the clock speed in there from

```
orangutan328p.build.f_cpu = 8000000 L
```

to

```
orangutan328p.build.f_cpu = 16000000 L
```

Then we use Arduino (which, remember, must be restarted after any edits to boards.txt) to once more upload a program into the AVR: Arduino causes a recompilation, again taking into account the clock speed change and our program runs as before, but now the processor is running at 16 MHz, a full sixteen times faster than when we first installed it.

As I stated earlier, in most projects my personal preference is not to use an external crystal because of the extra components required—though, of course, I use one if the project demands the fastest possible CPU speed. But in this case, I now elect to set the clock source back to the MCU's internal clock source, but with CKDIV8 unset so that my AVR is again running at 8 MHz.

```
avrdude -p m328p -c avrisp2 -P /dev/ttyACM0 -U lfuse:w:0xE2:m
```

I can now power down and remove the crystal and capacitors—and we're ready to move on.

Arduino and the AVR ID Problem

This section will probably only be of interest if you need or want to use some variant of an AVR device that is not supported—out of the box–by the Arduino software.

As we saw in Figure 3-8, Arduino talks to two entities, the compiler and AVRDude. It first uses the compiler to produce a hex file containing the developed program and then it commands AVRDude to upload that hex file into the AVR chip. In both cases Arduino has to supply the other piece of software with an -mmcu code; this indicates what kind of AVR chip is being compiled for, or uploaded to. Arduino obtains the value it uses from one single place, the mmcu entry for the programmer in boards.txt (see the earlier discussion on boards.txt).

When we want to use an AVR type that Arduino doesn't usually deal with, the problem we have is this: Although we can make new chips (or additional variants of existing chips) known to AVRDude by editing its avrdude.conf file (as we did in the previous section), there is no such easy way to make additional variants known to the compiler. We can get the compiler to list the AVR parts it knows about with the following command:

```
avr-gcc -target-help
```

Because we can't add parts to this list (unless we want to get into hacking the compiler—which is way beyond our scope in this book) we have to "dress up" our unknown AVR variant as something that the compiler *does* know about.

The compiler is only interested in building a body of machine code that is tailored for the characteristics of the stated MCU type, and placing that code in a hex file. It *never* actually talks to the AVR programmer device, or the AVR itself. AVRDude, on the other hand, makes very sure (using the device signature) that the AVR to which it is uploading is of precisely the type specified on its command line. Thus, we can get away with telling a lie to the compiler about what kind of chip we are using, but if we want to fool AVRDude we have to go in for a little subterfuge!

We'll stick with our previous example in which we want to use the micro power consumption ATmega328pu instead of an ATmega328p. The ultra-low-power version does not appear on the list of MCU parts that the compiler knows about. However, the mainstream ATmega328 and the ATmega328p (used on several Arduino boards) do appear. So, suppose we do have some ATmega328 chips, but we don't have any ATmega328p chips, we can modify the entry in avrdude.conf for the ATmega328p. In fact the only thing we need to change is the signature byte value line from:

```
    stk500_devcode     = 0x86;
    # avr910_devcode     = 0x;
```

```
signature          = 0x1e 0x95 0x0f;
pagel              = 0xd7;
bs2                = 0xc2;
chip_erase_delay   = 9000;
```

to

```
stk500_devcod      = 0x86;
# avr910_devcode    = 0x;
signature          = 0x1e 0x95 0x14;
pagel              = 0xd7;
bs2                = 0xc2;
chip_erase_delay   = 9000;
```

Now, when we want to program our ATmega328pu chip, we just call it a -mmcu 328p and both AVRDude and the compiler will be happy. Similarly we just put the entry for an ATmega328p into Arduino's boards.txt file. Of course, we'd have to do things differently if we wanted to use ATmega328p and pu chips, but this gives you the idea of how we can rig things up to work with a nonmainstream device.[8]

This issue of dealing with unusual part numbers stems from the fact that Arduino provides no mechanism for providing different part numbers to AVRDude and the compiler. It would become a nonissue if Arduino had separate configuration entries for upload.mmcu_type and compiler.mmcu_type–at the moment, though, it does not.

Pin Name Translations

If you've seen or used an Arduino you'll know that, whereas AVR data sheets refer to individual I/O pins as names like PortB3, the Arduino software uses names like Digital Pin 11. This is all part of the excellent way in which Arduino tries to make it simple for nonhardware people to learn to program.

On an Arduino board the connectors are labeled with Arduino specific labels for the AVR pins—see examples in Figure 3-13.

Figure 3-13. *Arduino port connector*

Since we are using the Arduino software, we also have to use Arduino's name for the I/O pins.

---

[8]In reality, although this example shows how you can make one part seem like another to AVRDude, it's a moot example. The ATmega328pu returns the same code as a full power ATmega328. So, if we wanted to use the pu version, we'd just configure it as ATmega328 and neither AVRDude nor the compiler would know the difference!

This means that we need a quick and easy translation between Arduino pin names and the actual physical pin numbers of our Arduino chip—and here it is! Figure 3-14 gives an easy reference that will let you see at a glance what physical pin number on the chip equates to the Arduino pin name you'll use in your project software. Make a photo copy of Figure 3-13 and keep it somewhere handy!

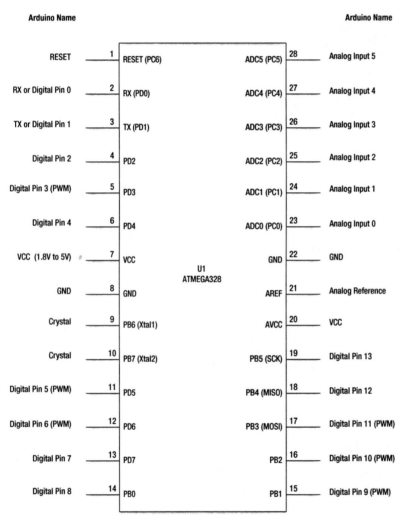

**ATmega328
AVR to Arduino Pin
Names Translation***

Arduino Name					Arduino Name
RESET	1	RESET (PC6)	ADC5 (PC5)	28	Analog Input 5
RX or Digital Pin 0	2	RX (PD0)	ADC4 (PC4)	27	Analog Input 4
TX or Digital Pin 1	3	TX (PD1)	ADC3 (PC3)	26	Analog Input 3
Digital Pin 2	4	PD2	ADC2 (PC2)	25	Analog Input 2
Digital Pin 3 (PWM)	5	PD3	ADC1 (PC1)	24	Analog Input 1
Digital Pin 4	6	PD4	ADC0 (PC0)	23	Analog Input 0
VCC (1.8V to 5V)	7	VCC	GND	22	GND
GND	8	GND	AREF	21	Analog Reference
Crystal	9	PB6 (Xtal1)	AVCC	20	VCC
Crystal	10	PB7 (Xtal2)	PB5 (SCK)	19	Digital Pin 13
Digital Pin 5 (PWM)	11	PD5	PB4 (MISO)	18	Digital Pin 12
Digital Pin 6 (PWM)	12	PD6	PB3 (MOSI)	17	Digital Pin 11 (PWM)
Digital Pin 7	13	PD7	PB2	16	Digital Pin 10 (PWM)
Digital Pin 8	14	PB0	PB1	15	Digital Pin 9 (PWM)

U1
ATMEGA328

* = Details are the same for an ATmega168

Figure 3-14. *AVR ATmega328 to Arduino pin name translation*

Bear in mind a few points about these translations.

- Pins 2 and 3 can actually be used as general I/O pins if you don't need the hardware serial channel. However, the moment you execute Arduino's Serial.Begin() function, the pins are reconfigured as TX and RX lines (output and input, respectively) and should only be used for those purposes.

- The supply voltage for the chip on pin 7 can be anywhere in the range shown for various ATmega328 variants. If you're planning to run your AVR on batteries, please check the data sheet for the version *you* have, to see what voltage it can work from before assuming it will work down to 1.8 V.

- If you don't use the crystal pins 9 and 10 for a crystal you can't use them for anything else.

- The pins with PWM (pulse width modulation) after their name are the only ones on which the Arduino supports PWM. PWM is used to control the brightness of LEDs or lamps, to control the speed of motors, or to set the angle of intelligent servo motors. We'll be visiting these topics in the several of the projects.

- The six analog inputs can in fact be used as outputs as well and can double as digital I/O lines if you want them to.

- The Analog Reference input (pin 21) is most often just tied to VCC. However, if you want analog voltage inputs to be compared relative to some other voltage, you would tie pin 21 to that voltage instead. See the chip's data sheet for more details on voltage limits.

AVR: Speak to Me!

If you've programmed in a full desktop environment, you'll be used to having lots of lovely facilities that help you debug your programs. Using things like Java NetBeans or Microsoft Visual Studio you can pause your program at pretty much any point you like, examine the value of variables, change variable values and then resume the program from where it paused. You have a veritable armory of debugging tools at your command.

When programming AVRs, the debugging facilities are a lot more limited! If you are using Atmel's AVRStudio (on a Windows PC) you can, with some minimal additional hardware, use the AVRs debugWire facility to get some debug capability. However, if, as we are here, you are using Arduino, your principal debugging tool is the serial channel. If your program isn't doing what you expect, you temporarily add Serial.print() statements to your program, so that you at least gain some idea of where the problem might be:

```
Serial.print("message");
```

You can print out text messages, or you can print out variable values that help you gradually track down what the problem might be and rectify it. This is not always easy, and it feels like hard work if you're used to something more sophisticated. However, using this method you can get to the bottom of most problems without too much trouble; it's just a longer haul. So, having some way for your AVR to push messages out to your desktop is a high priority.

In the simplest case, one where we have a programmer that offers an additional TTL level serial channel, we make the connections shown in Figure 3-15 in which we see the serial connection pins from the AVR on the test bed connected to the programmer's TTL level serial channel. As Figure 3-15 shows, we connect the TX of the AVR chip (pin 3 on an ATmega328) to the programmer's RX input, and connect the RX of the AVR chip (pin 2 on a '328) to the programmers' TX. Then, on the desktop, we use the Arduino software IDE as before, but we also start up a terminal emulator window (see below) which we point at the second serial channel (in our ongoing example of using the Pololu USB programmer this will be something like /dev/ttyACM1 on Linux and perhaps COM3: on Windows).

We can then include stuff in our Arduino sketches that gives out useful debug information. The Arduino sketch "Serial_Example 01"(listed below) shows how to send messages to the AVR's serial channel so that they show up in the terminal emulator window.

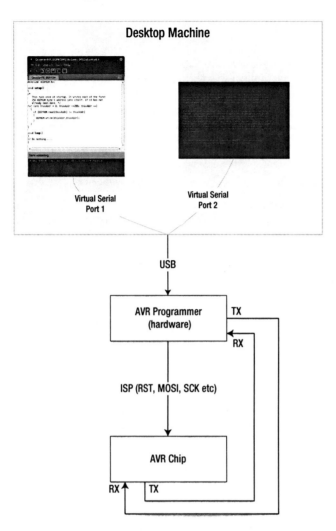

Figure 3-15. *Overview of serial connection scheme*

Here's an example of a program that would send messages from the AVR into a desktop machine's terminal window.

```
// Serial_Example_01

int theCounter = 0;

void setup()
{
    Serial.begin(9600);
}

void loop()
{
    Serial.print("The counter now = "); // msg without a new line
    Serial.prinln(theCounter);          // msg with a new line.
    theCounter++;
```

```
delay(1000);  // Sleep for one second (1000 milliseconds).
}
```

The Serial_Example_01 program declares an integer called theCounter (which being outside both the setup() and loop() functions is global in scope, meaning that it can be used from anywhere in the program. Then, in the setup() function (which is run just once when the program starts) the Serial channel is initialized. If you remember from an earlier discussion in this chapter, this is the moment when the TX and RX pins on the AVR stop being general-purpose I/O lines and instead begin usage as serial data transmission and reception pins.

With the setup complete, the program now executes the loop() function round and round forever. Within that loop

1. We send the message "The Counter Now =" out to the serial port, but notice that we user Serial.Print() and not Serial.println()–the first form doesn't cause the receiving terminal's cursor to move down to the next screen line, the second form *does* do a new line.

2. Then, we use Serial.println() to output the current value of theCounter and do a new line. The first time through, this makes the message "The Counter Now = 0" appear on the screen because we initialized the variable theCounter to zero when we first declared it.

3. Next, we increment the counter by 1 (that's what ++ on the end of a numeric variable means). Finally, we use the delay() function to put the program to sleep—in this case for 1,000 milliseconds, which to you and me is one second.

4. Then, as always in an Arduino program, having reached the end of the loop, the loop starts all over again. Only this time through the loop our variable theCounter will contain the value 1 (because we incremented it), next time through it will be 2, then 3 and so on.

As this program executes on the terminal emulator running on our desktop machine we should be seeing this kind of output.

```
The Counter now = 39
The Counter now = 40
The Counter now = 41
The Counter now = 42
The Counter now = 43
The Counter now = 44
The Counter now = 45
The Counter now = 46
The Counter now = 47
The Counter now = 48
The Counter now = 49
The Counter now = 50
```

This will continue forever, or at until we stop it! Eventually (after about nine hours) we'll start to see some strange numbers come from the counter, because it will overflow and eventually start again from zero—but that's another story!

You've probably noticed that the Arduino software interface offers a serial monitor which looks like it should be able to show the input from a serial channel. Unfortunately, the serial monitor expects to use the *same* virtual serial port that is used for programming—because that's how Arduino hardware works. None of the USB programmers work in this way, however, so for most purposes the serial monitor facility of Arduino is useless to us.

If you're using an ISP programmer that does not offer an additional TTL level serial channel, how can you tap into the essential serial chatter emerging from your AVR? There are two ways.

- If your desktop machine does have a "real" serial port that uses RS-232 signal levels (usually this is a nine-way D-plug on the side or back panel of your machine) you could go down the route of fitting a level translator chip (such as a Maxim MAX 235) to your test bed rig and connecting to your serial channel through that. That will take up space on your test bed rig that you might eventually need for other purposes, and a level translator chip can cost you a few bucks, perhaps more than your AVR chip did! See Appendix B for more info on RS-232 and signal-level conversion.

- Another—and I think preferable—alternative is to buy a USB to TTL serial dongle. As the name suggests, this plugs into a spare USB port on your desktop machine and sets itself up as one or more additional virtual serial ports (you sometimes have to install a driver, sometimes not). At the non-USB end, it presents TTL level TX, RX, and ground connections that you can connect directly to your AVR (remember that to protect against damage to your devices, *always* make the ground connection first and the others afterward). You can get these devices from a variety of places. For example,

  - `http://www.sparkfun.com/products/9717` (United States); and

  - Numerous Internet sellers sell these via auction sites.

In one or other of these ways, even if your AVR programmer does not provide the facility, you should be able get yourself the serial channel that you are going to need for debugging your projects and code.

If you're thinking ahead, you could be wondering how to deal with the situation where your project needs to use the serial channel for a purpose other than debugging. Suppose you are doing a project that requires you to send out a constant stream of information (e.g., a temperature reading derived from an AVR-connected sensor). Perhaps you want to send this information stream to a desktop application that paints pretty graphs of the information from moment to moment! In such an application it's not ideal to have to send debug information over that same channel, yet, your AVR chip only has one serial channel; so what can you do?

SoftwareSerial Library, a free download based on work by Mikal Hart, is available.

`http://arduino.cc/en/Reference/SoftwareSerial`

This library lets you turn any of the general purpose I/O pins on your AVR into an *additional* serial port. This means that you can use your hardware serial port for your application purpose and create a software serial port for debug or some other purpose (e.g., send info as a log stream to a data logger device with a TTL level serial interface). It's even possible to create *multiple* extra software serial ports, though there are some limitations on multiple ports—see the foregoing link for details and examples of using software serial.

Terminal Emulators

Up to now we've spoken blithely about using a terminal emulator window on your desktop machine. We intend for this to be the on-screen termination point for messages being put out by your AVR. But, what are these terminal emulators, where do you get them from, if you don't already have them?

On a Mac system you should find the terminal app that is built in sufficient for anything we need to do in this book.

On a Windows system you might use Hyperterminal (Windows XP and earlier) or you can use the downloadable version of Hyperterminal (for Windows Vista or W7) from

`http://www.hilgraeve.com/hyperterminal-trial/`

You might also (for Vista and W7) like to try puTTY—a free terminal emulator that you can get from

`http://www.chiark.greenend.org.uk/~sgtatham/putty/`

For Linux, and Windows systems, check out coolterm at

`http://freeware.the-meiers.org/`

For Linux systems you can use Minicom—a free terminal emulator. Have a look at `http://alioth.debian.org/projects/minicom/` for a kit.

On Ubuntu you can usually install Minicom with the command

`"sudo apt-get install minicom"`

Minicom, of course, has its own Wikipedia page.

If none of these possibilities works out, do a search of the Internet for a "terminal emulator with serial port support." You'll turn up lots of possibilities—many of them free to download.

Once you've got your terminal emulator running, you'll need to configure it with the following settings:

- The name of the serial port you want to communicate with (see the section "AVRDude: Getting Started" for tips on how to find out this information if you don't know it— remember, if you have a programmer that offers two serial ports, the second port will always be the TTL serial port). The port name will be `/dev/tty?????` on Unix and `COM?` on Windows. The `?` will vary from system to system.

- A send and receive data rate (a.k.a. the baud rate). This is the speed you set when—in the Arduino programming environment—you include a statement like `Serial.begin(2400);` in your code. That example sets the baud rate to (guess what!) 2400 baud (which means 2,400 bits per second).

- A bits-per-byte length. This is always eight bits.

- A number of stop bits: you should always use one stop bit.

- A parity setting. We use `None` (or `n`).

If you use your terminal emulator's settings screen to set these values, you should be able to communicate very happily with your AVR via whatever serial port method you are using.

Summary

This chapter has covered a lot of topics, most of them quite low-level and detailed ones. Congratulations if you've bashed through it all! If you didn't read it all, I quite understand! Use it as a reference as you proceed through the rest of the—more fun parts—of this book.

We began by comparing the MCU approach with using a dedicated chip to implement a timer. Then we looked at how the "naked" AVR approach works and how all the pieces go together. We looked at some of the basic characteristics of AVR chips and using external clocking components. Then, we looked at AVR fuses and what they can do for us. AVRDude was next—a very useful piece of software for our purposes but initially hard to get to know. We looked a numerous examples of AVRDude usage (including for programming fuses). We looked at the complexities of AVR part numbers and some methods for being able to use nonstandard AVR parts if we want to. We compared the native AVR pin names with the names for those same pins that Arduino uses (don't forget to make a photo copy of Figure 3-13 and keep it handy!). Finally, we looked at how we can use serial links to allow our AVR to talk to the desktop, for debug purposes or for application specific communication—or both.

Coming Up Next

Moving On: making things that move, in which we look at how your AVR can become a shaker and shifter!

■ ■ ■

CHAPTER 4

Moving On!

Your AVR chip is a silicon nerd! It's a very smart little beast, but it's very puny. You may as well ask it to calculate the square root of infinity as to directly energize a motor, or activate a solenoid. It's all a question of electrical muscle: even a small electric motor will want to consume about 500 milliamps of current, whereas an MCU port pin starts to sweat at about 20 milliamps. So, for all that the AVR is smart, translating that smartness into making real-world things move or happen at the right time is not within its direct capabilities. It needs help.

That's the main thrust of this chapter—how we deliver the help that an MCU needs to be a shaker and shifter in the real world of movement and motion.

Making Things That Move

I love looking at books and magazines that show the endless novelty and invention that MCUs inspire, I really do. However, you have to note a certain sameness about many ideas: such a large proportion of them are about making little LED lights flash, or making messages appear on neat little screens. Nothing wrong with that, of course, the world needs pretty things and neat solutions: I've created a few projects like that myself for this book and elsewhere! But, I often feel the lack of more muscular MCU applications that interact with the world of moving things in a more direct way, and I wish there were more published projects that did stuff like that.

In this chapter I get my wish. We look at how we can control everything from servo motors all the way through to allowing our MCU to do grown-up stuff, like turning mains appliances on and off.

Clearly, an exhaustive treatment of the myriad methods used to activate and control real-world items would fill many books: so, it's obvious I cannot do very complete coverage in one chapter of one book, but I do single out some examples at several levels of muscularity so that you have a feel for how the interfacing works and what's involved in controlling things. You'll look at creating movement and also a little bit at sensing movement.

The Servo Motor

First introduced some years ago for controlling moving parts in radio-controlled model planes and boats and trains, servo motors are an absolute gift for MCU applications. A servo motor contains the motor itself, plus a small internal control board (ironically, this board often has an embedded MCU on it). A typical servo motor has three connections.

- A voltage supply (+ and -) that is used to power the on-board electronics inside the motor as well as the motor itself. On almost all servo motors the + supply wire is red, and the – supply wire is black–be sure to check the documentation that came with your motor though.

- In most products a servo control input is a logic level input (between 0 and 5 volts) which needs to be pulsed at a constant rate. This wire is usually white, but sometimes it's yellow.

The basic idea of a servo motor–and the reason it is so ideal for MCU projects–is that the control entity (in this case our AVR MCU) can interface to the motor control input directly, just as if it was another logic device, not a power-gulping beast of a motor! The servo motor has the built-in electronics to drive and control the motor. For other types of motors the MCU needs to be far more involved in the control process, but generally, the MCU tells a servo motor what to do, and it does it. Since many servo motors can run from the same +5-volt supply that the MCU itself runs from, the servo motor and MCU partnership is indeed a marriage made in heaven!

Servo motors come in two main flavors.

- Positioner motors that rotate to a commanded angle. Individual servo motor products will have slightly different parameters, which belies the common name of "standard servo motors," but a typical baseline product will have the capability for somewhere between 150 and 180 degrees of rotational movement.

- If you pay more, you can get positioner servo motors that are able to give your MCU positional feedback–though these can command quite a high premium and they are not always needed. Many applications don't need positional sensing at all and some only need minimal sensing (such as end-of-travel detection) which can be done cheaply and effectively with limit switches or opto-sensors.

- Continuous servo motors offer full 360-degree rotation (in other words, they rotate at some number of revolutions per minute, just like any other motor) and you set the speed of rotation with the control input.

The electronics inside a servo motor has two parts: the control part and the driver part. The driver part is responsible for actually moving the motor into position. The control part consists of

- A sensor that gives a different voltage for every point of rotation of the motor.

- A circuit that converts incoming control pulses into a "target" position voltage

- Circuitry to signal the driver section to rotate the motor toward the target position.

- A control loop that monitors the motor's position sensor and cuts power to the driver section and locks it down when the target position is reached.

A servo motor's control input expects to get control pulses somewhere between 30 and 50 times per second. It's a sensible idea to use something close to 50 per second because there are some motors around that are not happy if you deviate too far from there. So, each second is chopped up into 50 slots each of which lasts for 20 milliseconds. Each slot is a "frame" (or a "servo frame"). To make the motor move to the desired position, all you have to do is vary the portion of each frame time slot when the control signal is high. So, you vary the pulse width but *not* the update frequency. MCU chips have the capability to produce PMW signals very precisely: for many of them it is built into their hardware, but unfortunately (because it is intended for multiple purposes) the frame rate is often rather higher than we need for controlling a servo motor. So, we have to write or use different software that will produce precisely the right kind of PWM signals for a servo.

Figure 4-1 illustrates the general idea of a PWM signal. The diagram in Figure 4-1 represents a complete 20 millisecond frame. At the start of the frame the pulse occurs, this is just a logic level pulse–active high. The servo motor's key interest is in the duration of the high time of this pulse. Figure 4-1 is not drawn to scale; if it was, the empty part of the slot would be even longer than that shown!

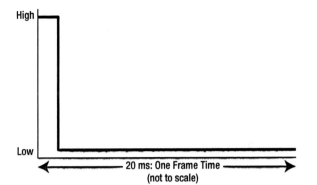

Figure 4-1. *One servo frame*

In Figure 4-2, you can see how this waveform looks over half a second (500 ms). Again, the ratio of the highs to the lows is exaggerated; the highs would be even shorter as compared to the lows if they were shown in true proportion.

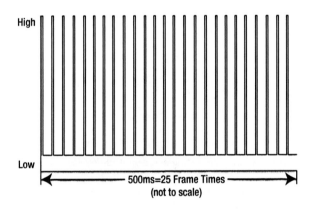

Figure 4-2. *A set of 25 servo frames*

In summary, then, at the start of each frame there is a small pulse, and it is the length of this small pulse that the motor reads and acts upon. If you analyze the specs of a range of servo motors, you'll find that there is variation between different manufacturers as to what range of pulse lengths the motor controller expects to get. The supposed standard pulse lengths are between 1 millisecond and 2 milliseconds, but many products deviate from this.

Even between supposedly identical products there is likely to be some small amount of variation between pulse lengths to get the same amount of rotation. This is because some analog-ness is involved here. Inside the servo motor the positional sensor is provided by a potentiometer (a rotary action variable resistor–see Appendix A). This potentiometer is turned by the motor's central spindle and it provides the control electronics with an analog voltage that varies according to the position of the motor.

As we saw earlier, the motor's internal electronics converts the control pulses we send into a voltage, and a comparator circuit (or sometimes an MCU) is used to generate a difference voltage between where we want the shaft to be and where it is now. This difference voltage is amplified and used to turn the motor in the appropriate direction to lessen this difference voltage, to the point where it reaches zero (meaning the motor is on-station at the commanded position). This arrangement is an elegant one (in an engineering sense) because it means that when the motor gets close to where it should be, the difference voltage gets less and less and the drive power to the motor falls away gracefully, making the motor decelerate as it gets close to the point where it must stop. This ensures that there will be very little, if any, overshoot. However, since there are analog voltages involved and a mechanical coupling between the potentiometer and the motor spindle, there are bound to be small amounts of electrical variation–even among otherwise identical products.

So, look carefully at the specifications for the servo motor that you buy, because there are variations; however, in the general case, the servo motor will react to pulses between 1 and 2 milliseconds: The motor will be positioned centrally at the midpoint of the pulse length (1.5 ms in the standard case).

The spec for one servo motor, the one pictured at Figure 4-3, says that it reacts to a pulse length of between 0.75 ms (which sets the motor positioned fully clockwise) and 2.25 ms (sets motor positioned fully counter-clockwise). So, a pulse length of 1.5 ms (the midpoint) should set this motor pretty much to the center of its travel. Let's see what the frames for that might look like.

Figure 4-3. *Servo motor example*

Figure 4-4 visualizes (but not to scale) a couple of servo frames implementing a midpoint pulse. We use pulse lengths to set the position, but the position we set for any given pulse length will vary between products and even (to a lesser extent) between individual units. You may already have experienced this variation at the product level. If you have ever owned a radio-controlled model, such as a car, boat, or plane, there is always some kind of mechanical adjuster to make it run true. Such adjusters are making up for (among other things) the variations of the individual servo motor installed in your model.

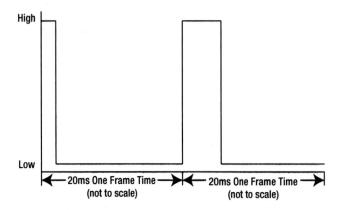

Figure 4-4. *Close-up on two servo frames*

But don't go away yet, there are more great things about servo motors. Once you have set the position, unless there is quite a lot of mechanical pressure on the motor, most motors will stay in the position you set, even when power is removed. When on power, the motor will resist any forces that try to take it off-station.

Additionally, they come with standard mounting arrangements. This means that you can shop around for the best priced motor, but if one motor proves unequal to the task you have for it, you can very often slot in a replacement without having to redo the mounting arrangements or power linkages. You'll find that many outlets which sell servo motors also sell mounting kits for them, and these can be very useful. Generally, then, servo motors are not too hard to install.

The mountings for a servo motor are pretty standard and the overlays to the photo in Figure 4-5 illustrate the approximate center distances and dimensions. These do vary a tiny bit from product to product, but not enough to make much difference. You can mount your servo motor in your project in a number of ways, though obviously the details vary each time. You can mount the motor in any orientation that suits your project, vertically, horizontally, or upside down, the motor will still work fine.

Figure 4-5. *Servo motor mounting centers and dimensions*

When fixing a servo into a wood-frame project I always use self-tapping screws with so-called cheesehead tops as in Figure 4-6. I always drill tap holes at about two-thirds the screw size if it's near the edge of the wood, if you don't do this, the wood tends to split.

Figure 4-6. *Using self-tapping cheesehead screws*

The really essential thing is that the motor is held securely so that it can't twist about, thus changing the distance to whatever it is driving. Also, in lightweight projects, you need to take account of the rotational force the motor will generate and add grip or deadweight into the box or enclosure of the project. You don't want the centrifugal force generated by the motor making your project walk off the desk, instead of what it's supposed to be doing. Figure 4-6 shows a fixing with self-tapping screws.

If your project doesn't offer any convenient or properly spaced fixing edges, which often happens, you may need to use mounting brackets (as mentioned earlier, the same outlets that sell the motors usually offer the mounting brackets); mounting brackets usually offer extensibility, which you can use to extend the motor's mounting points to a suitable dimension for your project needs.

If all else fails, you may need to go in for cutting out a hole in a piece of wood, plastic, or metal into which you slot your motor. This simply consists of drawing the outline for the motor body (excluding the mounting tabs) onto the place you want your motor to go: then, use a 0.75" (19 mm) drill bit to drill a couple of holes in a straight line within the outline - (the adjacent diagram shows this idea). Then, using the large holes as the start points for a small pad saw (a.k.a. a keyhole saw), cut neatly around the outline (indicated by the dotted line in the diagram). Smooth and clean off the resulting edges and drop your motor in–of course, remembering to fit screws or nuts and bolts into the fixing tabs–and you're done!

Translating the rotary movement of the motor shaft into other kinds of movement–such as a push–pull motion–is very often essential when using a servo motor. This involves fitting an attachment to the motor shaft. These types of attachments are known as "horns" and many, but not all, motors will come with a selection of them (see Figure 4-7). If your motor didn't come with any horns, or nothing that matches your needs, then you should find that the same vendor will sell a selection separately. Robotics and model making stores usually have a very large selection that should provide what you need.

Figure 4-7. *Servo motor "horns" package*

Giving a Servo Motor a Testing Time

In most projects you want to use a servo motor to provide fairly precise service. The problem is that using a servo motor is fraught with variables. We've already seen that, due to the analog elements inside a servo motor, there is some minor variation, even between how apparently identical units will act upon a given control signal. The other more difficult variable is how your MCU will provide precisely timed pulses to the motor; fairly precise timings are easy to do in a test program, but rather harder to do when your AVR is doing lots of other things too.

Let's look at the mechanical side of the precision issue: the variations between motors may only result in fractional differences of motor shaft rotation, but if you think about how these motors may be used, it's possible that those small differences could become a problem. Imagine if the motor is being used to power the short side of a lever, a small movement on one side will make a larger movement on the other side. Let me show you how that might look in a real situation.

Refer to Figure 4-8, in which a servo motor positions a ball guide gate in a game. In this game the ball has to be guided into a certain direction set by the position of a plastic paddle. The actuation mechanism is using leverage (with the screw on the paddle as the fulcrum) to make a fairly small movement of the motor (transmitted through the push rod) which will result in a comparatively large movement at the far end of the paddle. This means that any variation on how the motor positions itself will make quite a difference to the position of the end of the paddle. In this usage we would want the positioning of the paddle to be repeatable; it has to be much the same every time. You would, at the very least, want the paddle to return to a known rest point when the game was reset.

Given that any small variations of position are amplified, you would perform some testing and characterization of the overall paddle positioner assembly to make sure that the software's "idea" of where it is positioning the paddle is close enough to the reality. If you only cared about the paddle getting accurately back to its "rest" position (which is how it's shown in Figure 4-8), then you could install a sense switch that the paddle hits when it resets. Your program would then just send pulses to the motor to make it go back to the rest position and monitor the sense switch. It would stop sending pulses when it "sees" the sense switch close and the "at rest" position would always be the same–determined by the switch activation and not the motor characteristics which will alter slightly with wear and tear.

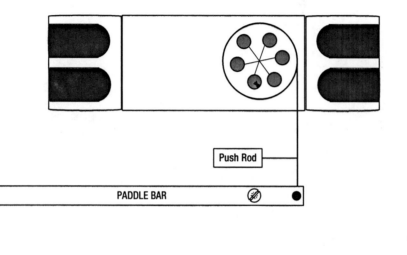

Figure 4-8. *Small motor movement—big effect!*

All this adds up to the fact that, when you use a servo motor in a project, you often need to have a good idea of the real limits of the motor movement: you need to know how well your positioning commands translate into what the motor actually does.

Servo motors that do not rotate 360 degrees have built in mechanical limiters that stop them from rotating too far. The nasty sound you get when the motor hits one of these hard is not a nice one; that sound you can hear is the mashing of internal plastic gears. However, it is possible, with care, to gently explore the limits of your motor, without much chance of damaging it.

It may be that your motor, when operated within the pulse lengths specified by the manufacturer, offers enough rotational movement for your project. If the movement is sufficient and accuracy is not especially an issue, then you're all set to go. However, if you want to get the maximum amount of rotation from your motor, and/or you want to do some testing to see how accurate your control can be, then you need a test program.

The Great Thing About Standards…

…is that there are so many variations of them to choose from! Servo motors were originally all meant to be the same. If one breaks, you just put in another one and everything works as before. Nice theory! But what are the variable points?

I have found most servo motor specifications to be quite conservative, meant to protect your motor against damage (and no doubt protect the manufacturers against a tidal wave of warranty claims). When I used a program to test the motor shown earlier on, I only got about 120 degrees of rotation using the stated pulse lengths. However, by very gently increasing the pulse lengths using a test program I managed to get the full 180-degree movement from it.

Here's the test program I used (within the Arduino IDE which is not shown).

```
/*
  Servo Motor Sweep. Makes a servo motor sweep from one end of
  its travel to the other.
*/

int motorPin = 4;                    // Name the motorPin

/*
  Constant values used through the program
*/

/*
  Pulse length (in microseconds) for fully counter clockwise
  and fully clockwise. Customize to your servo motor's specs.
*/
const int fullCCW =750;
const int fullCW = 2250;

const int frameRate = 50; // How many servo frames/second
const int msPerFrame = 1000 /frameRate; // Millisecs per frame
// Do the setup
void setup()
{
  pinMode(motorPin, OUTPUT);        // Make the pin an output
  Serial.begin(9600);
  Serial.print("msPerFrame=");       // Say the frame length val.
  Serial.println(msPerFrame,DEC);
}

// Now loop round this forever and ever.
void loop()
{
  /*
  We start from the fully counter clockwise value, then each
  time through the main program loop we lengthen the pulse
  by 5 microseconds. Then, we pause for enough time to allow
  the rest of the 50 ms frame time to pass. This is not going
  to be 100% accurate due to execution delays and latency, but
  it's easily accurate enough (about 98% accurate) for the servo
  motor - which in any case varies from example to example.
```

```
   To make this 100% accurate we would need to hook up an
   oscilloscope or a digital analyzer to the motorPin and tweak
   the program values until we had it exact, however that would
   be overkill for this purpose.
   */
 for (unsigned int myDelay = fullCCW; myDelay < fullCW; myDelay++)
 {
   // Frame start
   digitalWrite(motorPin, high);    // The pulse starts.
   delayMicroseconds(myDelay);      // pause for current pulse microseconds
   digitalWrite(motorPin, low);     // The pulse ends.
   /*
   Now wait out the rest of the frame time which is our
   frame time (in milliseconds) minus the pulse length in
   milliseconds (1000 milliseconds to a microsecond)
   */
   delay(msPerFrame-(myDelay/1000));
 }
}
```

Let's do a quick code walk:

- It starts by declaring constants for the control pin you will use to send pulses to the motor. In this case it's Arduino digital pin 4 (assuming using an ATmega328, this translates to physical pin 6–refer to the pinout chart from Chapter 3 figure 14). Then you get declarations for the minimum and maximum pulse lengths and these take the values specified by the manufacturer for this motor, which were 0.75 milliseconds and 2.25 milliseconds, respectively. In the program you translate these into microseconds (remember one millisecond = 1,000 microseconds).[1]

- Next, set the frame rate you want to use. In this case, you need 50 servo frames per second. Then create a constant that tells you how many milliseconds there are per frame.

- In the setup (which, remember, only runs once at startup), all you do is make the motor control pin into an output. You could add some stuff in the setup to call out the constants: for example, you could add

  ```
  Serial.begin(9600);
  ```

  and

  ```
  Serial.print("The frame time in milliseconds is ");
  ```

  and

  ```
  Serial.println(msPerFrame,DEC);
  ```

  if we have a serial connection into a desktop machine.

---

[1] Also remember that if, like me, you are mathematically challenged, you can use Google to perform conversions for you, with a query like "What is 0.75 milliseconds in microseconds?"

- Then, it's time to get into the main program loop–which, as you remember, loops around until you remove power from the AVR. Within the main program loop we run a for loop. This outputs servo frames on the motor control pin; inside each successive frame the motor control pulse gets longer by one millisecond starting from the minimum and continuing until it reaches the maximum. When the full range of pulse lengths has been output it starts all over again. Following are the steps within the main loop:

  - We initiate the for loop. This sets the fullCCW value as its start and the fullCW value (see the previous code) as its end. Each time through the loop the variable myDelay is incremented by one, using myDelay++.

  - We use digitalWrite to set the motor control pin to high.

  - We use the Arduino software's delayMicroseconds() function to wait for whatever the current pulse length is; delayMicroseconds() pauses the program for the stated number of microseconds.

  - We use digitalWrite to set the motor control pin to low–which ends the pulse.

  - Then, we use the delay() function of Arduino to pause the program for the rest of the current servo frame. The delay(XXms) function expects to get XXms as the number of milliseconds to pause. The calculation we do here works out the frame time remainder by taking overall frame time and subtracting from it the number of milliseconds we have already spent on the control pulse. The program is then paused for whatever the remainder is. So, if the pulse length is currently 1,000 microseconds (which is 1 millisecond) and the frame length is 20 milliseconds, this line of code will translate into:

    delay(20–(1000/1000)) = 19

    Meaning that the program will pause for 19 milliseconds.

  - When the delay completes, the next time through the for loop begins . . .

  - When the for loop completes, the main loop() begins again–and the pulse length will again start from the lowest value.

Although it's fairly basic and leaves out some things it might do, the program gives you the means to test your motor within the given parameters. The program timings won't be absolutely accurate because, of course, the program itself takes some time to run and so this will cause variation in the timings, though not enough to make any noticeable difference unless you are measuring it with a frequency meter or oscilloscope. If, using the values provided by the manufacturer of your servo motor, you get the movement you need from your motor, you'll most likely be content to leave it there.

What do you do, if you are not getting as much movement as you want, or as the spec says you should get from your servo motor? Well, you may want (at your own risk of course) to try some margin testing. To do this, you need to repeatedly tweak the fullCCW and fullCW constants in the test program by small amounts (5 microseconds *at most* each time) and reupload the program into your Arduino to find out what the true minimum and maximum values are for your individual motor.

How will you know when you have reached the actual minimum or maximum values? If you look and listen to your motor in motion, while the test program is running with the manufacturer's values, you will see that it moves in little staccato bursts in a strict rhythm. When it reaches the end of one cycle it quickly rewinds to the start position and the beat starts again. However, when you extend the times (up at one end or down at the other) you will see that, eventually, the rhythm is broken; there will be a dead time at the start or the end of the travel; the movement rhythm will miss one or more beats. This may also be accompanied by a tiny "click" sound that the motor doesn't normally make (which is it gently hitting the end stop). When you get to that stage, *do not* continue adjusting the timings: In fact, you should immediately undo your most recent changes and reupload the program into your AVR as quickly as you can or just remove power from the motor. In other words, having established the absolute limits of the movement for a particular motor, don't leave the motor tapping its end stops for very long.

By *gently* adjusting the min and max pulse length values you should be able to find out the full range of pulses that your motor can manage without any serious risk of damage. I have two examples of the motors pictured earlier and I performed this margin testing with both of them. Remember, these are supposedly identical products from the same manufacturer; I think also from the same batch if I read the labeling correctly. One motor was okay with pulses from 550us to 2600us, the other's range was 610us to 2450us. I have another motor, a completely different type from a different manufacturer, and the pulse lengths quoted in the spec for that one also proved very conservative.

One final word on this subject: if you are (I say again, at your own risk) operating your motor outside the specified limits, leave some margin. For example, if you have established that your motor is okay with pulse lengths between 800us and 2900us it's not wise to operate it with exactly those values because if–as the motor ages–the spec drifts a little, you have no margin for error and it's likely to start hitting the end stops on a regular basis (perhaps initially without you even realizing it) which is, mechanically, bad news. It is better to allow some safety margin at either end for future wear and tear and operate it at, perhaps, 900 and 2800, respectively.

Margin testing is one aspect, but what about accuracy? Suppose our application requires the motor to rotate 90 degrees from its start position. We could just assume that if the motor rotates 180 degrees when we send it a maximum length pulse, a pulse at half the maximum length will make it go to 90-degree rotation, but will it? We need a test program for that too!

Adding Some Library Code

At this stage we should make our task easier by introducing some ready-made library code into the picture. One of the glories of Arduino is that there are so many complete functional code libraries that are yours for the asking. This one is called the Servo library and it does everything we have looked at so far, but far more easily (I know, I should have said so, but I wanted you to see how the low level worked first!). The Servo library comes as part of the Arduino kit. The following Arduino sketch shows how to use it.

```
// ServoStepper1
#include < Servo.h>

Servo myMotor;
void setup()
{
  myMotor.attach(4);
}

void loop() {
  for (int i=0;i<=180;i++)
  {
    myMotor.write(i);  // Set angle to current value.
    delay(100);
  }

  myMotor.write(0); // Command back to home
  delay(1500);      // Wait for rewind.

}
```

As you can see from the listing, using the Servo library makes short work of controlling the motor. The code walk need not detain us for long!

- The program starts by including the Servo library code.
- We then declare a Servo called myMotor.
- In the setup() we attach this servo to Arduino pin 4 (the same pin as we used previously).
- In the program's main loop() we use a for loop to step between 0 and 180 in steps of 1.
- We use the servo's write method to write out the required angle of rotation for the motor
- We delay by 100 milliseconds, just so that we can see the motor do the steps; otherwise it would probably be too fast to see the individual steps and–depending on speeds of processor and motor–it might not have time to complete the move.
- When the for loop ends, we command the motor to return back to 0 degrees of rotation.
- We wait for 1 1/2 seconds for the motor to do its reset, and then the loop starts again.

Pretty straightforward stuff, no? Rather easier than what we were doing before. However, astute readers will have deduced that the Servo library must, under the surface, be translating the angle of rotation we supply into the appropriate servo pulse lengths on the designated pin. That is indeed what the library code does, and it assumes that your servo motor is using the "standard" pulse lengths for servo motors.

So, what do you do if your servo motor is one of the many that uses slightly different timing values? In this case, you simply use a different control method of the Servo library. Instead of using myMotor.write(angle) you use myMotor.writeMicroseconds(uSecs) and instead of the for loop using value 0 to 180, it uses the minimum and maximum pulse length values that your motor needs –as in this modified version of the program.

```
// ServoStepper2
#include <Servo.h>

const int fullCCW =550;
const int fullCW = 2250;

Servo myMotor;
void setup()
{
  myMotor.attach(4);
}

void loop() {
  for (int i=fullCCW;i< fullCW;i+=10)
  {
    myMotor.writeMicroseconds(i);  // Set angle to current value.
    delay(100);
  }

  myMotor.writeMicroseconds(fullCCW); // Command back to home
  delay(1500);      // Wait for rewind.
}
```

As you can see, this is more or less the same program, except the loop uses values derived from the minimum and maximum pulse length constants at the top of the program, and we use myMotor.WriteMicroseconds(). So, by using the Servo library we can (as so often when using Arduino libraries) make our task of creating a calibration program a lot easier.

Next, we'll create an Arduino program that takes three simple commands from the serial channel "u," "d," "h," and "z" (for up, down, halfway, and 0, respectively). Our program will look at the serial channel and if it sees any of these characters coming in it will increase, decrease, or set to 90 or 0 the servo setting appropriately.

```
// This program allows you to step the motor manually by sending keyboard commands
// "u", "d", "z" and "h" meaning up, down, zero and halfway respectively.
#include <Servo.h>
Servo myMotor;
int theAngle=0;

void setup()
{
  Serial.begin(9600);
  Serial.println("Servo Calibrator V1");
  myMotor.attach(4);
}

void loop() {
  if (Serial.available() !=0)
  {
    // Something has been received.
    int inChar = Serial.read();

    switch (inChar)
     {
     case 'u':
       theAngle++;
       break;

     case 'd':
       theAngle--;
       break;

     case 'h':
       theAngle=90;
       break;

     case 'z':
       theAngle = 0;
       break;

     default: // Default case, say what...
       Serial.println("use u, d, h or z only");
       break;
     }  // End of switch...case block
    if (theAngle < 0)
    {
       theAngle=0;
    }
```

```
  if (theAngle > 180)
  {
     theAngle = 180;
  }
  Serial.print("Angle is now set to ");
  Serial.println(theAngle,DEC);
 }
myMotor.write(theAngle);
}
```

Let's do a code walk for this program:

- As before, we include the servo.h library. Then we declare our Servo which we call myMotor. We also create an integer called theAngle which will hold the current servo angle that is to be set. This is just for clarity, the servo itself could hold the angle–see the Servo library read() method.

- In the setup() we open (begin) the serial channel and we put out a message so that anyone listening knows the program has started. We then, as before, use attach() to use Arduino pin 4 to control the servo motor. Then we get into the main loop.

- At the top of the main program loop() we check to see if any data are available from the serial channel (i.e., have any characters typed on the desktop been received in the Arduino)? If yes

    - We read the first received character from the serial channel and store it in a variable called inChar (input Character).

    - We begin a switch...case table. This uses the value of inChar as its switch value, and we check for each of the allowed characters in turn, changing the value of the variable theAngle appropriately. For example if the character received is a "z" we set theAngle to zero. A switch...case table works like this: When it finds a matching value it carries out all the program statements until it gets to a break, and it then exits the switch...case and moves onto the next statement in the program (in this case that will be the

        if (theAngle <0)...

down below the closing bracket. If none of the cases provided match the switch value (the value of inChar, in this example) the default case actioned. Here, we just make it send a message to the serial channel to say that what they sent was not valid and remind them of what we are looking for from them.

    - By the end of the switch...case code block, our variable theAngle is very likely to have been altered. So, next we check it to make sure that our changes to it have not taken out of the allowed range of 0 to 180. If it is out of range, we correct it. Doing this check after every command is received ensures that the angle we set can never go over 180 and never go below 0–no matter how many "u" or "d" commands are received from an overenthusiastic user!

    - We then send out the new value to the Serial channel so that the user can see some visible reaction on screen, as well as knowing the angle which the motor is being commanded to. This allows the user to compare what the software thinks it has done with what is actually happening in reality.

- That's the end of the code block that's conditional on there being something received from the Serial channel

- Finally, we write out the value of theAngle to the servo.

That program was a little larger than the previous ones, but I hope it contained nothing too complicated or hard to understand. So, how would you use that program? Well obviously it's quite fun to fool around with it for a while, but the serious use for it is to give you a way to relate the angle values that the software sends to the actual physical position your motor adopts when you send them. For example, does it really rotate to a position that is 90 degrees different from its start point when you send the "h" command? Using this program you can calibrate your motor as in Figure 4-9.

Figure 4-9. *Motor calibration at 0, 45, 90, 135, and 180 degrees*

In this photo sequence the calibration software starts from 0 degrees and progresses by 45-degree increments (taking photos left to right and progressing down) until it reaches 180 degrees. As you can clearly see in Figure 4-9 (thanks to the colored push pin inserted into the horn wheel), this motor–which is the same one that has slightly nonstandard timings that we saw earlier on–actually rotates a little more than 180 degrees. If this motor was going to be used in an application where accuracy of angle was very important, we would have to make note of the values we have to send the motor to get it to go to the correct angle. However, in other contexts it might be quite handy to have a servo motor that can rotate more than 180 degrees!

The Gem Light

By this stage I can almost hear readers saying "neat stuff, but what can you use it for?" Well perhaps it wasn't you saying that, perhaps you've already got some ideas in mind? Just in case, let's do a quickie project using a servo motor to get you started. You don't have to build this if you don't want to; it is not intended as a finished project, it's just a rough and ready thing to give you an idea of how to make use of a servo motor.

The Gem Light demonstrates the beauty of a moving light source when shone through crystals: to build this quickie project you will need

- A servo motor: I *know* you know what one of those is.

- A powerful LED light (e.g., a 1 Watt Luxeon LED) mounted on a heatsink: these are available from most electronics stores:

    - www.sparkfun.com/products/10179 (United States)

    - www.maplin.co.uk/1w-high-power-led-with-pcb-511367 (UK).

- The cardboard tube center from a used-up roll of kitchen wrap.

- Some cheap gem-like stones such as you would get from a new-age store or online from beadwork and crystal suppliers. If you can find them at an attractive price, square-cut glass crystals such as miniature "Swarovski" crystals are very suitable–but almost any transparent glass beads should look good.

- Some 1" (25 mm) black electrical tape masking tape.

- Two very small nuts and bolt sets with washers if possible. The smallest you can find.

- Some scrap bits of smooth (planed) stick wood 2" x 1" (45 mm x 24 mm) or so– dimensions not critical. You only need about 2' (60 cm) of this. A couple of small bits of 2" x 1/2" (46 x 12 mm) wood. None of these sizes are critical; you're just looking for any bits of wood that you may have hanging around that are around about these dimensions.

- Some heat-resistant food wrap film (a.k.a. cling-film). This *must* be fairly heat resistant stuff (the labeling on the box will usually tell you what maximum temperature it can take). You want something that can take 220 f (105 c) or more. Since the high-power LED gets quite warm, don't take chances with wrap for which you don't know the melting point. It could be a *fire hazard*–so please don't use it if you're not sure.

Begin by making the gem holder. Using some strong scissors, cut the cardboard tube from the kitchen roll down to about 2" (about 50 mm). Keep the 2" section and discard the rest.

Take your black insulating tape and neatly lap it round the outside of the roll, making an overlap at the top and bottom that you can neatly fold over the ends to hide the cardboard-ness! Then, cut a small piece of kitchen wrap and lay it over the end of the tube. Carefully use your fingers to push about an inch (24 mm) down into the end of the tube to make a small nest for your glass crystals to sit inside.

Using the scissors, carefully trim around the outside of the tube to cut away excess film. Leave a skirt of about 2" (50 mm) around the outside so that you can add more tape around the outside of the roll to secure the film to the tube. Figures 4-10 and 4-11 show the finished gem holder. It doesn't have to be especially pretty, but it should be as dark as possible, so use lots of black tape!

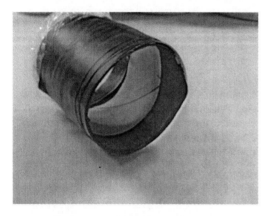

Figure 4-10. *Gem holder tube bottom end*

Figure 4-11. *Gem holder tube top end*

Figure 4-11 shows the top end of the gem holder, with the film-cradle for the glass beads to sit in.

Next, we need to mount the high-powered LED onto a suitable horn on the servo motor. This is shown in the photo sequence in Figure 4-12, in which the existing horn is first removed. This reveals the motor shaft on which you can see the gripping splines so that attachments don't easily slip—even under considerable load. Then a more suitable horn attachment is selected. Some appropriate mounting holes are drilled in the new attachment. These have to be sized so that you can use those very small nuts and bolts to fix the high-powered LED to the attachment securely. You will get a better effect if the LED is mounted a little off center, as this makes the light direction change all the more as the motor rotates and gives a more pleasing effect. Two wires are then soldered onto the Luxeon LED; be very careful not to overheat the LED while doing this.

Next, the horn is fixed onto the servo motor, and then the LED, on its heatsink, is fixed onto the horn using two nuts and bolts.

Figure 4-12. *Assembling the Gem Light*

Then, a strain relief tie-on is used (I simply used a strand of some wire cut out from an old CAT5 network cable) so that the wires flex as the motor moves, but the solder joints are not flexed. Finally, the LED is tested by hooking it up to a +5V supply with a 15 Ohm resistor in the positive lead. This particular LED is okay up to 350 ma so using a 15 ohm resistor limits the current to 333 ma. Maximum currents vary a lot from product to product. If you're going to try this project, make sure you know your LED's current rating and don't exceed it. The vendor of your LED should be able to tell you the maximum current it can take. In the final photo of the sequence in Figure 4-12 we see the LED alight and the motor ready to use.

Now we have to make a simple frame out of scrap wood to mount the motor and the gem holder upon. Obviously the details of how you do this will depend on what scrap wood you have available, but the goal is to make a cradle that can support the motor assembly and on top of that a transverse mounting for the gem holder. Figure 4-13 shows what my quickly knocked together assembly looked like.

Figure 4-13. *Gem Light support cradle*

It won't win any prizes for woodwork, but hey! We're just prototyping here. The idea is that the gem holder can be wedged between the two transverse beams, just above, but not touching, the LED/motor assembly as shown in Figure 4-14.

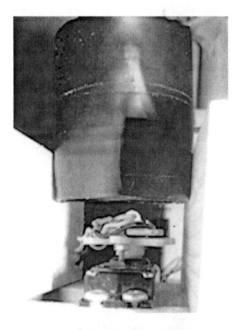

Figure 4-14. *The gem holder in place*

As you can see in Figure 4-14 the gem holder sits pretty close to the rotating LED light. The rotating light shines up through the holder from a varying angle, so that the contents of the holder scintillate in the moving light.

Now, we need some software to make the motor sweep back and forward slowly from 0 to 180 degrees and back again. The following Arduino sketch does this:

```
// ServoSlowScan_GemLight
// This program sets a servo motor to slow scan so that
// when a Luxeon LED is lashed to it, off-centre, and
// the whole assembly is placed under a transparent crystal
```

```
// holder filled with glass crystals they will scintillate!
// You can stop the scan by sending sending keyboard command
// "s" or start it by sending "g"
#include <Servo.h>
Servo myMotor;
int theAngle=0;
boolean countingUp = true;
boolean doMovement = true;

void setup()
{
  Serial.begin(9600);
  Serial.println("Servo Slow Scan for GemLight");
  myMotor.attach(4);
}

void loop() {
  delay(75);
  if (doMovement == true){
    if (countingUp == true)
    {
      theAngle++;
      if (theAngle >= 180)
      {
        countingUp = false;
      }
    }
    else
    {
      theAngle--;
      if (theAngle <= 0)
      {
        countingUp = true;
      }
    }
    myMotor.write(theAngle);
  }
  if (Serial.available() != 0)
  {
    // Something has been received.
    int inChar = Serial.read();
    switch (inChar)
    {
    case 's':
      doMovement = false;
      Serial.println("Gemlight Stopped.");
      break;

    case 'g':
      doMovement = true;
      Serial.println("Gemlight Started.");
      break;
```

```
    default: // Default case, tell them what we need.
      Serial.println("use s for 'stop' or g for 'go'");
      break;
    }
  }
}
```

This is largely an adaptation of the previous sketch for setting a random motor position, so we won't do a complete code walk on this one. Briefly:

- The program scans in one direction at a fairly slow speed (alter the delay() value at the top of the loop() if you want to increase or decrease speed) until it gets to the end of travel, then it starts back toward the opposite end.

- You can send it "g" (go) or "s" (stop) commands via the serial channel. If you send it a "s" command, it sets a Boolean variable called doMotion to false, and this causes the movement section of the code to be skipped each time the loop comes around. When you send a "g" command the doMotion Boolean is set to true and motion resumes.

Other than these points there is nothing new from the previous sketch.

Figure 4-15 shows the circuit diagram for this quickie project. This shows the necessary additions to the test bed rig we built in Chapter 2.

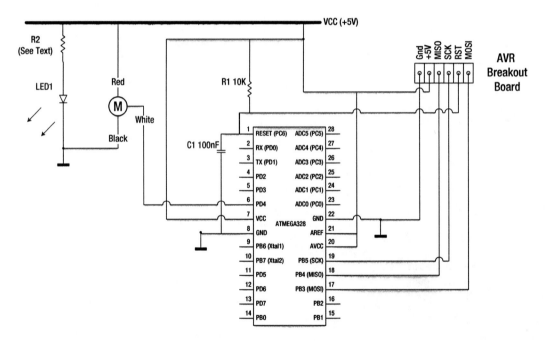

***Figure 4-15.** Gem Light added on to the test bed rig*

All we've added is the high-powered LED1, the current limiting resistor R2 (the value of which, as previously discussed, will depend on the current limit of the individual high power LED you buy). The servo motor is driven from pin 6 (Arduino pin 4) of the ATmega328.

In my case, I elected to cut the plug off the servo motor (instantly invalidating my warranty) and make solder ends on the wires that push nicely into the breadboard holes. You may want to keep the connector, in which case you will want to use a three-way section of header pin strip to allow you to plug the motor into the breadboard (see Figure 4-16).

Figure 4-16. *Header pins for servo motor connection*

If we were building a permanent version of this project we would probably want to add additional features such as

- Giving the MCU the capability to turn the light on and off, or perhaps control its intensity with PWM.

- Providing the ability to dynamically change the speed of the motor's scanning action in response to an additional command.

- On the mechanical side, changing the arrangement so that the gem holder is rotated by the motor, while the LED stays fixed underneath.

But, this project is just to give you an initial idea of a practical use for a servo motor so, we'll leave it there. I will show you some more servo motor usages in the main projects section of this book.

Now, how does it look when we put all this together? Figure 4-17 shows some views.

Figure 4-17. *The gem holder underlit by the moving LED*

The first photo in Figure 4-17 shows the gem holder in place on the frame, but unlit. Then it's lights out! LED on.

Drive On!

Small low-power LEDs and servo motor control inputs are among a very few things that a microcontroller can drive directly: it's far more normal for the MCU to need some help. In many designs you'll see individual transistors used as helpers to an MCU to drive some kind of load.

This is how it works (refer to Figure 4-18): the logic level signal from an MCU output is fed, via a resistor, into the base of an NPN (negative positive negative) transistor. The signal from the MCU flows through the resistor and down to ground through the transistor. The purpose of the resistor is to prevent too much current being drawn from the MCUs output.

The flow of current from the MCU, through the resistor to ground makes the transistor flip into its ON condition. The transistor terminal with an arrow coming out of it is the emitter; the transistor terminal at the top is called the collector. When used in the way shown in Figure 4-18, a transistor behaves as an electronically controlled switch. If current is flowing from its base to its emitter, then a much larger current can also flow from the collector to the emitter (which is connected to ground). Since the "load" is in the pathway from the +V supply to the transistor, when the transistor switches ON, the load is energized.

In this way, a small amount of current (a logic level signal from the MCU) is made to control a switch (the transistor) that is capable of handling much more current than the MCU ever could.

Although it's convenient to think of the transistor as being equivalent to a switch, always remember that it is actually a semiconductor device. It can be damaged by static electricity, it can overheat, and, unlike mechanical switches, it can be destroyed in a moment if you put more current through it than it can handle. So think of it like a switch, but treat it better!

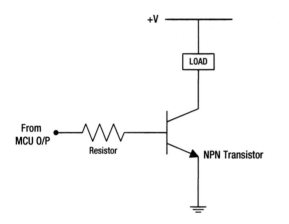

Figure 4-18. *Basic transistor driver circuit*

The "Load" in the circuit of Figure 4-18 can be whatever you like, provided the transistor can handle the current that the load draws. You calculate the load current using Ohm's law:

current = voltage over resistance
Suppose +v in the diagram is +5 volts and the load has a resistance of 100 ohms Then we have:
Current = 5/100
or

$\dfrac{5}{100}$ = 0.050 (which, when we ask Google "what is 0.050 amps in milliamps" we discover is 50 milliamps!).

The key parameter to look for in the NPN transistor used as a switch is the iCMax parameter, which says how much current the transistor's collector can handle. Allow a generous margin. When run at the limits of their spec, transistors will run hot, which is to be avoided wherever possible. For example if you need a transistor to handle 50 milliamps of current, choose a transistor that has a maximum collector current capability of 150 milliamps or more. Most transistors are very cheap, so until you get into high current devices (tens of amps, or more) there is no particular penalty to an overspec!

Typical loads for this kind of driver circuit are things like

- *High-powered LEDs*: the MCU cannot provide enough current to drive them directly.

- *Relays*: Essentially a set of switches activated by a small moving coil.

- *Motors*: We've already see one motor, but that had its own driver. When we use a motor that has no internal circuitry, then we'll need to use a driver transistor.

- *Solenoids*: When we want to create point-to-point movement (e.g., a door lock which has only two positions open and closed) we would use a solenoid.

All those are power-thirsty beasts and we need a driver transistor to allow our MCU to control them.

In Figure 4-18, we were using an NPN transistor which switches on when its base voltage rises. In MCU work, when we use transistors, we most often use NPN types. However, be aware that there are also PNP (positive negative positive) transistors which switch ON when the base voltage is low and OFF when it is high–these can sometimes also be useful and work perfectly well with MCUs.

An extra consideration when driving components that use windings of wire around a magnet (relays, motors, and solenoids principally) is something called back-EMF (Electromotive Force). You probably already know that when we apply power to a coil of wire wound round a metal core–which is basically what the aforementioned devices all use some variation of–we get a magnetic force, which persists until the power is removed. This is called the electromagnetic effect. However, when the power is removed, the magnetic force persists for a brief time and just for a few instants, the process works in reverse: the collapsing magnetic field (or the briefly continued motion of a motor coming to a stop) now generates voltage in the coil. The problem is that the voltages created by the collapsing magnetic field, although they are usually quite brief, can be large and are highly likely to damage any unprotected electronics they encounter back on the driver board. This is why we use "snubber" diodes when we use transistors to drive wound components. I'll return to this subject soon.

Suppose you wanted to use a transistor to enable your MCU to control a 12-volt relay? Your MCU only runs on +5 volts, so would this work? Yes, definitely it will work. Figure 4-19 shows how.

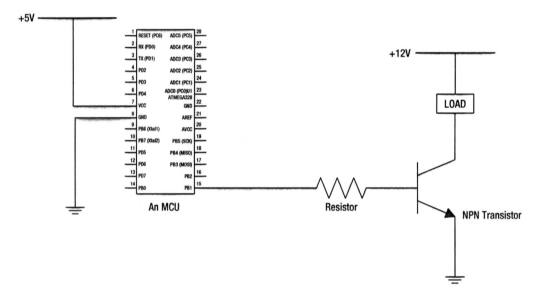

Figure 4-19. *Using a +12V load*

In Figure 4-19 you can see the MCU on the left. It is getting its normal +5 V supply and ground. One of the MCU outputs is connected to the transistor circuit–as we saw in Figure 4-18. This time, however, although the transistor's emitter is connected to ground and the load is still connected to the transistor's collector, the topside of the load is connected to +12 V. When the transistor is turned ON by the MCU outputting logic high, current flows from the +12 V rail through the load and to ground. Making the relay click on, or the solenoid fire–or whatever it is. So, as you can see, it's perfectly easy for an MCU (a +5-volt device) to control a +12-volt device. The only caveat is that the ground connections must be common. If you connect the transistor and the MCU to two completely different power supplies, they won't work, and you will very likely damage or destroy one or both of the semiconductor devices.

Now, let's revisit that back-EMF issue: this occurs when power is removed from the coil of a relay, a solenoid, or the windings of a motor. The collapsing magnetic field, or the residual mechanical momentum of such components, generates this nasty spike of voltage that we call back-EMF.[2] Even in a low-voltage application, these spikes can reach several hundreds of volts, albeit for just a few micro seconds. Even such a short burst, however, can completely destroy a driver transistor or a logic circuit. To counteract and nullify this problem we use a diode. These are usually just general-purpose diodes, but when used in this application they are variously called a snubber, a Freewheeling, a suppressor, a clamping, or a flyback diode. Figure 4-20 shows how they are used.

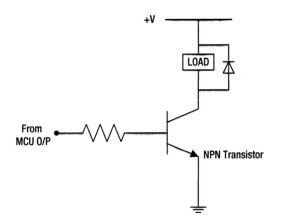

Figure 4-20. *Diode protecting against back-EMF*

In this version of the diagram shown in Figure 4-19, we have added the snubber diode (I like that name best, but you can choose what you want to call it). Because the back-EMF is always in the reverse polarity to the voltage used in the circuit, this diode basically starts to conduct when a back-EMF voltage is generated and shunts that voltage away from the driver transistor back to the supply rail. The diode you use should be capable of handling high voltages but need not be a high-current device. For currents below 200 ma most people use tried and tested diodes as snubbers, typically the 1N4148 or the 1N4001. In higher-current applications, the 1N4003 or 1N4007 is more often used. The crucial parameters are the switching speed and current handling ability of the diode–but the diodes quoted previously suffice for most applications.

So, you can use individual transistors to drive your power-hungry MCU peripherals. However, this does mean that for each thing you want to drive, you will need a transistor, a base resistor, and a snubber diode. If you're only driving one item then that's probably okay, but when it's two or three or more items, the component count starts to get a little bit unwieldy. Fortunately for projects where we want to drive loads that are under half an amp the semiconductor industry offers arrays of driver transistors on a chip and these often (but not always) include snubber diodes, and (when they are specified to have logic compatible inputs) you don't need to use a base resistor. Better yet, these chips are not overly expensive and will save you quite a lot of wiring and (if you're going to go ahead and design a permanent project board) board space.

One transistor driver array chip that has been very widely used for many years is the ULN2803A. This chip offers eight driver channels, each with logic signal compatible inputs, and each output has a snubber diode built in (though on the data sheet it's called a clamping diode). Each driver channel inside this chip actually uses two transistors in what is called a Darlington configuration–this basically increases the drive capability and

---

[2]Interestingly, in some contexts back-EMF is a problem, but in others it is useful. In smart motor control applications, the driver electronics may turn off the drive current for a very short interval and sample the back-EMF voltage in order to learn how fast the driven motor is actually running. It then resumes supplying power at an increased or decreased level according to whether the actual motor speed is greater or lesser than the desired speed. This technique is widely used where fine speed control is required—like in automotive applications, industrial machines and even in model railroad control systems.

speed over using just a single transistor. Each driver channel is capable of sinking 500 ma of current, though, if you ever did use them all at that maximum simultaneously you would run into severe heat problems. It's probably realistic to say that you could use all eight channels at about 200 ma simultaneously without too many problems–especially if you fitted a heatsink to the chip top (see adjacent picture). Since lots of companies make the ULN2803A, check the specific data sheet for your flavor of it, especially if you plan to use it up to its limits.

The ULN2803A is actually available in many different packagings; the 18-pin DIP packaging is the one you would want to use, because it is easy to use on your test rig breadboard. The diagrams in Figure 4-21 show the pinout and the functional block diagram of the chip.

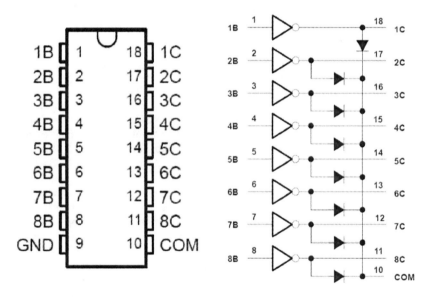

Figure 4-21. *2803A chip: pinout and block diagram (courtesy of Texas Instruments)*

As you can see, the array has eight inputs and eight outputs. Each output has its own snubber diode, but one end of all the diodes are brought out to one common pin (pin 10) which, in most applications, you would simply tie to the +V rail.

The invertor symbol for each driver (the right-pointing triangle with the roundel on the end) represents a pair of transistors in the Darlington configuration. When an input (say 1B) is taken to a logic high level, the corresponding output (1C in this case) will turn ON and start sinking current. The diagrams in Figure 4-22 show some common ways in which we use the drivers on this chip.

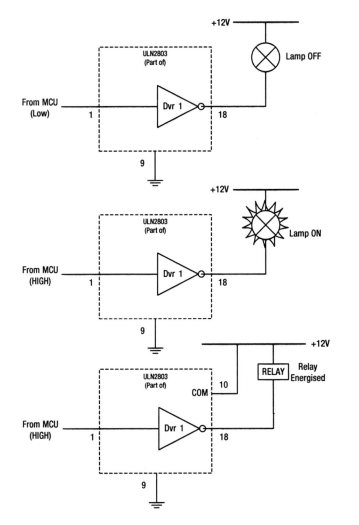

Figure 4-22. *Example uses of a ULN2803A driver channel*

- In the first case depicted, a lamp connected to the output of driver #1 is off because the signal from the MCU port at driver #1 input is low.

- In the second case, the MCU signal has now changed to high, and the output stage has turned ON and is now providing a path to ground for current coming through the lamp. In other words because the MCU signal changed from low to high, the output stage begins sinking current. In these first two cases, there is no need to use the snubber diode because lamps generate no harmful back-EMF.

- In the third case, a relay is connected to the output in place of the lamp. As before, the MCU is sending a logic high signal which means that the output is on and sinking current sufficient for the relay coil to be energized. In this application we expect that the relay will generate back-EMF when it is de-energized so we make sure that the COM pin (10) of the chip is connected to the +V rail of the supply.

In fact, in the normal case you would tie the COM output to the +V rail anyway, whether or not you were driving devices that required snubber diodes.

If we were doing a project that needed eight drivers, this one chip would potentially replace 24 individual components (8 resistors, 8 transistors, and 8 snubber diodes) and save us from a lot of fiddly intercomponent wiring. That does of course assume that none of the eight drivers had to drive anything that needed more than 500 ma and that the total capabilities of the chip were not exceeded. In practice, not all that many MCU projects actually need to drive so many peripherals, so it's pretty common to include a chip like this in a project but to only use half of the drivers it offers–but that's okay: it's still a lot easier, in most cases, than using the discrete component approach and the cost difference is negligible. We will use this chip a lot in the projects section of this book.

The ULN2803A is one of a range of integrated driver chips (numbered ULN2800 to 2812), so if for any reason your normal vendor doesn't have stock of 2803s, the vendor may be able to offer an alternative which will do just as well.

MOS-What?

Metal Oxide Semiconductor Field Effect Transistor (MOSFET). Not a name to set the pulses racing is it? But if you're interested in using your MCU to make stuff move, it definitely should get you at least just a little excited! For our purposes, where we usually want to use a transistor as a switch to do the bidding of our MCU, the trouble with the older bipolar transistor types (NPN and PNP) that we have touched on so far is that they are hot. Their ON resistance is still quite high and anything that resists the flow of electricity warms up, and the more current that's involved, the hotter they will get.

Suppose that we weren't turning on nice friendly little relays or comparatively tame little lamps. Suppose we were switching on a big, bad 12VDC heating element–such as you might use in a truck or in a trailer? Such a device would have an internal resistance of perhaps two or three ohms which means that it would be pulling somewhere between 4 and 6 amps from a 12V-volt power source: suddenly, we're not in Kansas anymore! We certainly could not use our ULN2803A chip for this job. We now need a switching element that can switch on and off something around 12 amps (since we still have to abide by the rule of allowing some headroom in the spec to ensure we don't overstress or overheat the device).

Over the years several standard transistors became an electronic designer's default go-to devices whenever some serious "muscle" was needed; one such device is the 2N3055. Although it first appeared in the 1970s it's still being made today and you can still buy it from most electronics outlets. It comes in a "TO-3 package," which is a metal case with two pins (the base and the emitter) sticking out of the base. The overall "can" of the transistor itself forms the collector connection. Almost always these transistors have to be mounted on big heatsinks that have metal fins and tend to look a little like the outside of a motor cycle engine. Figure 4-23 shows one of these assemblies: the transistor is in the middle of that big heatsink. You can get a sense of the scale from the diode and resistor to the left of the heatsink. It's not small.

Figure 4-23. *2N3055 transistor on a heatsink*

The 2N-3055 is a great old workhorse, if you were able to use x-ray vision to look inside all the electrical stuff around your house, garage, and car you'd probably find you actually own a few 3055 s: they've been built into power supplies for everything from TVs to welders and into car electronics and audio and video kit for several decades–though they are now used less and less.

The 2N3055 is capable of switching up to 15 amps, as long as it has the best possible heatsinking and heat bonding, so it could easily handle our example of the 6 amp, 12-volt heater. But, when using the 3055 (or any bipolar technology transistor) in a high amperage application we lose quite a lot of energy as heat and we need a lot of space in our project box to accommodate the heatsinking arrangements required; we might even have to add a cooling fan in some cases. This heat is generated because, even when fully ON (a state which for transistors is often referred to as "saturated") a bipolar transistor will still offer some resistance between collector and emitter and will heat up because of it. This heat problem is one major reason that bipolar transistors like the 2N3055 have been slowly but steadily losing ground to MOSFETs in power-switching applications over the last decade.

MOSFETs came onto the scene in a serious way in the early 1990s and gradually gained ground through various refinements and improvements. For example, there are now many MOSFET devices which can interface directly to logic circuits, which was not always the case. For our purposes, the great thing about MOSFETs is that when they are in a saturated ON state, they have almost no resistance and so they run a lot cooler than a bipolar transistor ever could. MOSFETs also offer faster switching speeds; however, when driving motors, solenoids, and other inductive components you still need a snubber diode–although some of the latest MOSFETS have one of those built in as well.

The diagram in Figure 4-24 shows two basic AVR-controlled MOSFET switch arrangements. The MOSFET depicted is an N-channel device, which means that the gate lead of the MOSFET has to be taken high to make the drain to source resistance fall to near zero (in other words, turn on the MOSFET). A P-channel device would have the opposite characteristic.

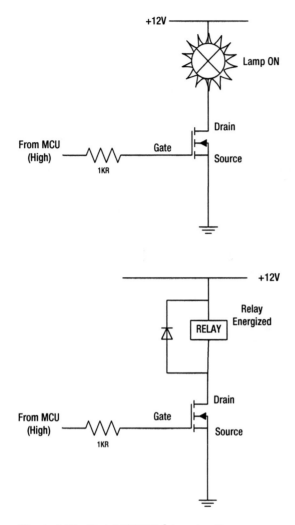

Figure 4-24. *Basic MOSFET driver circuits*

Figure 4-24 shows a resistor in the path from the MCU to the gate of the MOSFET: you can regard this as optional, it's not functionally necessary, but it does provide a modicum of protection for your MCU in case the MOSFET should ever fail and start feeding +12 volts back down the line toward it.

Unlike a bipolar transistor, where actual current must flow from base to emitter to turn the transistor ON, no current flows from gate to source on a MOSFET; it is the presence (the field) of voltage on the gate that causes the MOSFET to switch ON, not the flow of current through it to ground. The gate connection acts rather like a tiny capacitor that has to charge up. The gate resistor is therefore only there as a firebreak in case of a MOSFET malfunction; it's not there to protect the MCU port from having too much current demanded from it (as would be the case on a bipolar transistor equivalent), since there is no path to ground via the gate and therefore no current flows.

Somewhat surprisingly there are–as yet–not many MOSFET array chips that provide multiple drivers. There are a few; for example, Texas Instruments has the TLC59210 and TLC5920, which provide MOSFET drivers on the output stages and also provide logic data latches. However, the current handling capabilities of the devices available so far don't seem to be as good as using individual MOSFET transistors.

We'll look at some MOSFET driver circuits in the sections on motors and solenoids.

Relays

A relay is simply a switch that is activated by an electromagnet. You apply power to the coil of the electromagnet (as we did in Figure 4-24) and the movement of a part called the armature is made to close or open one or more sets of contacts. So the question may occur to you, since we already know we can do switching using transistors why would we use a relay? Why not just use various transistors? There are several answers to that question.

- Most relays are quite small and can accommodate quite a few switch contacts. Consequently it's often more space effective to use a relay than a half dozen semiconductor switches.

- Isolation is the main reason, in this age of semiconductor wizardry and wonder, the humble electromechanical relay is still in widespread use. Hear that small click when you turn your 68" flat-screen 3D, LED TV on or off? That's a relay. Hear that little click when you start your bread maker? That's a relay too. Why are we still using them?

  In many products or projects it is desirable to have electrical isolation between the different subsystems that make up the whole. Suppose you wanted to use your MCU to turn a mains powered light on and off. You *could* use a semiconductor switch (perhaps a triac or maybe a thyristor) to be the switching element, and control this from your low-voltage MCU circuit. But when (as it someday inevitably would) a fault develops in this circuit, or somebody miswires something on the lighting circuit or a 101 different problem conditions develop, there's a possibility that mains voltages are going to find their way into your MCU circuit and destroy every device in it and maybe give a bad electric shock to some poor person in the process.

  Relays (of various sorts) provide a mechanical rather than an electrical linkage between elements of a project. Stray voltages or earthing problems on the circuits connected to the contacts of a relay in no way affect the relay coil, since the coil is electrically isolated from the contacts. So a relay makes a great firewall against problems in one part of a product or project affecting or damaging other parts.

- The switch contacts of even small relays can handle quite a lot of amps. A relay with 13 amp contacts is going to be a lot smaller in area than the 2N3055 transistor and its heatsink which we saw earlier on.

In recent years, the trend in relays has been to get smaller and to be encapsulated into sealed, plug-in packages. Older relays–such as the one shown in Figure 4-25–were either open or encased in a transparent plastic hood. This makes it easier to explain how they work. In this picture you can probably see the actual contacts on the left. And the relay coil on the right. When the coil is energized, the yoke (which is the metal bit in the middle) moves to the left and uses plastic insulating push-rods to bend the center contacts away from the position shown in Figure 4-25 and over to the left-hand set of contacts. Therefore, these contacts are what are known as changeover contacts; they act like a double-pole single toggle switch–but one that is operated by an electromechanical hand.

Figure 4-25. *An open relay*

A relay that you would buy now uses exactly this same kind of internal arrangement (though the contact details vary a lot between products–offering more or fewer contacts than the one shown in Figure 4-25), but it will likely be inside a sealed unit with contacts emerging (like this one) at the bottom. Most modern relays are quite low profile, not tall like this one.

Another kind of relay, one that I have used quite a lot, is the "Solid State Relay" or SSR. SSRs now come in many shapes and sizes. This kind of relay has the following benefits:

- It can switch appreciable amounts of mains current at any common mains voltage (typically from 24VAC to 250VAC which means you can use an SSR whatever your domestic supply voltage may be).

- The control side stays 100 % isolated from the mains voltages being controlled

- Power is only switched at the moment when the AC supply is at its zero point of the cycle, meaning that an SSR doesn't generate any switching spikes on the mains supply. Electromechanical relays can't do this and thus there is often a tiny spark as their contacts close. This, eventually, makes the contacts on a mechanical relay wear out due to pitting and can generate small spikes on your mains supply. An SSR does not suffer from this problem.

- SSRs are very easy to use; most of them don't need any driver, the MCU output goes straight into the SSR control side–no driver transistors needed.

But there are also downsides to SSRs:

- An SSR is never truly OFF. Even when OFF it still leaks a small amount of current through. This is an important safety consideration (i.e., the SSR may be OFF, but unlike a mechanical switch, the device it controls is still getting a very small amount of current). In some circumstances it's also an economic consideration; the device attached via the SSR is always consuming a few milliamps of power.

- SSRs are more expensive than conventional relays–though, as always, you can find bargains on Internet auction sites if you look regularly.

- The mounting and guarding arrangements can be slightly more complex than for normal relays–especially for the larger SSRs.

- When an SSR fails it usually fails in a "full on" mode. If what it is controlling is something that should never, ever, be always full on (such as a water heater with no integral safety cutout) then this is a problem. In my experience SSR failures are rare. I have personally never had one fail in a project of mine, but that doesn't mean it never happens. So, be safe and make sure to guard against failure by using equipment with integral safety cutouts as your backstop against disaster. Also use an SSR that's capable of switching more current than you really need. I always use an SSR rated at double (or more) than what I apparently need.

  If your application is one where failure would have very bad results you can add extra features. You could feed power to the SSR via the "normally closed" contacts of a conventional relay, which your MCU controls. You give your MCU a way to sense whether the controlled device is on or not. If the MCU detects that the load is still on-power when it should not be, it energizes the relay (breaking mains power to the device and rendering it safe) and bleeps an alarm of some kind to show a fault condition.

  Where larger amounts of electrical energy are in use and safety has to be the first priority these kinds of fail-safe measures are worth taking.

Figure 4-26 contains a picture showing two examples of the larger kinds of SSR. This style of package is, due to its overall shape, known as the hockey-puck style–but there are other much smaller packagings for lower amounts of power switching. The left-hand device shown here is rated to switch 25 amps of mains current and the right-hand device is rated for 40 amps.[3] So, even if you wanted to switch power on and off to a 2 or 3 kilowatt water heater, you could find an SSR that was more than capable of handling it (with heatsinking and the all-important safety considerations taken into account–see Figure 4-27). These hockey-puck SSRs are normally bolted to a metal rail or chassis which helps with heatsinking. The metal case is isolated from all the terminals and so can be earthed via the mounting rail or the containing metal box. SSRs in this format sometimes come with a clip-over plastic hoods that help keep their potentially deadly mains terminals inaccessible. However, these, for some reason, are sometimes sold separately, so make sure if you're buying SSRs you get the hoods one way or another.

---

[3]40 amps is by no means the beefiest SSR: you can routinely get 70 amp and 80 amp devices. Specialist industrial electronics resellers stock even higher values. You can also get SSRs in the same hockey-puck formats which allow you to switch large DC loads.

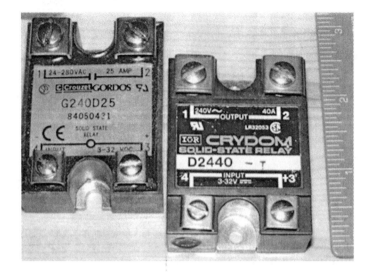

Figure 4-26. *Two examples of a solid state relay*

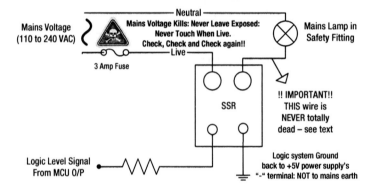

Figure 4-27. *Basic use of an SSR*

The hockey-puck format SSR has four screw connectors, which are intended to be used with spade or ring connectors. The bottom two connectors are the control "input," which only needs a low-voltage DC signal such as the 5-volt output from an MCU or some other logic level chip. Inside the SSR this low voltage is used to light up an LED. The other two terminals are the mains switch connections. The switching element inside the SSR is enabled or disabled by detecting the LED light turned on or off by the low voltage at the control input. In other words, the control side and the mains side are opto-isolated. There is *no* common electrical connection between them; the ON/OFF command is transmitted by the presence or absence of light inside the SSR. This provides great protection for the control circuit and–provided you keep the mains wires and control wiring runs well apart from one another–never the twain should meet!

Figure 4-27 is a diagram of how an SSR is used: in this case we are switching mains power on and off to a mains lamp, under control of an MCU. On the control side, the MCU sends a logic level signal into the + terminal and the other terminal goes to ground. You may or may not need the resistor: SSRs designed to be used with logic level control systems will not require an external resistor, but other types of SSR might require a 270R resistor to limit the current pulled from the MCU. Consult the data sheet for your particular SSR.

■ **Caution**   As Figure 4-27 makes very clear, when mains electrics are involved you cannot be too careful. Make sure you use a fuse in the circuit in case of mishaps or malfunctions, make sure that all of your mains connections are covered up and well insulated so that you, other people, or family pets cannot accidentally touch them. Preferably enclose all the mains handling side of your project into an earthed metal box. *Always* design in a mechanical, insulated, isolation point at which you can totally disconnect your project from the mains: This may be a double pole mains isolation switch, a removable cartridge fuse, or a plug you can pull out from a mains outlet socket.

So you have looked at a few types of relays–but of course there are hundreds of different variations, types, and sizes. A look through the relays and contactors section of your favorite electronics vendor's web site or catalog should show you that there is one for every possible use.

Solenoids

A solenoid is a fairly brute-force device that uses electromagnetic force to shift a movable part from one position to another. It normally has a return spring of some kind to return it to the original position when power is removed, though the same effect can be had by feeding power to it in reverse polarity. Solenoids usually have an "at rest" position which they revert to when no power is applied to their coil and an activated position which they reach when power has been applied. You activate at least one solenoid every day of your life. You will find them in

- Various parts of cars; for example, they have been regularly used to engage the drive from the starting motor to the engine.

- In the door of your dishwasher or washing machine; it's a solenoid that engages to stop you from opening the door when it's running.

- If you have an electric door lock at your workplace it will almost certainly be a solenoid-operated lock.

- In your electric toaster, the release mechanism that pops up the toast when it's ready is quite likely to involve a small solenoid.

- Your central heating system will have at least one mains-powered solenoid in it. It is used to turn water supply to various bits of the system and on and off. If it's an oil-fired system, then it's quite likely to have two or three solenoids in it.

- Your electric shower will use a solenoid to allow or block the flow of water through the miniature heating tank. Do you hear a clunk when you activate the shower? That's the solenoid kicking in to open the water flow valve.

- The device that locks the read-write heads into their at-rest position when you power down the hard drive in your desktop computer is often a very small solenoid.

So, you'll find a solenoid in a great many of the things you use regularly. Some solenoids are made to work from AC voltages (such as the mains supply) while others are meant to work from DC voltages. It is the latter we are mainly concerned with for our projects.

Activating a solenoid from your MCU is not very different from activating a relay. You are switching power on so that it can go through a wound coil that will create electromagnetism so, of course, you'll need a snubber diode. The only real difference is that whereas a relay only needs to move perhaps 1/8th of an inch (3 mm), a solenoid may have to move an inch or more to do the job that's intended. That means that a lot more current needs to go through the solenoid's coil to make things happen. The coil of a +5 V relay may have a resistance of 150 or 200 ohms and require less than 50 milliamps to activate: a DC solenoid will often have a coil resistance of no more than 10 ohms and so will require something in excess of ten times more current than a relay.

Figure 4-28 shows a typical DC solenoid. This has a wire coil (with two connection wires emerging from it) and a "bullet" that is pulled into the core at the center of the coil when the coil is energized. By fixing the bullet to a pull wire or a directly to some other device (such as the bolt part of an electrically operated lock) the solenoid is made to mechanically control something.

Figure 4-28. *Example of a DC solenoid*

Let's try to make this more real by doing another quickie project, just to demonstrate how a solenoid can be used. In this project I used the following:

- A 12-volt solenoid.

- A 12-volt battery.

- Some wooden pulleys fitted with spacers as spindles (see Figure 4-29).

- An old shelf joiner bracket that I had lying around.

- A few small nuts and bolts.

- Some bits of scrap wood to act as a base for the brief life of the project.

- Some "fireline" thread (used for fishing line and for beading projects among many other things). If you don't have any of this, just use very thin steel garden wire or something similar.

- A return spring–sourced from a "spring kit." You may already have a suitable spring hanging around somewhere; if not, your favorite tech vendor will sell an inexpensive box of assorted springs that you will find invaluable in making projects involving movement.

Figure 4-29 shows how the project looked when assembled.

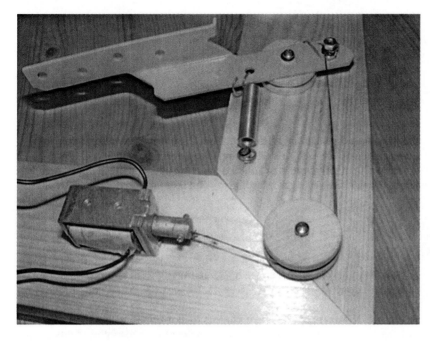

Figure 4-29. *Quickie example of using a solenoid*

The solenoid is fixed to the wooden base by a couple of bolts (not visible in the picture). The end of the solenoid's bullet has the fireline tied securely to it. The fireline is wound around a wood pulley which is fixed to the baseboard. The shelf bracket (which is being used as a lever to increase the travel obtained) is fixed to another pulley and the spring is fitted between its midway point and the baseboard to make it want to come back toward us as we look at the photo. The other end of the fireline is wound tightly around a nut and bolt that go through the end hole of the bracket and a top nut clamps the fireline winding in place.

When the solenoid is energized it pulls the fireline, which exerts leverage on the end of the bracket, overcoming the spring tension. The pull action of the solenoid (about half an inch or so) makes the far end of the bracket travel about 2 inches in the "away from us" direction, which is a very useful amount of movement and could be used for various purposes. When power is removed from the solenoid, the spring takes the bracket back to its rest position. It is a simple mechanism, effective for all kinds of uses.

The wooden pulleys are available in various sizes from various sources, mostly robotics and educational outlets. They are usually sold in packs of ten for a very reasonable price. To use them as we do in this solenoid demo project, we have to fit them with something to make them turn easily when fixed to a baseboard, namely, a steel stand-off (also called a spacer). These tubular steel stand-offs are used to separate a printed circuit board from the box it is housed in. What you need is a stand-off that is slightly longer than the vertical height of the wooden pulley you buy and which has an unthreaded center. You'll have to decide what stand-off length you need, but following are some examples:

- www.sparkfun.com/products/10739 (United States).

- www.maplin.co.uk (UK) (available in a kit).

You drill out the center of the pulley so that the stand-off can be gently tapped into place with a small hammer, without splitting the pulley. The spacer should protrude a little underneath: this is essential to stop the underside of the pulley from rubbing on the mounting surface and keeping it from turning. You then use a self-tapping screw of sufficient length to form the spindle of the assembled pulley. The following photos should make this clearer.

Screw the spindle screw into the baseboard until it's tight, then back off a half turn. The pulley should then spin nicely and freely around the spindle screw. For many uses, this kind of arrangement works well. However, where the pulley is likely to be subject to a lot of force, you may find that the screw will tend to get pulled over. In such cases you have to use a bolt right through the baseboard, secured top and bottom with nuts, washers, and lock washers.

Motors (Non-Servo)

We looked earlier at servo motors. Now, let's turn our attention to other kinds. As you would expect, there are dozens of kinds of motors, so let's narrow it down to DC motors and specifically we will look at using simple motors and stepper motors with your MCU.

A simple DC motor is the sort that, when you apply power to it, runs up to its maximum speed and stays there until you remove power, or you make it do some work which slows it down. Almost all motors of this class are sold as either three-pole or, sometimes, five-pole motors. Such motors are usually quite small and very often inexpensive. They show up in everything from toys and novelties to battery-driven cooling fans. If your phone vibrates when you get a call, there could be a subminiature motor making that happen too.

The speed of DC motors is proportional to the voltage used to power them. Any motor has a rated voltage which should never be exceeded, but you can always run a DC motor at *less* than its stated voltage and it will still run, the speed will just be slower (in proportion to how far under its rated voltage the supply gets). When a motor is under load, its ability to maintain its speed is, in part, due to how much current is available to it–though mechanical factors also play an important part.

Earlier in this chapter we looked at how we could use PWM signals to tell a servo motor at what angle to set itself. We saw that the built-in hardware PWM that the AVR offers is not suitable for servo motor work and we ended up using a library package to produce the signals we needed. That was because the PWM features of the AVR are optimized for producing PWM at frequencies required for direct motor control.

PWM control of motors involves giving them little bursts of power at their preferred voltage: the longer the bursts are, the faster the motor will turn. Finally at "full throttle" there are no gaps between the bursts and the motor is getting full DC power. At the other end of the spectrum, if the motor is getting only very short bursts of power it will turn very slowly if at all. In a short while we'll build a proving circuit to try out this PWM approach, but first let's look at some different DC motors.

Figure 4-30 shows three motors. The one in the foreground with multiple wires coming out of it is a stepper motor. You'll be looking at how to use those a little later. The other two motors are simple DC motors; they have just two wires coming from them and they expect DC power at a certain maximum voltage. As you may be able to make out from the photos, the two non-servo motors are actually in two sections. The lower section is actually the motor itself, whereas the upper section is a gearbox that gears down the RPM (revolutions per minute) generated by the motor to a slower speed. This is a very common arrangement in motors; it's used so much because it provides fine speed control of the spindle and can give the motor mechanical advantage in turning larger loads that it directly could do.

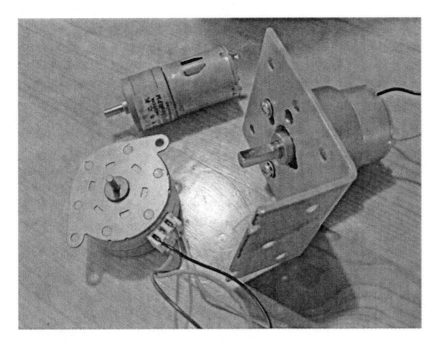

Figure 4-30. *A selection of motors*

I have fitted the motor on the right-hand side with a mounting bracket. As you can tell, this is a conversion of a corner shelf bracket bought for not much from a DIY store and just drilled and filed out to fit this motor's mounting points. This particular motor seemed not to have a mounting bracket available for it; however, when you are buying a motor it's always a good idea to see if you can buy a mounting bracket for it from the same source–it can save you some metal bashing. If you have to make your own mounting bracket it's not hard, just find something that's roughly the right size and (assuming you have a safe working place with a vise and workbench to hold the item steady) drill the required holes and slots in it.

One other point to note about the motors in Figure 4-30 is that the motor at the right-hand side has a shaft with a flat spot on it; this makes it easy to secure pulleys on it. The other two motors have perfectly round shafts: this means that, under heavy load, a pulley might not grip the motor shaft tightly enough and the motor shaft might start slipping. To counteract this occurrence, many people file a flat spot on the motor shaft to give the pulley a better grip. If you plan to do this, solder a wire across the two terminals of the motor (if it's a two-terminal device and not a stepper motor) which should help prevent the filing action from turning the motor. Also, try very hard not to let any of the filings get into the motor mechanism, since they can play havoc with the smooth running of the motor's gearbox or motor bearings.

Now, let's build up a DC motor driver on the test bed rig and try out some PWM control for it. If you want to try this for yourself, you will need

- Your test bed rig (as built in Chapter 2).

- A MOSFET driver transistor. You can use an IRL540 or a VNP10NC6 or any MOSFET that has a logic level compatible input threshold.

- A DC motor of some kind. If you can get a 6-volt motor you can run it from the same +5 V supply as your test bed rig; it just won't go quite as fast as it otherwise would. If you can't find a +6 V motor, you can use a +12 V motor but you will have to use an additional supply from a 12 V battery or another mains supply with a 12 V output. Figure 4-31 demonstrates how these wire.

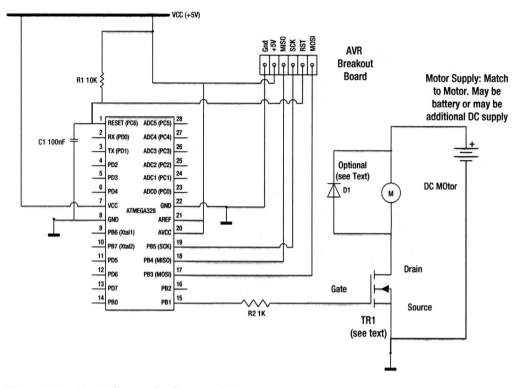

Figure 4-31. *Circuit diagram for the motor driver*

- If your MOSFET does not include a snubber diode, you will need to add one (a 1N4002 will be okay, unless you are using a very large motor). The VNP10 MOSFET mentioned previously includes a snubber, internally.

If you are using a different supply for the motor and the MCU, be *very* sure to connect the two ground connections before you power either of them on (see earlier discussion about dual rail power supply).

Now we need a test program to try this out.

```
/*
Motor PWM Tester V1
This program uses PWM to control a motor via a driver
 transistor. It cycles through all possible PWM values (0 to 255)
 at a rate of one speed step every MS_BETWEEN_STEPS milliseconds.
 It will recognize and action a few single-letter commands sent
 via the serial channel. (In these descriptions, SS means Speed
 Stepping)
"a" toggles SS on/off - initial state is ON
"d" decrements the current pwm value.
"f" sets pwm value to 255 (full on) & disables SS
"u" increments the current pwm value.
"z" sets pwm value to zero (stops motor) & disables SS
*/
```

```
const int MOTOR_PIN = 9; // Must use a PWM capable pin for this.
const int MS_BETWEEN_STEPS = 500; // Millisecs between speed steps
byte pwmVal = 0;
byte lastPwm = 0;
int msCounter = 0;
boolean incPwmEnabled = true;

void setup()
{
  Serial.begin(9600);
  Serial.println("PWM tester V1.0d");
  pinMode(MOTOR_PIN,OUTPUT);
  analogWrite(MOTOR_PIN,pwmVal);
}

void loop()
{
  delay(1); // Wait a millisecond.
  if (++msCounter >= MS_BETWEEN_STEPS)
  {
    msCounter = 0;
    if (incPwmEnabled == true)
    {
      pwmVal++;
    }
  }
  if (Serial.available() != 0)
  {
    // Something has been received.
    int inChar = Serial.read();
    switch (inChar)
    {
    case 'a':
      Serial.print("Speed Stepping is now ");
      if (incPwmEnabled==true)
      {
        incPwmEnabled = false;
        Serial.println("OFF");
      }
      else
      {
        incPwmEnabled = true;
        Serial.println("ON");
      }
      break;
    case 'f':
      pwmVal = 255;
      incPwmEnabled = false;
      break;
```

```
  case 'u':
    pwmVal++;
    break;

  case 'd':
    if (pwmVal != 0)
      pwmVal--;
    break;
  case 'z':
    pwmVal = 0;
    incPwmEnabled = false;
    break;

  default: // Default case, say what...
    Serial.println("use a, u, f, d or z only");
    break;
  }
}
// If the value has changed, check it, correct it and write it out
if (lastPwm != pwmVal)
{
  if ((pwmVal >= 255)  && (incPwmEnabled == true))
  {
    pwmVal=0;
  }
  analogWrite(MOTOR_PIN,pwmVal);
  Serial.print("pwmVal is now ");
  Serial.println(pwmVal,DEC);
  lastPwm = pwmVal;
  }
}
```

This program's basic task is to take the motor from very slow speeds (low PWM values) to full speed (high PWM values) in a never-ending cycle of "Speed Steps." At its heart it uses the Arduino's analogWrite() function (see Arduino reference page for full details) to output a constantly varying PWM signal on the chosen AVR pin:

```
analogWrite(PIN, PWM_Value);
```

However, it also allows you, via the serial channel, to override this basic behavior with your own commands. If you only want to see the motor speed vary up and down, you don't need anything connected to the serial port.

The following is a code walk of this program:

- The program starts by declaring a number of constants and variables. The constants provide values for the Arduino pin number via which we are exerting PWM control over the motor (Arduino pin 9, physical pin 15 on the ATmega328), and a constant value for the number of milliseconds between speed steps.

- The variables are the current pwmVal the lastPwm (which remembers the previous pwmValue so that the program can tell if it has changed) and counter that counts milliseconds and a Boolean value called incPwmEnabled, which allow or disallows the speed stepper from proceeding.

- In the setup() function (which, remember, runs just once) the serial channel is initialized and a banner test output to it. Then the motor pin is initialized as an output and the initial value of zero (motor stopped) is written to it.

- In the main loop() (which runs over and over forever, until you stop it)

  - The program delays for one millisecond and then increments its millisecond counter. If the counter reaches a value that indicates that it's time for a speed step, then the counter is zeroed and if speed stepping is enabled, the speed value (pwmVal) is incremented.

  - Next the program checks for input from the serial channel. If any input is found, then it is parsed and actioned inside a switch ... case table (if you're not familiar with this construct, refer back to the earlier code walk for an explanation). See the comments at the top of this program that explain what the available single letter commands actually do here.

  - At the end of the switch...case table, the program checks to see if the pwmVal (the motor speed PWM value) has been changed by any of the previous code as compared to the remembered pwmValue last time through the loop. If a change has been made, then it checks that the value is still legal (hasn't gone outside the range 0 to 255) and resets it to zero, if required. Then, the new pwmVal is written to the motor control pin and a message sent to the serial channel indicating the new value.

  - Finally the program memorizes the new pwmValue into lastPwm–ready for next time around the loop, which now begins again . . .

With +12-volt DC motor I used for my testing, the motor started to turn very slowly at a PWM value of about 26–obviously this will vary between motors and supply voltage quite a lot. It's handy to know where the stall point is for your particular motor though, because when you use these things in real projects you know a start value for any soft start routines and don't waste time on cycling through PWM ratings that your motor can't use. With the VNP10 MOSFET transistor I was using I left the tester running my motor at PWM = 128 for an hour and found that the transistor was only very slightly warm to the touch–so, clearly, there was no need for a heatsink in that case. However, you will be using a different motor and possibly a different MOSFET, so you will need to make this check for yourself and fit a heatsink, if needed.

The Motor PWM Tester V1 program does what it says on the packet; it lets you play around with and observe the results of PWM driving a DC motor. However, it lacks a couple of things that every motor control program needs–namely, a RampUp and a RampDown function. Most projects benefit functionally or stylistically from having motor-driven movement that starts and stops smoothly rather than abruptly: if we wanted to go from 0 to full revs and back again almost instantly we'd just use a relay to connect and cut power.

In the imaginatively named "Motor PWM Tester V2" we add some ramping functions and single-letter commands to trigger them. This is the first time in this book we have used a program that has more than just the setup() and loop() functions–but it's not too hard to understand. All that we do is add our new functions *after* the end of the loop() function, making sure that they have the right structure of balanced brackets, and so on. If you're new to programming, take a while to study this example, so that you understand it. A mini-code walk follows the program listing.

```
/*
Motor PWM Tester V2
 This program uses PWM to control a DC motor via a driver
 transistor. It cycles through all possible PWM values (0 to 255)
 at a rate of one speed step every MS_BETWEEN_STEPS milliseconds.
```

It will recognize and action a few single-letter commands sent via the serial channel. (In these descriptions SS means Speed Stepping)
"a" toggles SS on/off - initial state is ON
"d" decrements the current pwm value.
"f" sets pwm value to 255 (full on) & disables SS
"r" ramps from zero to full in 5 seconds & disables SS
"R" ramps from zero to full in 1 second & disables SS
"s" ramps full to zero in 5 seconds & disables SS
"S" ramps full to zero in 1 second & disables SS
"u" increments the current pwm value.
"z" sets pwm value to zero (stops motor) & disables SS
*/

```
const int MOTOR_PIN = 9; // Must use a PWM capable pin for this.
const int MS_BETWEEN_STEPS = 500; // Millisecs between speed steps
const int MOTOR_SPEED_DELAY = 1000; // Motor 0 to full ramp time
byte pwmVal = 0;
byte lastPwm = 0;
int msCounter = 0;
boolean incPwmEnabled = true;

void setup()
{
  Serial.begin(9600);
  Serial.println("PWM tester V2.0d");
  pinMode(MOTOR_PIN,OUTPUT);
  analogWrite(MOTOR_PIN,pwmVal);
}

void loop()
{
  delay(1); // Wait a millisecond.
  if (++msCounter >=  MS_BETWEEN_STEPS)
  {
    msCounter = 0;
    if (incPwmEnabled == true)
    {
      pwmVal++;
    }
  }
  if (Serial.available() != 0)
  {
    // Something has been received.
    int inChar = Serial.read();
    switch (inChar)
    {
    case 'a':
      Serial.print("Speed Stepping is now ");
```

```
    if (incPwmEnabled==true)
    {
      incPwmEnabled = false;
      Serial.println("OFF");
    }
    else
    {
      incPwmEnabled = true;
      Serial.println("ON");
    }
    break;
case 'f':
  pwmVal = 255;
  incPwmEnabled = false;
  break;

case 'u':
  pwmVal++;
  break;

case 'd':
  if (pwmVal != 0)
    pwmVal--;
  break;
case 'r':
case 'R':
  // Do 5 or 1 second ramp up
  incPwmEnabled = false;
  if (inChar == 'r')
  {
    doRampUp(5000);
  }
  else
  {
    doRampUp(1000);
  }
  pwmVal = 255;
  break;

case 's':
case 'S':
  // Do 1 or 5 second ramp down
  incPwmEnabled = false;
  if (inChar == 's')
  {
    doRampDown(5000);
  }
```

```
      else
      {
        doRampDown(1000);
      }
      pwmVal = 0;
      break;

    case 'z':
      pwmVal = 0;
      incPwmEnabled = false;
      break;

    default: // Default case, say what...
      Serial.println("use f, d, r, R, s, S, u or z only");
      break;
    }
  }
  // If the value has changed, check it, correct it and write it out
  if (lastPwm != pwmVal)
  {
    if ((pwmVal >= 255)  && (incPwmEnabled == true))
    {
      pwmVal = 0;
    }
    analogWrite(MOTOR_PIN,pwmVal);
    Serial.print("pwmVal is now ");
    Serial.println(pwmVal,DEC);
    lastPwm = pwmVal;
  }
}

void doRampUp(int rampLenMs)
{
  /*
    Stops the motor. Waits MOTOR_SPEED_DELAY ms for motor
    to actually stop, then ramps up the motor to full pwm
    speed in the number of milliseconds required by the caller.
  */
  int msVal = int(rampLenMs/255);
  analogWrite(MOTOR_PIN,0);
  delay(MOTOR_SPEED_DELAY);
  for (int myLoop =0; myLoop <= 255; myLoop ++)
  {
    delay(msVal);
    analogWrite(MOTOR_PIN,myLoop);
  }
}

void doRampDown(int rampLenMs)
{
  /*
    Ramps down the motor from full to zero pwm in the number of
```

```
  milliseconds required by the caller.
  */
int msVal = int(rampLenMs/255);
analogWrite(MOTOR_PIN,255);
delay(MOTOR_SPEED_DELAY); // Wait for full speed
for (int myLoop =255; myLoop >= 0; myLoop --)
{
  delay(msVal);
  analogWrite(MOTOR_PIN,myLoop);
}
}
```

A code walk through the changes from the first version of the program might help.

- The additional new commands are bolded in the initial comments of the program.

- Inside the switch...case block we are using a slightly different syntax. In the case of the "s" and "r" commands we're checking for the uppercase versions of the commands too. You can actually check for as many cases as you want in this fashion. The code to handle these commands is pretty much the same, except for the ramp length we want to set (1,000 or 5,000) so bundling them together can save a small amount of space[4] by preventing duplication.

  The new "s" and "S" commands call one of our new functions, doRampDown() and the "r" and "R" commands call the other, doRampUp().

- The new function doRampDown() does not need to send back any information or results to whoever uses it, so it is prefixed with the word void. It expects to be sent just one piece of information ("an argument"), which is an integer value indicating how long the caller wants the motor's power ramp down to last. The function calls this integer argument rampLenMs.

  Inside the function, a new variable msVal is declared and set to contain the ramp length required divided by 255. This value is used to determine the duration of each of the required 255 PWM steps to get down to 0 (motor stopped). So if the caller wants the ramp down from full speed to 0 to take 5 seconds (which is 5,000 milliseconds), msVal will get set to:

  5000 /255 = 19.6 milliseconds

  since we have specified in the code that msVal be rounded to an integer (that's what the int before the brackets instructs the compiler to do) the value will be rounded down to the nearest whole number–in this example, 19. The program sets the motor speed PWM value to maximum.

---

[4] In this instance it probably has not saved much, since there is not an awful lot of code needed to implement these commands, but if the code to implement the commands was more extensive, the potential savings would definitely be worth having!

Since the motor cannot reach full speed immediately the program waits for a while to allow the motor to reach speed (you want to change the constant value MOTOR_SPEED_DELAY to better match your particular motor). Then, the program goes into a countdown loop, counting down the pwm value from 255 to 0, at intervals set by msVal. This loop should complete in approximately the time requested by the caller. When the loop completes, the doRampDown() function is completed; control passes back to the loop() function at the point immediately following where it called doRampDown().

■ **Heads-up**   Using ramp lengths of less than 2550 is likely to have strange results, since msVal will be rounded down to 0.

- The new function doRampUp() is also declared as a void because it does not need to send back any information or results to whoever uses it. It also expects to be sent just one argument—an integer value indicating how long the caller wants the motor's power ramp up to last.

  Inside the function, a new variable msVal is declared and set to contain the ramp length required by 255. This value is used to determine the duration of each of the required 255 PWM steps to get from 0 (motor stopped) to 255 (max speed).

  The program sets the motor speed PWM value to 0 and waits a while to allow the motor to actually stop. Then, a count-up loop begins, counting from 0 to 255, at intervals set by msVal. Again, this should complete in approximately the time requested.

  As before, using ramp lengths of less than 2550 are likely to have strange results, since msVal will end up as 0.

And there you go, that's a quick look through how to do PWM to control a DC motor.

The other kind of motor that is used often in projects involving movement is called a stepper motor. This motor is used when more precise speeds or positioning are required. The name of the motor indicates how it works; rather than running continuously when power is applied, this kind of motor has two or more electromagnetic coils which are wired separately to allow it to be moved in individual steps. If you own an inkjet or a laser printer, a document scanner, a DVD or Blu-Ray player, or a hard drive, then you own a stepper motor: stepper motors are found in all these products, and many others.

The coils on a stepper motor are arranged around the motor shaft in such a way that, when energized in certain ways, the coils act in equal opposition to one another and the motor shaft is held stationary (in stasis). When the motor is told to rotate by a certain amount (e.g., to position the print head inside a printer to a required position), coils are deenergized or their polarity reversed, in the required sequence to make the motor turn by the required number of steps to get to the new position.

A good way to think about this is to imagine a roundabout in a play park–the old-fashioned kind that the kids have to push round for themselves. Imagine this roundabout to be the motor shaft. Now, imagine that there are two identical kids, who will act as our motor coils. If they both grab a handle and pull in opposite directions, nothing happens. The roundabout stays still. If one of them lets go, until the next handle comes around, then the roundabout moves–but only to the next handle: when the next handle is grabbed and the pulling is again equal in both directions the roundabout stops again. Next, they decide that one will push the roundabout handles as they pass and the other will pull. If they both work in perfect alternation, the roundabout soon gets going. This is conceptually very similar to how the motor coils in a stepper motor act.

What kind of circuit do we need for driving a stepper motor? It depends in large degree what kind of stepper motor we are using, but let's assume we are using what is known as a bipolar motor which has two coils, with four wires coming from it. We saw a photo of such a motor in Figure 4-30, earlier in this chapter. Figure 4-32 shows how such a motor is arranged electrically.

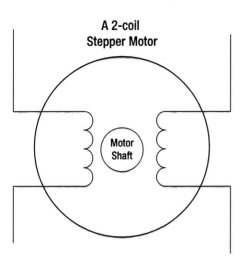

A 2-coil Stepper Motor

Figure 4-32. Two-coil stepper motor wiring

A wire is brought out from each end of both coils. This allows the control electronics to do two different things.

- Apply or remove power to a coil.

- Change the polarity of the power applied, thus using a coil to attract or repel the motor's central shaft.

By changing the polarity and/or the presence of power in each coil in a repeating sequence, it becomes pretty easy to make the motor move by tightly controlled amounts and to put the coils in equal opposition to one another to hold it steady. The circuit we use to apply power in these various ways is called a double H switch. Let's see what a single H switch is all about before we go on from here.

An H switch is an arrangement of transistors around a motor that form the shape of the letter "H" on a circuit diagram. Figure 4-33 depicts an H switch, made from MOSFET transistors. If it was using MOSFETs that have snubber diodes built into them, this is pretty much what such a circuit might look like. The gate of each MOSFET is driven by a logic level line coming from an MCU. Using the logic lines we can turn each transistor on and off independently by taking the logic line that drives it to a high condition (transistor on) or low (transistor off).

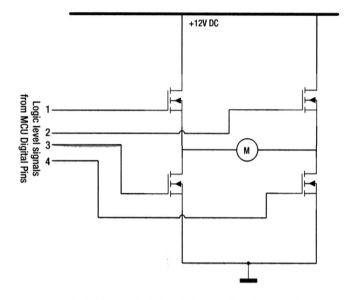

Figure 4-33. *Motor control H switch made from MOSFETs*

But you have to be very, very careful. What happens if you take line 1 and line 3 high at the same time? Yes, you turn on the top left and bottom left transistors and make a perfect short circuit across the power rails! Ouch: the fuse blows, things get hot, and possibly they have to be replaced. So *do not* do that (or make 2 and 4 high at the same time, which would have the same effect).

If you make line 1 high and line 4 high at the same time (with lines 2 and 3 remaining low), you turn on the top left transistor and the bottom right transistor. This puts +12 volts on the left-hand side of the motor and ground on the right-hand side. The motor turns clockwise.

If you then make all the digital lines low again, then you make lines 2 and 3 high, you turn on the top right and bottom left transistors. You've now put +12 volts on the right-hand side connection to the motor and ground on the left-hand side. The motor turns counterclockwise.

So now, with this single coil motor, you can stop it (all lines low); you can make it run clockwise (lines 1 and 4 high) and you can make it run counterclockwise (lines 2 and 3 high). If you add in some PWM (using an extended version of how you did it before) at the same time, you have complete control over the speed and direction of this motor.

When you have stepper motor that has two coils, you control each one with an H switch. By coordinating the use of the H switches you can precisely control the motor's step rotation. Building a pair of H switches out of eight transistors is not ideal; it's a lot of transistors and wiring! Luckily there are lots of ready-made chips around that simplify the task by providing everything required for driving a stepper motor on a single chip.

Chips like the SN754410NE and the L293D are very widely used for controlling small- and medium-power stepper motors. The possible downside is that cramming all those power transistors into one chip can lead to heat problems, especially if the motor you use needs a lot of current, or if your application involves constant movement of the motor. In such a case you would be better off using a driver chip rated for higher current use (e.g., the L298) or taking the trouble to build the H bridges out of individual MOSFETs if your motor is a real power guzzler.

In Figure 4-34, you can see a circuit using an L293D to control a four-wire stepper motor. This is just for illustrative purposes; it's based on a particular motor so don't try to build this unless you really want to. It would be wise to fit a heatsink if you were building this circuit. You should also check that the coils of any motor you buy are comfortably within the current range of the L293D. These kinds of chips tend to melt or burn up if you overstress them. Be safe, not sorry.

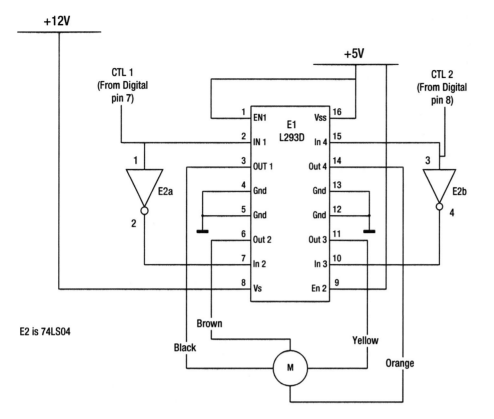

Figure 4-34. *Stepper motor control using the L293D*

This example uses only two lines from the MCU to control the motor. We are using a 74LS04 (we could also use a 74HC04) to provide two logic invertors. This is in recognition of the fact that when input 1 is high we *always* want input 2 to be low, and vice versa, and similarly we always want input 4 and 3 to be at opposite logic levels. We could use four lines from the MCU, but this arrangement means we can save those I/O pins and use them for something else. This circuit diagram is for use with the stepper motor that we saw pictured in Figure 4-30, which has black, brown, orange and yellow wires coming from it. It is an Astrosyn B355 motor, but there are hundreds of makes of stepper motor so it's unlikely that your electronics vendor will stock exactly this one. However, your vendor will stock something equivalent if you want to use this circuit as a basis. If you do buy a stepper motor, make very sure to get a copy of its data sheet; you will need it for making the connections and configuring the software that you will use to drive it. Some example stepper motor products are

- www.sparkfun.com/products/10551 (United States).

- www.rapidonline.com (UK) (order code 37-0507).

You can easily find the L293D datasheet and a pinout diagram of the 74LS04 online.

So how does this circuit work? When CTL 1 line is high, the OUT 1 is pulling (sinking) current and OUT 2 is pushing current. When CTL 1 is low the opposite happens. When CTL 2 is high the OUT 4 pin is pulling (sinking) current and the OUT 3 pin is pushing current. Again, the opposite happens when CTL 1 is low. By changing the inputs to this H switch in the right sequence, we can use software to step the motor in one direction or the other, or make it stay where it is. Because of the physical arrangement of the coils, each step will rotate the motor shaft exactly the same number of degrees: from this we can work out how many steps make a complete revolution.

Writing software to flick I/O bits up and down in the right sequence to make a stepper motor turn is not the most exciting stuff in the world. Fortunately, we're connected to Arduino-land and there is, of course, a library available to take all the drudge work out of this for us. The Stepper library is a standard part of the Arduino distribution and if you browse the example sketches that came with the Arduino software set you'll find there are several example programs that you can use if you want to play around with steppers. In any case, do have a look at the library home page to get a feel for how you would use the library software:

http://arduino.cc/en/Reference/Stepper

Stepper motor specs will usually not quote RPM figures, but the stepper software wants you to specify an RPM value for the motor. The stepper motor specification will usually quote two useful figures; these are the angle of rotation per step and the maximum number of pulses per second (pps) that the motor can action. Here's how you use these.

- You calculate the number of steps required for a full rotation of 360 degrees. A common value for degrees per step is 7.5 degrees, so such a motor would take 48 steps to do a complete rotation:

  $360 \div 7.5 = 48$

- The maximum RPM is: The number of pulses per second, times 60, divided by the number of steps per rotation. So, if the pps is 300, then this calculation is:

  $(300 x 60) \div 48 = 375$ RPM

This doesn't mean you could definitely get that RPM from your motor, it is a theoretical maximum. In normal operation you would probably set the RPM to something just over half this value–say 200 RPM–to get reliable operation.

We don't make much use of stepper motors in this book, but in specific kinds of projects they are very useful and you can expect to find them included in far more projects in future, because they are getting cheaper and easier to use than they have ever been.

Sensing Movement

So far in this chapter we have looked at how to create movement, but that's not the whole story. Very often, creating movement is only useful if you can sense the progress of what is moving, or if you can use movement as a trigger. Two classic examples are a sliding door (you have to know when to turn off the motor that drives it when it reaches its closed or open position) and a burglar alarm (you can have the smartest alarm in the world, but it is useless without its movement sensors).

In this section we'll look at ways to sense movement motion and position. We'll look at sensor types, how they talk to your MCU, and how and where you might use them.

Sensor Switches

The simplest sensors are mechanically activated switches. Switches were the first kind of sensors used by control systems and they are probably still the most common. Figure 4-35 shows some common types. The pictures show a miniature PCB switch, two microswitches each with a different actuator arm, a rotary switch, a flip switch, and a slide switch. These are all very common switches. Microswitches with actuator arms are commonly found in many contexts, sometimes as absolute limit detectors on moving parts (i.e., backups for optical detectors) but also as the primary detectors. Door switches are often used in security applications, but they may also be used for switching on lights in store rooms where it's only a requirement for the light to be on when the door is open.

Figure 4-35. *A selection of various switches*

Mechanically operated switches have some useful advantages as sensors over any other kind of approach.

- They are cheap.

- They don't need to be fed with power; they close or open a circuit just by mechanical pressure being applied to the switch actuator.

- Because they don't need power there is no need to worry about things like potential earth loops and voltage differences between the sensor and the control system.

- There are no complex signaling compatibility requirements, as can occur with more complex sensor types.

Of course, there are some issues with mechanical switches, when used as sensors. Principal among these are wear and tear on the mechanical aspects and contact bouncing. Wear and tear occurs simply because switches are mechanical devices and they have to be struck by something to activate them. That means that due to repeated mechanical contact things can change over time (e.g., actuator arms can bend slightly). These changes can, especially in a high-speed system, subtly change the timings involved–meaning that things can stop working. This is not often a problem, but it's not unheard of, and it can cause system failures.

Contact bounce (also known as contact chatter) is a major consideration. To humans, the action of most switches appears to be a snap action that happens in an instant. In fact, in all switches there is a brief moment of the contacts settling into their new position during which they bounce on and off one another, somewhat like a table tennis ball dropped from just a small height onto a tabletop might do, but much faster.

Where a switch is directly controlling power flow to some lights or a motor contact bounce is not really a problem. However, if the switch is signaling a logic high or a logic low to a microcontroller, a problem arises. One or two milliseconds of contact bounce is imperceptible to a human being, but to a device that is–easily–capable of sampling the state of a switch input 5,000 or 6,000 times per second, these bounces look like the switch being turned on and off repeatedly.

You can deal with debounce at the hardware level by fitting small capacitors between the inputs concerned and ground. However, this arrangement requires some experimentation and as switches age this arrangement can stop working unless you build in a lot of leeway, which can make switch inputs insufficiently responsive for situations in which a switch needs to be repeatedly activated at short intervals by some other mechanism. The usual software solution for "debouncing" the signal from a switch is to artificially slow down the microcontroller by making it do a long wait loop whenever the switch activation is detected–as in the following steps:

- Program reads the switch and recognizes status change from last reading (was open, is now closed or vice versa).

- Program delays (does nothing, just waits) for 10–12 milliseconds.

- Program reads switch again: if the value is still at new setting then this is counted as a valid switch closure.

This approach works fine, the software effectively ignores contact bounce and only "sees" one switch state change per operation. However, the approach can have some downsides. Main among these is the fact that while the microcontroller processor is doing nothing, waiting for time to pass while debounce dies down, it can do nothing else. In an application with real-time requirements–for example, where multiplexing of LED displays is being performed by software, or where incoming characters from a network are being received at rates in excess of 10 million bits per second–this approach can be too disruptive and can stop other things from working properly.

In applications with real-time or near real-time requirements, a different approach is needed–one in which switch handling cannot block out other activities. The flowchart in Figure 4-36 indicates one such approach.

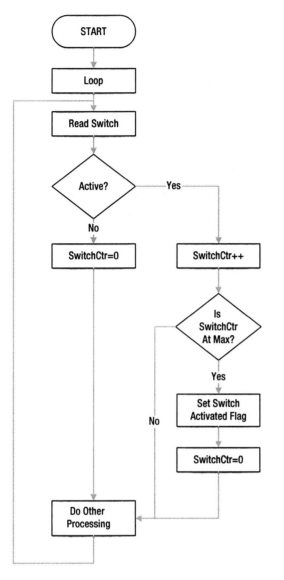

Figure 4-36. *Switch handling without blocking*

In this way of handling switch activation, a counter is used to remember how many consecutive switch reads have found the switch "active." When the switch contacts are settling into their new position, their bouncing will mean that the switch gets incremented a few times, but then zeroed and then incremented some more. Only after the contacts finally settle into their final position does the counter reach some preset level (found by experiment or by working out precise timings based on software profiling) that qualifies the event as switch activation. When the preset level is reached, the program might immediately perform whatever action is required for the switch closure, or it might (as shown in the flowchart) just set a flag to say that a switch closure has been detected. This latter approach means that the action required in response to the switch can be carried out at some convenient point in the rest of the application–which is represented by the "Do Other Processing" box in Figure 4-36.

By using this approach, other processes (e.g., the LED multiplex progression, mentioned earlier) still get carried out at their required regular rate, but also the switch is properly debounced and bogus multiple switch activations are avoided.

Of course, many other approaches are possible: you could, for example, do a version of the flowchart based on time, in which the software remembers the current time when it first saw the switch active and–after going away to perform other regular duties–it looks again 20 milliseconds later: if the switch is still active on the second sample, then a switch activation is said to have occurred. These kinds of approaches are a little more complex than the wait-delay method, but they do work better in applications where any stalling (blocking) of processing disrupts other aspects of the system.

One other aspect of using switches as sensors is that of noise. Where a switch is to be attached to a microcontroller by a long cable it's often unwise to simply extend two wires out to the switch, one wire carrying ground the other being (effectively) an extended microcontroller input pin. With long cables (more than a couple of feet or less in an electrically noisy environment) airborne electrical noise or interference can generate ghost switch activations that make systems malfunction. Logic circuit inputs are high impedance and therefore only need small amounts of current to activate them. This means that when they are extended out to longer lengths (especially in unscreened wiring near moving parts) they are easily fooled by passing transients into temporarily registering an incorrect logical level. There are a number of ways to deal with this situation; my favorite is to use a 20 ma opto-isolator loop. Figure 4-37 demonstrates the essential idea.

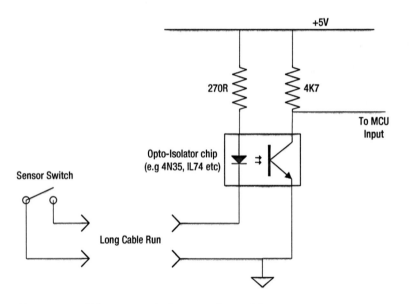

Figure 4-37. *Using an opto-isolator on a long cable run*

This arrangement uses an opto-isolator chip; this would be on the same board as the MCU chip. Opto-isolator chips (also called opto-couplers or photocouplers) come in many forms, but the one depicted would be a small chip, usually a six- or eight-pin device, which contains an LED and a phototransistor. These are not electrically connected inside the chip in any way, but they are physically arranged so that the LED can shine light on to the opto-sensitive base of the phototransistor. Thus, when LED light is present, the transistor is driven into its ON state and current can flow from its collector to its emitter. This is the same kind of arrangement as we saw in the SSR in Figure 4-26, except that here we are turning on a small, very low-power, transistor rather than a mains switching element such as a triac.

In the arrangement depicted in Figure 4-38, when the switch closes, it offers a path to ground for the LED which comes on–switching on the transistor as previously described. This allows the transistor to pull the MCU input (previously held high by the 4K7 resistor) to low.

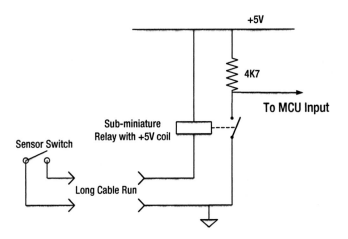

+5V

4K7

To MCU Input

Sub-miniature
Relay with +5V coil

Sensor Switch

Long Cable Run

Figure 4-38. *Using a small relay to isolate a logic input*

This widely used technique has two main advantages. First, the switch circuit is no longer subject to spurious noise: because it takes quite a lot of current to make the LED light up, interference from other electrical sources or radio frequency airborne noise has no effect. Second, it allows good electrical isolation between the application system and the outside world to be maintained: a comparatively vulnerable MCU input is not being extended out into the wider (and potentially hostile) world of mains wiring, back-EMF from motors, telephone wires, and radio signal sources. Plainly, these advantages are achieved at the cost of needing some extra components for every switch interfaced in this fashion. Opto-isolated mechanical switch signals do still need to be debounced though, because the LED/phototransistor combination is fast enough to faithfully reproduce the bounce pulses and present them to the MCU. There is a wide variation in the maximum speeds of opto-isolators, all of them are easily fast enough for switch interfacing, but if you plan to use one for high-frequency purposes (e.g., to opto-isolate connections in a serial communications channel) you will need to use fast couplers (e.g., the 6N137 which can handle 10 MHz throughputs). Be sure to check data sheets to verify an opto-isolator's viability in your application before buying.

If you need to isolate several inputs you can reduce the component count quite a lot by using device families like the IL74 family, which offers single, dual, and quad opto-isolators in one package. These are widely stocked items and there are plenty of equivalent alternatives from Texas Instruments, Toshiba, and others.

In applications where speed is not an issue, you can achieve the same level of isolation using a subminiature +5-volt relay instead of the opto-isolator chip. In such a setup (see Figure 4-38), the relay coil simply replaces the resistor/LED combination and the relay contacts replace the phototransistor. The 4K7 pull-up resistor is still required on the logic input and under some circumstances fitting a snubber diode across the relay might be advisable.

The use of simple switches as detectors has many variations. For example, a reed switch is a pair of contacts (usually encased in plastic) which are hypersensitive to magnetism. When they are subjected to a magnetic force, the contacts close and the switch is on. A Hall-effect switch fills the same function, except its sensitivity to magnetism is more acute, because it is a semiconductor device that uses electronics to amplify the effect, so it can detect smaller amounts of magnetism. These are very often used to detect door or window openings and Hall-effect switches are used to detect speeds of moving parts: to do that a small magnet is fixed to the moving part and a Hall-effect switch is placed near a point on the moving machine where the magnet will pass as the machine moves.

Then there are mercury switches, often used to allow a device to know when it is on a level or inclined surface. A small amount of mercury is driven by gravity up or down a small tube with contacts at strategic points. Since mercury conducts electricity, when the mercury is at the right end of the tube to indicate the required orientation of the unit in which it is contained, the contact is made. As inclinometers, mercury switches were very widely used, though less so now because of the invention of accelerometers – which we will be looking at in the next section.

Various kinds of float switches are used to close a pair of contacts when a liquid reaches a certain level. Some of these use plastic-encased magnets to close an equally waterproofed reed switch; others use a float ball attached to a "long arm" to mechanically activate a switch that is mounted well above the fluid level.

There are pressure switches, wind-operated switches, temperature-operated switches (simple thermostats), direction switches, and a whole subgenre of rotary switch types. But, suffice it to say that the switch may be the second oldest electrical component (after the battery), but it's still alive and well.

So, switches can be used in various ways to provide sensing inputs and to indicate the position of moving mechanical parts in the project. Their obvious limitation is that they can only provide one piece of information– their mechanical state, activated or not activated: it is up to the systems to which they are connected to make sense of what the ON/OFF signals a switch produces actually mean. Often, for MCU projects, we need more than just ON/OFF or YES/NO–at that stage we turn to active sensors.

Active Sensors

An active sensor is often a complete electronic subsystem in its own right. It requires power and it has some degree of embedded intelligence. It may be able to signal various conditions to other subsystems and in some cases it may be able to receive commands to adjust its operational parameters and scope. In this section we look at just a few examples of the many hundreds of kinds of active sensors that exist.

One type of sensor we have all become familiar with is the PIR (passive infrared) sensor. Although it is mainly used to sense movement, a PIR sensor can actually only sense temperature. Simply put, a PIR sensor can sense any significant amount of variation in the average temperature within the scene that it "sees." It begins by establishing a "norm" of temperature for everything in its field of vision. When something with a significantly different temperature enters the scene (you or me) it senses an "event." It has no idea what has actually happened: It could be that the sun has suddenly come out, or a fire has started, or a dog, a cat, or a person is just crossing its field of vision. A basic PIR sensor will simply signal an event to some superior system when it deems that sufficient change has occurred to constitute an event. Various types of PIR sensor have different event thresholds. For example, a PIR sensor in a security application in a sealed-up warehouse, where nothing at all is supposed to move, may trigger an event for even a very slight variation. In a security system for a house the sensitivity may be less, since although the humans may all be out to work, the cat or the dog may be still wandering around the house–and having pets trigger false alarms several times per day gets old very quickly. In an application like detecting a vehicle entering a space such as a garage, the sensitivity would likely need to be even less, since you don't want sunlight suddenly streaming into a window or a boiler prewarming the house to trigger events.

Figure 4-39 shows a typical PIR sensor: these kinds of devices, in many variations, are used extensively in homes and offices around the world. These are used to provide sensory input for burglar alarms and to position sensing systems and automated lighting systems. This one has an LED inside that briefly lights up to show when it has been triggered. These kinds of sensors are widely available and can often be bought for just $3 or $4.

Figure 4-39. PIR sensor

Figure 4-40 shows the inside of one of these sensors. As you can see, there's quite a lot inside a small package. Furthest away from us is the PIR sensor element, which is the heart of the device. It emits invisible bursts of low-energy infrared light, while simultaneously measuring how much of it comes back. The "activated" LED can perhaps just be seen beside it. Then there is the control chip, which is the brains of the device, interpreting and processing the signals from the sensor element and controlling the LEDs and relay. There are then a few capacitors. On the right-hand side, a "power on" LED is almost hidden behind the "tamper" switch– which is the thing with the spring attached to it. When the sensor's top cover is on, this spring is compressed, closing the tamper switch. In an alarm application, if a would-be robber tries to take the sensor cover off the switch to disable it, then the tamper switch would be activated. Then, next to the screw connector block is the miniature relay. This relay is clicked on whenever the sensor is triggered–the relay's contacts are extended on to the connector block.

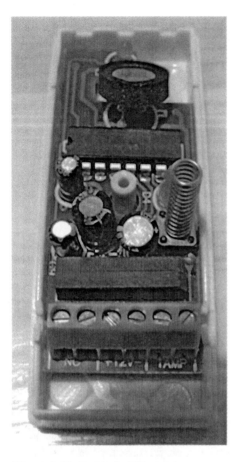

Figure 4-40. *Inside the PIR sensor*

Nearest to us in the photo is the connector block. This is a six-way screw terminal block and there are three pairs of connections. The first two–as you may be able to see–are labeled "NC," which stands for normally closed. These are the contacts from the relay. These contacts are made when the sensor is inactive, but they open when the sensor wishes to signal it has detected an event. It is these contacts that would normally go back into a superior system so that it can take some responsive action. That superior system might be a security system of some kind, a home automation system, or just a stand-alone MCU-based project. We'll being using this arrangement in a couple of the projects in this book. The next two contacts are for the +12-volt supply (+ and -) that this particular sensor needs to power the sensor element, the control chip, and the relay.

The final two connections on the right-hand side are the connections to the "tamper" switch. These connections are normally made, but they open when the sensor's cover is removed. In a security application these would also go back to the control unit.

These kinds of packaged PIR sensors are very useful in a number of applications, including home automation, power savings schemes to turn off lights in unoccupied rooms, security systems, and helper-call systems where they could be configured as part of a system that would allow an aged or infirm person to summon help by waving their hand in front of a sensor. However, although they feature a degree of built-in intelligence, they still only provide very simple information to other components of a system–namely, they close a pair of contacts to indicate that there has been "an event"–but that's all. Other types of sensor allow the control system to get a little more information.

Sharp has a range of infrared distance sensors collectively known as the IR Rangers. These are widely used in industrial automation systems and robotics. They come with lenses which give each sensor an optimum sensing range. Let's look at the GPD12 sensor which is a midrange sensor from this product set. This particular model is fitted with optics that allow it to focus on objects between 4" (10 cm) and 31" (80 cm) away from it.

Figure 4-41. Sharp GP2D12 distance sensor

The photo in Figure 4-41 shows how the device looks, a little spooky isn't it! It has two of what look like "eyes": it sends out beams of infrared light from the IR emitter on the left and senses with the sensor on the right. When the light is striking something within the sensor's focus zone, the amount of infrared light it senses changes. So far this is quite similar to what we saw with the last sensor, but this sensor doesn't package or process the sensor information, it just makes it available as a constantly varying analog voltage at its output, which means that some other system can log or interpret the raw signal and take any actions, based on its own judgment. This is different from the previous sensor, which only gave out an active/not active indication.

The sensor usually, but not always, comes with a cable (as shown in the picture) that you can use in conjunction with a three-way header pin strip to connect into your breadboard. The cable is sometimes sold separately. The sensor has three pins (numbers indicated in photo) and these are:

- Pin 1 is the output signal. For a +5 volts supply this will vary between about 0.45 and 2.5 volts for objects at the near point and far point of the distances for which the sensor is optimized.

- Pin 2 is ground.

- Pin 3 is the +V input. The sensor can work on voltages between 4.5 and 5.5 volts. Its peak current requirement can briefly be as high as 200 ma, but usually it uses a lot less, somewhere about 50 ma in my testing. Many sources advise using a 50 uf or 100 uf electrolytic capacitor across the sensor supply to maximize its sensitivity and prevent these peaks from making it give misleading readings.

Since the output from the GP2D12 is analog, we have to feed it into one of the analog inputs of our AVR–as in the diagram in Figure 4-42, which shows it attached to the test rig breadboard.

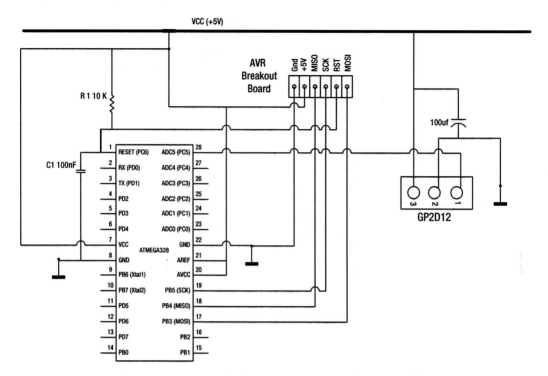

Figure 4-42. *Connecting a GP2D12 sensor to the test rig breadboard*

And by using the following short Arduino sketch we can see the average output from the sensor on the serial channel. Since this is an analog device it is advisable to compile an average value from it, rather than just read it once.

```
// Sharp Sensor Program
const int SAMPLES_PER_PASS = 10;

void setup()
{
  Serial.begin(9600);
}

void loop()
{
  int avg=0;
  for (int i=0;i<=SAMPLES_PER_PASS;i++)
  {
    delay(50);
    avg += analogRead(A5);

  }
  Serial.println(avg/SAMPLES_PER_PASS,DEC);
  avg=0;
  delay(150);
}
```

The code walk for this program is pretty simple:

- The program declares a constant value SAMPLE_PER_PASS that defines how many samples are used to make up each average value.

- In the setup() the only thing done is to initialize the serial channel

- In the main loop() the average starts off as 0. Then, a loop starts, inside which the current value read from the sensor is added to the rolling total for this time through the loop(). Since the sample update rate of the device is reckoned to be 45 milliseconds or so, the loop waits 50 ms between each sample collection so that it doesn't just grab the same sample value over and over again.

- After all samples have been collected, the program works out the average value that was read. It does this by dividing the total held in avg by the number of samples collected.

- After a short delay, the loop begins again.

In a real application the sensor would most likely be read frequently as part of the main processing loop and its current average value stored somewhere so that various other routines (e.g., the navigation routines of a robot's control system) could access it and make use of it.

There are many other types of opto-sensors. For example, there are beam-interruptor sensors. These are often used to sense rotation speeds. For example, a motor may turn a flywheel on a sewing machine and behind the flywheel a disc could be attached that spins on the same shaft or axle, at the same speed. If the spinning disc has a hole cut in it and a light is placed one side of the disc and a light sensor at the other side, the sensor will generate a pulse every time the hole lets some light through. By timing the pulses, software can accurately compute the current RPM of the whole assembly and increase or decrease PWM pulses to the motor accordingly.

Reflective sensors are also widely used. Reflective sensors are usually one piece devices, but they include an infrared emitter and a sensor. Figure 4-43 shows an example of a miniature reflecting sensor.

Figure 4-43. *Miniature reflective sensor*

As you can see, the sensor has two elements in one component: the emitter and the sensor. It is functionally very like the GP2D12 sensor we just looked at, but a lot smaller and without the focal length ability. Some examples can be found at

- www.sparkfun.com/products/246 (United States).

- www.maplin.co.uk (UK) (stock number JA26D pictured).

These kinds of sensors have many uses. They can be used to sense spin speed, simply by mounting the sensor close to the revolving part. A small dab of paint (of a contrasting color) is put onto the revolving part. As the paint dab passes the reflecting sensor, the returned amount of light seen by the sensor briefly changes and it generates a pulse. Again, this allows software to work out the speed of the revolving part by measuring the time between sensor pulses. These same kinds of sensors are widely used in automated production facilities.

One of the oldest types of sensor is the light-dependent resistor (LDR). This venerable member of the sensor family has been upstaged now by the phototransistor, but it is still used for some purposes. As its name suggests, the LDR has a resistance which changes according to how much light is present. LDRs have a wide range of sensitivity, most have a variation of at least an order of magnitude in resistance between total dark and bright light.

Where light direction is important, or extraneous light sources need to be blanked, an LDR can be placed into a thin tube of appropriate length to ensure that only light coming from the desired direction reaches it. The general arrangement for using an LDR is shown in Figure 4-44.

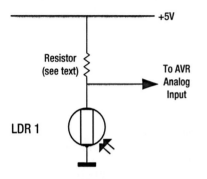

Figure 4-44. LDR usage

The LDR forms the bottom half of a two-stage potential divider; the fixed value resistor forms the other half. The voltage at junction of the two resistors is fed into one of the AVR's analog input pins. The value that you read from that pin (for testing purposes you could use pretty much the same program used for the GP2D12 sensor) will vary up and down according to the light level.

The value of the top resistor should be about 50% of the maximum resistance of the LDR. So, for example, if the LDR resistance in total darkness is 1 megohm, then the fixed resistor should be something like 500 K. This is highly dependent on the characteristics of the LDR, however, and you may need to experiment a little bit. You are aiming to choose a value for the fixed resistor which maximizes the difference that you see at the AVR input pin between the LDR brightly lit and in darkness (i.e., with your finger clamped over it).

To end this whistle-stop tour of sensor land let's look at a sensor that conveys a lot of information, an accelerometer. An accelerometer is essentially a device that measures acceleration and deceleration. Everything in the world is affected by gravity, which is a uniform force that causes everything to try to fall to earth at a uniform rate. The accelerometer makes use of this to measure acceleration.

Accelerometers are essentially devices that can sense changes in the speed of movement–usually in multiple planes (up/down/left right, etc.). However, since they also sense gravity, they are often used to sense "horizontality" (is that a real word?) and verticality. In other words, in leveling applications the uniform force of gravity is used as a constant that allows the device to measure how far out of true in both X and Y direction it is and to indicate those values as set of analog voltages. The result is that when you include one of these in a project or product, you get a gravity-sensitive device that can tell what orientation it is in and whether it is moving or tipped in certain directions.

Accelerometers are used in all kinds of things. If your car decelerates hard because it has hit something, it's going to be an accelerometer that triggers the airbag inflation. When you use your game controller to hit that phantom tennis ball, it's an accelerometer inside that tells the game code how "hard" you hit the ball. If you have an orientation-sensitive camera, phone, tablet, or game controller, there'll be an accelerometer of some kind providing that sensitivity. Sounds like fun, no? Let's look at one of these and see how we use it.

Accelerometers come in many grades and types, and a wide range of price points. Most current devices are tri-axis accelerometers which means that they can sense tilt forward and backward (Y axis movement), tilt left and right (X axis movement), and have up and down movement (Z axis movement); older devices only sense X and Y planes.

Almost all current generation accelerometers come in surface-mount packages only. Finding an accelerometer in a DIP package is hard (and will be *very* expensive if you do find one[5]), so vendors serving the hobby market have taken the pragmatic step of designing breakout boards for the most popular low-cost accelerometer chips. One popular chip is the MMA7260Q from Freescale Semiconductor. See the datasheet and product at

www.sparkfun.com/datasheets/Accelerometers/MMA7260Q-Rev1.pdf.

- www.sparkfun.com/products/308 (United States).

A complication, from our point of view, in trying this out is that most accelerometers don't work from +5 volts, but from +3.3 volts. If you want to use a 3.3 V device (such as the one we will look at here) with the test bed rig we built in Chapter 2, then you have two options. First, you can add a 3.3 V supply capability to the test bed by adding a 3.3-volt regulator that takes its input from the existing +5 volts and use a LD1117V33 or a TS2950CT-3.3 regulator–these, respectively, are

- www.sparkfun.com/products/526 (United States).

- www.maplin.co.uk (UK) (stock number N68CA).

Alternatively, if you have followed through on the idea of getting a USB attached TTL level serial port, you should find, if you look closely, that it does offer a 3.3 V pin that you can take some power from. Internet auction and electronics sites are awash with low-cost products that match the search criteria "USB To TTL Serial." Almost all of these seem to be based on the CP2012 chip and I can't find any of those that *don't* offer a 3.3 V output, so take your pick! Sparkfun has something very similar (search for "BOB-00198" on its site). Figure 4-45 shows the Sparkfun product and a generic product bought from the Internet:

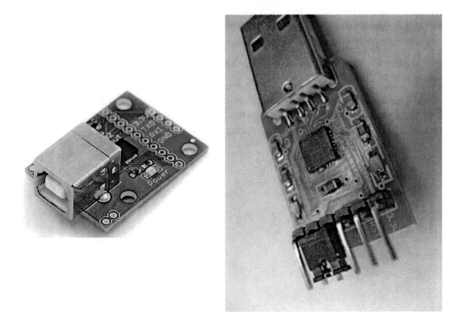

Figure 4-45. *Accelerometers purchased from the Internet*

---

[5]At the time of writing, ADXL206HDZ is available in an eight-pin DIP package, but it costs an outrageous $1,380. This is not even a tri-axis device, only dual axis!

The power requirements of accelerometers are very small–typically a lot less than one milliamp–so you should have no problem with loading if you want to grab power from a USB to serial device like those just mentioned.

The MMS7260Q (or more precisely Sparkfun's breakout board for it) has eight connection points.

- +Vcc–as previously mentioned, this needs to be fed a supply of + 3.3 volts at a maximum of 1 milliamp.

- Ground.

- X–an analog voltage representing the current X plane value.

- Y–an analog voltage representing the current Y plane value.

- Z–an analog voltage representing the current Z plane value.

- G-Select 1 & G-Select 2–you set up a binary code on these pins; the code you set determines the sensitivity of the accelerometer to gravitational force. You can set one of four ranges. The possible input codes are

  - 00 = 800 mV/g (800 mVolts change in output per unit of g-force applied)

  - 01 = 600 mV/g

  - 10 = 300 mVg

  - 11 = 200 mV/g

  In fact, the G pins have tie-lows internally to the chip, so you only need to tie an input to a high level if you want a 1; unconnected G inputs will default to 0 with no connection needed. If you were also running your MCU from 3.3 volts, you could set this sensitivity from software by allocating a couple of digital I/O pins to drive these inputs.

- SLP (sleep mode)–this pin effectively enables or disables the accelerometer. For continuous operation, just link it to + Vcc.

Figure 4-46 shows the general idea for connecting the accelerometer on its breakout board to the test rig breadboard. Note that the ARef (Analog reference voltage) pin 21 on the AVR is now connected to the 3.3 V supply, rather than +5 V as previously. This is essential for things to work properly.

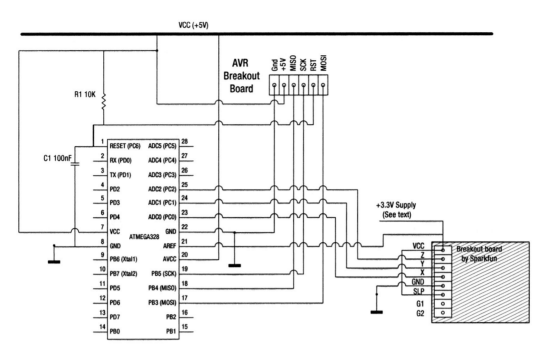

Figure 4-46. *Connecting the MM7260 breakout board to the AVR test rig*

Finally, the following is a simple test program that pushes out a continuous stream of data to the serial screen to say what the current values of X, Y, and Z are. Move the test rig breadboard with the accelerometer breakout board on it in order to see the numbers change.

```
/*
This sketch is to interrogate and continuously display the output values
from an MM7260 Accelerometer. The X, Y and Z outputs are attached to
analog inputs 0,1 and 2 respectively. A 3.3V source is needed to supply
AREF and to power the chip - since that is the supply voltage required.
See book text for more details. */
#define X_IN 0
#define Y_IN 1
#define Z_IN 2

void setup()
{
  // Not much to do here.
  Serial.begin(9600);
  analogReference(EXTERNAL); // Use the voltage on Aref pin as ref for analog inputs
}

void loop()
{
  Serial.print(" Accelerometer Values: X = " );
  Serial.print (analogRead(X_IN),DEC);
```

```
    Serial.print(": Y = " );
    Serial.print (analogRead(Y_IN),DEC);

    Serial.print(": Z = " );
    Serial.println (analogRead(Z_IN),DEC);

    delay(100);
}
```

Summary

In this wide-ranging chapter on the subject of movement we have looked at a number of things that can be used to make things move under the control of an MCU. We looked at several different types and classes of motors and how to drive them. We looked at solenoids and how they can be used in real situations.

Then, we looked at sensing movement in various ways and with various devices. You saw that the ability to make things move in an intelligent system is not enough–that movement has to be sensed so that it can be properly directed and/or controlled.

Although we covered a lot of ground in this chapter, the truth of the matter is that we only really scratched the surface. However, I hope it has been enough to get you started on the road to discovering more about these subject areas. I hope it has left you enthused enough to go ahead and start making your own projects that use intelligently directed movement and force, projects that do useful and (even more important) fun things.

Coming Up Next

Smarten up! Building in intelligence.

CHAPTER 5

■ ■ ■

Smarten Up!

This book deals with making things that are provided with embedded intelligence. My hope is that this book will inspire you to develop your own ideas to enhance projects discussed in these pages, and that you will go on to design and build your own projects for many years to come. If you're new to electronics, or you've never dealt with programmable devices before, you may wonder why this approach is better than just using single-purpose devices. So, it seems only fair to prime the pump by looking at some basic ideas about embedded intelligence. Why would we want it? What does it buy us? Where is it useful, and does it have a dark side?

So, in this chapter, we are going to look at the benefits of building in intelligence to things around us. We're going to see why we do it, how we do it, and how to avoid some traps of overimplementation and assumption. We're also going to look at the benefits of connecting intelligent devices, and throughout we will look at some concrete examples applicable to home automation. Some of those ideas are incorporated into buildable projects later in this book.

Intelligent Devices

Clearly, since everything from jumbo jets, the cars we drive, festive lighting rigs, and even birthday cards now contains programmable controllers, there must be benefits to having microcontrollers built into things. But what exactly are those benefits? How is, say, a car with built-in intelligence superior to one without? And who reaps those benefits?

Well, some things are obvious when you see them: open the door of a modern car, and if it's dark outside, the indoor light comes on for just the door you opened–not all the others doors too and the interior light (or lights) fades up to full brightness. Close the door and the inside light of the car doesn't snap off, it slowly and stylishly fades out. But, it didn't take a computer to do that; with some smart wiring and some very simple electronic or electromechanical components an old-style car control system could have done that.

But, how about this: your car is not feeling too well, you've inadvertently put some poor-quality fuel in it and the engine is not firing too smoothly: But, no problem, the engine control unit (ECU)–which is based around a microcontroller–is on the case.

Using its sensors, the ECU discovers that the engine is not running normally and it automatically adjusts the frequency and duration of the spark plug activations to optimize the firing to suit the poorer-quality fuel, and it does so very quickly–quite likely without you, the driver, ever being aware there was a problem. On an old-time car that did not have an ECU, such an adjustment would probably have meant a trip to the workshop to have a skilled mechanic equipped with various analyzers make the necessary adjustments. It's even possible that you may have spluttered to a stop at the roadside and had to call for assistance, so the ECU's ability to adjust to this new situation saved you a heap of trouble.

Here's another example: picture a digital scale, such as you might use to weigh ingredients for cooking in the kitchen, or for weighing letters and packets to find out how much they are going to cost to send. An electronic scale uses a sensing device generically known as a strain gauge. This is an electronic component whose resistance changes according to tiny changes in the amount of pressure placed on it–an extremely sensitive little gizmo.

As a strain gauge component ages, its characteristics change: in other words, the electrical resistance it offers at the point where it has no pressure on it (its zero point) will change quite a lot over its lifetime, due to usage and environmental factors such as humidity. If the output of the sensor were just displayed as is, you would not get a reliable measurement. So, in such products there is built-in intelligence which, when the device is powered up, reads the current "no load" resistance of the sensor, and automatically uses that as its zero point for the current weighing session. In other words, the scale's zero point is automatically recalibrated every time it is powered up–much better and more convenient than the user having to reset the zero point each day, as would have been the case using older designs.

The central point about both of the previous examples is that the embedded intelligence makes the product concerned function more conveniently and with less need for any human intervention or adjustment. However, there are far more benefits from embedding intelligent devices than our examples so far have shown. In the following sections we'll look at a fuller list of what embedded intelligence can deliver in the following areas:

- Increased functionality

- Adaptive behavior

- Increased efficiency

- Improved problem management

- Capacity for repurposing

- Greener products

- Support from the mother ship

Increased Functionality

Why do some older people have such problems using things like phones and remotes? I have a theory: although they grew up in a world with TVs and radios and cars and telephones, they also grew up in a world in which these things did not have embedded intelligence.

Before we started building computing power into pretty much all commodity consumer devices (something that happened from the early 1990s onward) a button on a consumer device usually did just one thing. If you had a button on a TV that said "Power" you only pressed it to power the TV on and off. With embedded intelligence, our devices started to be able to do lots more things: For example, on a modern TV it's just as likely that if you press the "Power" button for a short time, the TV will go into standby mode, whereas, if you press the power button for a longer time, it will power the TV off completely. Hold it down even longer and you get into a technician's service menu! So, individual buttons can do different things according to context and different user actions. Modern consumer device rarely have single-function buttons–and my theory is that some older people just can't get used to that! Nice theory...

Industry analysts (such as McKinsey[1]) believe that most of the advanced features of modern consumer goods are not used by most of the people who buy them. If this is true, or even partly true, then why do manufacturers keep on providing so many options and extras on their products? Simple answer, because with the advent of embedded intelligence in consumer products, it became easy (and relatively cheap) for them to do so.

In the days when there was no embedded intelligence, any additional functions in a product had to be provided by extra hardware. Take the example of an early digital-era alarm clock that played a tune when the set alarm time was reached. Such a product would have had a dedicated clock chip inside it, a chip that made the

---

[1] www.mckinseyquarterly.com/Consumer_electronics_gets_back_to_basics_2454.

alarm tone (probably it only just made one kind of buzz) and a chip to drive the display. If the manufacturer had wanted to offer an enhanced version of the product that played tunes rather than just buzzing, it would have had to add more chips to the product–adding to the manufacturing cost of *each and every unit produced.*

By contrast, in the modern equivalent of the alarm clock product, alarm tunes would be implemented in software; there would be no buzzer or "tunes" chip. That means that adding more tunes becomes just a matter of developing more software which is a one-off cost but does not add anything at all to the manufacturing cost of the product. This is why so many modern products have such a plethora of features and functions–they are implemented in software. If you're a global corporation making several million of these clocks, this is a very attractive approach, since doing things in software has comparatively little effect on the per-unit production cost. Also, it's known that "features" sell a product–the longer the list of features you can put on the packaging, the more attractive consumers will seem to find it (even if none of them ever use those features).

Similarly to the preceding example, it's now common for products to be manufactured for use globally and for user interface texts, in lots of different languages, to be built in. Again, it's far more cost-effective for manufacturers to do this because it's just software. There is no need for additional chips or to produce country-specific versions of the product.

Adaptive Behavior

In a previous example we saw how the embedded intelligence in a car might compensate for poor-quality fuel–an example of adaptive behavior that products and projects can display when they have embedded intelligence. That was a fairly simple example, but the uses for adaptive behavior can get far more complex.

In microcontroller-based systems, adaptation of behavior is almost always driven by sensory or data inputs. The behavior of a product might be adapted in response to

- *Environment*: For example the microcontroller might have a sensor that tells it the outside air temperature. Or, it might have a rain sensor that tells it whether rain is falling. An intelligent MP3 player might use information from an ambient noise sensor to know when to increase the headphones volume to compensate for lots of outside noise.

- *Performance*: Sensors might allow the controller to assess performance of the entity it is controlling. As in the car example we looked at previously, the ECU was able to infer from sensor inputs that the engine was not firing optimally and take appropriate action to rectify the problem.

- *Presence*: Some devices only need to function when certain conditions are true. Lights are a good example. Often they only need to be on when someone is in the room. The weighing scales we looked at earlier are another example. The scales only need to stay powered on if there is something present to be weighed. If nothing is present to be weighed, they can power off after a while.

- *User input*: As in our previous example about functionality, a device might present all user information and user prompts in the Latvian language, if the user has indicated that as his preference.

- *Location*: Because more and more consumer products now feature a GPS receiver, devices have the ability to know precisely where in the world they are. This allows them to adapt their behavior accordingly. For example, a car might have headlights whose maximum beam-height can be adjusted by the car's control system. Since the maximum legal "throw" of headlights varies from country to country, an intelligent car could automatically adjust the headlight height, based on GPS location, during a drive across Europe.

- *Data received*: The days of the truly stand-alone device are passing. Very often an intelligent device will need to work in concert with other intelligent devices. This means that it must be able to respond to data provided to it from external sources. Most sensors provide fairly limited information about one thing. Having the ability to receive various kinds of data from a whole range of other devices allows an intelligent product, or project, to perform as part of a coordinated set of devices, not just unilaterally.

  Home automation systems are a prime example of this need for concerted activity through data sharing. It's very useful to have a lighting controller that puts lights on only when someone is the room, but it's even more useful if that controller has the intelligence to react to a message from the home security system that says the house is now in "nobody's home" mode. That sensor activation is probably just the cat, and she can see in the dark anyway! Let's save some electricity.

The ability of devices with embedded microcontrollers to respond intelligently and adaptively to data received from peer devices is something we look at in more detail in some of the project sections.

Increased Efficiency

In these pollution- and energy-aware days, we all want to consume less energy. But, we also want our devices to do more things for us, to provide us with more information and to manage our resources more effectively. Embedded intelligence is one of the means whereby these apparently conflicting desires can be met.

Efficiency, in this context, is not just about reducing the carbon footprint of devices: it's also about getting things done better, faster, and cheaper. For example, by embedding microcontrollers in devices such as dishwashers and washing machines, manufacturers have been able to make them consume less power and water, while giving equivalent or better results.

How does embedded intelligence deliver these benefits? It's really a question of awareness and memory. If the controlling software program in a device is aware of its environment it can respond appropriately. A nonintelligent control system will initiate just one action in the presence of any given set of inputs. An intelligent system can make inferences not only from its sensory inputs but also from data it has remembered or learned previously.

To take the electronic alarm clock example mentioned earlier, a nonintelligent version of this device will look at the time now, it will look at its set alarm time, and if they match, it will sound its bleeper. An intelligent version of the same device would be very likely to have additional abilities. For example, it might have the ability to sense the outside temperature and sound the alarm 30 minutes early if the outside temperature has fallen below freezing level overnight. It might also have the ability to randomly select among a collection of alarm tones so that the sleepy user does not become immune to the wake-up call. In a fully integrated home automation (HA) system, the clock might have the ability to send "alarm time reached" messages to other intelligent devices. For examples it might

- Send a message to a home heating system 30 minutes before the alarm is to sound—so that the home is warm when the user rises from bed, but the heating is not running unnecessarily early.

- Cause other HA system components to turn on lights, open curtains, or make beverages.

- If the user is disabled or infirm, it might automatically send a message to a pager or call unit for a helper to assist with washing or dressing.

- Cause an information display next to the user's bed to light up, showing outside temperature, house systems status, and so on.

- Send a wake-up message via the house network to boot up the user's PC so that she can check her e-mail before she starts for work.

In essence, an intelligent alarm clock can behave just a little more like a thinking thing then a dumb machine, but it can also make things more efficient. If you set your alarm for a little later than usual, your heating system will come on later than usual, if you need help from someone after you get up, that person is not called until he is really needed, the information display comes on when you need it, not at some preprogrammed time that doesn't synch with you waking up.

So, in addition to energy efficiency embedded, connected intelligence also delivers efficiency of other kinds in a way that nonintelligent devices would not be able to do.

Improved Problem Management

Embedded intelligence is—as we have seen—a way of enabling products and devices to work around problems that occur in normal operation, but there's more . . .

A nonintelligent device needs to have fault-detection hardware built into it. For example, in an alarm clock made from standard logic chips, a "snooze" button which is stuck in the pressed position is likely to cause the clock to inexplicably stop working. The designer could have built in extra logic chips to detect if any of the buttons were stuck, but it would involve extra cost of materials and manufacture and increase the physical size of the circuitry required.

By contrast, stuck-down button detection in a software-controlled intelligent device is far easier and does not significantly affect the cost of each unit manufactured. Better yet, the software can put a message on the display (or send off a message to a superior system, in a connected environment) to flag up that there is a stuck button problem, making the fault easy to identify and rectify. This concept of preemptive problem management has been taken up enthusiastically by the automotive industry and, although not without its problems (as we shall see later in the "Downsides of Intelligent Devices" section) it has, in general, made modern vehicles far more reliable and easy to service.

With embedded intelligence, devices and systems can do more than identify problems when they occur; they can also identify issues *before* they become problems. For example, some sophisticated home and office lighting management systems use embedded intelligence to collect statistics about the "on" time of individual lamps, or groups of lights. Coupled with the manufacturer's data on lifetime of the lamps concerned, it becomes possible to raise "change lamp" alerts when lights approach their true end of life but before they actually fail. This is a much better approach than just slavishly changing the lamps on a fixed maintenance cycle when they could easily still have a lot of useful life remaining. Similar techniques can be used to deal intelligently with replacing batteries in various kinds of devices.

Capacity for Repurposing

As human beings we love to second-guess ourselves. We always have second thoughts about things we make. In conventional electronics, when you build something, it can be quite hard to subsequently make substantial modifications to what it does or how it behaves. In many microcontroller projects you can endlessly alter, refine, adapt, reuse, or repurpose your creations, since a great many changes simply require making a modified version of the software and reprogramming the microcontroller with it. However, to realize the full benefits of this feature, you do have to think ahead a little bit at the time you design and create your project.

Outside Light—Without Intelligence

Let's imagine a situation where we need to control a light fixed to the outside of a house. Without involving electronics, we could just fit a switch to turn the light on or off manually, as shown in Figure 5-1, in which we see the mains power source (a wall outlet probably), the switch (probably mounted on a wall near the door leading outside the house), and the light itself.

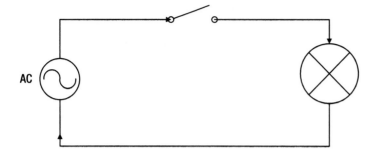

Figure 5-1. *Outside light controlled by simple switch*

This approach, although simple, is not ideal. The light might be left on for whole days even when not needed, or we might forget to put it on and leave visitors or family members groping around outside in the dark looking for the door to the house. So, perhaps we might add a mechanical timer to make the light go on and off at preset times of the day (Figure 5-2)–probably sunset and sunrise.

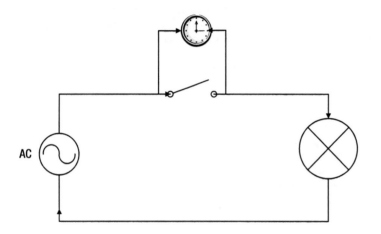

Figure 5-2. *Outside light control by switch and/or timer switch*

Again, this is not totally satisfactory because, as the daylight hours vary through the year, we would have to keep adjusting the timer's on/off cycles too.

If we get electronics involved, we can use an ambient light sensor (used, in this case, as a darkness detector) to keep the light off when it's daylight but turn it on when it gets dark–as shown in Figure 5-3, in which a mains-powered light-sensitive switch is used to allow power through when there is no light.

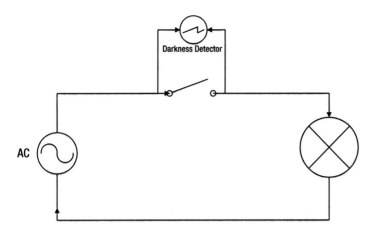

Figure 5-3. *Adding a darkness detector*

This is a lot better; the light only comes on when it really is dark outside. However, we still waste a lot of power, because the light is always on during darkness hours, even if there is no need for the light to be on because nobody is around. So, we retain the darkness sensor, but we also add a proximity sensor as in Figure 5-4.

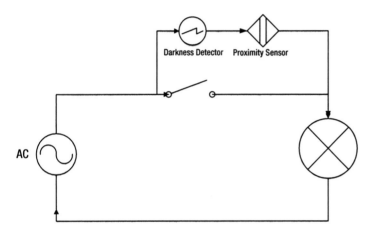

Figure 5-4. *Darkness and proximity version*

This provides us with a motion-triggered light that only puts the light on when it detects movement near it during darkness hours. Such a sensor will usually incorporate a timer that keeps the contact made for, perhaps, 30 seconds after any movement is detected. Mains-powered motion-triggered lights are, of course, widely available.

So now, the light comes on only when we need it, doesn't waste power, and doesn't need constant adjustment through the year. Oh, and we also retain the ability to use just the conventional switch in case we want to put the light on manually (e.g., to make sure the lamp is working).

Although we now have a very useful setup, it only does just this one set of combined functions: daylight detect; movement detect; and light on/off.

Outside Light—With an Intelligent Controller

What if, instead, we connect the light to a controller that has embedded intelligence and communication capability? What if, as previously discussed, it remembers how long the lamp has been on for and can send a message to some other system when the lamp gets close to the end of its predicted life? What if, when triggered at dawn or dusk, the light only comes on as brightly as required, not at full wattage? What if the light could also serve additional purposes?

These could be useful additions to the functionality of such a light; but what if this intelligence was connected to other intelligent devices in the house? For example, if the owners of the house were away from home for the week, what if the security system could command the controller to switch on the outside light for a few minutes every hour to simulate occupancy? What if, when the security system sent out an "Intruder detected" message, this outside light controller could be programmed to fast-flash the outside light as an indication to anybody nearby that something bad was going on? Wouldn't it be nice if, instead of just plopping on and off, the outside light could stylishly and gently fade up and down when triggered? All of this would be perfectly possible with the arrangement shown in Figure 5-5.

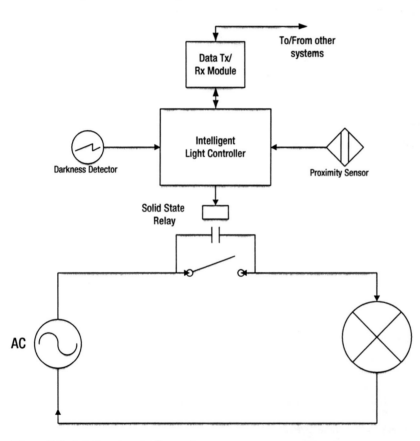

Figure 5-5. *Intelligent controller version*

In this version of the outside light, the sensors themselves no longer directly control the flow of power into the light. Power flow is now controlled by a solid state relay (which is does the same job as a conventional mechanical relay, but with no moving parts, and is much faster, meaning it can be pulsed on and off quickly to achieve dimming).

We still have light/dark and proximity sensors, but instead of being devices suitable for use in mains circuits they are now low-voltage types, suitable for interfacing to a microcontroller, a device that only directly connects to low-voltage DC sources—never, ever, directly to the mains power! Software running inside the light controller's microcontroller chip constantly scans the sensor states and activates the SSR whenever the mains light is required to be on.

Notice also that in this arrangement we have added a data transmitter/receiver (Tx/Rx) device. This might be a very short-range radio module; it might be a Zigbee radio receiver, a Wi-Fi module, a wired connection to your CAT5 or CAT6 home LAN (local area network), or perhaps a plain old RS232 serial cable back to the serial port of your desktop machine. The exact connection method is, for now, immaterial. The point to take on board here is that it allows this controller to communicate with other intelligent devices in some way.

Because the microcontroller chip contains nonvolatile flash memory (which retains its contents even if the chip is powered down), the controller can maintain a count of how many minutes the lamp has been powered on for. If the software is written such that it can know the expected lifetime of the type of lamp being used, then it's a simple matter for it to send a message via the data Tx/Rx module to some other entity (e.g., a PC HA application, or a smart phone message box) to say "Lamp change of outside light due."

Similarly, in this configuration, the controller has the ability to receive information from other devices. It may receive regular updates from a time server, so that it always knows the correct time of day. It may receive commands such as

- Light on.

- Light off.

- Respond only to movement.

- Respond only to darkness.

- Light on for x seconds.

Intelligent Light Controller Enhancements

The main point in this example is that once you have put intelligence into your light controller, provided you have designed your controller properly, you can add all kinds of enhancements to it without changing the hardware. It simply becomes a matter of updating the software that the microcontroller runs to make it do things differently, to do additional things, or to respond to additional remote commands. That is the essential difference between an intelligent and a "dumb" device.

General-purpose microcontroller platforms such as Arduino are the perfect embodiment of this idea that you can use generic hardware building blocks for many purposes simply by changing the software they run. However, while this approach works very well, it isn't perfect because, to be generally applicable, general-purpose microcontroller building blocks often have to provide more computer hardware (e.g., more input or output pins) than many permanent projects need, but still require the addition of external drivers and helper chips.

Greener Products

As we have seen previously, embedding intelligence into your product or project can make it less power hungry, and thus more environmentally friendly.

However, this has to be by design, it won't just happen. When developing software you have to bear this in mind. Ensuring switch-off of power-hungry lights, displays, motors, solenoids, and so on when they are not needed is essential to realizing these benefits.

Support from the Mother Ship

We're all now familiar with the idea of "over the wire" support services. Our desktop machines find and install updates for us. In many locations our cable and satellite boxes and our broadband routers get software updates without us even realizing it has happened. In many places, our electricity or gas meters are read remotely over the wire.

All this is only made possible because these devices contain embedded intelligence and are equipped with a communications channel of some kind that allows them to request or receive information from a superior controlling entity–their mother ship, if you will.

In a smaller way, it's possible for our microcontroller projects to "phone home" when we give them the ability to connect to the wider world–as we saw in the earlier lighting controller example of Figure 5-5. That had the possibility of reporting back to an application in our home PC to raise a "lamp change due" alert.

As well as reporting to control devices, though, intelligent devices can extend their capabilities by requesting and receiving sensory data from their peers. The intelligent alarm clock idea we discussed previously in this chapter is one example of such a usage: it was receiving outside temperature readings from another intelligent controller.

Embedded Intelligence Benefits

So, in summary, making your product or project device "smart" not only can increase functionality, reliability, and efficiency but, when coupled with the ability to communicate with peer devices, can confer the ability for classes of devices with embedded intelligence to act as a cohesive system, in which truly the sum of the whole is greater than the sum of all the parts.

But the news is not *all* good; there are some consequences to smartening up devices by including microcontrollers in them.

Downsides of Intelligent Devices

You'll probably have experienced the downside of putting intelligence into products. You may get a fault light on your car for no apparent reason. You may find that your GPS lapses back into Latvian prompts and information displays because it lost power. Your super-smart burglar alarm system may prove just too complex to be usable by anyone who doesn't have several days to study and restudy the manual. Yes, the news is not all good.

Embedded intelligence should be used just as much to facilitate maintenance and usability as adding additional functionality. When designing, as we do in this book, projects that make use of embedded intelligence, you should always focus on the user experience that the project will deliver. If the project has a user interface, is the device easy to use, is it obvious what the device is telling or asking the user? If not, it's not doing its job properly. If the project does not need to have a direct user interface, can it provide diagnostic information to other systems, so that troubleshooting is made easier?

These are all issues you need to keep in mind if you want to avoid developing smart devices that nobody wants to use.

The Anatomy of a Smart Device

A smart device will have one or more digital processors in it. As well as the processor, there will also be some amount of digital memory, and an I/O system that allows sensor and communications data to flow into and out of the processor section.

The digital memory will house

- The processor's operating program.

- Temporary data used by the operating program.

- Possibly some history or context information that will allow the software program to make inferences. For example, the intelligent alarm clock that we outlined earlier in this chapter might store the last 16 half-hourly readings from the outside temperature sensor, so that it can tell if the waking-up and commute time is unexpectedly or unusually cold.

The processor(s) will have an execution unit that will execute the software code at power on and keep running it until power is removed. Unlike a desktop computer, smart devices typically "boot up" very quickly, and you almost never need to perform a formal shutdown procedure–you just power them off when you're done.

A smart device will have an I/O subsystem that allows it to interface with the outside world. This I/O system may be an all-digital interface, or it may be a mixed analog and digital system. Most members of the AVR microcontroller family, with which we are concerned in this book, provide digital and analog I/O facilities– meaning that an AVR can interface with many kinds of real-world devices, without the need for additional support chips.

A smart device also needs sensory input. One of the most fascinating things about the microcontroller revolution is the simply enormous range of sensors that have become available to interface with them. Broadly, sensors fall into the following general categories:

- *Presence detectors*: This might be the kind of motion sensor we discussed earlier in connection with the smart lighting controller. Or, it could be a sophisticated video analysis system that provides a digital trigger to our microcontroller when it detects something moving in the view of one its CCTV (closed circuit TV) cameras. Or, it might be a very simple sensor such as a pressure pad concealed under a doormat which is activated when someone steps on it.

- *Temperature and pressure sensors*: These typically provide the microcontroller with data about some condition in the outside world. Such conditions might include

  - How hot is something?

  - How cold is something?

  - What pressure is present?

  - What is the noise level?

- *Speed and distance sensors*: How fast are we moving? How fast is that spinning? How long did something take to get from point A to point B? How far away is that object?

- *User interface sensors*: A switch was pressed, a touch screen was touched, a pedal was pressed down, a mouse was clicked, a gesture was made, and a controller was tilted to the right.

- *Color and light sensors*: What is the light level? What color is that? Is it daytime, or is it nighttime?

- *Specialist sensors*: These can be magnetic field detectors, radiation sensors, electrical field detectors, and many more.

A look through any good electronics catalog will provide hundreds of examples of sensors–almost all of them created specifically to interface with microcontrollers.

Smart devices, then, are defined as those that have some level of sensory ability and some level of embedded intelligence. They respond to real-world events and data in various useful ways, always appropriately to context.

The purpose of this book is not to allow you to build some fantastic single smart device but, rather, to show you that additive intelligence can be built up in easy pieces when you embed AVR microcontrollers into things and give them the ability to interact with people, or with other systems.

Summary

In this chapter we have looked at the methods whereby intelligence can be built into everyday objects. We have seen the benefits it can confer as opposed to conventional approaches and we have seen the possible downsides that can ensue if intelligence is not designed thoughtfully and with due regard to the user experience.

Coming Up Next

Digital conversations: MCU shall talk unto MCU!

■ ■ ■

CHAPTER 6

Digitally Speaking

In the last chapter we looked at the benefits of enabling devices with intelligence to communicate with one another and also with overseeing control systems. Now, let's look at the specifics of how this communication happens, at some of the connection methods that can be used. We'll also look at why, especially if you have big plans for what you want to achieve, you might need a fully worked out object model.

If you are completely new to the concept of serial digital communication, you might like to read Appendix B before continuing with this chapter. In this chapter we look at how interdevice communication happens and glimpse some of the many uses for it in modern intelligent devices.

When Intelligent Devices Speak

What happens when intelligent devices talk to one another? What do they say? Well, actually, if you created the devices that will do the communicating, it's up to you! Once the communication channel is established, your devices can exchange any kind of message that is needed. The intelligent alarm clock we discussed in Chapter 5 might request the current accurate time from a time server by sending a message as simple as "Time?" as long as the time server it's requesting from is programmed to understand that message. The server might respond with "18:01.30" (meaning 30 seconds past 6:01 p.m.). Likewise, the software running in the alarm clock would have to understand how to unpack the response it got, in order to make use of the received information.

Given that microcontrollers (and computers in general) do not have unlimited resources or capabilities, it is necessary to limit the number of messages that can be sent and received for any given application, so any idea that devices can message one another about anything at all are, for the moment, purely science fiction: often, it is also necessary to closely prescribe the actual sequence in which messages will be sent and received. In the previous example, if the alarm clock received a message "18:01.30" when it had *not* sent a "Time?" request, and wasn't expecting any message, it might get confused, or more likely it would just ignore the message.

Such systems need extensive provisions to deal with the unexpected. If your intelligent alarm clock sends a message to get the "Time?" but never gets a reply, because its message (or the reply) has somehow gotten lost along the way, it needs to be programmed to give up eventually—it can't wait forever. Similarly, messages that don't make contextual sense need to be handled correctly. If your clock has sent a "Time?" request but due to some error receives a date string like "2012-08-31", or an invalid time value such as "25:12.01", it needs to do something other than crash and restart.

For all the previous reasons, interdevice communications need to be carefully designed and documented in order to work well. Such a design is usually called a communications protocol, and you'll be designing a simple one later in this chapter.

It's important to know that for AVR microcontroller applications that need to communicate with other local entities, a full networking protocol (such as TCP/IP) is not always practical or necessary. It can be impractical because of resource limitations in the AVR chip: if the TCP/IP (Transmission Control Protocol/Internet Protocol) network suite takes up all of your on-chip program memory and doesn't leave enough for your application program, then the whole exercise is pointless! Also, network stacks do a lot of things, and their complexity may amount to massive overkill for basic uses. So, bear in mind, as you read the next section, that simpler applications can, many times, get away with using simpler means of communication.

Communications Channel Types

Device-to-device communication is not only about the messages carried; it's about the communication channel itself. For example, when you send an e-mail, *your* main concern is getting the content of the e-mail correct and making sure that you have the correct e-mail address for the recipient . However, after you click that "send" button, a lot of other (largely invisible) stuff goes on to make sure that your message is delivered, or to let you know if there is a problem getting it there. It's the same with messages between intelligent devices.

It's important to appreciate that communication channels can operate at various different layers. These can be summarized as

- *The physical layer*: There has to be a continuous pathway of some kind between the sender and the recipient. This pathway might be wires inside a cable (e.g., a CAT5 cable, as widely used by computer LAN networks), it might be a Wi-Fi link between a wireless router and a Wi-Fi card or dongle on the receiving device, or it might be something like a radio data sender/receiver board which then connects directly to a microcontroller chip.

- *The network layer*: This is the layer that uses the physical medium most closely. In a majority of networks this is provided by IP (Internet Protocol). You need this layer in environments where it's not possible merely to send a message directly over the network. For example, what if the link is a wireless network? It's likely that you are sharing it with other devices and your message might collide with theirs. Both messages would be garbled and lost. In complex networks where it's necessary to forward messages from one network segment to another, it is the network layer that takes on this task.

- *The transport layer*: It is often the job of the transport layer to chop up large application messages into smaller chunks for sending (and to reassemble message segments received from others) and to realize when messages—or segments of messages—have not made it to their destination and resend them if required. In the IT world, the combined capabilities of the TCP and IP protocols (thus TCP/IP networking) most often provide the transport and network layers.

- *The application layer*: This is the level we initially looked at; it is the actual message sending and receiving that is visible to the application itself (in our earlier example, this was the intelligent alarm clock and the time server).

Figure 6-1 summarizes these ideas and shows how (in cases where all these layers are needed) they combine to take a message, push it over a wire, and deliver it to another intelligent system.

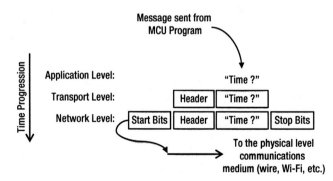

Figure 6-1. *Packetization of a message*

The sequence starts from the top of the diagram and flows downward. This is the sequence depicted:

1. Your Microcontroller application program needs to send the text "Time?" to another device connected to the communications medium. For the purposes of this explanation, the communications medium could be a point to point cable, a wireless link of some kind (e.g., Wi-Fi) or even a USB point-to-point cable.

2. Your application makes a "Send" call to a transport layer software library—which might be an AVR implementation of a standard transport level protocol such as TCP or FTP (File Transfer Protocol). The transport protocol takes the message you want to send (which, in networking terms, is called the payload) and it constructs its own header for the message. The header contains information such as how many bytes long your payload message is, the segment number (in this case, since your message is not long enough to need breaking up into segments for transit over a link, this will just be segment 0), a checksum value (see "Error Checking" section, below), and various other descriptive items.

3. The transport layer hands on the complete packet to the next layer down, which is the network layer. This is the level that actually sends out the data packet, bit by binary bit, over the physical communications medium. It first sends out its own start bits (see Appendix B), then the header and payload from the previous step, then some stop bits, and perhaps an additional checksum or other checking data.

In most eight-bit MCU applications, the foregoing illustrates the most complex scenario that will be used for communication. However, communications between larger computers, such as your desktop machine or the many servers at your Internet server provider's data center, use a seven-layer communications model called the OSI Model. We won't be using it in this book, but if you're interested to see the details of a full-blown network stack, take a look at http://en.wikipedia.org/wiki/OSI_model.

Error Checking

Networking protocols of all kinds make extensive use of checksums. A checksum is a total obtained by simply adding up the value of each byte sent in a data packet. So, a checksum means, "This is the total value of all the bytes I just sent you."

Let's look at a simple example. Suppose I wanted to send five bytes of data across a network link, and these bytes had decimal values as follows: 5, 4, 3, 2, and 1. Now if we add them all up, we get a total of $5+4+3+2+1=15$. So, the checksum value would be 15. Table 6-1 indicates what would be sent and the checksum value at each stage. Notice that the checksum is only the bytes being sent; it does not include its own value.

Table 6-1. Simple Checksum

Byte Number	Value Sent	Checksum Value
-	-	0
1	5	5
2	4	9
3	3	12
4	2	14
5	1	15
Checksum	15	

The checksum gives a reasonably robust way for a data receiver to ensure that what she received is the same as what was sent. The receiving device computes its own checksum of the bytes received and compares it to the received checksum—if they differ (either because one of the data bytes was corrupted in transit, or perhaps the checksum itself was) then some error has occurred and the accuracy of the received data packet cannot be trusted.

Checksums are always limited to some number of bits, which means they have a maximum possible value. For example, an eight-bit checksum is limited to 255 (in binary that's 1111 1111). So, what happens if we send this two-byte packet? See Table 6-2:

Table 6-2. Packet Checksum

Byte Number	Value	8-Bit Checksum Value
		0
1	255	255
2	2	1
Checksum	1	

We got an overflow of the checksum counter and we discarded the carry. In other words, the checksum calculator did the following binary sum, but discarded the carry to the ninth bit

Thus, the golden rule is that checksum overflows are always discarded to keep the checksum value within its allowed number of bits.

1111 1111
0000 0010
ɫ 0000 0001

Although they are good enough for most applications, checksums are not an infallible check on the integrity of received data. Consider what would happen if we sent the same data packet again, but this time some of the data were mangled in transit to the receiver; in Table 6-3 we show what the receiver saw as well).

Table 6-3. Checksum Failure

Byte Number	Sent Value	Senders Checksum Value	Received Value	Receiver's Computed Checksum
		0		0
1	5	5	5	5
2	4	9	4	9
3	3	12	0	9
4	2	14	3	12
5	1	15	3	15
Checksum	15			15

In this case, the received checksum still matches the computed checksum, even though bytes 3 to 5 in the data packet have been received incorrectly. In practice, this kind of undetected error is rare, though not unknown. In many cases even if the checksum mechanism failed to detect an error, the faulty data delivered to the application would not make sense and would be rejected. It was once estimated that many streaming media failures on the Internet are due to this cause, a quite feasible hypothesis since streaming media involve the transmission of enormous numbers of data packets over multiple networks.

A whole armory of other checking information can be used to validate data packets passing between computers (such as longitudinal parity checks and error correcting codes, or ECC), but these can add unacceptable overheads or complexity, so they are not always used.

The key is to ask what the consequence of undetected errors might be; if the consequence is that a returned time value for an intelligent alarm clock is garbled, then that's not so terrible—the clock's application code will probably perform some kind of checking on the returned time value anyway (and reject a corrupted time value of "09:2\.w}") and it will request the update again. If we were designing communications between control devices within a nuclear power station and the result of a corrupted error message could be a meltdown, then we'd probably want to incorporate as many checks as possible. Fortunately for us, our usages for communications all veer toward the former rather than the latter examples.

So, in the previous diagrams and explanations, we saw the most complex case we are likely to encounter in eight-bit MCU land. If you wanted to have the full facilities of a network stack, they are easy to obtain; you can get very useful ready-made communications libraries from the Arduino Playground (at http://arduino.cc/playground/Main/LibraryList) which will allow you to implement networking without having to create it for yourself. However, as ever, the devil is in the detail. In AVR projects we are often constrained by the comparatively small size of the memory we have available for our program code. This means that we sometimes have to make some hard choices about how we do things.

For example, Adam Neilsen's SLIP (Serial Line IP) library—available from the Arduino Playground site mentioned previously—will give you the capability to do TCP/IP networking over the AVR's built-in serial line. This library needs about 9 KB of code space on the AVR chip. If we are using an ATmega328 AVR microcontroller, which offers 32 KB of program memory and intended to use most of the facilities the library provides, then it would be worth dedicating that much space to the library. However, if we were using an ATmega168, which only offers 16 KB of program space, then it would be far harder to justify, especially if we were only going use part of the functionality on offer. Of course, if we were using one of the Tiny AVR ranges, such as the ATtiny13, which only has 1 KB of program memory, then using most libraries (let alone one of 9 KB) is simply not going to happen.

In summary, if your project really demands it and the hardware can support it, and your budget allows it (not all Arduino libraries are free; some are offered commercially) then using libraries is a very good way to compress your project development time and acquire communications functions "off the shelf." However, in many instances we need a solution that is more along the lines of the KISS principle.

Microcontroller KISS Communications

If you can't justify using communications libraries and the requirements are fairly simple, then it's possible to build in the things you need from within your own code. This approach will still increase your code size, but by far less than using a library containing a full network suite.

So, what does this simpler approach look like? In the case in which you are exchanging messages between your own projects, or between a desktop machine application that you created or can control, it's really a matter of inventing a protocol that is simple but fairly robust.

Let's stick with the example of the intelligent alarm clock requesting a time check. First, we'd need to connect our AVR project to the logic level serial port that is provided by the AVR programmer (see the "TTL Level Serial Port" section in Chapter 2). Figure 6-2 shows the hardware setup we might use.

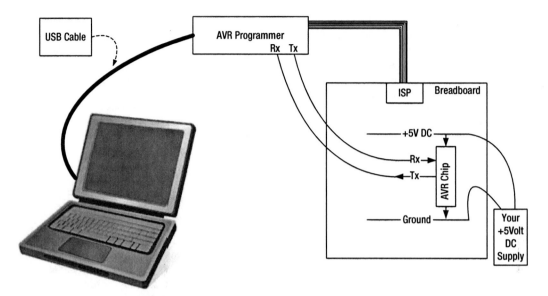

Figure 6-2. *Serial connection to the laptop via AVR programmer board*

Going from left to right in this diagram we have a laptop computer, on which the AVR programming environment is installed and on which you would run the "laptop side" software. By the way, this is only shown as a laptop for illustrative purposes, we could just as easily use a desk-side/desktop machine, but I just like this laptop picture!

Hanging off the laptop, via its USB cable is the AVR programmer: the programmer gets its instructions from the Arduino software running inside the laptop and its power supply through the USB cable. Then we have the AVR programmer. The programmer's cable connects to the ISP (in-system programming) port that we created on the breadboard when we set it up and the ISP cable also links the breadboard and the programmer's ground planes. Finally, on the breadboard (which is powered by the +5-volt supply that we also added in the setup phase) is the AVR chip.

The RS-232 Connection

In the previous example, we saw how to make the connections using only logic level signals. However, when you connect via a "real" serial port, the signals are conditioned to a standard called RS-232. For more details about serial ports and RS-232 refer to Appendix B.

If you are using an AVR programmer that doesn't offer a logic level serial interface, you may want to know how to create an equivalent setup that will connect to an RS-232 port on your desktop or laptop machine. Older machines will likely have an RS-232 port built in (this will be indicated by the presence of one or more nine-pin serial port plugs on their connector panels). For newer machines, you may need to add a "USB to serial port" adaptor, which is readily available at computer and electronics stores.

■ **Warning**   You should *never* connect your AVR chip directly to the RS-232 serial port of your desktop or laptop machine. You will very likely destroy the AVR chip and will probably cause expensive damage to the main board of the larger machine. Only connect your AVR to an RS-232 port using an interface chip—as described in this section.

Refer now to the diagram in Figure 6-3 which shows the general scheme for connecting an AVR chip's serial port to a larger machine's RS-232 port, using a level shifter chip.

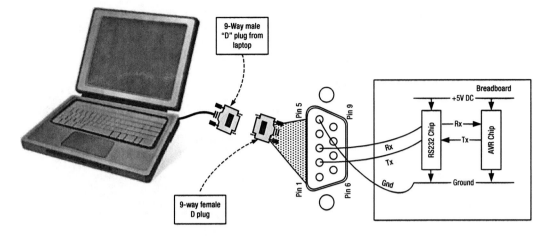

Figure 6-3. *Connecting your AVR project to an RS232 port*

The desktop or a laptop (as shown in the diagram) presents a male nine-pin serial port (also called a DB9 connector). This DB9 connector may be built into the machine, or it might be on the end of a USB to serial converter dongle.

The serial port will be using RS-232 voltage levels, which are quite a lot more than those used by the AVR (anywhere between 9 and 15 volts). So, on the AVR side, we need an RS-232 level converter chip (such as Maxim's MAX232 or MAX233 chip) to convert to/from the 5-volt logic levels that our AVR chip uses to RS-232 levels.

The MAX232 and MAX233 chips require only a +5V supply, but internally they use a circuit called a charge pump to develop the higher voltages that RS-232 requires. The MAX232 requires four additional capacitors to make it work, but the MAX233 does not need any external components for its voltage converters—so it's easier to use but more expensive. See Appendix C and the website for this book more detailed information on these chips.

The blow-up in Figure 6-3 shows the pin numbers of interest on the DB9 connector. The diagram illustrates the *solder* side, *not* the pins side. Figure 6-4 shows an actual connector with labels indicating the pin numbers. You may just be able to see that the pin numbers are etched into the plastic shell too: not all DB9 connectors have such etched pin numbers, but most do.

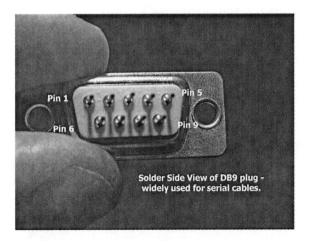

Figure 6-4. *DB9 connector, solder side pin ID*

For your development rig and test bed, remember that the recommended programmer for use with this book, the Pololu AVR–ISP programmer, features a serial channel that talks in logic levels rather than RS-232 and this *can* be directly connected to your AVR chip without the need for RS-232 level conversion.

RS-232 or Direct Logic Level Connection?

So, we have a technology choice: but, there are some circumstances where that choice is dictated for us by what we must connect with.

So, just where would we use an RS-232 setup, and where would we just use the programmer's built-in serial channel? Essentially it is a per-project choice. You would use a full RS-232 setup if

- The completed project has to talk directly to a desktop or laptop machine on a regular basis.

- You need to debug the project over a long period of time by making it send messages into a larger machine that can store an appreciable archive of messages on a hard drive or some other persistent storage device.

On the other hand, you would use the AVR programmer's logic level serial port if

- You plan to use the serial port for sending out debug messages while perfecting the project but do not have a requirement for the completed project to do so.

- Your project doesn't have the space for an RS-232 driver chip, or it won't bear the cost of one (such chips often cost more than the AVR).

After a project is completed and deployed, it's quite common to want (or need) to do an occasional update, or to need to briefly monitor the deployed project in situ via the serial channel to deal with some problem that emerges after deployment. For each project you do, you'll need to decide whether you would just temporarily reconnect the programmer for those debugging sessions or whether a more permanent arrangement will be needed.

Designing the Time-Getter Protocol

Now that we've looked at ways of actually connecting your AVR and your laptop or desktop machine, we need to look in detail at a simple communications protocol design that could use such a setup.

In this example we have the exclusive use of this communications medium (the serial cable), so we don't have to cater for the complexities of sharing the link with other users. However, we still need to allow for the possibility of errors and problems because, although it's a lot less likely, it's still possible that the data could be corrupted in transit and problems will always eventually occur due to disconnections, system errors, and so on. In this example, we deal with that issue very simply, by pausing between reads of the serial port, and by ignoring any messages that don't conform to our protocol specification.

Designing an application-specific communications protocol is quite detailed work, but, as long as you are absolutely clear on what you want your application to do, it's not overly difficult. Your aim must be to create a clear and unambiguous specification. Clearly differentiate between things that "shall" happen (mandatory things) and things that "can" happen (optional things). Specify exactly what message will be exchanged, what character set will be used, and—where applicable—the timescales that will be allowed for transactions to complete before an error or an abort occurs.

You can express the specification as a bullet list of requirements (as I do in the following list), or if it's something more complex , you can do it as a more formal document involving detailed "use cases" (intended to specify what will happen in all possible uses of the thing being specified). There are very good and detailed Wikipedia pages on use case diagrams and development.

We're keeping it simple here and now, so here is your specification as a simple bullet list:

- All messages shall be seven-bit ASCII coded text strings, terminated by a newline character (ASCII code 13).

- When it starts up, the AVR shall send a message containing the text "ALIVE" to the laptop. This is for information purposes only and the laptop does not need to make a response.

- The AVR can request the current local time from the laptop by sending the string "TIME?" followed by a newline character.

- The laptop shall respond to the "TIME?" message with a message containing the current local 24-hour clock time. This response shall contains hours, minutes, and seconds in the format "HH:MM.ss"—for example, for exactly 6 seconds past 3:20 p.m. it would send "15:20.06".

- The AVR can, optionally, send a message containing the string "ACK" when it correctly receives the time value, but the laptop does not wait for this or make any response to it.

- The laptop shall only respond to "TIME?" messages from the AVR. All other messages are ignored.

- The laptop shall send a message containing "HELLO" (followed by a new line) to the AVR at least once per hour. This is intended to allow it to discover if the AVR is still connected. On receipt of this message, the AVR shall send back "ALIVE".

- The AVR shall respond only to the "HELLO" message; it shall ignore any other message initiated from the laptop side.

We'll call this the time-getter protocol (for want of a better name). The flowcharts in Figure 6-5 show some possible software flows for the AVR and then the laptop-side software that might implement it.

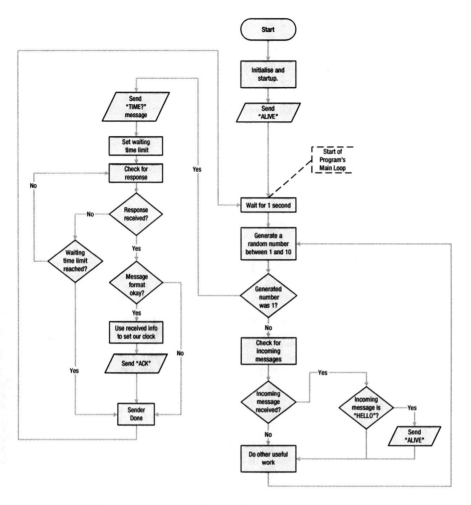

Figure 6-5. *AVR side flowchart to implement the time-getter protocol*

In the flowchart we see that the AVR software starts up, sends out its initial "ALIVE" message, and then begins its main loop, where first it waits and does nothing for one second. This pause is partly to allow messages to get sent, but also to make sure that the receiving process has a little time to do whatever it needs to respond to them before any additional messages are sent.

Next, in the main loop, we use a random number to simulate the need to occasionally fire off a "TIME?" request to the laptop. In the real thing, of course, we would probably do this based on the progress of time, perhaps once per hour. For the purposes of this example we need to do it a little more often. So, a random number is generated between 1 and 10:

- If the generated number is *not* 1, then a check for incoming messages is done. If any message has been received, we look to see if the message was "HELLO"; if it was, we fire off an "ALIVE" response message and rejoin the main loop flow at "Do other useful work."

- If the generated number *was* 1 (which of course it should be on average once every ten times) a "TIME?" request message is sent. Then, a time limit is set as to how long to wait for a response: this is a necessary complication. Without this refinement, if a response was never received, this wait loop would last forever and the whole AVR application would stop!

If the waiting time is eventually exhausted, we just abandon the effort to get an update and rejoin the main flow at "Do other useful work." If we *do* get a response message, we parse (check) it to make sure it is in the right format and contains sensible values. If it seems okay, we use the received info to update our local clock time. We then send an ACK message and return to the main flow at "Do other useful work."

Since this flowchart only represents a portion of what an AVR alarm clock would have to do, the "Do other useful work" box on this flowchart would contain a lot of other functions. These might include updating a display, checking to see if the set alarm time has been reached, sounding alarms, responding to key presses, requesting data from other sources, and so on.

Now let's look at what the laptop end of this protocol would look like (see Figure 6-6).

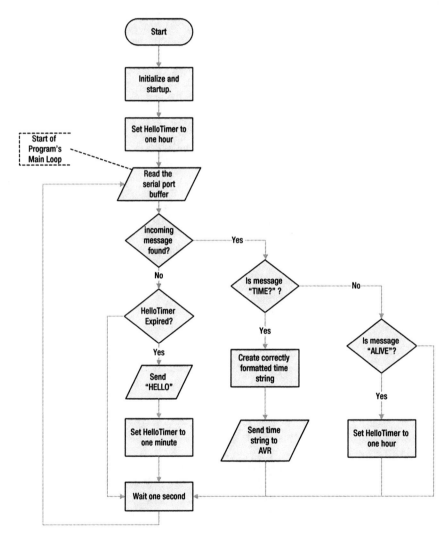

Figure 6-6. *Laptop (or desktop) side flowchart to implement the time-getter protocol*

This flow begins by initializing and then setting a timer called the HelloTimer. The HelloTimer counts down seconds until it's time for the AVR to be sent a "HELLO" message. Initially, the time is set to expire in one hour (3,600 seconds).

Entering the main loop, the laptop-side flowchart reads the serial port's buffer to see if there is a complete incoming message in it. If a complete message is ready to be processed, then the flow looks to see

- If the message is a time request (i.e., checks to see if the exact message is "TIME?"). If so, then it reads the current local time from the laptop operating system and converts it (if required) into the format required by the time-getter protocol specification. It then sends the formatted time string to the AVR.

- If the message received was not "TIME?" the flow looks to see if the message was "ALIVE"—which would be a response to a "HELLO" message that it had previously sent. If the message is not "ALIVE", then the message is ignored and control passes on to the "wait one second" box at the bottom of the main loop.

- If the received message was "ALIVE" then the flow resets the HelloTimer to 3,600 seconds so that it will not expire again for another hour. This meets the specification's requirement for at least hourly "HELLO" messages.

If there was no incoming message found, the main loop now checks to see if the HelloTimer has expired. If it has expired (time's up) then it sends the "HELLO" message and sets the HelloTimer to one minute. This gives the AVR one minute to respond before the laptop tries again. If the expected "ALIVE" response is received during that minute (it would normally be received back within a second or two) then the message handling portion of the flow will deal with it, as described previously. If no response is received, then after one minute, the main flow will try again.

At the bottom of the main flow there is a "Wait one second" box: this is intended to ensure that the protocol handler will take a nap now and again to let other processes in the system have some CPU time. It can happen that some problem makes continual data (usually gibberish) arrive at a serial port. This can be the result of a crashed or faulty AVR, or just a disconnected serial cable (which can act like an aerial and make the serial port hardware think it is seeing start-bits, resulting in spurious random characters appearing to arrive). Putting this wait time into the loop ensures that our protocol handler can't continuously chew up huge amounts of CPU time, if such a fault occurs. This kind of "good citizenship" is always a requirement for software that will run in a multitasking environment, such as is found in a laptop or desktop machine. As you can see from Figure 6-6, all possible flows are routed through the wait box to ensure that the program pauses regularly.

So now, we have a specification for our protocol and some flowcharts that could be used as guide to creating implementation software. It's often tempting, even with a relatively simple requirement like the time-getter protocol, to skip the specification and flowcharting stages and just dive straight in and start coding (been there, done that!) but you often find that it ends up taking you longer than you thought: it's a lot easier to see fundamental flaws of logic and approach in a flowchart than it is in screens full of code—and usually far easier and faster to rectify them: I know, I *was* that programmer!

Talking Tokens

So far in this chapter we've looked at protocols that involve sending messages that are in plain text (such as "HELLO"). However, we've also seen that microcontroller software must often be about making the most of limited memory and code space resources. In more complex projects than the examples we've used thus far, the cumulative overhead of storing, sending, parsing, and using human-readable messages can be quite large—albeit that such protocols are very easy to test and debug because the messages are easily understood.

There are various approaches to making application-to-application messaging more efficient. For example, in larger computers and in data networks compression techniques are used to minimize the amount of data that has to be stored or moved around, based on the fact that the processing power you need to compress and decompress data is a lot more abundant than either network bandwidth or memory capacity: the consumption of both of these latter resources can be minimized by using compression. However, microcontrollers are not large computers and while they have useful amounts of processing power, it's nothing like as much as you would find in a larger machine such as a desktop or a server computer.

Another method for minimizing the overhead of application messaging is through a process of tokenization. In this method, messages are reduced to a common set of tokens that all participants know about. Tokens are not unique to information technology; in fact, when you look around, humans have created many systems that use tokens. Money is a token system; originally, coins and later banknotes were tokens for gold.

Think about a theme park. In many such places, when you go in, you buy a set of "ride tokens." When you want to go on one of the park's rides, you hand over one or more tokens to the person running that ride. He doesn't tell you out loud how much the ride costs, he doesn't have to ask you for money, and he doesn't have to give you change. You just hand over tokens and everybody knows what it means—you can take the ride. It's a much faster system and needs less communication than not using tokens. In essence, it is a simplified, single-purpose version of money, intended to increase the efficiency of buying and selling one thing—theme park rides.

A theme park ride token scheme is a pretty simple one. There's only one thing to be handled and the only response required to presenting a token is to be let through onto a ride. However, the token concept can be put to good use in helping us with making communications to and from MCU applications as efficient as possible. If a set of tokens can be developed which all participants in an application environment agree on and can understand, then communication can be simplified and streamlined. For example, if all participants agree that, in their "ready" state, receiving a message containing a single byte with the value "01" is a token that means "HELLO" we have reduced the message size by about 84%[1] and the message parsing processing time and storage overhead are reduced too. This is a trivial example, but in a message-heavy application such as HA or machine control applications, the savings add up and are worth it.

How, then, would we develop a tokens model suitable for general use in various MCU projects that require communication? Many methods and tools are available for this development. In our case, we'll start by developing a simple object model. If you have a well-defined object model that all of your cooperating, communicating projects know about, then you can tokenize that communication. But first, you need to take a detour and walk through the topic of object models.

Object Models

Object-oriented programming kind of took over the world of computer programming during the 1990s. Until then, computer programs had been largely procedural; that is, the focus was mainly on the tasks and procedures to be performed rather than the objects involved.

For example, if the aim was to create a payroll system for a company, there would often be completely separate programs for different functions (paycheck printing, employee detail changes, report compilation, etc.). Each of these programs would make or use entries in the company database, but the database itself would—in programming terms—be just a passive participant.

Also, there would be a lot of duplication between the different programs (e.g., several of them would perform edits to employee records). If somebody left the company, the employee changes program would not automatically trigger the print out of her final paycheck. That would have to wait until the paycheck printing program was next run.

---

[1] Assuming that the actual message would be "HELLO"[newline] makes it six bytes long.

In an object-oriented approach to the same application, the database becomes an active object that can intelligently respond to changes: objects themselves can contain action methods; they are not merely the subject of the procedural actions. An object's methods can initiate messaging to other components of a system to do things automatically. The diagram in Figure 6-7 is an implementation of an object-oriented approach to the employee leaving scenario.

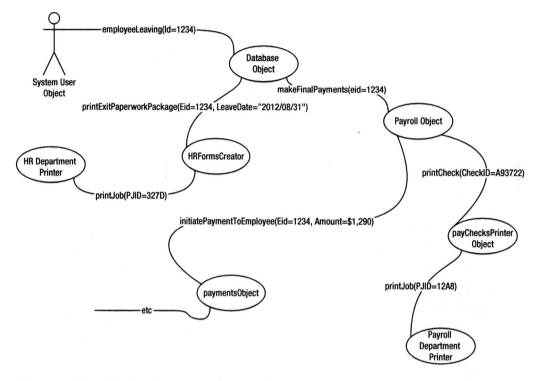

Figure 6-7. *Example of an object-oriented approach*

In this example, the various physical and logical entities that might take part in the "employee leaving" scenario are abstracted as objects. The database itself and the system user (in our example this would probably be the leaving employee's manager, or a human resources team member) are depicted as system objects, and there are objects representing functions within the human resources (HR) and payroll departments of the company.

Following is one possible sequence of events to enact the "employee leaving" scenario:

1. A system user, using a provided GUI on his computer, invokes the database object's "employee leaving" method. He provides the method with the employee's employee identification number (EID), which is 1234, and a leaving date (August 31, 2012).

2. The database object uses its internal resources to make the required changes to the employee's records and uses its internal methods to

   a. Instruct the HR forms creator object to create a set of exit paperwork (exit interview questions, return of company equipment form, etc.). The forms creator is supplied with the employee's EID and her leaving date. The form creator then marshals together the electronic forms that it knows should be part of a leaver's paperwork package and inserts the leaver's details and leave date onto them before using the print object's `printJob` method to create printed versions.

b. Invokes the Payroll object's makeFinalPayments method, again providing the EID. The payroll object uses the paychecksPrinter method printCheck to print off the employee's final paycheck and uses the paymentsObject's initiatePaymentToEmployee method to begin a bank to bank transfer of the required amount to the leaver's designated bank account.

In this object-oriented approach, some advantages are immediately apparent. For example, the software that implements the printCheck, initiatePaymentToEmployee, and printJob methods don't have to be duplicated within a "run Payroll" program and an "Employee Leaving" program, they are usable for both those purposes and any others that may require them, now or in future.

Of course, for the sake of simplicity, Figure 6-7 ignores additional detail. For example, in order to calculate the value of the final paycheck, the PayRoll object would need to invoke a method on the database object that returns employee 1234's leave date. Similarly, the HRFormsCreator object would probably need to use a database method to retrieve employee 1234's job role, since it's likely that the ExitPaperworkPackage contents would vary slightly by job type.

Nevertheless, it should be clear that objectifying elements within an application environment can confer many benefits. However, it does require some very careful thinking about the objects involved, and it's most important of all when objects must cooperate and communicate with one another to provide flexible, reusable solution components, as in the example we just looked at. The best way to structure such thought processes and to document the results produced is to build an object model.

Generally speaking, then, object-oriented programming (which is now the norm for most commercial programming) treats every component of a system as an object capable of intelligently reacting to changes to its environment, to itself, to other objects, and to contact from other objects. Inside, it works by giving objects the means to communicate events to one another and to offer method interfaces to one another, using protocols and messages that conform to an object model to which they all adhere. Most important for our purposes, the object model itself can be tokenized to minimize the communications and overhead necessary for its implementation.

Object models come in all shapes and sizes.[2] Also, there are many ways to actually implement an object model. Here and now, we're going to "imagineer" a small, simple, incomplete model—but one which nonetheless could be extended for use in HA projects. Let's imagine the SHOM (Smart Home Object Model).[3]

Smart Home Object Model

There are lots of ways to build and document object models. Unified Modeling Language (UML) provides a set of standards, techniques, syntaxes, and symbology for building object models. UML was originally aimed at programming activities, but it can be applicable to developing all kinds of object definitions. There is an excellent Wikipedia page on UML, and that contains a frequently updated list of links to tools (commercial and open source) that provide various UML-based object design packages.

Since our aims in this section are rather more modest than learning all about UML, we'll use a somewhat simpler approach to developing SHOM.

The two essential parts of an object model are

---

[2] If you want a look at a fully developed object model, take a look at things like Microsoft's COM (Component Object Model), the DOM (Document Object Model), or GNUStep which is based on the earlier NeXTSTEP mode: Wikipedia has umbrella pages for "Object model" with links to many different models.

[3] This is something that we are inventing for this book, it's not a standard object model for smart home/home automation, nor will it ever be! In fact, incredibly, there doesn't seem to be a single ready-made object model in the public domain for this purpose. There actually *are* quite a few home and building automation object models, but these have either been produced by commercial organizations that regard them as proprietary information which they don't release, or by international industry bodies that charge for them at rates way outside the price range of the average hobbyist. So, it seems as if we have to make our own.

- *Information about how objects are organized*: This is usually expressed as a hierarchy, which allows objects to be grouped together in such a way that traversing down the hierarchy takes you from the very general ("SHOM") through the less general ("Appliance") and through to a general class ("Electric Heater"), and down to the particular ("Space Heater"). The hierarchy model that we can use is superficially similar to the filesystems that we are all accustomed to using on our computers. We'll see the SHOM hierarchy soon.

- *Object definitions*: These consist of three sections, the object's properties, the object's methods, and object events.

The relationships implicit in the object hierarchy simplify the complexity of providing exhaustive property lists for every object type. Object types can inherit a great many common properties from the objects above them in the hierarchy. For example, an electric space heater object would inherit the generalized properties of all appliances and all electric heaters, (they can turn on and off, they can be uninstalled, they can be portable or nonportable, they have various settings, they have a color, etc.), as well as having its own particular properties (manufacturer name, model number, and manufacture date).

Likewise, an object's methods can be a mixture of ones that it inherits and specific ones. For our example, the electric space heater, the inherited methods will probably be things like `turnOn` and `turnOff`; its specific ones might be `setOnTime` and `setOffTime`—if it was of a type that had a built-in programmable timer.

Object events are things it can notify the world (well, the network) about. For example, our space heater might want to send out an event message to say `"offTimeReached"`, or it might send out an event message to say `"manualOn"` if someone had switched it on locally. For some object types, events can be triggered by using object methods that alter an object's properties. For example, calling our space heater object's `setState` method might result in the `SpaceHeater` object changing its `currentState` property to `On`, thus triggering a `"HeaterOn"` event message.

As you can tell, even from this brief description, things can be slotted into object models in many different ways, and there is never a 100% "right" answer; there will always be exceptions in matching the complexity of the real world to such a logical model.

The key to building a good object model is to classify objects by what things *are*, rather than what they *do*. A space heater is best classified under appliances rather than under the name of the space it heats: if you classify it under `\SHOM\Indoor\Space\AtticRoom\SpaceHeater` then you have classified what it does (heats the attic room) rather than what it is (a space heater). In this example case it's much better for the `SpaceHeater` object type to have a property called `CurrentLocation` that can be updated as needed.

So what would the SHOM hierarchy look like? Figure 6-8 shows a tree view of one possible version. Obviously, this is just a starting point, it would need a lot of work to complete, but it shows the general idea of a hierarchy of objects and how they relate to one another.

Let's just look at one object definition:

`\SHOM\Fitting\Electrical\Security&Access\Doorbell\BasicDoorbell`

If we were designing a basic doorbell using an AVR and we knew that it would be used as part of an HA setup, what properties, methods, and events would we want to give it? Table 6-4 lists them.

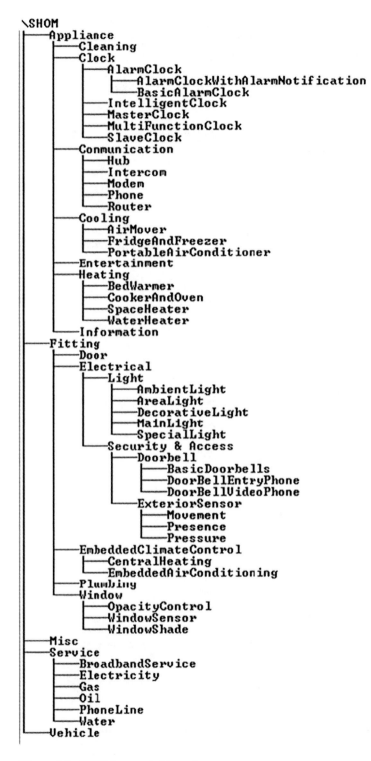

```
\SHOM
├──Appliance
│      ├──Cleaning
│      ├──Clock
│      │      ├──AlarmClock
│      │      │      ├──AlarmClockWithAlarmNotification
│      │      │      └──BasicAlarmClock
│      │      ├──IntelligentClock
│      │      ├──MasterClock
│      │      ├──MultiFunctionClock
│      │      └──SlaveClock
│      ├──Communication
│      │      ├──Hub
│      │      ├──Intercom
│      │      ├──Modem
│      │      ├──Phone
│      │      └──Router
│      ├──Cooling
│      │      ├──AirMover
│      │      ├──FridgeAndFreezer
│      │      └──PortableAirConditioner
│      ├──Entertainment
│      ├──Heating
│      │      ├──BedWarmer
│      │      ├──CookerAndOven
│      │      ├──SpaceHeater
│      │      └──WaterHeater
│      └──Information
├──Fitting
│      ├──Door
│      ├──Electrical
│      │      ├──Light
│      │      │      ├──AmbientLight
│      │      │      ├──AreaLight
│      │      │      ├──DecorativeLight
│      │      │      ├──MainLight
│      │      │      └──SpecialLight
│      │      └──Security & Access
│      │             ├──Doorbell
│      │             │      ├──BasicDoorbells
│      │             │      ├──DoorBellEntryPhone
│      │             │      └──DoorBellVideoPhone
│      │             └──ExteriorSensor
│      │                    ├──Movement
│      │                    ├──Presence
│      │                    └──Pressure
│      ├──EmbeddedClimateControl
│      │      ├──CentralHeating
│      │      └──EmbeddedAirConditioning
│      ├──Plumbing
│      └──Window
│             ├──OpacityControl
│             ├──WindowSensor
│             └──WindowShade
├──Misc
├──Service
│      ├──BroadbandService
│      ├──Electricity
│      ├──Gas
│      ├──Oil
│      ├──PhoneLine
│      └──Water
└──Vehicle
```

Figure 6-8. *SHOM example hierarchy*

Table 6-4. *Hypothetical SHOM Doorbell Object*

Property	Method	Event	Possible Values and Description
DoorbellLocation			Freeform string: for example "Front Door" or "Side Entrance"
HasMultipleTunes			True or False
CanTurnOff			True or False, can be commanded to go inactive (vacations, night times, etc.)
CurrentState			0 = Disabled 1 = Enabled
IsRinging			True or False
CurrentStatus			Bitmask indicating Boolean values as follows: Bit 0 = Battery Low Bit 1 = On Mains Bit 2 = Has sounded since last power on Bit 3 = Bellpush Button Stuck Detected Bit 4 = Bellpush Illuminated
VersionInfo			Returns the current firmware version string from the doorbell MCU.
	EnableDoorbell()		When called, this method ensures the doorbell is enabled.
	DisableDoorbell()		When called, this method ensures the doorbell is disabled and will not respond to the Bellpush. Do not disturb!
	SetTune(tuneNumber)		Sets the doorbell to play the indicated tune (if available) when the Bellpush is pressed.
	TestDoorbell()		Rings the doorbell as if someone had pressed the Bellpush
	SetBellPushLight(State)		Set the Bellpush's internal light to the indicated state (on or off).
	DoReset()		Do a complete restart of the doorbell hardware and software.

(*continued*)

Table 6-4. (*continued*)

Property	Method	Event	Possible Values and Description
		DoorbellActivated	Someone has pressed the Bellpush, or a TestDoorbell() method has been used.
		DoorbellDisabled	The doorbell has been disabled.
		DoorbellEnabled	The doorbell has been enabled
		DoorbellBatteryLow	The doorbell has detected its batteries are almost out of power.

And this is for a simple, basic doorbell. This is why the SHOM differentiates between this and the—even more complex—entry phone types.

In fact, pretty much all the properties, methods and events in the foregoing list will be common to all doorbells, so in a real implementation it's likely that the BasicDoorbells object type would inherit all these from the Doorbells object definition, or the nodes above that. The DoorbellEntryPhone object type would probably have all the items in the table too, plus additional characteristics, specific to its audio and/or video capabilities.

Object Tokenizing

So, to bring the thought streams of tokenization and objectification together . . . how do we gain the benefits of both by reducing an object model to tokens?

There are lots of ways to do this; we'll look at just one that is particularly suitable for use in MCU land, because it minimizes resource usage. Various object models do it by assigning huge, long GUID (Globally Unique IDs) to each object type. However, that is—in our terms—a resource-hungry approach (since GUIDs tend to be very long strings of numbers and digits). Because we don't need our IDs to be unique except within our own project space, we can take a simple approach.

As we saw in the previous section, to be useful, an object model has to be adhered to by all the participants in a particular application environment; otherwise they'll all be talking at cross-purposes. Clearly, then, the first thing to do is to develop and finalize your object model. You can grab one of the free UML object modeling packages (such as Umbrello) if you want to do a formal design that you can later share, or export files to your favorite programming language.

If your model is very simple or if you're happy to manually implement the software expression of the model yourself, then you can do it "old school" on pencil and paper, or just use your desktop machine to mock up the hierarchy part using a file tree (this is how I did the rough layout for SHOM: I just created the required object names as a hierarchy of directories, then used the tree command, which is available at the Unix and Windows command line prompts to get the tree display we saw earlier). You'll find, whatever method you use, that actually seeing the model in front of you and fleshing it out makes you think much more clearly about the whole approach you are taking.

To build our model, what we need to do is assign a sequential index number (starting from zero) to each item at each level in the hierarchy. This is rather like assigning an address to every house in a street that's just been newly built. That's what we do in Figure 6-9.

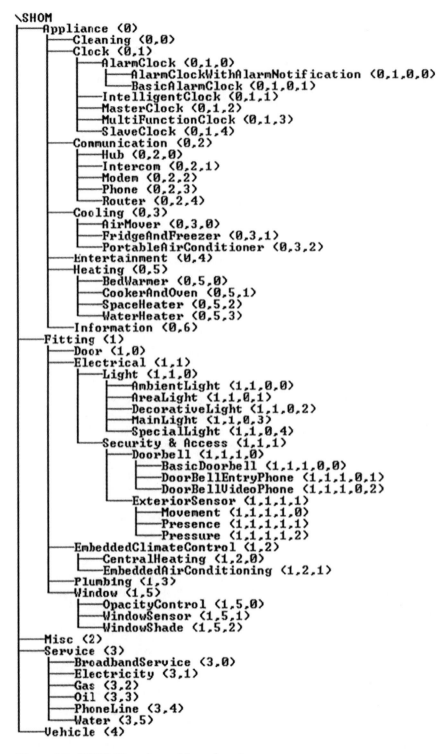

```
\SHOM
├──── Appliance (0)
│      ├──── Cleaning (0,0)
│      ├──── Clock (0,1)
│      │      ├──── AlarmClock (0,1,0)
│      │      │      ├──── AlarmClockWithAlarmNotification (0,1,0,0)
│      │      │      └──── BasicAlarmClock (0,1,0,1)
│      │      ├──── IntelligentClock (0,1,1)
│      │      ├──── MasterClock (0,1,2)
│      │      ├──── MultiFunctionClock (0,1,3)
│      │      └──── SlaveClock (0,1,4)
│      ├──── Communication (0,2)
│      │      ├──── Hub (0,2,0)
│      │      ├──── Intercom (0,2,1)
│      │      ├──── Modem (0,2,2)
│      │      ├──── Phone (0,2,3)
│      │      └──── Router (0,2,4)
│      ├──── Cooling (0,3)
│      │      ├──── AirMover (0,3,0)
│      │      ├──── FridgeAndFreezer (0,3,1)
│      │      └──── PortableAirConditioner (0,3,2)
│      ├──── Entertainment (0,4)
│      ├──── Heating (0,5)
│      │      ├──── BedWarmer (0,5,0)
│      │      ├──── CookerAndOven (0,5,1)
│      │      ├──── SpaceHeater (0,5,2)
│      │      └──── WaterHeater (0,5,3)
│      └──── Information (0,6)
├──── Fitting (1)
│      ├──── Door (1,0)
│      ├──── Electrical (1,1)
│      │      ├──── Light (1,1,0)
│      │      │      ├──── AmbientLight (1,1,0,0)
│      │      │      ├──── AreaLight (1,1,0,1)
│      │      │      ├──── DecorativeLight (1,1,0,2)
│      │      │      ├──── MainLight (1,1,0,3)
│      │      │      └──── SpecialLight (1,1,0,4)
│      │      └──── Security & Access (1,1,1)
│      │             ├──── Doorbell (1,1,1,0)
│      │             │      ├──── BasicDoorbell (1,1,1,0,0)
│      │             │      ├──── DoorBellEntryPhone (1,1,1,0,1)
│      │             │      └──── DoorBellVideoPhone (1,1,1,0,2)
│      │             └──── ExteriorSensor (1,1,1,1)
│      │                    ├──── Movement (1,1,1,1,0)
│      │                    ├──── Presence (1,1,1,1,1)
│      │                    └──── Pressure (1,1,1,1,2)
│      ├──── EmbeddedClimateControl (1,2)
│      │      ├──── CentralHeating (1,2,0)
│      │      └──── EmbeddedAirConditioning (1,2,1)
│      ├──── Plumbing (1,3)
│      └──── Window (1,5)
│             ├──── OpacityControl (1,5,0)
│             ├──── WindowSensor (1,5,1)
│             └──── WindowShade (1,5,2)
├──── Misc (2)
├──── Service (3)
│      ├──── BroadbandService (3,0)
│      ├──── Electricity (3,1)
│      ├──── Gas (3,2)
│      ├──── Oil (3,3)
│      ├──── PhoneLine (3,4)
│      └──── Water (3,5)
└──── Vehicle (4)
```

Figure 6-9. *SHOM hierarchy—addressed version*

As the diagram shows, each item at each level now has a unique number sequence by which it can be found, For example, we have assigned the BasicDoorbells type a unique numbered sequence of (1,1,1,0,0) which would allow us to refer to that object type as, 11100 which is a five-byte token. So instead of having to specify the following, which is 68 bytes long, each and every time we want to use such an object, we can now use just 5 bytes to identify our BasicDoorbells object type:

\SHOM\Fittings\Electrical\Security & Access\Doorbells\BasicDoorbells

Similarly, we could refer to a SpaceHeaters (object 0,5,2) by the three-byte index 052 instead of

\SHOM\Appliances\Heating\SpaceHeaters

which, again, saves us precious memory space and communication bandwidth. We would also tokenize the method and event IDs and ultimately, instead of a

\SHOM\Fittings\Electrical\Security & Access\Doorbells\BasicDoorbells

object generating a

DoorbellActivated

event, our MCU-based doorbell would be a 11100 object that has generated a type 0 event (since the DoorbellActivated event is the first listed event for that object type in Table 6-4.

Implementing a Tokenized Object Model on AVR

You've now seen some examples of how to build and tokenize an object model. In a situation where you were building a large set of cooperating projects you might very well use this kind of scheme. Let's round off this chapter by looking at the general considerations that might apply if you were to actually do a full SHOM implementation using HA nodes run by AVR microcontrollers.

A detailed implementation of a tokenized object model is probably another book in itself, but essentially, the idea would be to use the Arduino software compiler's preprocessor (essentially the WINAVR preprocessor) to process header files that contain a human-readable version of the object model, including the object hierarchy and the methods and properties of each node in the hierarchy. The preprocessor would produce a binary file containing data structures that express the object model as a compact binary map. Then, the AVR of each application merely has to have a copy of this map in its EEPROM memory.

In a real implementation (such as one for SHOM) the following additional considerations would need to be taken into account:

- Provision would need to be made for all participating devices to get an update of the object map, as, inevitably, there would be fairly frequent updates to it.

- To allow for updates, the object model itself would need to have an embedded version number. This could either be done by replacing the \SHOM at the top of the map (see Figure 6-9) with a name that includes the version number (e.g., \SHOM_V2.1.7) or simply by prefixing the \SHOM root with a version number. and bumping that number whenever necessary. For example, referring to Figure 6-9, instead of communication hubs being 0,2,0 they would (in, say, SHOM version five) be 5,0,2,0.

- In a full implementation it would probably be necessary to use some kind of object coordination server as an always-on network node. Possibly, this would be a program running as a service inside a desktop machine, but it could be a single-purpose AVR module, or even a real Arduino(!), equipped with multiple communications interfaces (serial port(s), CAT5 shield, etc.). SHOM-compliant devices, when starting up, would send out a message via their communications interface declaring their object type and relevant properties and the server would grant them permission to operate in the environment, give them required local information (such as the time and date, or the SHOM version in use across the configuration) and also provide them with SHOM updates if needed.

- There would need to be a discovery mechanism, perhaps via the object server, for participating devices. For example, in this full implementation an intelligent alarm clock (0,1,1) might want to dynamically discover an accurate time source, a master clock (0,1,2). Such an alarm clock *could* just be hard-coded with the details of a master clock, but a dynamic discovery mechanism would be better because it is more proof against changes in the configuration, and more reusable—you could slot it into any equivalent environment and it would just work.

- The model, as developed in this chapter, would probably need some tweaks. For example, if we fully expanded the \SHOM\Appliances\Entertainment node of the object map, it's conceivable that now, or in future, there would be more than 256 classes of home entertainment device (PVR, VCR, DVD Player, CD Player, MP3 Player, Record Player, Cassette Player, RtR tape, Mini-Disc, Satellite Receiver, DVB-t Receiver, VCR/DVD Combo, etc.). This would mean that, in a full implementation, it *might* be necessary to find ways to accommodate bigger per-node number ranges.

Clearly, a full implementation of a tokenized object model would be a complex business. Normally these kinds of schemes are implemented by building "include files" that all participating programs use to pick up the standard set of addressing and token values. You could also use TCP/IP methods (such as object IP addresses or port numbers for each object or class of object). So, there are a number of ready-made and well understood and supported ways in which your object model could be built.

Summary of Object Models and Tokenization

To summarize, cooperating objects need to operate to a known communication protocol, and to an agreed object model. Because of the memory resource constraints inherent in eight-bit microcontrollers, and the need to keep messages as short as possible, using a tokenized version of the object model is a very good fit. Although it's quite a chore to put it all together, it does pay off in the long run and there are numerous tools and standards to help you do it.

Summary

In this chapter we have looked at examples of messaging between AVR microcontrollers and their peers and between microcontroller and desktop machines. We've looked at a couple of connection methods and how the hardware for those looks. We have seen some of the ways in which communication can be made more reliable and how errors can be detected. We have looked at the resource requirements for sophisticated network software stacks, and seen how that can sometimes be a problem in MCU land.

We've seen how to simplify application-level messaging back to basics and we have developed the specification and flowcharts for a simple, serially interfaced, AVR clock application. Finally, we have seen how an object model suitable for use in Smart Home/Home Automation projects could be developed and how the use of tokenization could make such a model usable in MCU projects and summarizes the kind of considerations necessary to grow it into a full-fledged application support infrastructure.

Coming up

Part 2: Introduction to the Projects Section. Please fasten your safety belt.

The Projects

■ ■ ■

CHAPTER 7

Introduction to the Projects Section

(Stephen Leacock) "Writing is not hard. Just get paper and pencil, sit down, and write as it occurs to you. The writing is easy—it's the occurring that's hard."

I think microcontrollers can be a bit like that. You have a world of possibility–a blank page if you will–and you can combine the intelligence of your MCU, your own imagination, and the fantastic toolkits you have at your disposal to build pretty much whatever you can imagine. But, what will you build?

For some people, amassing the tools and the parts to build MCU projects can turn out to be most of the fun. Like a "wannabe" chef who spends ages sharpening knives, polishing silverware, and finding neat and tidy places for every little implement, it's easy to get mesmerized by the tools and the processes and lose sight of what it's all for. For other people it's the other way around: they have a plethora of ideas, but no clear idea how to break the overall task down into manageable steps to make it happen.

So far in this book we've looked a lot at the "how" and the "why" but not so much at the "what"–as in *"What am I going to make with all these fancy new capabilities, tools, and components?"* So, in this section of the book our focus is definitely on the "what." We're going to run through a number of projects, small ones and not so small ones, that I hope will give you ideas if you need them. I also hope you'll gain a few perspectives on the different activities concerned with MCU projects and their possible sequencing. Another possible side effect may be that you'll start to see the contents of your plastics and cardboard recycling bin in a whole new way!.

Project Bases

In most projects in this section you have a simple choice about what base to build upon. The choices are one of the following:

- Building the project on the test rig that we built in Chapter 2.

- Building the project on a piece of solder board of some kind (see The Duck Shooter game in Chapter 12 for an example of doing it this way).

- Using a freeware package like Eagle or Fritzing to design a printed circuit board for the project and building your version of the project onto that. Of course, this can be quite an expensive option, since although the software mentioned is free (and there are other free software packages, too), when you use them to design a PCB you still have to pay someone to make your circuit board from the design that is produced by the package.

Deciding which project to build in which way is going to be largely determined by whether you regard the project in question as a "keeper" project. In other words, do you plan to build up the project, get it working, stand back in awe of its wondrousness for a while, and then tear it down and reuse the components for something new? Or, do you plan to deploy the project to your home, your office, or your car as a permanent fixture? If the former, then you'll want to build the project on the test rig breadboard. If the latter, then you'll want to build your project on something that you can build into a box and have it become a piece of "set and forget" infrastructure in your home or office.

Building up the project on the test rig has the advantage that necessary things like the power supply, power rail smoothing capacitors, and the all-important ISP connector for updating the MCU software are already in place; if you're building a custom project board, you will have to provide these things as part of your build. So, it's your decision as to what base you use for the electronics side of the projects. The circuit diagrams mostly assume you'll be building a custom board, so if you're building on the test rig, simply ignore the elements previously listed above (PSU, ISP, etc.), since you already have them.

Project Chapter Formats

In general, the format of each project chapter is

- A description of the project: what it does, why you might want to build it.

- A design discussion, detailing the trade-offs and features of the design.

- A "maker" section, which deals with how to make any mechanical elements of the project and where you might find the parts you need.

- A circuit diagram for the electronic aspects of the project (including the MCU).

- Details of the project software. In most cases the software is too long to reproduce in full, so there is a summary of the software and the full software listing is available for download.

- A code walk of the software that names all the software's functions and provides a short commentary about what each one does. This code walk is intended to help you understand the full software listing when you download it from the book's web site (http://www.apress.com/9781430244462).

Each project is illustrated with diagrams and photos that should help you build one of your own, or more likely make your own adaptation of it. Even if you start by building the project as presented here, you'll learn a lot more from modifying it later on to meet your own needs. In many cases you'll probably make improvements or enhancements to my original design in the process of customization.

The difficulty of legibly reproducing circuit diagrams with lots of small detail in a printed book is something that authors and publishers have always struggled with. Fortunately, the Internet makes it possible to offer you an alternative. If there is detail in a circuit diagram that you can't make out in this book, go to the book's web site where you will find electronic versions of all the diagrams in formats that will enable you to enlarge details that may be hard to see on the page. As mentioned previously, the full software listings are available on the web site too.

All the circuit diagrams have been reproduced here from my original completed designs, so they should work for you just as well as they did for me. However, if you find any mistakes please let me know via the publisher, so that we can verify the error and put corrections on the web site to help other people. Similarly, if any components or parts used in the projects should become unavailable between the writing of this book and when you need them, we will put information on the web site about possible workarounds or replacement products that may serve the same purpose.

Be aware of static electricity. Get yourself an anti-static work mat and wrist band if you can. Think about this. You'll have had a static shock yourself at some stage, perhaps from a car door, from a door handle, or from touching some piece of earthed equipment. So you, at whatever size you are, can get static electricity shocks from things. But you get static shocks all day every day from things; it's just that most of them are much too small to register with your nervous system. But now, reflect that you are handling chips that have millions of transistors inside them, many of which are less than one millionth of an inch across. On that scale, the tiny shocks that you don't even notice seem like lightning bolts to those tiny components and can destroy or weaken them in an instant.

Of course, most modern semiconductors have a certain degree of inbuilt protection on their external pin connections, but we need to help things along by being aware that we bring static electricity to the work bench with us and generate more while we're working. So, using an anti-static kit is a good habit to get into. Don't get paranoid about static, but don't pretend it doesn't exist: You may not zap your semiconductors outright, but a lack of static control can shorten their life span and/or make them operate unreliably.

Finally, please **work safely**. You are dealing with electricity in these projects and electricity should *always* be treated with respect; even if you are only dealing with 5 volts, respect and care should be the watchwords. Ensure that your power supply is a safe one. It should be appropriately fused on the mains side and on the DC output side. Inappropriate fuse values are a major safety hazard. Fitting a 10 amp fuse to a device that only ever uses 1 amp is crazy and potentially dangerous: if a fault occurs in the device then it could heat up nicely and even catch fire before it blows the fuse. Try to fuse your devices at no more than what they need plus perhaps 10% extra. Appropriate AC-side fusing should ensure that, should anything go wrong, you'll have a dead device on your hands, not a house fire. Appropriate DC-side fusing might make the difference between having to replace the fuse and having to replace a whole board full of components.

When you are soldering, wear goggles if you can, to protect your eyes from the smoke. Always make sure your work area is well ventilated so that you don't have to breathe in the solder fumes and smoke; use a desk fan set on low to waft smoke away toward the window. Use a soldering iron that (as described in Chapter 6) has some kind of holster or holder so that you don't burn holes in your carpets or furniture or yourself. Never, ever flick solder around; it stays hot for a long time after it leaves the iron. If you need to remove solder from the iron, use a damp (but not wet) ball of tissue paper or scrap cotton material.

If you need to remove solder from your project board (e.g., because you put a little too much on and it has bridged two contacts when you didn't mean for that to happen), get yourself a solder sucker. These are quite cheap to buy, and they are really a manually operated suction pump with a heat-resistant tip that can be used to suck molten solder away from a board.

So, work safe, use a helping-hands project gripper if you have one and be sensible and very careful about soldering iron usage.

Project Scope and Difficulty

The projects are presented in no particular order. Some of the projects are large and some are small. They're also of various types–some are purely electronic, but many include some degree of "makery"–using easy-to-get materials (such as stick wood) or adapting or reusing stuff such as discarded plastic packaging or materials.

So, if you have a preference for starting with, say, a simple project, choose one that you can build up on the test bed rig. If you're inclined to build something that has more of a mechanical element to it, you'll probably want to start with a project like the sliding panel which is heavier on construction and not so heavy on electronics.

The simple fact is that the only thing that the projects truly have in common is that there is an AVR embedded in each and every one. But, that's why we're here! I hope you build at least one of the projects in this section and I hope enjoy reading about them all.

■ ■ ■

CHAPTER 8

Project 1: Good Evening, Mr. Bond: Your Secret Panel

We're in at the deep end with this project. There is some fairly complicated mechanical making and woodwork in this project. There is no reason at all why you should do this project first, so if it seems a bit daunting and you want to build up to it, have a look at some of the simpler projects first.

This project celebrates that old favorite of certain movie and story genres–the secret panel–the kind of panel that unexpectedly opens in the wood paneling of a classic country house library when you touch the contacts embedded in both eyes of a portrait on the wall, or turn the head of an apparently immobile statue! But what's behind the panel . . .? Well, that's rather up to you.

A Life Ruined by Movies and TV

I admit it. When I was younger, I watched way too much Batman, Thunderbirds, Scooby Doo, Secret Service movies, and body-in-the-library mysteries. Mystery and secrets are the themes that tie these entertainments together. All of them (at one time or another) featured a secret door or a secret panel, inside which was variously concealed an underground silo full of advanced technology, a crazy janitor named Jameson, a control panel with switches marked "Launch Missiles," or a bloodstained murder weapon. I always wanted a reason to have a secret panel in my own house, but I always struggled to think of a use for it in my own real life.

The shameful truth is that, if I'm honest, I *still* struggle to think of what I am really going to use it for–but the good news is that now that I have built my "secret panel," I will finally have to give it some serious thought!

Making It Real

Oh boy, there are so many ways to do this, but the most obvious ones are not necessarily the best. Let's start by stating the basic requirements, which are these:

- A small panel is to be dragged about 9–12 inches and back again by using an electric motor under the control of an MCU.

- The panel must slide smoothly (but not too quickly, you want to savor the moment of movement and revelation) between its open and closed positions.

- The panel must always return to the same open and closed positions; these positions cannot vary by more than very small amounts.

- The panel must be of a size that is easily concealed, or it must blend in as much as possible with whatever it is set into.

- The panel must only be activated by a concealed activation method (a hidden button, etc.).

- The secret panel assembly as a whole must operate in vertical or horizontal orientation. It must be able to be set in a wall or into a desk.

- The panel should be safe–that is, its mechanism should not be strong enough to cut off somebody's finger!

- The panel, when it opens, must reveal something utterly astounding!

I'm afraid that although I have some ideas, the revelation is mostly going to be up to you!

The Fireline Fiasco

My first attempt at this project involved a convoluted system of pulleys and used fireline (a very strong plastic thread that's used for jewelry and fishing line) which allowed a single motor with two spools to push *and* pull the panel into position (see Figure 8-1).

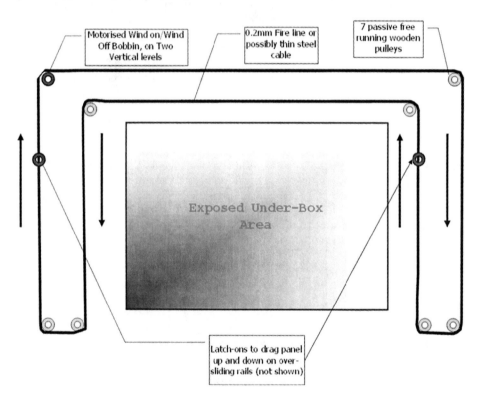

Figure 8-1. Thread and pulley version (failed)

This worked pretty well, but only for about a day! It turns out that fireline, at least for this use, stretches slightly and with a fairly long run like this, it meant that the push-pull motor arrangement (top left in the diagram) was not viable since the thread got progressively longer and thus looser. After a day or so of use, it got slack enough to jump off the winding spools and wreck the whole scheme!

Next, I tried using some steel garden wire in place of the fireline, but this idea was a nonstarter with the motors that I had on hand. Steel garden wire is not very flexible, and when used with the required number of right-angled turns, it exerted more drag than the motor could handle. With a more powerful motor and a slightly thinner wire, this idea might work. The other problem that I became aware of, before I gave up on this approach, was that the wooden pulleys (I used the same arrangement as described in the Solenoid leverage example in Chapter 4) started to chew through the wooden mount and go off the true when subjected to the force required. So, no prize for this approach! I have no doubt that with a metal frame, some metal pulleys with smooth bearings, and a powerful motor, it probably could work, but it would get pretty expensive, pretty fast!

My next idea was a simple one. The panel is pulled open by the motor, again just using fireline threads. Then, when the motor turns the other way, a counterbalancing weight pulls the panel from the other end to return it to the closed position. Since, in this arrangement, the fireline is not pushing *and* pulling, it doesn't matter if it stretches a little. However, this scheme would presuppose that the panel will be mounted in a place where there would be space for this counterbalance to travel up and down, and, actually, I struggled to envisage many installation scenarios where that might be true. Similarly, I tried out but discounted the idea of return springs; the kind of return springs you would need would be quite long and might be hard to fit into the overall mechanism space. Also, you would have to tether the panel to the springs with something lightweight but strong, and if that something stretched . . . then again you would encounter the precision problem.

Thinking Again

The absolutely ideal solution would be a helical spring. This is the kind of rotary spring that's built into extensible measuring tapes, or extensible "queue barriers," the kind you often see in stores, museums, or stadiums. However, I tried using the helical spring from a measuring tape (the most obvious low-cost source of such a spring) and found that it's not nearly strong enough for this purpose. Springs with the kind of return force required are meant for use in things like elevator car doors, and they come with a very unattractive price tag of several hundred dollars. Curses! Foiled again!

Next, I tried some steel-threaded rod. This stuff can be bought in almost any hardware store and is used for a variety of things in the building trade. It's also pretty cheap. If you put a nut on the threaded rod and turn the rod while holding the nut still, the nut slowly moves up or down. You do have to spin the rod fairly fast to get a decent speed of movement–but the amount of force required to turn the rod is actually quite small due to the immense amount of leverage involved. So this idea was promising.

After a search on the Internet, I found that many model makers and woodworking sources have a "threaded insert," which you can put inside a block of wood and which presents an internal thread suitable for use with a threaded rod. Figure 8-2 shows one of these.

Figure 8-2. *Threaded insert*

This insert in Figure 8-2 has a metric M6 thread through the center–but you can get these in various metric or imperial sizes from the following sources:

- www.amazon.com (United States). Search for "threaded insert" in "Industrial and scientific" category.

- www.modelfixings.co.uk (UK).

On the outside, the insert has a coarse thread that can chew its way into a suitably sized hole through a wooden block and an Allen key head to help you screw it into the wood.

My idea was to use a couple of these fixed onto some small wood blocks on each side of the sliding panel. I built this idea up, but it has two crucial drawbacks. First, it's far, far too slow; I started with a 60 rpm motor and the panel movement was positively glacial! I tried using a 500 rpm motor, but the panel still moved too slowly. Worse (and this is the second problem), when you spin the threaded rods at that speed you really do need proper metal ball-race bearings at each end. Using holes in the wood at each end of the rod really doesn't work when those spin speeds are involved. Since these threaded rods are almost never quite straight, they generate vibration when spun at any speed–especially at the lengths required here; in short, the mechanism would shake itself apart in no time. The threads on the standard rods are too fine.

Again, there is a fix for this. You could use "Acme" threaded rods (or the similar "trapezoidal threaded" rods) and nuts. These kind of threads are much more suitable and high precision. The rods are usually thicker and the threads are more coarse, but deeper. These are intended for exactly this kind of use. If you look at the thread on a bench vise or a manual car jack, you'll likely find one of these threads in use there. The problem is that if you elect to use one of these threads you increase the cost of the project by something like an order of magnitude–they are not cheap. You'd also have to find a source of Acme or Trapezoidal threaded inserts–which I have not yet managed to do. So, this approach comes close, but it seems to run into the sand on details and cost.

Racking Up a Success

Finally, I settled on something intended for robotics or model vehicle use. There are lots of gearboxes made for driving wheeled vehicles. Here, a motor/gearbox assembly is mounted in a robot, or a model vehicle, and provides controlled drive to its wheels. If we hold such an assembly captive in a frame, and fit it with cogs instead of wheels, it can drag a panel back and forth. This is effectively a rack-and-pinion system. The panel is fitted with tracks on its underside that mesh with the cogs, as in Figure 8-3.

Figure 8-3. *Sliding panel underside*

Many suitable gearboxes and motor assemblies are available:

- www.pololu.com/catalog/category/34 (United States and global).

Or, for a very low-cost example–the one I used, in fact:

- www.mindsetsonline.co.uk/product_info.php?products_id=200 (UK).

You can get the rack parts from

- www.robotmarketplace.com (various products–search for rack).

- www.technobots.co.uk (search for part numbers 4600-024 and 4600-110).

The exact details of the woodwork part of this project will vary. The essential requirement is to make the panel that you want to slide and build everything else around it. The panel should be as symmetrical as you can make it, it should be as smooth and flat as you can make it, and it should be fairly lightweight. If the panel surface will be visible, it will have to match the surrounding surface if it's not to stick out like a sore thumb. If you're lucky enough to have a wood-paneled room (or, even better, be building one), you might be able to find a way to set your project into the paneling–everybody's idea of a classic secret panel.

Probably (as in my prototype), it will have to be of a size that can easily hide behind a "concealer," which might be a picture, a mirror, or a drape or wall hanging of some kind. If it's set into a horizontal surface like a desk, worktop, or shelf, it might be concealed beneath a mouse mat, a desktop CD-ROM, a blotting pad, a writing surface, an "in tray," a clock, a large ornament, a small loudspeaker, a desk tidy–really the possibilities are endless.

The sticking point is usually going to be space; you'll need space behind or under your secret panel to allow for the mechanism and the concealed compartment. Hollowing out such a space in a brick or concrete wall can be done but is problematic. There may not be enough space back there for what you need. However, it can be a lot easier to accommodate in a less solid structure, such as the following:

- A drywall.

- A large walk-in closet or an enclosed shelving unit.

- The kind of custom cabinetry often made for a home-theatre setup.

- A desk or work surface.

Of course, always bear in mind that your panel doesn't have to be a sliding one (although that's what we're building here). It could be a flip-open panel that looks like a picture or a decorative molding; one that flips open when you activate a solenoid via your AVR.

Once you have your panel made, you need to design a frame. The frame must

- Be rigid enough to remain square and not distort when you mount it behind something else.

- Be suitable for fitting a backbox or under-box onto.

- Be suitable for mounting the motor on.

- Provide a slideway for the panel.

The photo sequence in Figures 8-4 through 8-6 shows my version of the project parts; luckily I had a drywall that I could play around with so I was able to cut a hole, right through into a closet on the other side. This meant that I could keep everything hidden from view. I'll go into some of these parts in more detail later in the chapter.

■ **Caution** Are you making a permanent version of this project for serious use? It's important to ensure that if the panel jams, its fuse blows, or its power supply fails, you can still access the mechanism and electronics in some way. You don't want to have to smash the thing apart if somebody fools around with it and blows the fuse. It's meant to be secure by virtue of being secret; it's not meant to be impregnable!

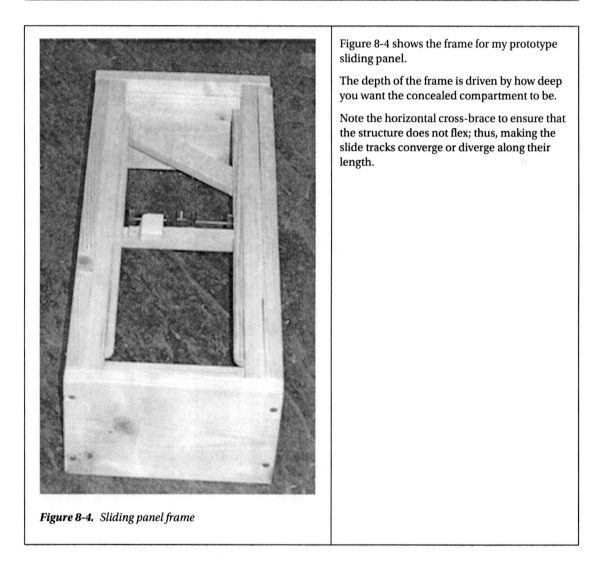

Figure 8-4. Sliding panel frame

Figure 8-4 shows the frame for my prototype sliding panel.

The depth of the frame is driven by how deep you want the concealed compartment to be.

Note the horizontal cross-brace to ensure that the structure does not flex; thus, making the slide tracks converge or diverge along their length.

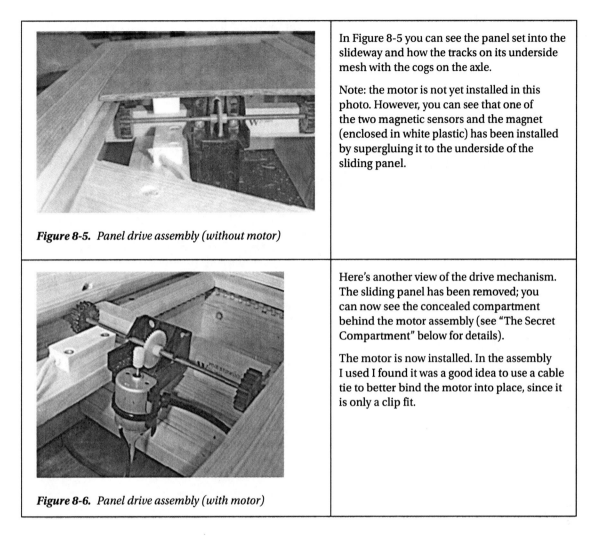

	In Figure 8-5 you can see the panel set into the slideway and how the tracks on its underside mesh with the cogs on the axle.
	Note: the motor is not yet installed in this photo. However, you can see that one of the two magnetic sensors and the magnet (enclosed in white plastic) has been installed by supergluing it to the underside of the sliding panel.
Figure 8-5. *Panel drive assembly (without motor)*	
	Here's another view of the drive mechanism. The sliding panel has been removed; you can now see the concealed compartment behind the motor assembly (see "The Secret Compartment" below for details).
	The motor is now installed. In the assembly I used I found it was a good idea to use a cable tie to better bind the motor into place, since it is only a clip fit.
Figure 8-6. *Panel drive assembly (with motor)*	

Hiding the Button

Of course, it's pointless to have a secret panel if you have an obvious activation button for it. So finding a nonobvious method of activating your secret panel is quite important.

You *could* just have a hidden keypad that sits alongside the panel, but that's a bit, well, tedious. In all the best movies, it just takes a finger jab at a cunningly concealed button to make the panel slide or flip open. So, where can we hide the button? I investigated several possibilities.

- Inside a figurine of "The Stig" (the mystery test driver from the BBC TV series "Top Gear"). This started out life as a novelty gift. It contained shower gel. When it was empty I decided not to throw it away but to keep it as a shelf ornament. Actually, though, having washed it out, it occurred to me that if I could thread a pair of wires through it and mount a tiny push button under Stig's removable head (the lid for the shower gel)–well, that might work!

- Inside a clock. I have a carriage clock that has its own secret compartment behind the face. How about hiding the button in there? The clock seldom needs to move, so hiding the wires is pretty easy.

- Inside a hollow book, the kind sold as a "security safe" or "book safe" on numerous web sites and stores. It's an old idea, but still a good one. The problem is the trailing wires. You could go for the additional complication of battery operation and a wireless sender inside the fake book; however, if you're really that serious about security, this would have to send an encrypted activation signal. Of course, you'd also need a receiver and decoding software at the AVR board end of things.

  Without resorting to wireless, you're going to have wires trailing when you pull the book off the shelf. You could do it another way; use a piece of reflective foil on the back of the book and a reflective sensor built into the back of the book case that recognizes when the book is removed, but that makes you dependent upon several assumptions, such as that the book will always be in the same position and that when the room is in darkness the light doesn't give away the position of the device, and so on. So, the hollow book idea is do-able, but it has a lot of snags to work out.

- A pair of touch contacts disguised as screw heads or random furniture features. I actually tried this with an old chair that had its covering fixed on with metal furniture studs. I tried wiring one stud into one of the AVR's analog inputs and the other to ground. The idea is that when you use one finger from each hand to bridge between the two, the panel opens. Unfortunately, as you can't use adjacent studs which might be discovered accidentally by anyone sitting on the chair, the cable lengths get a little too long and you get a lot of noise which can result in random activations even just because somebody walks past the chair. I also feared that it might not be long before static electricity might zap the AVR input. Somebody in nylon clothing shuffling around on a chair can probably generate quite a lot of static and that static might well want to escape through the AVR input. It might be possible to resolve these issues with a different electrical arrangement and smarter discriminating software, but it seemed like a long job and, well, there were other, more attractive, alternatives.

In the end, I built the shower gel Stig version and the clock version. Unfortunately, the owners of the Stig copyright were unable to give us permission to use pictures of that version, but take it from me, it looks very cool! The clock version (which we can show in a picture) is also pretty good. Figures 8-7 and 8-8 show the clock normally and with secret frontage opened to reveal the push-button box.

An unassuming modern-day repro carriage clock.

But this clock houses not one but two secrets!

Figure 8-7. Just a clock

First, it has an opening front which reveals a set of tiny storage shelves.

Second, on the bottom shelf is a tiny box with a button in it. Guess what happens when the button is pressed? Aw! you're no fun . . .

Figure 8-8. The clock of secrets revealed!

Position Sensors

I briefly considered the idea of using some distance sensors to allow the software to know the panel position. However, the cost of using these is not really justified here. All we really need is a momentary switch closure when the panel reaches its fully open or fully closed position. This could be done with mechanical switches with long actuation arms–as we looked at in the section "Sensing Movement," in Chapter 4 of this book. However, I was not keen on this approach because

- I wanted to avoid anything that might impede the panel's movement, or have the potential to do so as the mechanism wears.

- Mounting physical switches on the prototype frame was actually going to be problematic.

In the end I went for a contactless approach. I found some small magnetic security sensors which used encapsulated reed switches that can detect a magnet being within about 1/2" (12 mm) of them. These products are made to be used as simple door or window sensors in alarms and security systems.

All I had to do was mount a small magnet on the lower–unseen–side of the sliding panel and mount one reed switch at the fully open point and another at the fully closed point of the panel's travel. The software is written such that it continually polls the switches whenever the panel is in motion, so it won't miss the switches being activated as the magnet passes.

These small magnet/switch products are widely available, for example

- www.amazon.com (United States) search for "magnetic window alarm sensor"–you'll find lots of examples.

- www.maplin.co.uk (UK)–search for stock number MM08, or look on B&Q web site, etc.

The Secret Compartment

When the sliding panel has slid gracefully aside, it will reveal the secret compartment. This is the nub of the whole thing–the reason for doing it; I think that means it deserves to have some magic about it!

I built a small wooden box sized to fit snugly inside the frame. I made quite a wide brim for it out of wide flat wood. Underneath the brim I put two flexible LED strips (blue ones) and fixed them on with twists of garden wire drilled through holes in the side of the box (similar to the technique used to fix the LED strips in the waterfall passageway light project).

When seen from straight on (as it normally would be once installed), you can't see the LED strips–you just see a circle of blue light fading up (thanks to the software) as the panel opens. It looks superb. Figures 8-9 and 8-10 show the backbox made and ready to be installed in the frame, with LED strips installed.

Figure 8-9. *The compartment before installing in the frame*

Figure 8-10. *The compartment showing LED strip*

Obviously if you're building one of these for yourself the size of your backbox or under-box is going to depend on how much space you have and the size of the frame. Finally, with the backbox installed in the frame, the motor fitted, and the panel in place and ready to slide we have the mechanical side of things settled; it's time to look at the electronics.

The Electronics

Figure 8-11 shows the circuit diagram for the electronics side of the secret panel project.

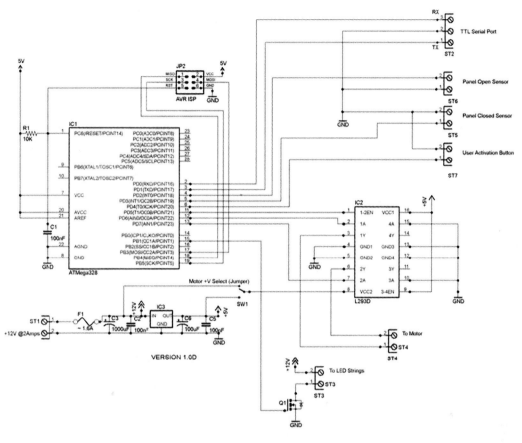

Figure 8-11. *Secret panel circuit diagram*

In my version of this project a +12-volt supply is needed for the LEDs and the +5V is derived from that using a 7805 voltage regulator. That regulator should be fitted with a heatsink. If you are using a LED string product that needs only +5V (as many SMD (surface mount device) LED strings do) and your motor is happy running on +5V, then you can simplify this design quite a lot.

░ **Caution** It's *very* important to make sure that you use a fuse—as indicated in the Figure 8-11—nasty things can happen if something goes wrong and there is no fuse to blow! This is especially important in any device with moving parts where fingers may get caught.

Whichever side of the power supply (12V or +5V) is running, the motor should have C3 on it. This is a fairly large capacitor, which is there to counteract the motor's startup demand. It's shown on the +12V side on the diagram, but swap around C3 and C6 if you're running your motor from +5V.

The electronics for this project consists of two chips, one voltage regulator, and one transistor. The first chip is of course our trusty ATmega328 (you could easily use ATmega168 instead if you wanted to–the code for this project is quite small). As with all our projects, the AVR has to be running at 8 MHz (as detailed in Chapter 3). We of course have our usual ISP jack for programming the AVR and the reset RC network across the RESET pin and we have the TTL level serial port. If you're building the circuit on the test bed breadboard (which is what I did) then you'll already have all these items. If you're building this on a solder board or some other way, you'll need to provide these things.

The second chip is an L293D chip; this was the one we messed around with in Chapter 4 when we looked at "H" switches and push-pull drivers for use with stepper motors. Here, though, we're only using a single coil motor so we're only using half of the chip–we disable the other half. The chip can drive a motor up to about 600 ma, so you'll need to make sure that your motor is not going to overload it. The L293 does feature over current protection, though, so if you are in any doubt, try out your motor and see what happens.

Three I/O lines go from the MCU to the L293D

- AVR pin 11 (Arduino digital pin 5) connects to the enable input we are using (pin 1). The AVR has to make this pin HIGH for the L293D to be enabled.

- AVR pin 12 and pin 13 (Arduino digital pins 6 and 7, respectively) are used to set the polarity of the power going to the motor (i.e., which of the "Y" outputs is pushing and which is pulling). If they are both set to LOW then the motor gets no power. The software PWM pulses whichever is the positive lead to make the motor ramp up. The enable pin overrides these signals.

Pin 8 of the LS293D is the motor supply pin. As shown in the diagram in Figure 8-11, you can use a simple wire jumper to provide power from +5 volts or +12 volts, depending on the voltage your motor requires. The L293D spec says you can use up to +36V as the motor supply. The unused half of the L293D simply has its inputs tied to ground. As you may remember from our previous encounter with the L293D, we don't need to use snubber diodes or any current limiting; the chip has all that built in.

The AVR's pin 15 (Arduino digital pin 9) interfaces to the MOSFET, and that drives the LED strings. The MOSFET used is over spec for this purpose, which means that you could add a lot more LED strings to your own creation.

The two limit switches (in the software these are called PANEL_FULLY_OPEN and PANEL_FULLY_CLOSED) connect to AVR pins 4 and 5 (Arduino digital pins 2 and 3, respectively). These are simple magnet-operated reed switches which connect to ground when the magnet attached to the moving panel passes near them. The internal AVR 20K pull-ups are enabled on these pins, so there is no need for external pull-up resistors.

Finally, the user's push button (wired across from inside the clock–as shown earlier) interfaces via AVR pin 6 (Arduino digital pin 4). This is, again, a simple connection to ground with a pull-up enabled on the AVR. The software only activates this push button when it is released; this is to prevent a user from holding it down to make the panel cycle continuously, which it is not meant to do (the L293D would go over temperature and shut down, for one thing).

That's it for the electronics, all the external connections in the prototype are–as shown–made by screw connectors, but you could use something else if you wanted to. I used PCB mounting screw connectors with fairly long pins because they can plug nicely into the testbed breadboard.

Sliding Panel Electronics Troubleshooting

You can find out quite a lot by connecting to the TTL level serial port (see Chapter 3 for details) because the software outputs quite a few messages as it goes about its work. It will indicate each operation as it starts and ends; it also indicates fault conditions and sensor events.

You'll find that the reed switches used as limit detectors do tend to bounce quite a lot. The software counteracts this bounce by reacting to the first "sighting" of the limit switch it is expecting to close. For example, if the software is commanding the panel to close, it continuously monitors the fully closed sensor and reacts to the first pulse it sees from the PANEL_FULLY_CLOSED switch and then stops looking at that switch.

If you are having problems, there is provision in the software for fitting a "fault" LED provides additional assistance (it's not shown on the circuit diagram in Figure 8-11 because I never needed it and hopefully you won't either). If you want additional indication of what the MCU is doing, attach an LED with its + lead to AVR pin 14 (Arduino digital pin 8) and its negative lead through a 330R resistor to ground. When this LED lights up it means that a panel transit has taken too long. During building you'd see messages about this on the serial channel. However, once installed and working it could be handy to have an LED indicator showing there is a problem.

If the LED comes on (or you see a panel transit time-out message on the serial channel) it could be caused by several things.

- The panel is stuck due to some blockage or mechanical jam.

- You're using a slower motor than I did (in which case, adjust the time-out value MAX_PANEL_MOVE_TIME).

- You've adjusted the parameters of the ramp-up function within the software which has altered the total transit time of the motor.

In most cases you'll know if the mechanism jams; it will make a ghastly noise. If it used to work but now times out, maybe the panel slides need cleaning and are slowing down the panel movement? In my design the panel is held captive in its slides by the wall or surface onto which you fix it. If the surface has warped slightly so that it's squeezing the panel and restricting its ease of movement, that can easily cause a problem.

If you're having problems with the electronics of a newly built panel it may be because your motor has different startup characteristics than the one I used and it's spiking your power supply or momentarily dragging it down (if the power supply is not providing enough power). Such a problem can have many negative effects, such as a complete software restart whenever the motor is commanded to start, or garbled text coming out of the TTL serial port, or the motor starting for a moment then stopping again.

If you do suspect that the motor is causing problems, try modifying the rampPanelMotorUp function within the software to make a softer, more gradual, start.

If the problem remains, in many cases the answer will be to add a larger reservoir capacitor across the supply rail supplying the motor. Try duplicating the existing reservoir capacitor (in my design this would be C3) to see if that fixes the problem, or at least changes it a little which would indicate that you're on the right track and just need to increase the capacitor value. Also, try adding some duplicates of C2 and C5, placing them near the L293D. If you can, try a different power supply which offers a little more amperage, or try a different motor.

Software Commentary

The software is–downloadable from this book's web site (www.apress.com/9781430244462). The following is a code walk through the main functions of the program.

Function	Commentary
Declarations Header Section (args: none)	In this initial section the Arduino pin numbers for the various external connections are defined (see previous text) and various constants are declared. Of special interest are: • MAX_PANEL_MOVE_TIME which defines (in milliseconds) how many seconds the panel is given to complete its transit from open to closed (or vice versa). This is set at a default of five seconds; you should customize it for the motor you are using. Don't allow too long because if there is a problem with the mechanism or a blockage, the motor will grind away for longer than it needs to. Don't make it too short, or the software will start issuing time-outs and give up on moving the panel. The value should be about one second longer than the panel transit would normally take. • LED_DELAY is used to slug the LED strings fade rate so that it happens more stylishly, slowly and gracefully. Increase this value to slow the fade, or decrease it (minimum = 1) to increase. • limitSwStates is an array of two items which hold the latest state of the limit switches. These are updated regularly in the main loop so they are always up to date.
setup() args: None	The setup() function initializes all the I/O pins as required (including enabling pull-up resistors for inputs) and initializes the serial port. It then collects the initial sensor states. Then, it fades the LED strings up and down to provide a visual verification that they are working. Finally, if the panel seems to be open, it is closed.
loop() args: None	The main loop() function of this program is pretty simple. If the user button has not been pressed then it just updates the limit switch states–and that's it! If the user switch *has* been pressed then it checks to see if the panel looks as if it is closed; if so, it opens it. In any other case (the panel is open, or neither sensor is active) the panel is closed. All user button press actions result in a message going out to the serial port.
closePanel() args: ledFaderStart AND openPanel() args: ledFaderStart	These functions command the motor to ramp up in the required direction to open or close the panel. They then wait until either the appropriate sensor is activated (e.g., closePanel waits for the PANEL_FULLY_CLOSED sensor to be hit) or a time-out occurs. The LED strings are faded in or out while waiting for the panel to complete its transit. The LEDs are left fully on (panel open) or off (panel closed) at the end of the function. The motor is always turned off when these functions end. LED fading doesn't start until ledFaderStart milliseconds after the function is called. This allows an adjustment point to allow fading and panel movement to be better synced when using different motors and processors. Messages are issued to the serial port, and the failStateLed pin is put ON in the case of a time-out.

(*continued*)

Function	Commentary
rampPanelMotorUp() args: pwmLead	This function does a feathered start on the motor. Electrically and mechanically, this works a lot better than just putting full power on the motor straight away, and in this application it looks classier! The function takes one argument which is pwmLead. As detailed earlier in this chapter (see "The Electronics" section earlier.) there are two control lines into the motor driver. By setting one or other of these to low and the other to high you control the polarity of the power supplied to the motor. pwmLead in this function specifies which of the possible two Arduino pin numbers is to be the positive. The polarity setup is actually done by the setMotorControls() support function. We initially increase the PWM pulses into the motor quite gently but more aggressively as the PWM pulses get longer. You'll probably need to tune the point at which this happens (as per comment in the code) to best suit your chosen motor.
motorOff() args: None	Sets both motor leads to LOW so that no power flows through the motor. Used to stop the motor quickly when the panel movement is over. As an alternative to this you could also add a rampPanelMotorDown() function which slow-stops the panel, but that depends on how much momentum your mechanical components have and whether they might overshoot too badly.
progressLedPwm() args: fadingUp	This function progresses a LED string fade up or down (the Boolean argument fadingUp indicates which type of activity is in progress). In order to make sure that fading is pretty and doesn't happen too fast, we use a ledDelayCtr (a static variable). This effectively counts how many times this function is called and only does a fade step every LED_DELAY calls.
Various Others	The other remaining functions are very small and self-explanatory.

All Together Now!

So, finally, it is time to put it all together. I made a hole in the drywall. On the panel side that was just large enough to let the secret compartment become visible. On the other side, it had to be big enough to mount the frame into the wall, so it was quite a large hole (but inside the closet mentioned earlier). I put a frame around the hole on the front side and secured the frame assembly on the rear side mounted so that the secret compartment lined up to be visible. After making sure that the panel could move back and forth freely, which involved a tedious amount of smoothing of the rear face of the drywall (which had to be dead flat to ensure that the panel stayed trapped in its slide run and could not jump out), it finally all came together. I used a picture as the concealer to hide the panel under normal circumstances.

The sequence in Figures 8-12 through 8-15 shows the final installation.

<table>
<tr>
<td>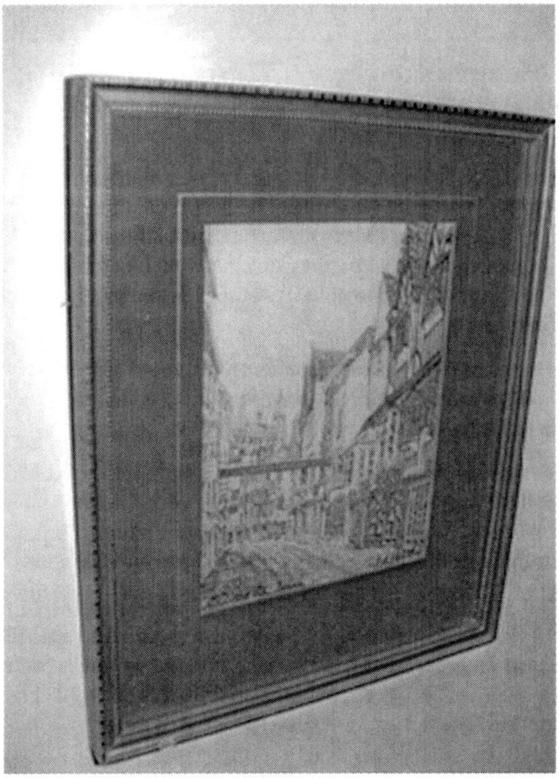
Figure 8-12. A picture of innocence</td>
<td>A picture hanging on the drywall.</td>
</tr>
</table>

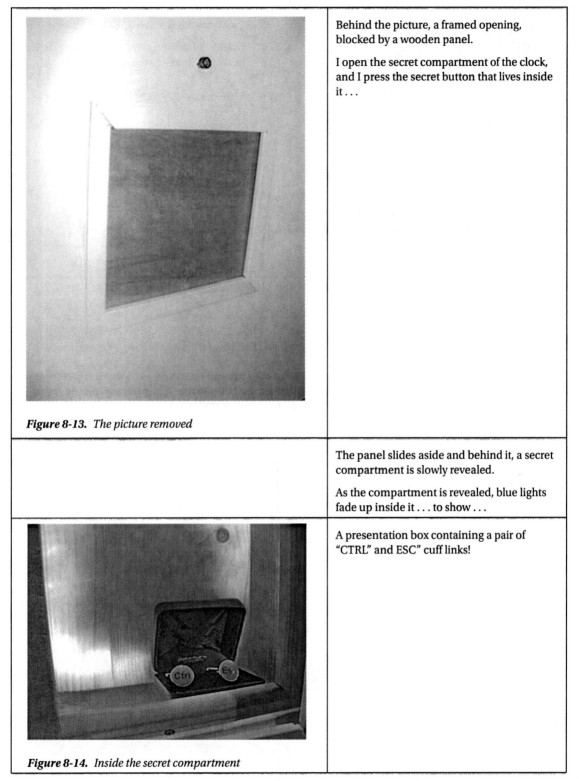

Figure 8-13. *The picture removed*

Behind the picture, a framed opening, blocked by a wooden panel.

I open the secret compartment of the clock, and I press the secret button that lives inside it . . .

The panel slides aside and behind it, a secret compartment is slowly revealed.

As the compartment is revealed, blue lights fade up inside it . . . to show . . .

A presentation box containing a pair of "CTRL" and ESC" cuff links!

Figure 8-14. *Inside the secret compartment*

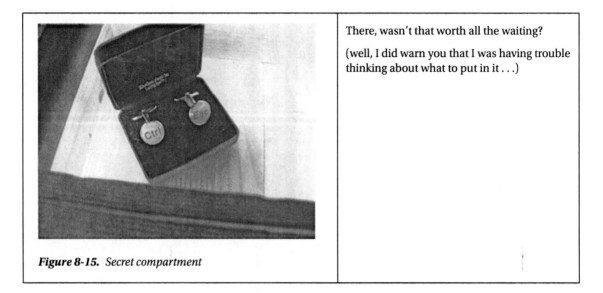

There, wasn't that worth all the waiting?

(well, I did warn you that I was having trouble thinking about what to put in it . . .)

Figure 8-15. *Secret compartment*

Summary

This was a great project for me, I learned a lot from doing it and had frustration and fun in pretty much equal measure.

Who knew there would turn out to be so many different ways to do it! I guess the beauty of it is that there is not a single "right" way to do it; if it works, it works–whatever method you use. It's an unusual project for an electronics book because it has as many dependencies on where you install it as on what components and parts you use.

This project was one that I have always had in the back of my mind to do. Finally, this book gave me an excuse to do it, and it did not disappoint!

However, I'm afraid I still don't know what to keep in my secret compartment.

Coming up Next

Here Kitty, Kitty: Random laser beams to drive your pets crazy.

■ ■ ■

CHAPTER 9

Project 2: Crazy Beams—Exercise Your Pet!

In this project we are going to try to give your pet (your cat or your dog) hours of harmless fun and exercise. This project is a little like the gem light project we looked at in Chapter 4. This time, though, we're not out to do something ornamental; this time we have a functional aim in mind: keeping the animals entertained!

The idea for this project came from observing how much fun it can be to watch a cat or dog trying to catch the light spot cast from a presentation pointer. You've seen these things; they are very low-powered laser lights, usually no more than 5 mw and often built into a pen or a key ring. They are used to put a pinpoint of red light on a screen—usually to indicate a point or area of interest during a live presentation that uses a computer or a stills projector. A dog or a cat will happily spend a long time skittering around the floor chasing one of these light spots, while you, sitting comfortably in your chair, shine the light all around the room. The animal pounces on the light spot triumphantly. But then, the light spot escapes its grasp and it's off again. Then the light disappears altogether. Where has it gone? It's behind you! Your dog or cat can have hours of fun. The trouble is that the human wielding the pointer light usually gets tired of the game before the animal does!

So, what if there was a machine to do the light shining? One that could move the light around, casting multiple light spots, randomly speeding up and slowing down, making the light disappear and reappear again somewhere else. Endless fun! And, since a machine never gets tired, it goes on and on until the animal has had enough!

The Project

This project uses two very low power lasers attached to two servo motors. These motors allow the beams of light to be moved around in the horizontal plane. However, the laser and motor assembly are mounted on a spindle which allows them to be moved in the vertical plane by a third motor; this allows the AVR controlling the whole thing to move the beams around quite a large area.

The second laser and its associated motor are optional, you can just build the project with one laser and servo motor if you want to. Although the effect is better with two beams, the software doesn't care if any (or all) of the motors are not really there. Commodity-priced servo motors don't offer any positional sensing capability to the host computer, so unless you use far more expensive motors the Crazy Beams software has no way to sense the motor positions. This is not a problem, however; as we saw in Chapter 4, servo motors are pretty good at doing what they're told!

If you have multiple animals to entertain, you could add a third or even a fourth motor and laser. That would make lots of beams for your pets to chase. If you're scaling up the project in that way, though, you need to make sure your power supply arrangements are sufficient. The power requirements for each laser are low, but each additional servo motor adds quite a lot to the power supply load. Scaling up the project from a hardware point of view is not hard; there are lots of spare I/O pins on the AVR MCU chip and the software makes use of a motor descriptor array which can be extended.

Another way to scale up the project without extra motors and lasers would be to add prismatic diffusers, to split the beams multiple ways, although at reduced intensity. You can get some very pretty room lighting effects in this way too, but that's beyond the immediate scope of this project.

Sourcing the Lasers

Presentation pointers that incorporate low-power laser diodes are widely sold and cheap, so my first thought was to try to extract the laser diodes I needed from two of these. Having tried this, I can't recommend that approach. The problem is that those kinds of products are really not meant for disassembly: they seem to be put together as a friction fit under a lot of pressure. That means that you have to cut your way into them, making jagged edges and (in my case) deforming both the lens assembly and the laser diode in the process. My laser didn't focus properly afterward and stopped working shortly after that. So, on the whole, pillaging a presentation pointer for its laser module seems like an unexpectedly tricky job that could take a lot of tries to get right!

Fortunately, you *can* buy just the laser diode and lens assembly separately and ready wired for use with a power supply; it does cost a little more, but it's ready to go when you get it—and this is the route I eventually took.

Example products can be found at

- `www.sparkfun.com/products/9906` (United States).

- `www.maplin.co.uk` (UK) (search for LE07).

You can also get these from various eBay vendors (search for "laser diode module"). Make sure you get +4.5V or +5V lasers, which will simplify your power supply arrangements. Don't get anything more powerful than 5 milliwatts because it will be too bright and possibly dangerous to your eyesight.

■ **Caution**   *Never* regard a laser as harmless. Using one with the recommended power level is as safe as we can make it, but *do not* ever shine the laser directly into your own eyes or anyone else's. Sight damage *will* occur. Also, make sure that the laser stays slightly unfocused when you set up your *Crazy Beams* project. This will diffuse the laser light slightly so that your pet's eyes, if they happen to look at the unit, cannot be overexposed.

The lasers I used consume about 40 ma each, which is not a lot, but about twice as much as you would want to take from an MCU pin.[1] So, we have to include our old friend the 2803 transistor array chip (see Chapter 3) to provide the drive that the lasers need. You could use just use NPN transistors, such as a couple of BC548s if you prefer—but by the time you've added a base resistor they'd probably take up almost the same amount of board space.

Project Build

The project consists of three major assemblies.

- A simple wooden frame.

- The horizontal motor/laser assembly.

- The electronics board. I just built the project on the test bed rig, but you could easily make a solder board version of it—it's really just two chips.

---

[1]In fact an ATmega328 pin could sink about 40 ma, but it's an absolute maximum value which—since we would be doing it on two pins (one per laser)—is not advised.

The frame has to be fairly deep, but not very long or high. So, I made this up out of some short lengths of 7" (180 mm)-wide pine plank (see Figure 9-3).

The horizontal motors frame is made from a couple of stiff plastic strips (something suitable in plastic or metal can be obtained from your usual home supplies superstore) and a couple of thick wood blocks (I used some short lengths of 2"-square table leg that I had left over from a previous project).

The horizontal assembly is mounted on a spindle so that it can swing back and forth. The spindle is made from a couple of 0.25"/M6 bolts which clear through the sides of the frame and then loosely fit into some appropriately sized threaded inserts, which screw into the side of the blocks. Figure 9-1 shows a threaded insert (see the "Secret panel" project in Chapter 8 for more details and links to where to get them).

Figure 9-1. *Threaded insert*

The horizontal motors are mounted on the assembly and the lasers are mounted to the top of those motors. This means that the motors can sweep the laser lights that they carry back and forth to move the light spots in the horizontal plane. Figure 9-2 shows the completed assembly with the two servo motors mounted in place but no lasers fitted yet; you can see a threaded insert at the end of the assembly. There is no "right" size for this assembly because the size depends on some variable factors:

- Whether you are going to use two horizontal motors and lasers (as per the picture) or just one.

- How far apart you want the traveling light spots to be. If you have several pets to amuse, it may be that you want greater separation, in which case the motors will need to be mounted wider apart to increase the distance. You may also want space for scaling if you have more additional pets to amuse and want to add more horizontal beams.

- The maximum rotation of your servo motors–as we saw in Chapter 4 there is actually some quite surprising variation in this supposedly "standard" factor.

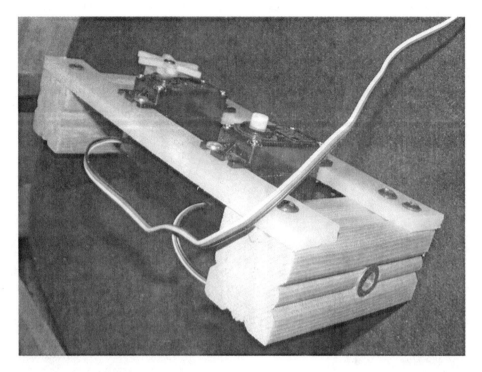

Figure 9-2. *Completed horizontal assembly*

Obviously, a little servo motor pushing and pulling is going to have a much easier job if the horizontal assembly swings freely. It's therefore pretty important that you make sure to place the threaded inserts as centrally in the end blocks as you can get them.

When you put all this together you should have a free-swinging assembly that the vertical motor (via the linkage mentioned earlier) can easily move to and fro, under control of the MCU. Don't over tighten the bolts through the threaded inserts, and make sure the clearance holes through the frame sides are just large enough to allow the bolt to rotate freely.

The vertical motor is built onto the frame, raised up by appropriately sized wooden blocks–as shown in Figure 9-3. The motor needs to sit at a height where, via a linkage made with stiff wire bent into shape, it can push and pull the horizontal assembly back and forth, affecting the vertical position of the laser spots. It doesn't have to provide a large amount of movement, since a small change in the angle of the lasers makes quite a big difference to the beam's position. The software on the prototype only needs to move the vertical motor over about 30 % of its possible travel, and this makes a perfectly adequate difference to the beam positions.

Figure 9-3. *Crazy Beams project frame (vertical servo motor in place)*

You could, if you wanted to make the project "disappear" better, paint the frame in black or some other darker color. I left mine white, since it lives in my office/workshop area so appearance is not a big issue.

Assembly

Before you begin assembly it's a good idea to make sure that each servo motor you plan to use is reset to its zero degrees position. This is essential for getting the laser mounting right and for getting the wire link set up correctly.

I've found that some motors reset to their zero position as soon as you connect their voltage pins (almost always black and red wires) to a +5V source, but leave their servo lead (usually either white or yellow) disconnected. Some motors don't reset, though, and for these you should use the servo motor reset program (you can also download this program from the book's web site (www.apress.com/9781430244462). To use this, you'll have to jump ahead a bit to the circuit diagram in Figure 9-7 and Figure 9-8 and connect your motors up as shown there.

The servo reset program is very simple, as follows:

```
/*
 Servo Motor Reset Program:
 Reset all listed servo motors to zero degrees
 */
#include< Servo.h>
#define HORIZ01_PIN 6
#define HORIZ02_PIN 9
#define VERT01_PIN 10

Servo horiz01;
Servo horiz02;
Servo vert01;
```

```
void setup()
{
  Serial.begin(9600);
  Serial.println("Resetting motors");
  horiz01.attach(HORIZ01_PIN );
  horiz02.attach(HORIZ02_PIN );
  vert01.attach(VERT01_PIN);

  horiz01.write(0);
  horiz02.write(0);
  vert01.write(0);
  Serial.println("Reset done");
}

void loop()
{
  // Main loop left intentionally empty!
}
```

This servo reset program just uses the servo library (see Chapter 4 for details) to set each motor to zero degrees; it uses only the setup() function, and the loop() is empty. When you upload and run the program, you may find that nothing appears to happen. This could mean you have not wired up the motors correctly, but more likely it means that the motors are already at their zero degrees position. To be sure, try temporarily changing the

```
"....write(0)"
```

lines to something like

```
"...write(100)"
```

and try again. That should make some movement, if your wiring is right. Don't forget to change the code back to zero and run it again to make sure your motor is reset to zero degrees before you install it. The main program for this project also includes numerous features that can be useful during setup and alignment of the mechanical elements. See the section "Crazy Beams Software Code Walk."

It's *important* that you make a note of which way your motor turns when it goes from angle 0 to angle 100. You'll need this information to better visualize positioning the laser diodes and setting the linkage from the horizontal assembly to the vertical motor.

Once the motors are reset you can begin mounting the laser modules on the servo motors. I used the longest and widest of the horns (the plastic wheels and fittings that usually come with the motor are the "horns") and some 22 SWG[2] (0.7 mm) tinned wire to bind the lasers to it. You can use various kinds of wire for this purpose–piano wire or garden wire might be suitable. Any metal wire in the range 20 SWG to 25 SWG should work well.

You need to bind the laser to one side of the center so that you can still access the center screw on the horn to tighten it up. The photo in Figure 9-4 shows how this looks when it's done. Twist the wire up tight with a pair of pliers. Make it tight enough to hold the laser very securely, but don't go crazy. The wire will snap or the laser casing might deform. The wire actually does hold the lasers very securely; however, when the setup alignment is done, you can put a dab of glue between the plastic horn and the laser module to make extra sure it stays in place—but don't do that before you have aligned the laser.

---

[2]SWG = Standard Wire Gauge.

Figure 9-4. *Laser diode mounted on servo motor*

The next job is to install the linkage from the vertical motor to the horizontal assembly. Mount it so that, with the vertical motor at its reset position, the horizontal assembly is held such that the laser light will just shine *inside* the frame. This gives the software the ability to reset the beams so that they don't leave the frame. The linkage from the vertical motor to the horizontal assembly is made of a dual strand of 22 SWG (0.7 mm) tinned steel wire—again, you can use anything comparable. As long as your horizontal assembly swings freely this linkage should be plenty strong enough. You'll need a small hole through the lower plastic crossbar so that the linkage has a good anchor. As before, the vertical motor is fitted with the longest of the plastic horns it came with (this maximizes the swing the motor can exert).

Figure 9-5 shows the linkage in place, in this photo the motor is set at about 70 degrees of travel; when it's set to less, the motor will turn counter clockwise and pull the assembly back toward us, lowering the vertical setting.

Figure 9-6 shows the overall assembly.

As long as you have made sure the motors are all reset to their zero degrees position, aligning the lasers is quite straightforward. You just need to put the horn on the motor such that the laser will point to a base position when at its "at rest" position. We can handle the rest of the positioning issues in the software (see "Crazy Beams Code Walk" section – below).

The Electronics

The diagram in Figure 9-7 shows the electronics for this project. This diagram is broadly the same whether you build it up on the test bed rig or whether you make a custom solder board for it. Of course, if you use the test bed rig, the ISP connector is already in place.

Note that because we are using motors, a fuse is a must-have: you need one somewhere in the + lead of the power supply.

We are again using a trusty ATmega328 chip. We are using it in its internal 8 MHz clock mode (see Chapter 3 for details on using AVRDude to set up this mode of operation) which is plenty fast enough for this application. In addition (as previously mentioned), we need a ULN2803A driver transistor array.

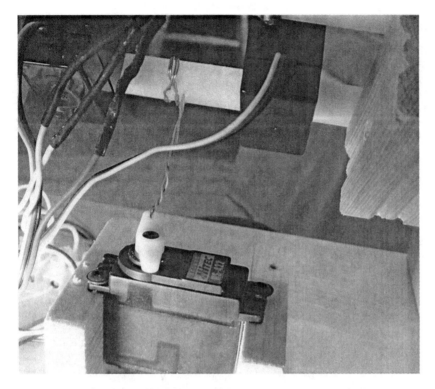

Figure 9-5. *Vertical motor to horizontal frame linkage (see also Figure 9-6)*

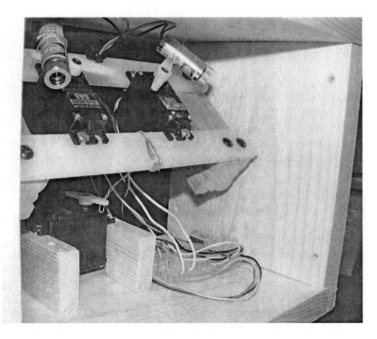

Figure 9-6. *Overall view of the Crazy Beams project*

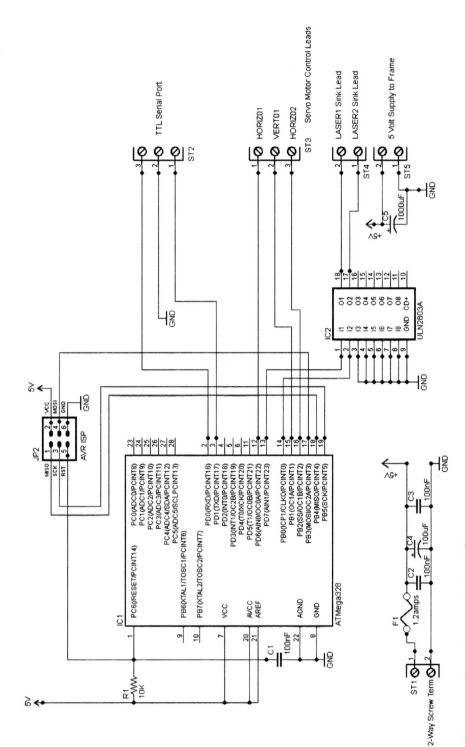

Figure 9-7. Crazy Beams main circuit diagram

Table 9-1 shows the AVR pins we use here.

Table 9-1. *AVR Pins Usage*

AVR Pin Number	Arduino Name	Usage
2	RXD	Receive data
3	TXD	Transmit data
12	Digital pin 6	Horizontal Motor 1 Servo Control Line
13	Digital pin 7	Laser1 (HIGH = ON)
14	Digital pin 8	Laser2 (HIGH = ON)
15	Digital pin 9	Horizontal Motor 2 Servo Control Line
16	Digital pin 10	Vertical Motor 1 Servo Controller Line

As previously discussed, this leaves lots of spare I/O pins free for adding more beams and motors.

Because they are electromechanical devices, even the comparatively well-behaved servo motors can be quite brutal to a power supply (as compared to purely electronic devices). Therefore, we add a couple of 1000 uF capacitors to the circuit in this project to better protect the logic circuits against power supply dips and spikes. C5 goes onto the main electronics circuit board (test rig) and the other, C6, goes inside the crazy beams frame box. One effect of adding this extra capacitance is that the rise time of the power supply will increase; that is, the time it takes at switch on for the PSU to reach +5V from nothing will be increased. This can cause problems with AVR reset. So if, after you add the capacitors, your AVR never (or sometimes doesn't) starts up, you may need to increase the value of C1 (e.g., to 0.47 uF) to make the power-on reset pulse at the AVR's pin 1 a little longer. That should solve the problem, if it occurs.

The power arrangement shown in the circuit diagram assumes that everything runs off +5 volts, which it probably will. Most small servo motors run on +5 volts as do the specified laser diodes. However, if you somehow end up needing a +12V supply as well, just reuse the power supply design from the sliding panel project from Chapter 8 which will do the job nicely.

As you can see, the connections to the crazy beams frame come off the board via seven screw connector terminals (not including the TTL level serial port, which you can optionally use for this project as you'll see when we get to the software description). Unless you're building a custom board that can live inside the frame, you'll need to make up a seven-way wiring harness to convey the signals from the board to the frame. You'll see in the photos how I did this; I just used a miniature plastic screw terminal inside the box.

The diagram in Figure 9-8 shows the wiring inside the project's wood frame. The essential connections are as follows:

- +5V to the + lead of each motor, and also to the positive side (red wire) of the two laser diodes.

- Ground connects to each motor (note: C6 doing the smoothing function described above).

- Each motor's servo lead is brought back to the board individually.

- The negative lead of each of the laser diodes is brought back individually to the board.

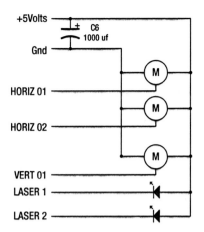

Figure 9-8. *Motors and laser wiring*

It's tempting to want to make the wiring run between the electronics and the frame as long as possible, but although I haven't tried it, I think that you might start to run into noise problems if the wires were more than about 18 inches.

That concludes the description of the physical aspects of the project. Let's now move on to the software.

Crazy Beams—The Software

The software for the Crazy Beams project is currently version 3. I did two previous versions (how did you guess!) but scrapped them due to various defects and shortcomings.

The final version uses a data structure (servoMotorDetails) to describe the properties and current state of each motor. An array instance of this data structure, motors, holds the descriptions of the servo motors and their state (see next section "Software–Positioning Parameters and Timing Constants," for more details). Various functions within the program play around with the contents of this array, and then they call setMotorAngles(), which is the only function in the main part of the program that writes to the hardware.

The main two components of the loop() function are to generate a random number which, based on the number generated, can change the pathways of the crazy beams in some random way. We'll see details of this in the section "Crazy Beams Software Code Walk." The other component of the main loop is just to progress the "animation" of the laser beams. They basically scan back and forth and a little bit up and down—which would get boring after a while, but the random number handler's actions break it all up and make the beams suddenly do something different. There is no predictable pattern to the pathway of the beams—they are, literally, crazy! Also within the main loop we check to see if any single letter commands have come in from the serial channel.

Software—Positioning Parameters and Timing Constants

Just before we take a code walk, it might be helpful to explain in a little more detail the function of the constants and values declared at the start of the Crazy Beams software.

In this project, we don't use the full rotation of the servo motors; we only need to use a part of each motor's rotational range to get the effects we want. However, that range will vary from build to build, affected by mounting arrangements, distances between motors and frame, and beam length. So, each motor has the following parameters associated with it. These are stored (along with some other items that add to the description of each of the three motors) in an array of C-structs called motors, which is of type servoMotorDetails.

- restAngle: This is the angle the motor will be set to when the project is not in use, or during initial reset.

- startAngle: This is the "home" position for the motor; it is the start point of its useful rotational range within this project.

- endAngle: This is the maximum rotation we need the motor to do within the context of this project. If the motor rotates further than this, then the laser (or mechanical linkage it controls) may hit something, or a beam may shine somewhere we don't want it to. The software will never send the motor beyond this point.

- maxAngle: This is the maximum angle to which the motor is capable of turning. It is never used by this software.

- currentAngle: This is the angle to which the motor is currently turned.

Two timing constants control the beam travel speeds: LOOP_DELAY_MIN and LOOP_DELAY_MAX. In the main loop, after each beam move, the program delays for a few milliseconds. One of the randomly chosen actions in the main loop is to change this timing value to a random value in order to make the beams move faster or slower. These two constants constrain the randomly chosen timing value to a range that makes sense for this application.

Crazy Beams Software Code Walk

The Arduino code for Crazy Beams is downloadable from the book's web site (www.apress.com/9781430244462). The code walk shown in Table 9-2 explains all the functions within the program.

Table 9-2. *Crazy Beams Software—Functions List*

Function	Commentary
Declarations Header Section (args: none)	In this initial section, the Arduino pin numbers for the motors and the lasers are defined and various constants are declared. This section also includes the servo library, which is what we use to provide the PWM values needed by the motors.
	The servoMotorDetails struct is declared, and the motors array filled with a mixture of constants, initial values, and references to instances of servo motors. Note that mtrsArrayTop needs to be declared here because, in Arduino's environment, there is no easy way for software to dynamically discover the upper bound of an array. This tells the rest of the program the highest index number of the motors array.
setup() args: None	The setup() function attaches the relevant pin numbers to the servo motor object instances. It then sets the motors to their rest position, then to their end positions, back to the rest position, and then finally to their start positions. This is intended to ensure a full mechanical reset and to ensure there are no blockages to movement over the full required movement range. Essentially, the theory is that users get used to how a machine resets, and if anything sounds different than usual they will investigate it before too much damage is done. Nice theory!
	Next, the laser pins are initialized and the lasers flash quickly four times to show they are okay.
	Finally the version message is sent out to the serial channel. Usage of the serial channel in this project is optional. However, having a TTL level serial USB dongle on a laptop or desktop does give you extra control over the unit. See Chapter 2 for more detail on USB serial dongles.

(continued)

Table 9-2. (*continued*)

Function	Commentary
loop() args: None	As previously described, the main loop of this program progresses movement of the horizontal beam motors and the vertical motor in a nice smooth fashion; each one will scan from its start position to its end position and back again, over and over. The code to do this is located near the end of the loop() function. However, in order to get to that, the processor has to get through a number of preliminaries. • First, the program checks to see if any characters have been sent in from the serial channel. If characters have been received, then the processKbInput() function (described below) is called to handle them. • Next, the value of the doNothing Boolean is checked. If this is found to be true, then the loop() is exited. As the name of this Boolean implies, this is the mechanism whereby the unit is disabled. The value of doNothing is toggled by receiving an "S" command from the serial channel (see description of processKbInput()). Next, we generate a random number. In the program as-supplied, this random number will be between 0 and 199. Most of the numbers in the range don't have any effect. However, within the main loop there is a list (in a switch-case set) of numbers that do cause changes to the beam paths to be made. Note that the beam path changes are made by changing items in the motors array, *not* by directly writing to the hardware. The contents of the array are used to write out positioning commands to the hardware, only at the very end of loop(). The random number matches do the following things: • Set the horizontal beam positioning motors to a random position (somewhere between its start and end position). • Set the vertical beam positioning motor to a random position (somewhere between its start and end positions). • Turn beams off and disable movement (by setting the selfDisabled Boolean). • Turn beams back on and re-enable movement (by clearing the selfDisabled Boolean). • Change the speed of operations by changing the delay value in the main loop. This changes the speed at which the beams will move around. The effect of injecting this randomness is that the beams will move around smoothly for a while and then suddenly change course or speed. Then they disappear and shortly afterward they reappear somewhere else. If you want less randomness, just increase the higher value in random(0,200) from 200 to a larger number. This makes it less likely that any of the defined numbers will come up in a random selection. Decrease it (no lower than 10 though) if you want even more randomness. Finally, we call the functions to progress the horizontal and vertical motion, and it is these that actually call the setMotorAngles() function, which positions the hardware according to the contents of the motors array.

(*continued*)

Table 9-2. (*continued*)

Function	Commentary
motorsHome() motorsRest() motorsToMax() motorsToEnd() motorsToStart() Args: None Return values: None	These functions all do similar things. They position each of the motors to a known position, such as its rest position or its end position. These were described in the previous section of the text. None of these functions take any arguments, or (since there is no sensory feedback from the servo motors used) return any values.
turnOnLasers() turnOffLasers() args: None. Return values: None	These functions turn both lasers on or off. They take no arguments and return no values.
progressHorizMotion() progressVerticalMotion() args: None. Return values: None	These functions progress the motion of the horizontal and vertical motors. They manipulate the contents of the members of the motors array that relate to the horizontal motors. For each horizontal motor the following processing is performed: • If the movingForward member is true then the currentAngle member of the array is incremented. If it becomes more than the value indicated in maxAngle then the end of travel in the current direction has been reached and the currentAngle is decremented again, and the movingForward flag for this motor is set to false. • If the movingForward member is false, then the currentAngle member of the array is decremented. If that makes it less than startAngle, then the motor has moved as far in the reverse direction as it can and movingForward is set to true. At the end of this processing, the motor position has been moved on by one step, and a reversal of direction made, if needed. Finally, the motor values are written out to the hardware using setMotorAngles()
horizontalMotorRandom() verticalMotorRandom() args: None Return values: None	These functions set the currentAngle member of each motor's entry in the motors array to a random value. The random value will be somewhere between the motor's startAngle and endAngle values.
setMotorAngles() args: int motorID	This function sets the angle of one or more motors, as defined in the motors array. It takes one argument, motorID, which is an integer that defines which member of the motors array is to be used. However, if motorID is sent as −1, then *all* motors are set. The currentAngle values held in motors are assumed to be in range and valid. This is the only point in the program where the motor positions are directly set from the software. All other functions that want to set the motor positions modify values in the motors array and then call this function.
lasersOn() lasersOff() args: None Return values: None	These functions turn both lasers on or off.

(*continued*)

Table 9-2. (*continued*)

Function	Commentary
changeLoopDelay() args: None return Value: None	This function changes the global variable loopDelay to a random value between LOOP_DELAY_MIN and LOOP_DELAY_MAX. As mentioned previously, this has the effect of changing the beam progress speed by changing the time delay in the programs main loop.
processKbInput() args: None Return value: None	This function is called from the main loop when it recognizes that something has been received from the serial channel. This gives a way for a user (using a TTL serial port on another computer) to exercise control over the Crazy Beams unit, and to see the message stream coming out of the unit. This function implements a number of single-character commands. Commands are not echoed and can be lowercase or uppercase, either will work. The commands are as follows:

- "S" = Toggles the state of the doNothing Boolean flag. When set, this flag sets the unit into inert mode. The lasers are turned off and all automated movement ceases.

- "L" = Toggles the state of the lasers. If they were on, they go off and vice versa. This is almost useless unless the unit is inert, since the laser state is regularly changed during normal operations. However, when the unit is inert it is a very useful guide to checking laser positions and focus.

- "1" and "2" = These comments cause only a single laser to remain on, for example "1" will put laser 1 on, but 2 will go off. Again, this is only useful when the unit is inert.

- "E" = Makes all motors go to their end position. Used in inert mode for checking motor limits.

- "S" = Makes all motors go to their start position. Used in inert mode for checking motor limits.

- "R" = Makes all motors go to their rest positions.

■ **Note**   There is no M command for setting motors to their max position, since often this can cause mechanical damage or impact.

- Any other command results in an error message listing the available commands.

So, that concludes our code walk for Crazy Beams, and indeed the project description.

Summary

This chapter has detailed the design, mechanical construction, electronics, and software of a Crazy Beams project. This is a project that is intended to provide unending entertainment for your pets, by giving them beams of light moving around the floor that they can chase, but never catch! If you are building the project you should take due note of the safety messages in the text around laser usage and fusing. The project is readily adaptable to a variety of configurations, either less or more complex (e.g., depending on the number of pets you have to entertain).

Coming Up Next

WordDune; a game of words.

CHAPTER 10

■ ■ ■

Project 3: WordDune

How Much Do You *Really* See?

This project is all about looking good! That is, looking and doing it well.

The quickness of the computer often deceives the eye. We're all quite used to thinking that we see moving images on a computer or TV screen when what we really see is very fast image manipulation and animation. In this project we use an LCD display to improve your looking skills.

The human brain is very good at pattern recognition; we can pick out a single familiar face in a crowd of hundreds of people, we can see pictures in apparently random clouds in the sky or in the flames of a fire, we can pick out somebody saying our name across a noisy room. Although we *all* have this ability to see order in apparent chaos, we have it in different degrees. How good are you? This game tests your ability to pick out complete words from a veritable dune of numbers, letters, and symbols. It's a really easy game–at first: but at each level it gets more and more difficult . . . see where you reach your limit!

WordDune is a game in which actual words or phrases are semihidden in an on-screen torrent of random characters and letters. The torrent gets faster and denser at each level of the game. Your task is to spot four words which repeatedly hide among the ever-changing random characters. At the end of each level, you have to be able to say what the four words were.

The Hardware

Aside from the ATmega328 AVR chip, the only additional hardware for this game is a four-line LCD display and a push button. This makes this an easy project to build on the test bed; if you want a permanent version of it, you could build it on a tripad or a strip board.

This project uses a 4x20 (4 rows by 20 columns) LCD display built around the Hitachi HD44780 LCD controller.

Example products might include the following:

- Sparkfun SKU: LCD-00256 (United States).

- Maplin Stock Number: N30AZ (UK).

- Various online auction site vendors.

I strongly recommend you solder a row of header pins to the display so that it can plug into a breadboard. Later on, if you ever decide to make a permanent version of this project you could use a socket header strip on your permanent board in which to plug in the display.

Figure 10-1. *Header pin and socket strips*

Suitable example products for header pins are

- Sparkfun SKU: PRT-10158 and PRT-10007 (United States).

- Maplin Stock Number: JW59P.

- The header sockets, which are usually available from various eBay vendors.

You can connect to the display by using just the lower four bits of the interface to save some MCU I/O pins and because it's fast enough for our purposes here. I use the LiquidCrystal library–bundled with Arduino–to do the detailed display driving.

There are two ways to update the game's dictionary (see section "WordDune Gameplay").

- You can simply modify the word set that's included in the code and reprogram the microcontroller–using the ISP connection.

- You can use a TTL level serial interface to use the game's embedded command set to remove and add items. We'll look at the command set in the section "WordDune Commands."

Figure 10-2 shows the circuit diagram for the game.

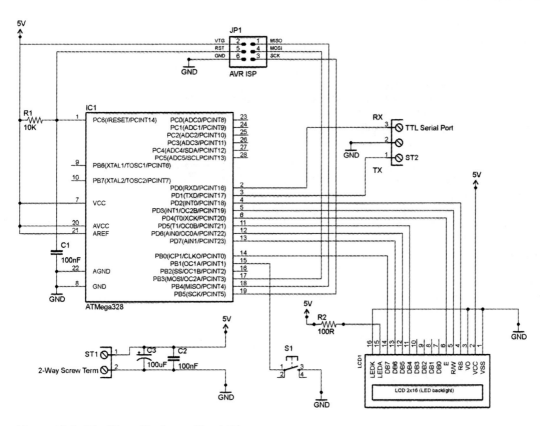

Figure 10-2. *WordDune Hardware Circuit Diagram*

As you can see, the WordDune hardware is pretty straightforward. The ATmega328 MCU is, as ever, center stage and is running without an external crystal, since an 8 MHz clock speed is plenty fast enough for this project. See Chapter 3 for details on setting the MCU's clock rate, if it's not already done.

There is an ISP jack. If you're building this on the test bed breadboard that we made in Chapter 2 you'll already have these connections made by the permanent striped jumpers. If you're building a permanent version of the project you'll just need to make JP1 out of two lots of three header pin sections.

There are two other screw terminal connectors shown. The first brings power (just +5V and ground needed): again, if you are building this on the test bed, this is already catered for by the +5V fused supply you sourced in Chapter 2. If you're building a permanent version of this game, you might want to make ST1 (screw terminal 1) a panel-mounted female DC power socket instead: this would have to be a physical match for the plug of whatever you use as your power source (see the Wikipedia article 'Coaxial Power Connector' for details about DC power plugs and sockets). You could use various kinds of +5V supply, such as

- An external +5V mains supply (a so-called wall wart) capable of supplying 500 milliamps or more.

- A USB to DC power lead. This project uses only about 350 ma, so a USB port from most desktop machines can supply this, as can devices like a mains to USB power supply, or a "charge mule" (a mains charger that has its own internal battery that you can later use to charge your USB kit if you are away from a mains outlet).

- A set of three AA batteries (alkaline preferred), supplying about 4.5 volts. You would be well advised to check with the vendor of your display before committing to battery operation, however; some (but not all) LCD displays I have tried lose brightness and contrast very quickly when operated even slightly below +5V. If you are not running on +5V you could replace resistor R2 with a slightly lower value. However, you need to refer to the data sheet of the LCD display that you buy to determine a new value for a different voltage. Make certain that you don't take the backlight LED over its maximum current, or else you will damage it. The data sheets for some LCD displays are strangely silent on the subject of maximum backlight LED current. If in doubt, 50 ma is a reasonably safe guess.

The capacitors C2 and C3 are to smooth out any fluctuations in the power supply, and, again, these are not usually needed if you're building the project on your test bed rig.

The TTL level serial port (ST2) allows you connect to an external terminal emulator running in your desktop machine. Your test rig probably already has this of course, but if not, or if you are building a keeper version of this game, take a look at the "Serial ports" discussion near the end of Chapter 3 to see how to easily setup a serial channel to a desktop or laptop using a USB to TTL serial dongle.

The press button (momentary action, single pole, push to make) switch can be any switch that suits. In this application I'd advise a nice "clicky" switch that gives you strong feedback when you press it: you press the button a lot during this game, so you need something that you can be sure you have pressed. If you're not keen on having the push-button switch mounted on the breadboard, or it doesn't have the right connector type to plug in, you can put long leads on the switch and mount it in a small plastic box (you may find something suitable going out for recycling).

WordDune: The Build

I initially built WordDune on the test bed rig. I started by installing the 4x20 LCD display (with header pins fitted) onto the test bed rig breadboard on the upper side at column 40. Then, I installed tie-high and tie-low jumpers as indicated on the circuit diagram; I also installed R2. Figure 10-3 shows this stage.

Figure 10-3. *WordDune: LCD display at column 40 with ties and R2 installed*

Next, I installed the seven "flying" jumpers that are required to link the signals between the MCU and the display. The photo in Figure 10-4 depicts this step.

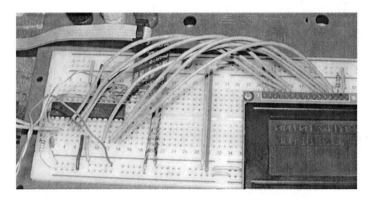

Figure 10-4. *WordDune flying jumpers installed*

The next step was to connect a push button S1 between ground and AVR pin 15 (see Figure 10-5). I took a button switch and soldered some wires to it (I had cut the wires out of an old CAT5 network cable). I've found that solid (not stranded) wires pulled out of old CAT5 cables make ideal connections because the stripped wire ends fit neatly into breadboard holes (see Figure 10-6).

Figure 10-5. *WordDune: The push button*

Figure 10-6. *Push button wired to the test rig*

The push button I used in fact has an LED indicator in it. I haven't used that in this version, but a spare pin on the AVR could easily be used to make the button light up to indicate times when the program is waiting for the button to be pressed. I leave this as an exercise for any reader who would like to take this extra step.

While doing the extensive testing for the game (it's a tough job, but somebody had to do it) I did in fact get tired of the push button flopping around, so I liberated a coffee jar lid from our recycling box, cut a button-size hole in the top of it, cut a wire-size hole in the side, spray painted the whole thing black, and mounted the button into it (see Figure 10-7). Hey, presto! A much more usable button mount, (see Figure 10-8).

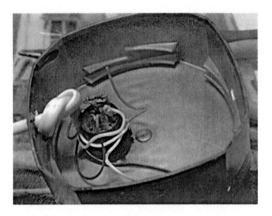

Figure 10-7. *The coffee jar lid button mount*

Figure 10-8. *Button holder complete*

So, for building the game on the test bed rig, that's about all there is to it!

WordDune Gameplay

A WordDune is a random jumble of numbers letter and symbols in which a set of four actual words is hidden, somewhere. The trouble is, this dune keeps shifting; the words appear but they are soon buried in the continuing onscreen torrent of random characters and letters. The torrent gets faster and denser at each level. You, as the player must spot the words. At the end of a level, you have to know what the four words were.

For each level, four words are randomly chosen from a list of words. You can add or remove words from this list to keep the game fresh. Each word is on screen at a random place for a few moments, four times during each level. However, as the levels progress, the onscreen time of each word gets less, and the clutter around the actual words gets denser, making it harder to spot.

The challenge is to identify the four words and–if you're playing against others–to say them out loud before the four words are revealed at the end of the round. You can play the game in a group, or just on your own as a personal challenge.

The game has two distinct splash sequences (animated sequences that play over and over while the software is waiting for someone to start off a WordDune game). The screenshots in Figures 10-9 through 10-15 show the game in progress at various levels.

Figure 10-9. *WordDune: Start prompt*

Figure 10-10. *WordDune: Level 0 in progress*

Figure 10-11. *WordDune: End of level 0 screen*

Figure 10-12. *Level 1: The introducer screen*

Figure 10-13. *WordDune: CLIFF in lowercase soup*

Figure 10-14. *WordDune: Level 3, Albatross disappearing*

Figure 10-15. *WordDune: The game end*

The first two screenshots show the start prompt that immediately follows the animated attractor sequence, and a game in progress at level 0. In level 0 words appear on the screen and are only gradually erased by spaces. It's so easy you could do it in your sleep!

When a game level ends you get a screen like the one shown in Figure 10-11. When you click, you get shown the four words that you were searching for in the level that just completed. Then, it's onto the next and slightly harder level. Figure 10-12 illustrates the Level 1 introducer screen.

As the levels progress, it gets harder to see the words, which are, first, among lowercase random letters and then later among random letters and numbers. And the words start getting overwritten faster and faster with each new level. In Figures 10-13 and 10-14, CLIFF is quite easy to spot and you can probably just about see where ALBATROSS was, but a short time ago!

So, it starts very easy, but gets harder and harder. On the easy levels it's worth remembering that, once you've spotted the four words, you can terminate a level early by clicking the button (see Figure 10-15).

WordDune: Game Software Setup

When you have the hardware ready (as per the circuit diagram in Figure 10- 1 and the build instructions) you can install the software. The installation of this software is a little unusual.

■ **Note**   You can download the sketch for this example at `www.apress.com/9781430244462`.

Setting up the game proceeds in two steps.

- You first open the WordDune sketch and compile and upload it into the AVR using the usual upload method within the Arduino IDE. This, as usual, performs a chip erase before uploading (which, of course, erases the EEPROM as well as all the flash memory).

- Next, you use AVRDude to put the contents of the file `WordDune_EEPROM.Hex` into the AVR's EEPROM memory. In WordDune, the EEPROM is used to hold a catalog of prompts and error messages: but the main use for it is to hold a dictionary of words that the game will use. As we shall see in the "WordDune Commands" section later on, you can add words, delete words, and list the contents of this dictionary using commands into the serial channel.

The idea of setting up the software in this way is to maximize the available space in EEPROM for the word list (which for, some reason, I misleadingly called a dictionary). The game works best when you have a large list of words. By adding new words you build up the size of the list; you can typically get about 90 words of average length into the space available in an ATmega328 EEPROM space. All words are entered and held in uppercase. If you try to enter a word that's already in the list it will be rejected as a duplicate. The maximum length of a word is 20 characters. You start off with a default set of ten words, but you can add to or take away words and list all the current words using commands into the serial port.

The EEPROM also holds the error messages catalog and the help text that reminds you of what commands are available (see section 'WordDune Commands"). We could hold all this stuff in flash memory (using PROGMEM) or we could use the unsupported EEMEM keyword in the code to specify EEPROM contents, but it's easier (and uses completely supported Arduino functions) to do it this way.

Here is the detailed procedure for installing the game, once you have constructed the hardware. You will need the `WordDune.PDE` file containing the Word_Dune V3 sketch. You will need the `WordDune_EEPROM.Hex` file (which actually contains just raw bytes, not a hex dump). You will need to use AVRDude to upload the contents of the hex file into the AVR's EEPROM.

First, you load up Word_Dune_V3 (see Figure 10-16) into Arduino. Press the "Upload" button to build (compile) the program and upload it into your AVR. The program itself should be approximately 15 KB in size.

Figure 10-16. *WordDune: Word_Dune_V3 sketch in Arduino*

Now, start up a terminal window and execute the following AVRDude command:

```
avrdude -p m328 -P /dev/ttyACM0 -c avrisp2 -U eeprom:w:WordDune_EEPROM.Hex:r
```

You'll need to adapt this command if you are using some other variant of AVR (e.g., an ATmega328p) and you'll almost certainly need to change the /dev/ttyACM0 port name to whatever one you are using for your AVR programmer. For example, on a Windows system, you would use a COM port number such as COM2 instead. The section "AVRDude" in Chapter 3 contains help on finding out your port number if you need it; Chapter 3 also contains help in other related areas regarding using AVRDude level MCU programming.

Once the EEPROM upload is complete (WordDune will restart after the upload because the chip is reset as the last part of that upload) you're ready to start playing–as per the earlier game instructions.

WordDune Commands

WordDune supports a number of commands that you can issue via the TTL serial channel. When you are typing these commands, you will sometimes experience a second or so delay before the characters are echoed back; this is because the AVR is doing things on the LCD screen that delay the response. Nothing is lost; it's just a very short delay in echoing the characters you type.

In summary,

- All commands and words are in UPPERCASE.

- You only need the first three characters of the command for it to be recognized, but you can type in the whole command if you want to (e.g., DIC or DICTIONARY will both work).

- If you make a mistake, you can use the backspace key on your keyboard to rub out characters.

- Pressing CTRL/R will show you what characters you have typed in your command so far.

- Press the return or Enter key when your command is complete.

The following table provides a list and description of each of the commands:

Command	Description
HELP	Shows a list of all the available commands.
ADD [Word]	Add a new word to the dictionary. All words will be uppercase. If word is already in the dictionary (the word list) then it will be rejected as a duplicate. If word was added, confirmation is given. The number of free characters remaining in the word list, after this word has been added, is also shown. Example: "ADD SPINNING."
DEPROM	Show a hex dump of the entire EEPROM: shows a hex dump (hex values plus actual characters) of the EEPROM contents. This is mainly a debug feature.
DICTIONARY	Show a list of the words in the dictionary. Gives a numbered list of the currently known words.
SWC	Show Word Count–shows how many words are in the dictionary (word list).
LEVEL [LevelID #]	If used alone, just shows the current game level number. If used with an argument, sets the game level to the indicated value. Game levels number from 0 (beginner) to 6 (Impossible!) Example: "LEV 2".
DELETE [Word]	Delete the indicated word. Example: "DEL SPINNING."

General Software Structure

The WordDune software comprises four blocks of data:

- The main body of code for the game. This is, as usual, stored in the flash program memory.

- A catalog of messages and prompts that the program uses to interact with and inform the user, both on the LCD screen and also via the serial channel, if active. This message catalog approach is useful because

- If messages are simply included in the main code (i.e., they just occur inline in the code in various println() function), then the strings of text comprising those messages have to be stored in the main flash memory. In the WordDune case it's not a problem, since there is plenty of spare code space when using an ATmega328. However, where the program code body is larger, and there are more than a few messages, this can soon eat up all your code memory to the point where your software no longer fits. You might think that you could declare the messages as static variables. However, it turns out that is an even worse alternative, since static values are held first in flash memory (as part of the program) but then they *also* get cached at runtime in RAM memory, which is a scarce resource on an AVR chip.

  - Having the program's messages in a catalog makes it easier to change the language the program "speaks." If you wanted to change all the program's messages to, for example, German, it would be quite easy to do, since most are in one place and not distributed throughout the code.

- The help text, which is put out to the serial port in response to a HELP command. Again this is, in MCU terms, quite a lot of data.

- The word list (called the dictionary in the software for reasons that now escape me). Although the code includes an initial set of ten words, the idea is that you will add a lot more words via serial channel commands once you have the game working.

In the WordDune implementation, the message catalog, the help text, and the word list are all held in the MCU's EEPROM. As you will remember, this is nonvolatile but reprogrammable memory on the AVR chip which is available to store user data.

In the game setup instructions we installed a ready-made EEPROM image using AVRDude (see "Game Software Setup"). This image was actually built by another Arduino sketch called CatBuilder (available from this book's web site, www.apress.com/9781430244462). This sketch programs the EEPROM memory from a set of text arrays. If you wanted to make alterations to the message catalog, this is where you should do it. The steps are as follows:

- Make your alterations to the data sections of CatBuilder and resave the sketch.

- Compile and upload your modified version of CatBuilder into your MCU.

- Let the modified CatBuilder run.

- Once it completes, use AVRDude to save your new EEPROM image into a new file with a descriptive name, something like

  ```
  avrdude -p m328 -P /dev/ttyACM0 -c avrisp2 -U eeprom:r:WordDune_German.Hex:r
  ```

  (Again, you will need to adjust the port name from /dev/ttyACM0 to whatever you are using, and perhaps use a different AVR part code if you're not using an ATmega328).

From the perspective of an Arduino sketch, the EEPROM is seen as a set of read-writable bytes, numbering from 0-n (where n is the last byte). These are accessed as follows:

```
EEPROM.read(x) ;  // Returns a byte value from EEPROM address x.
EEPROM.write(x,y); // Writes the byte value y into EEPROM address x.
```

CatBuilder fills the EEPROM space with a set of three catalog data structures, the message catalog, the help message catalog, and the dictionary (word list) catalog. The first six bytes of EEPROM contain pointers to the start address of each of these catalogs. Each pointer is a 16-bit value, stored in two bytes. Specifically, these are as follows:

EEPROM Bytes 0&1 = EEPROM address of the message catalogue (low byte first).

EEPROM Bytes 2&3 = EEPROM address of the help message catalogue (low byte first).

EEPROM Bytes 4&5 = EEPROM address of the start of the dictionary (low byte first).

The format of these catalogs is very simple. They use seven-bit ASCII characters. ASCII stands for American Standard Code for Information Interchange: a standardized Western alphabet and number coding scheme. See Arduino's help page on ASCII in the reference section or on the Wikipedia page

http://en.wikipedia.org/wiki/ASCII

Each catalog entry is a series of ASCII coded seven-bit characters, with the final character having bit 7 set, to indicate the end of the catalog entry. A byte containing 255 at what should be the start of an entry indicates the end of the catalog. The following table illustrates this arrangement.

Char	"H"	"E"	"L"	"L"	"O"	[Space]	"Y"	"O"	"U"	"O"	"K"	"A"	"Y"	NONE
Value (Dec)	72	69	75	75	79	32	89	79	213 (=85+128)	79	75	65	217(=89+128)	255
Offset	0	1	2	3	4	5	6	7	8	9	10	11	12	13

We have only two messages "Hello You" and "Okay" in this catalog. Each of the messages is terminated by a byte with bit 7 set: bit 7 is always 0 in ASCII codes, so to indicate that a character is the last one in the string, we retain the code, but we add 128 (binary weight of bit 7) to it to show it's the last character (as in the case of "U" and "Y" in Table 10-2). When we read the value 255 as the first byte of a message, it means we have reached the end of the catalog.

The help message is implemented as a catalog with just one single message incorporating newlines where needed, but the messages catalog and the word list/dictionary are multientry catalogs. To retrieve a message from a catalog you simply need to know the entry number (e.g., in Table 10-2, the string "Hello You" would be entry #0 and the string "Okay" would be entry #2). We'll see how this works in more detail in the section "WordDune Sketch Code Walk.".

Although CatBuilder reserves EEPROM space for the word list/dictionary catalog, it's actually the WordDune sketch that initializes it to the default set of words, if it hasn't already been done.

WordDune Sketch Code Walk

The following code walk summarizes each of the functions within the WordDune program. Please refer to the program sources themselves, available from www.apress.com/9781430244462.

WordDune: Declarations Section

This section sets up various operation parameters and constants. Of interest might be

- DO_FORMAT which causes the EEPROM contents to be reinitialized.

- WORDS_PER_LEVEL which allows you to set more or fewer words to be spotted at each level.

- The initial set of words comes from the declaration of the array firstWords. If you don't want to use the TTL serial channel to expand your word list you can expand this array with additional or different words and then set up the game again (as per earlier instructions).

- levelData, which is an array of values that set the timing parameters for each level of the game. See the comments embedded in the program code for what these mean.

setup()

In the setup function the serial channel is initialized, the LCD screen parameters set up, and the screen cleared. The switch port is made into an input, and the pull-up on it is enabled (by writing HIGH to it). Then, if there are no words yet in the dictionary, or DO_FORMAT is true, we format the word list area of the EEPROM. We then check if there are a usable number of words and output a message saying how many words there are using sayMessage(). The current game level is set to 0; the serial channel gets a "WordDune" prompt sent to it.

Because the game makes use of random selections at several points, we need a random element to seed the random number generator. What we do is read a value from the floating analog input 2 which will be some random value based on whatever electrical mush that input is picking up at that moment. We use that as the random seed to ensure we get different random numbers each time we play. Then, we transfer control to doSplashScreen() which does pretty stuff on the LCD screen, all the while inviting the user to click the press button to play a game. When a user does this, then, the splash screen returns control to setup(), we clear the LCD screen, and setup() ends, transferring control to the main loop().

loop()

In the main loop of the program, we select four random words (issuing an error message and going into a terminal loop if there are not enough words available to do so). Then, having selected the words, we call the level introducer, which does all the onscreen stuff to gently take a user into a game level. After waiting for the click switch to be released, we enter the main part of the level loop.

In the main part of the loop we loop around very fast, putting individual characters on the screen at random locations. To choose the individual characters, we use a switch case block, casing off the current game level, to choose a random character according to the game level: at first it's spaces and symbols, which makes it far easier to spot complete uppercase words among them, but for the higher levels it's a mix of lower- and uppercase letters and then eventually it's all uppercase letters, among which it's very hard to spot complete words. Every now and again, by seeing if a randomly generated number matches a preset value, we put one of our chosen complete words on the screen. Just before the end of each loop we check to see if the user has pressed the button. It's part of the game spec that they don't have to wait until the end of a level to see the list of words they were supposed to have spotted–they can end the level early if they think they already know the words. Also, at the end of each loop we check to see if there has been any input from the serial channel and we go process anything that has arrived.

When all four words have been shown for the configured number of times, the level ends. We do the levelEnd() function (which prompts the user to say what words he has spotted, and then shows him what words were actually duned during this level). We then clear the LCD screen and bump the level counter. If the level just ended was the last, highest level, the user is told game over and invited to play again and the game restarts at level 0. Otherwise we loop around again to play the next level in sequence.

format_EEPROM()

Args: `Size` and `StartByte`

This function fills the indicated section of the EEPROM with all ones (0xFF). The fill operation starts from `StartByte` and goes on until EEPROM address `Size` is reached.

addToDictionary()

Args: `theWord`

This function appends the provided ASCII-coded word to the end of the word list (dictionary). It fails if the word already exists, if it was invalid, or if the WordList catalog is full.

dumpEEPROMToSerialChannel()

Args: None

This function outputs a hex dump (Hex and ASCII format) of the EEPROM contents to the serial channel (see Figure 10-17).

```
alan@Ubuntu001: ~
0000: 06 00 ee 00 7d 01 0a 0d 0a 57 6f 72 64 20 44 75    ....}....Word Du
0010: 6e 65 3a 20 56 65 72 73 69 6f 6e a0 42 61 73 65    ne: Version.Base
0020: 20 64 69 63 74 69 6f 6e 61 72 79 20 72 65 62 75     dictionary rebu
0030: 69 6c f4 3d 3d 3d 3d 3d 3d bd 20 65 6e 74 72 69    il.======. entri
0040: 65 73 20 66 6f 75 6e 64 ae 20 46 72 65 65 20 73    es found. Free s
0050: 70 61 63 65 20 3d a0 57 6f 72 64 20 77 61 73 20    pace =.Word was
0060: 61 64 64 65 e4 57 6f 72 64 20 4e 4f 54 20 61 64    adde.Word NOT ad
0070: 64 65 64 3a a0 49 6e 73 75 66 66 69 63 69 65 6e    ded:.Insufficien
0080: 74 20 73 70 61 63 65 ae 44 69 63 74 69 6f 6e 61    t space.Dictiona
0090: 72 79 20 63 6f 72 72 75 70 74 bf 4d 69 6e 69 6d    ry corrupt.Minim
00a0: 75 6d 20 63 68 61 72 20 63 6f 75 6e 74 20 69 73    um char count is
00b0: a0 4e 6f 74 20 61 64 64 65 64 3a 20 45 72 72 6f    .Not added: Erro
00c0: 72 20 63 6f 64 65 20 3d a0 55 6e 6b 6e 6f 77 6e    r code =.Unknown
00d0: 20 63 6d 64 ae 4e 6f 20 73 75 63 68 20 77 6f 72     cmd.No such wor
00e0: 64 a1 57 6f 72 64 20 65 78 69 73 74 73 a1 43 6f    d.Word exists.Co
00f0: 6d 6d 61 6e 64 73 3a 0a 0d 41 44 44 20 5b 57 6f    mmands:..ADD [Wo
0100: 72 64 5d 3a 20 41 64 64 20 6e 65 77 20 77 6f 72    rd]: Add new wor
0110: 64 0a 0d 44 45 50 3a 20 44 75 6d 70 20 45 45 50    d..DEP: Dump EEP
0120: 52 4f 4d 0a 0d 44 49 43 3a 20 4c 69 73 74 20 64    ROM..DIC: List d
0130: 69 63 74 69 6f 6e 61 72 79 0a 0d 4c 45 56 3a 20    ictionary..LEV:
0140: 73 65 74 2f 73 68 6f 77 20 67 61 6d 65 20 6c 65    set/show game le
0150: 76 65 6c 0a 0d 44 45 4c 3a 20 44 65 6c 65 74 65    vel..DEL: Delete
0160: 20 77 6f 72 64 0a 0d 53 57 43 3a 20 53 68 6f 77     word..SWC: Show
0170: 20 77 6f 72 64 20 63 6f 75 6e 74 0a 8d 53 55 50     word count..SUP
```

Figure 10-17. WordDune: Output from the dump EEPROM (DEP) command

The DEP command is mainly useful for debug purposes.

dumpDictToSerialChannel()

Args: None

This function outputs a formatted list of words in the dictionary/word list to the serial channel. Figure 10-18 illustrates the output.

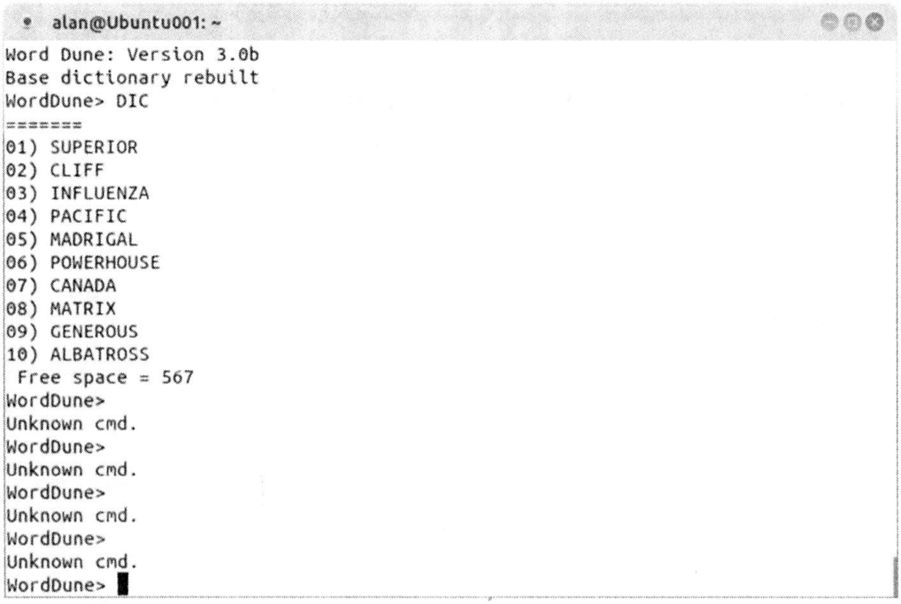

```
alan@Ubuntu001: ~                                    ⊖ ⊖ ⊗
Word Dune: Version 3.0b
Base dictionary rebuilt
WordDune> DIC
=======
01) SUPERIOR
02) CLIFF
03) INFLUENZA
04) PACIFIC
05) MADRIGAL
06) POWERHOUSE
07) CANADA
08) MATRIX
09) GENEROUS
10) ALBATROSS
 Free space = 567
WordDune>
Unknown cmd.
WordDune>
Unknown cmd.
WordDune>
Unknown cmd.
WordDune>
Unknown cmd.
WordDune> █
```

Figure 10-18. WordDune: Output from the Dictionary command

The table below describes the less major functions of the program.

NAME	ARGS	Description
returnDictWordCount()	None	This function returns an integer indicating the number of words currently in the word list/dictionary. It can return zero, if the list is empty.
getDictWord()	wordNum, byteArray	This function returns the wordNumth word from the list by writing it into the byte array. If there is no word at index wordNum then it returns -1 to indicate an error.
doInputBufferParser()	None	This function is called when a terminating character (return key) has been received via the serial line. This function looks at the contents of the input buffer and tries to resolve it into an actionable command. If it finds a command, it actions it with the appropriate program functions. If no match is found, it just puts out an "unrecognized command" response.

(continued)

NAME	ARGS	Description
processKeyboardChar()	theChar	Each time the serial line receives a character this function is called. If the received character is a normal printable character it is converted to uppercase (if it's a letter), it is echoed back to the serial channel and it is placed into the next available slot in the input buffer. If it's not a normal printable character then the function checks to see if it's a terminator (return), in which case doInputBufferParser is called. If it's a backspace then the rubout routine is run. If it's CTRL/R the contents of the input buffer are echoed back out to the serial channel.
sayMessage()	catNumber, msgNumber, outMsg, doNewLine	This function first retrieves the indicated message number from the indicated catalog. (0 = messages, 1 = help, dictionary = 2). If outMsg == true then the retrieved message is sent out to the serial channel, ending with a newline if indicated by the doNewLine arg. If outMsg is false then the message is only retrieved but nothing is done with it. This is purely to provide a debug tool for checking if a message exists. Returns an empty message if the requested message was found, or a generic error message if it was not.
returnZeroPackedNumberString()	number, desiredNumberLength	This function returns a string representation of the indicated number front-padded with zeroes to make it up to the indicated length. So, for example, returnZeroPackedNumberString (3,3) would return "003." Returns an empty string if there was a problem. Note: We could have used sprintf() for this, but that would have used more memory.
returnFreeEEPROMSpace()	EEPROM_LEN	This function returns an integer indicating how many free bytes remain in the EEPROM. The arg tells it the overall size of the EEPROM (since this cannot easily be discovered dynamically). In effect, due to the way the catalogs in EEPROM are structured, the number returned from this function indicates how many more characters can be added to the dictionary/word list.

(continued)

NAME	ARGS	Description
doDeleteWord()	wordToZap	This function deletes the indicated word from the dictionary/word list and fills in the empty space it leaves behind to maintain the integrity of the catalog. The argument wordToZap can be sent as "*" (asterisk) meaning delete *all* words. The user is appropriately prompted to confirm any delete action. The function returns true or false according to whether the word delete(s) went ahead or not.
returnWordLocation()	theWord	This function is a utility for other functions. It returns the EEPROM offset location of a word in the catalog. Returns -1 if the word was not found.
returnDictionaryBase()	None	This function is a utility for other functions. It returns the EEPROM address where the dictionary/word list begins.
doLevelIntroducer()	levelNumber, wordCount	This function does all the messaging and prompting necessary to introduce the user of the game to a new level. The level number being introduced and the number of words available for use are indicated in the args. The function only returns when it detects that a user has pressed the push button.
selectFourWords()	None	This function selects four unique words from the dictionary/word list. These are placed in the duneWords array. If there are insufficient words available it returns -1.
findNumberInWordArray()	numToFind	Utility function used by others. Returns true if the word array already contains the indicated word number.
chooseRandomWordIndexIndex()	None	Utility function used by others. Returns the index of a duneWord that has not yet been shown four times during the current level.
returnTotalTryCount()	None	Utility function used by others. Returns an integer indicating how many complete words have been shown during the current level.
doLevelEnd()	None	Utility function used by others. Does everything required at the end of a game level. Tells the user the level has ended, prompts her to click when she is ready to see the word list and then awaits a further click to proceed to next level or game end.

(continued)

NAME	ARGS	Description
showDuneWords()	onSerial, onLCD, pastTense	A function that shows the duneWords for the current level. The list of words is put out on the serial port and on to the LCD screen as indicated by the args. Uses current (words are...") or past tense ("words were ...") according to the arg. The latter is mainly meant for debug use.
sayThis()	whatToSay, onSerial, onLCD, serialGetsNewLine	A function that puts out a message on the serial port and and/or to the LCD screen as indicated by the args. The serialGetsNewLine arg allows partial messages to be put out and subsequently appended to by others.
awaitKeypress()	timeoutMs, returnWhenPressed, digitalPinNum	A function that will await a use key press for the indicated number of milliseconds (0 means wait forever). Returns either when the timeout period expires or when the button is pressed (returnWhenPressed == true) or when the button has been pressed and then released (returnWhenPressed == false).
doSplashScreen()	None	Does a selection of eye-catching and pretty things on the LCD screen while waiting for the user to press the button to start a game. In arcade game terms this is an attractor sequence.
fillScreenWithRandomCharacters()	None	A utility function used by doSplashScreen(). Does what the name suggests!
doSerialInput()	None	Checks for an incoming character on the serial channel, if any is found calls processKeyboardCharacter to buffer the received character. It calls the input buffer parses if the character is a terminator.

That concludes our code walk, and our description of the game WordDune. Have fun with it!

Summary

In this chapter we have looked at a game of observation called WordDune. We looked at the hardware, the game play, and the software. We looked at how you can customize the game by adding your own words to it. We also took a detailed code walk.

Coming Up Next

Project 4: The Lighting Waterfall.

▄ ▄ ▄

CHAPTER 11

Project 4: The Lighting Waterfall

Light the Way—Ever So Prettily!

In this chapter we look at a project that is not only useful but pretty. If you have a passageway or corridor or even a long, thin room in your home that could do with some nice lighting, then this could be the project for you.

People used to expect very little of the lighting in their homes. One nice bright light in the middle of the room, a simple on/off switch, and the job was done. The fact that our parents and grandparents were happy with this kind of lighting was probably a reflection of the fact that *their* forefathers had to spend their darkness hours trying to read or work by feeble gaslights or even candlelight: so, to them, being able to make a room as bright as daylight whenever they wanted must have seemed like a dream come true. Viva Edison and Swann!

But pretty soon people realized that controlled and varied lighting could greatly enhance and transform even a very plain room: the more chic lighting styles of the 1950s and 1960s were born. Semiconductor technology entered the scene when–in the 1970s–it became possible to make a light dimmer that would fit into the footprint of a standard wall switch. Now, you could not only place lights strategically to enhance a room, you could set their brightness to whatever you wanted. Why not have several lights? Have some with plain white lamps in, and perhaps some different colored ones to create different pools of light within the room.

A steady stream of incremental developments to lighting followed that continues to this day. If you could make a device that would allow people to manually control the brightness of their lights, why couldn't you give them an IR remote control, so that they could do it from their seat? If you could remotely control the state and brightness of all the lights in a room, why couldn't you give control of those functions to an automated system? If that system could be given access to "people sensors," why couldn't the lights automatically come on when someone entered the room and go off a little while after the last person left it? Do you need different lighting setups in the room for different times of the day, or days of the week? No problem; the control system could be made to remember "scenes": each scene can have preset color combinations, brightness settings, even light directions if you add a motorized direction setting to the light fittings.

In more recent times, the LED–previously thought of mostly as an indicator light or for making seven-segment displays for clocks or technical equipment–suddenly got brighter and jazzier. Developments such as Professor Shuji Nakamura's invention of the blue LED in the mid-1990s (he also perfected bright LEDs in green and white colors) made LEDs a serious contender for the filament lamp's crown as light source of choice. LED lights use a great deal less electricity than conventional lighting methods, and they have a much longer lifetime. However, LED lighting was initially far more expensive than traditional lighting. This is partly because LEDs work on low-voltage DC, not high-voltage mains AC and so the additional cost of providing a converter is involved, but the price difference is also due to higher production costs. Also, LED light gives a different, more directional light than the lights we have been used to, which has met with some consumer resistance. However, with innovations such as "warm" LED lighting, better diffusers, and ever higher intensity devices, plus the ever increasing cost of domestic electricity and desire for more lighting control, the advance of LED lighting has been slow but relentless–to the point where it's no longer impossible to imagine a time when most homes will be mainly lit by LED lighting.

One characteristic of LED lighting is that it often aggregates lots of small LEDs to form a light source. For example, the LED work light pictured (assembled and disassembled) in Figure 11-1 uses 72 pure white LEDs to provide a bright directional work light[1] from a 6V battery source. In the case of this particular light all the LEDs come on at the same time and brightness; this is just a work light. However, in other products, LED lights intended for use as disco light shows or ambient lighting components for restaurants, LEDs are organized into groups or banks of lights to give very fine control over lighting levels and sequencing.

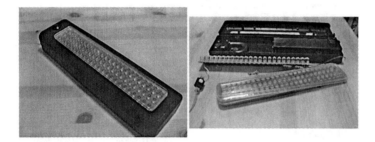

Figure 11-1. *72 LED worklight*

When you bring this together with the ability of an MCU to exercise detailed control over a large number of individual LEDs or sets of LEDs, you can suddenly see the possibility of exercising endlessly detailed variable control over room lighting schemes and doing things that, previously, were prohibitively complex or expensive.

The project we're about to see is but one example . . .

The Passageway Light

Most homes have some kind of hallway, corridor, or passageway, either inside or as a covered way outside. Some homes have long, thin rooms which can be difficult to light with any style. When we moved into our house, the 16-foot (5 meters) passageway that goes along the middle of it was lit by a single pendant, an unshaded bulb hanging from the ceiling. The switch for this light was at one end of the passageway. It let you see where you were going, but it received zero points for eye appeal, convenience, and style. I wondered what I could do to light this space better: this project (or, more precisely, projects, since we'll also see the design for a MKII version) was the result.

I'm a great believer in the interior designer's notion that if you want to give a room some style, you must light it with indirect light sources. Okay, you do still need to have a brash, bright light available for cleaning, decorating, looking for a lost key, and so on, but take a cue from the hospitality industry! Most clubs, restaurants, and bars have fluorescent tubes on the ceiling, but they're only there so that the cleaners and maintenance staff can see what they're doing—and those places can look pretty plain and ugly in that mode. There's a reason we refer to the "cold light of day"! However, when serving their main purpose, being a party place, the plain lights go off and the atmosphere lighting takes over—usually making the place look superb. Why should the relaxation rooms of your home be any different? Cold but bright lights for working in them (found that key yet?) and softer, more varied, lights for when you're relaxing in them. So, I started with the idea that these would be hidden, indirect lights.

Nobody stays in the passageway, people only pass through on their way to one of the other rooms, and so my next design goal was that the lights should come on when needed but automatically go off again after some fixed

---

[1] Such products are a very cheap source of LEDs by the way, if you are careful with your desoldering.

amount of time. Then, inspired by the long, thin nature of the space, I seized on the idea of a lighting waterfall; the lights would come on in sequence along the line of the passageway and go off in sequence again when the time-out was reached. Since there were entrances at both ends of the passageway, why couldn't the waterfall come on in the direction of travel? Could the lights fade in and fade out, rather than clicking on or off one by one? Whoa! Suddenly I had a spec in my head for this project!

I was convinced early on that this was going to be a LED lighting scheme. At this time, RGB (Red Green Blue) LED strips were still pretty expensive, but I was quite taken with some flexible LED lights strips that I bought from an online auction site. Being, I think, intended for used on vehicles, these run on 12V DC and seem to be completely waterproof. They can be flexed into pretty much any shape you might need.

I decided to use these for the project and so I bought some single color strips, like the one shown in Figure 11-2, from a well-known Internet auction site. These are available in different lengths containing 12, 24, 30, or 48 LEDs on a flexible PCB set inside a very flexible plastic gel casing. Alternative sources of supply are

- www.bestlightingbuy.com/motorcycle-led-strip-car-lights-flexible-grill-light.html (United States).

- www.brightlightz.co.uk/categories/led-strip-lights-flexible (UK).

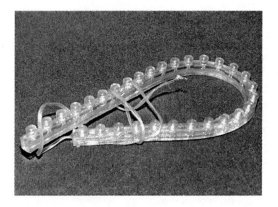

Figure 11-2. *Flexible single color LED strip*

There is, of course, no reason why you should not use SMD (Surface Mount Device) LED strips–cut to your desired length–in your implementation, in which case you would probably need:

- www.sparkfun.com (search for COM-10259; they do many others too) (United States).

- www.maplin.co.uk (search for stock number N56CF, and others) (UK).

This was so obviously a job for an MCU that I never considered any other implementation approach, but that requirement for the LEDs to fade in and out gave me a problem. The ATmega328 that I wanted to use for this project offers four pins with usable hardware PWM capability. These are

- Pin 5 (Arduino D3).

- Pin 15 (Arduino D9).

- Pin 16 (Arduino D10).

- Pin 17 (Arduino D11).

Pins 11 and 12 (Arduino pins D5 and D6, respectively) also offer PWM; however, as noted on the Arduino web site, the millis() and delay() functions of the Arduino software share the same internal timer used to generate PWM on those pins and so when used at low-duty cycles these pins may not fully turn off. Well, we need a reliable black level for this project and we make extensive use of the delay() function in its software; therefore, it seems sensible to stick to using just the PWM pins that can be guaranteed to behave as expected.

All of the above meant that I could only drive four LED strips from the MCU in the way that the spec called for. After a lot of thought, I decided that I would go ahead and build a four-way setup and see how it looked and revisit the project for a MKII approach if necessary.

The project requirements were

- To provide a set of four LED lighting strips (I eventually settled on warm yellow as the LED color, mainly because the walls of the passageway are painted white and would mix well with it).

- To have each lighting strip's brightness be independently software controllable and dimmable between nothing and full brightness using PWM.

- To provide a "person detector" at either end of the passageway which, when triggered, will turn on the lights for a preset 40 seconds.

- To have the lights to come on and go off in a waterfall sequence, starting at the end at which a person enters the passageway. At the end of the time-out sequence, lights go off in the same sequence they came on (i.e., first off is the one that was first on).

- To put the lights permanently on at full intensity via a manual button on the control box.

- To turn the lights off permanently, via a button on the control box, so that they cannot be triggered.

I elected to use two Paradox PA-461 PIR sensors as the "people sensor" elements in this project. These can be obtained at quite low cost if you shop around. We saw a lot of details about these sensors in Chapter 4 on page 60, so I won't recap here. Suffice it to say that you feed the sensors a +12-volt supply and they momentarily break a closed loop contact whenever anyone walks past them. If you can't get these particular sensors, it doesn't matter; your local vendor or favorite online source should be able to supply something similar.

For the purposes of this project I refer to the sensors as

- Sensor 1–also called the "near sensor" because it is near the control box.

- Sensor 2–also called the "far sensor" because it is not near the control box.

The physical layout diagram in Figure 11-7 makes this arrangement clear.

Proving Circuit

In order to develop the software for this project and to refine the hardware design I used the circuit diagram shown in Figure 11-2 to build up the design on the test bed–as built in Chapter 2. If you want to try this design out for yourself, follow this circuit diagram.

As you can see, there is nothing special about it; it uses a ULN2803A Darlington transistor array chip to allow the AVR to drive the LED strips. Each of my LED strips (24 LEDs per strip) uses about 220 ma at 12V, which is well within the capabilities of the 2803, but your LED strip consumption may vary, so check with the vendor before you buy. Some longer (48 LED) strips pull quite a lot more current, so you need to make sure you don't go above about 350 ma per driver or you may get into heat problems with the 2803 and start needing to fit a heatsink.

The circuit diagram shows the MCU as an ATmega328, but originally this used an ATmega168: they are pin-compatible devices, the 168 just has less memory, but that should not matter in this application: if you have an ATmega168 and want to use it, give it a try!

Whichever MCU you use, you should make sure it's running at 8 MHz. Running the MCU at the "out of the box" speed of 1 MHz is not sufficient in this application; it is too slow. If you're not sure how to set your AVR to run at 8 MHz, see the discussion on AVRDude and the CKDIV8 fuse in "AVRDude Out of the Box," in Chapter 3.

As the circuit diagram in Figure 11-3 shows, the four outputs of the AVR which are capable of hardware PWM are used to drive the inputs of the ULN2803A driver chip and therefore the LED strips. The remaining, unused, driver stages on the 2803 have their bases (5B-8B) grounded.

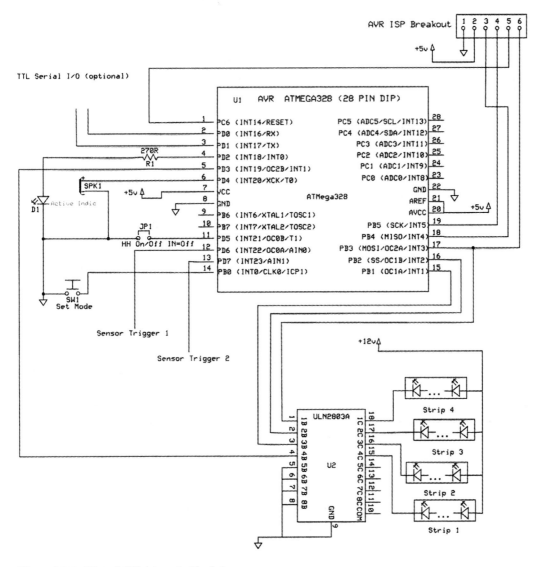

Figure 11-3. *Waterfall lights on test bed rig*

Mostly this will be used as an automatic system, and so the control box is tucked away somewhere unobtrusive. Therefore, rather than use multiple buttons, I decided to have just one push button and to use it to step through the three (plus one) possible controller modes.

- *Automatic mode*: Sensors trigger lights to fade up in appropriate order according to which sensor triggers them.

- *ON mode*: Lights come on and stay on.

253

- *OFF mode*: Lights go off and stay off–even if sensor triggers received.

- A *"pretties" mode*: The LED sets fade up and down in quick alternation. This is the "Easter egg" feature of this program–you get into it by holding down the mode button for about seven seconds until the unit bleeps. Nothing spectacular, but something to surprise your friends or family with, especially once they have gotten used to the normal functions.

The downside of using only one button is that the unit needs to signal to the user which mode is being selected at each button press. For this purpose I added a small piezo speaker. It can be directly attached to an AVR pin and can, if installed properly, be easily loud enough for making the required bleeping noises inside a box. The speaker emits

- A rising tone when a button press sets the unit into Automatic mode.

- A constant pitch tone when entering ON mode.

- A falling tone when entering OFF mode.

I did toy with the idea of having the unit do a short beep whenever the sensors sent in a trigger pulse, but I quickly concluded (based on experience in the past) that such a feature would quickly get to be annoying.

I added a heartbeat LED connected to pin 4 of the MCU (Arduino pin D2). This is just a single LED that is pulsed on and off once per second by the program (and just blips very briefly when the unit is in OFF mode). This is handy as a visual confirmation that the software is still running and on the rails!

I also added a jumper, JP1: This is intended to let the software know whether or not it is being used with an integrated home help "smart home" system. When this jumper is IN (i.e., the two contacts are bridged) then the software will not expect to output status information on its serial channel to a superior system. This is largely a future-oriented feature, not of immediate use.

Whether or not the unit thinks it is participating in a larger "smart home" setup, it will always accept incoming commands from the serial channel. Most of these were originally for helping with test purposes (e.g., to be able to simulate sensor activations when no sensors were actually wired up to the initial version built up on the test rig). However, many of them are useful to keep in the mix for troubleshooting the unit, should any problems occur. I originally envisaged just one or two commands, but by the time I had completed the software, the command set had grown. The following table lists the commands in the finished software,

Command	Effect
ALLOFF	All LED strips go off and stay off.
ALLON	All LED strips come on and stay on at full brightness.
BEEP	Makes the unit beep. Useful to ensure the unit is still operating properly.
CLOCK	Shows the system time, this is how many milliseconds since the unit started.
CYCLE	The unit enters FADECYCLE mode for 1.5 times the length of the period set for sensor triggering.
FDN	Fade Down: all LEDs fade from maximum brightness to off.
FUP	Fade UP: all LEDs fade up from minimum to maximum brightness.
Ixxx	Intensity. Sets all LED strips to the indicated intensity level, where xxx is a number from 0 to 255. Illegal values are ignored.
SPP	Show PWM Parameters. Prints a table of the current PWM settings for each LED strip.
Txx	Trigger: Simulates a trigger from an external sensor. xx should 01 or 02 according to the sensor to be simulated.

Waterfall Lights Software

The final software for the MKI waterfall lights (then still called the "passageway lights") was version 2.0a. The software is rather too big to reproduce in full here, but it is downloadable from the book's web site (www.apress.com/9781430244462). The following is a function-by-function code walk summary of the software:

Function Name	Args/return type	Commentary
Global header	None/void	In the global header section of this program a set of hardware related constants are declared. For example, these set pin numbers for items like the BUTTON and the SOUNDER.
		Then the constants for the three different available fade rates are set.
		The SEQUENCE_STAGGER constant is declared to be 500 milliseconds: this determines the speed of the waterfall effect (i.e., the time delay between each LED strip down the line being taken to its next level of brightness during a fade up or fade down).
		Then the sensor count is declared. You could just run this with one sensor if you wanted to.
		Constants are declared for the various light modes that the LED strips can enter. Only FADEIN, FADEOUT, FADECYCLE, and ON and OFF are actually implemented in this version.
		After explaining PWM, the main data structure used by the program–a LIGHT_STRUCT–is defined and an instance of it (the lights[] array) is created and filled with details such as pin numbers that control each light represented in the array. All PWM values are set to zero, meaning all lights start as off.
		Next, constants are declared to define things like how many lights are being controlled and how long they stay on when triggered.
		After defining the program modes and the push-button long press duration (for the Easter egg) and doing a few more initializations and declarations, the header is done.
setup()	None/void	In the setup() function the various pins required for the control button, the LED strip drivers, the heartbeat LED, the sense pin, etc., are all set to the appropriate pin type, INPUT or OUTPUT. All input pins have their pull-up resistors enabled by writing a HIGH to them.
		The smart home help jumper is read to see if that mode is needed.
		The serial channel is initialized and an announcement sent to it with the program version number and build date.
		Finally, the power up sound is made on the internal speaker.

(continued)

Function Name	Args/return type	Commentary
loop()	None	The program now enters the main loop. For various reasons, we don't want the loop() function to continually reinitialize at each loop in the usual way. So all the code in the loop() function is run inside a do-while loop that can never end. It will run round until forever, but without reinitializing any of loop()'s resources as it otherwise would. We could use static variables but . . . nah!
		The loop starts by calling the doSerialInput() function (see below in this table).
		Then, it looks to see if the mode button is pressed. If the button is NOT pressed now, but it was pressed last time we checked, then we check if it was a long press (Easter egg) or a normal press. If it was a normal length press, we call the shortPress() function, or the longPress() function if not.
		If the button IS pressed now, we check to see how long it's been pressed for and action a longPress() if that is called for.
		If the button is pressed now, but was not pressed last time we looked, then we remember the time now: this, when the button is released in future, allows us to know how long it was pressed for.
		Next the program checks the sensor inputs. If the program is in normal (automatic) mode and a sensor is found to have been triggered then the sensorEvent() function is called. The sensors used in the prototype stay active for about one second, easily long enough for the main loop to spot their activation. Different sensors with shorter activation durations might need some adjustment to this approach.
		Now, the program enters the lights processing loop. Inside this, the required state of the lights–as represented by the contents of the lights[] array–are made real by writing out each light's PWM state to the pin that controls it. Individual lights can be set to enter different modes in future, principally in the fadeCycle() function (see below in this table). We next check to see if any such change is pending for the current light and action it if so.
		Turn-off times for lights are processed, and the lights processing loop ends.
		If the 100th-of-a-second function is due to be run it is invoked now. The hundredthSec() function does fade advances and other things–see below in this table.
oneSec()	None/void	The oneSec() function is called once per second from hundredthSec(); it pulses the heartbeat (a.k.a. "active") LED at a rate appropriate to the current mode of operation (once per second for normal, very short bursts of light for OFF.

(*continued*)

Function Name	Args/return type	Commentary
hundredthSec()	None/void	hundredthSec() is a function that is called once every 100th of a second from loop(). It acts as a dispatcher for once per second events and for lights processing events (such as fade progressions and control changes). The various lighting modes (FADEIN, etc.) are implemented in a switch table within this function. Important to realize that this function only works on the lights[] array, it does not directly change the pin states– that only happens in the main loop() as we saw above.
doInputBufferParser()	None/Boolean	doInputBufferParser() is called from doSerialInput() when that function recognizes it has received a terminator character. This function uses a switch table to try to recognize one of the implemented command and checks the supplied command line arguments (if any are needed) before it calls the required command's implementation function. Unknown commands get the "unknown command" response, and commands that fail to return a success value, or command line arguments that are incorrect in some way all result in a "Cannot execute command" message. The function returns TRUE if the command succeeded or FALSE if not.
showPwmParameters()	None/void	This function simply prints a short report out to the serial channel showing contents of the lights[] array.
sensorEvent()	Int sensorNum / Boolean	The sensorEvent() function carries out the light sequencing when a sensor trigger is received. Triggers only have effect if the lights are currently OFF. If the lights are already active, nothing is changed and the function returns FALSE.
		The currentState of lights[0] is sampled to determine whether the lights are OFF at the time of the trigger.
		The lights are programmed to fade up in a time-staggered sequence starting from now.
		If the sensorNum is 1 then the lights fade in the array order 0,1,2,3.
		If the sensor number is 2, then they switch on in descending order.
		When a trigger has been accepted and actioned the function returns TRUE.
doBeep()	None/void	The sounder makes a steady one KHz tone for half a second.
setFadeCycleMode()	None/Boolean	If the current mode is not INACTIVE (i.e., OFF) then this function puts the lights into FadeCycle mode for one minute.
		If the unit is currently in INACTIVE mode, then the function returns FALSE.
		The function acts upon the lights[] array, not the hardware directly and returns TRUE when the mode has been set.
		This function is called from the longPress() function.

(continued)

Function Name	Args/return type	Commentary
longPress()	Unsigned long pressDuration / void	This function is called from loop() when a long button press is deemed to have occurred. In fact in this version it simply calls setFadeCycleMode() and doesn't use its arg.
shortPress()	None/void	This function advances the current program mode by one, wrapping back to the first mode if needs be. It invokes other functions to make appropriate bleeps and noises for the new mode.
doPowerUpSound()	None/void	This function sounds a rising note sound to indicate a power up or activation.
doPowerDownSound()	None/void	This function sounds a falling note sound to indicate a deactivation.
doSerialInput()	None/void	In this function we check for any incoming characters on the serial channel. It uses processKeyboardChar() to assess the incoming character (see below in this table).
		If the incoming character is a terminator, then the input buffer is tailed with a zero byte to make it into a complete zero terminated string and the parser (see above in this table) is called. Upon return from the parser, the input buffer is reinitialized, and a fresh user prompt is issued, to invite more commands.
processKeyboardChar()	Char theChar/int	This function actions an ASCII input character received as its arg. It buffers the char, if it's a printable one. If it's a control char, then it actions it if possible, or ignores it. It also processes backspaces (which it treats as a rubout character) and CTRL/R to show and reprint the input buffer contents. If it's a CR char, then the function returns 1, else it returns zero.
turnAllOn()	None/void	Processes the lights[] array to turn all the LEDs full on. This will be implemented shortly afterward in the main loop.
turnAllOff()	None/void	Processes the lights[] array to turn all the LEDs off. This will be implemented shortly afterward in the main loop.
showSystemTime()	None/void	Sends out a formatted message to the serial channel to show the system time–in this context, this means the number of milliseconds since the AVR was started, not the wall clock time.

So, having worked out the hardware and software the next step is the implementation and installation.

Moving to Making It

Moving into the maker stage of the project, the first thing I had to decide was how to house the lights. If you want to build this project you'll have to decide this too; your decision, like mine, will be based on the characteristics of the installation site.

In my case, the walls of the passageway are very uneven, being rendered in a style known as "roughcast," which does not provide a uniform, smooth surface. My original idea was to build a small wall-mounted pelmeted box out of long lengths of stripwood. This would hide the lights themselves but allow the light to shine downward from under the pelmet. However, I decided that an assembly of stripwoods might not be flexible enough to follow the ins and outs of my wall.

After some thought, I came up with the idea of using a square plastic wire channel with a snap-on lid (a.k.a. plastic cable trunking). This wire channel was not only flexible enough to follow the contours of my wall pretty closely, but it also came in white plastic, so it would blend in with the white painted wall better than wood. Although it is harder to find, I believe you can also get it in other colors such as brown and black. This kind of channel (which is often self-adhesive via sticky tape on the back) comes both in fixed lengths (usually 10- or 11-feet lengths) and in flat form, in a roll that you can make it up from. You can easily cut it to the required length with a hacksaw.

Figure 11-4 shows a section of this stuff, which is sold in most electrical contractor outlets, DIY stores, and even in more general online stores like Amazon.

Figure 11-4. *White plastic cable channel with snap-on lid in place*

I used a hacksaw blade and a safety craft knife to cut out slots in one side of this wire channel to form the light outlets–sized to the LED strips.

To suspend the LED strips from the top of the channel, I drilled pairs of very small holes–just enough to get a strand of plastic-coated (must be coated) garden wire through. I looped the garden wire around the LED strip and on the outside of the channel I twisted and knotted the two ends of the garden wire to securely hold the LED strip in place. These twists should be tight, but obviously not so tight as to chew into the LED strip. The strips protrude from the top, but since the assembly will be mounted high up, they cannot normally be seen. The diagram in Figure 11-5 shows the general idea (see also the photo later in Figure 11-16). You could simply glue the LED strips into place inside the assembly if you wanted to, but that would make any future maintenance, changes, or update activities harder than they need to be.

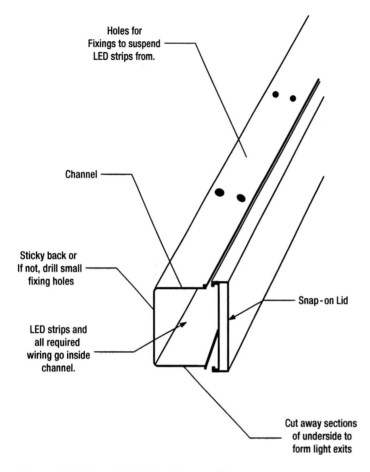

Holes for
Fixings to suspend
LED strips from.

Channel

Sticky back or
If not, drill small
fixing holes

LED strips and
all required
wiring go inside
channel.

Snap-on Lid

Cut away sections
of underside to
form light exits

Figure 11-5. *Waterfall light holder assembly*

Figure 11-5 visualizes these points.

Having installed the LED strips into the channel I then got a 5 amp wire and ran it the length of the holder. This forms the +12-volt feed for the four LED strips and the far-end sensor. I cut each LED strip's positive wire into this +12V feed wire. Of course, each cut-in point has to be taped up or shrink-wrapped to prevent any mishaps. In addition to the +12V feed wire, I then ran a six-way ribbon cable along the whole length of the holder and out the other side. The six conductors in this ribbon cable are used as follows:

- Wire 1 drops off at LED strip #1 and connects to its negative wire.

- Wire 2 drops off at LED strip #2 and connects to its negative wire.

- Wire 3 drops off at LED strip #3 and connects to its negative wire.

- Wire 4 drops off at LED strip #4 and connects to its negative wire.

- Wire 5 extends out to the far sensor and provides its "trigger" line back into the control box.

- Wire 6 carries a ground connection to the far sensor power feed, and to one side of its normally closed relay contacts. The +12V wire is also extended out to the far sensor to provide its power feed.

With the light holder assembly made, the next order of business is connections. The control box needed the following connection groups:

- A connector to bring in the signals from the light holder assembly–this had to be at least a seven-way connector. (+12V feed, four LED strip return wires, ground, and the far sensor trigger line).

- A connector for the near sensor–a three-way connector.

- A power connector to bring in 12V DC at about 2 amps. I decided that in the implementation, rather than having dual supplies or batteries it would be sensible to just feed the control box with +12V from a mains adaptor and have it incorporate a regulator that makes the MCU's required +5 volts from that.

If you're building your own version of this project you can decide to use whatever connectors you want, provided they can provide the right number of connections (as listed above) and each pole of the connector can carry at least one amp.

In my case, after initially considering a seven-way DIN connector from

- www.mouser.com (stock number 568-NYS323) (international)

- www.maplin.co.uk (stock number HH30H) (UK)

I decided to look for something with more connections, in case I decided to add more lights. I eventually settled on using a military style 14-way connector. I found out that these are very good quality and you can get the plug and socket for around $10 (delivered price) from several online sites. If you search for Y2M14-TK or Y2M14-ZJ you will find them for sale by many sellers[2]: you'll also sometimes find them listed as "Aviation connectors," "Y2M connectors," or "CA-Bayonet connectors."

If you do use one of these connectors, be aware that the plug hood has a left-hand thread, so you undo it the opposite way around (I wasted a couple of hours trying to figure that one out). Mate the plug and socket and while holding the locking collar tight with one hand, twist the cable grip clockwise (as viewed from the plug side) with the other hand.

Figure 11-6 shows a disassembled plug and the socket.

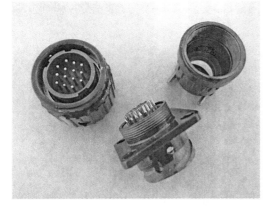

Figure 11-6. *Disassembled plug and socket*

---

[2] If you want different number of poles, you'll find these Y2M series connectors go up to very large pin counts. Check out the Y2M-65TK!

For the near-sensor connector, I just used a five-way DIN plug and bulkhead socket that I had handy (though it only needed to be a three-way plug, strictly speaking). The DC plug was a standard DC jack to match the 2.1 mm pin plug that the power supply came with. Examples of DC jacks come from

- www.sparkfun.com (sku: PRT-10785) (United States).

- www.maplin.co.uk (stock number JK09K) (UK).

Obviously, you should match the DC power jack that you use to the one that is already fitted to your +12V DC power supply. I'm afraid that DC power jacks are bit of a minefield because there are so many different pin sizes and barrel depths. I always find it best to take the one I am trying to match to the store and make sure it fits, there and then.

The power supply I used for my installation was just a 12V 3-amp unit that I got cheaply from an auction site. The project only needs 2 amps really, but this power supply (originally made for a flat-screen computer monitor) was brand new, unused, and very cheap. It works really well. You may already have something similar that you could use, but if not, a suitable power supply should not be hard to find at a good price.

Having settled on the connectors and drawn up the final circuit diagram and connection schedule I got busy putting it all together. Figures 11-7 and 11-8 show the final circuit diagram, with connector details and a pictorial view of the connections and installation layout. These are only provided as examples as, should you decide to build something like this for yourself, you will probably have to vary the details to fit your installation, your requirements, and the connectors you use.

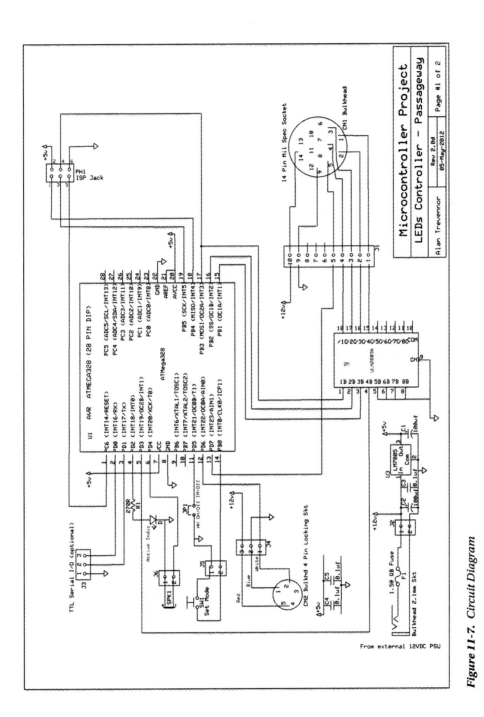

Figure 11-7. Circuit Diagram

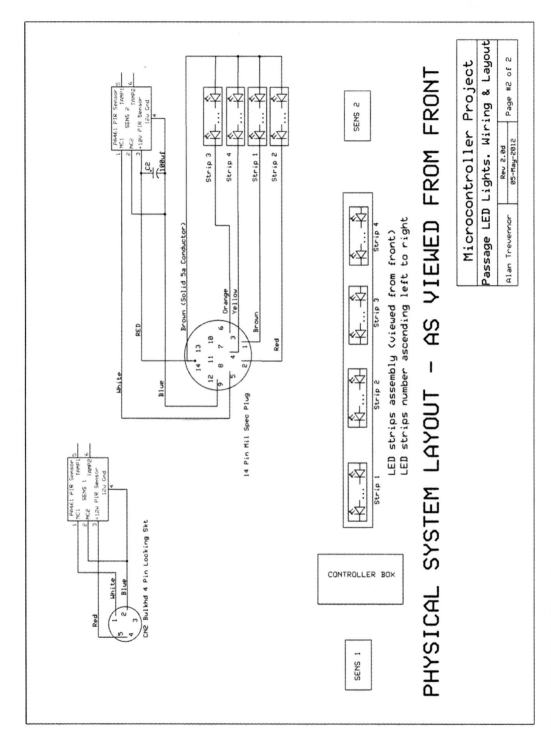

Figure 11-8. *Physical System Layout*

The following summarizes points of interest in these diagrams:

- In the finished version, the ISP connector is now a six-way ISP connector consisting of two rows of three pins, not the breakout board that was used for prototyping on the test rig. This should be made with two rows of three header pins.

  See Chapter 2 for an explanation of ISP programming. Adding an ISP connector to this project makes it possible to update the controller's software in situ, using your Pololu (or any other) ISP programmer. When viewed from the topside, this connector should be wired to look like Figure 11-9.

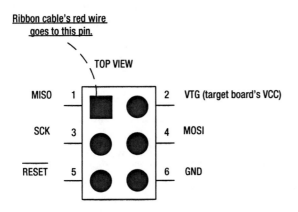

Figure 11-9. *ISP connector details*

- Note that, in this final version of the hardware design, the +5V regulator and associated capacitors have been added to allow the +5V supply to be derived from the +12V input.

- The +12V DC power supply coming in via the DC jack passes through a plastic cased inline fuse holder–inside the control box–before getting onto the board through a screw connector.

- The serial lines (TX, RX, and ground) are brought out to a three-way miniature screw connector. The signals from the near sensor (sensor 1) are also brought onto the board via a three-way screw connector.

- The signals coming in from the 14-pin mil socket are carried through to the board using a ten-way header pin strip and socket.

- The piezo electric speaker is held onto the side of the control box by two small bolts (see Figure 11-14). This results in a maximum loudness from it. You could drill a cluster of small holes in the box side to let more sound out, as I did, but I didn't find that made much difference in the end.

Figures 11-10 through 11-16 show photos of the various built pieces and the finished result.

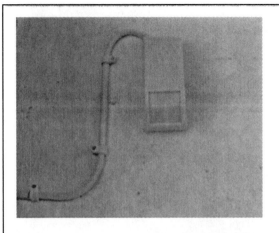

The sensors were both installed by fixing them to the wall with a small screw. Six-core alarm wire cable was used for the connections, though only three wires are used. The cable from the far-end sensor (pictured) was connected to the ribbon cable and +12V power supply inside the light holder assembly–as described earlier.

Figure 11-10. *The far sensor (sensor 2) installed*

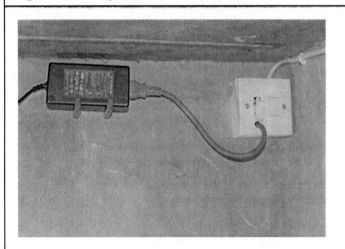

The power unit was hidden away in a space under the stairs. A small hole through the wall allowed the DC side of the power supply (exiting left in this photo) to get to the control box (see below in this photo sequence).

Note: It is *very important* to make sure with an "always on" project like this to correctly fuse the mains supply side of the power supply. In this case I was able to get a qualified electrician to fit a fused switch box in the mains path to this PSU. But, whatever the arrangement used, it is absolutely necessary to make sure that a low-amp fuse (3 amps at most) is in the mains path. Any malfunction in the PSU will simply then blow the fuse, maintaining your safety.

Figure 11-11. *The 12V DC power supply*

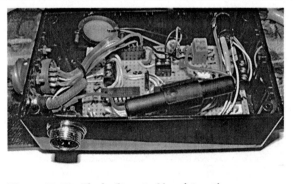

The box used was a plastic project box measuring about 5" x 3" (127 mm x 76 mm); holes were cut out of the sides for the 14-way connector, the DIN connector, the DC jack, and the push button (the button is shown in this photo at top right).

The circuit was built up on a piece of tripad solder board which was then mounted on spacers into the box.

Figure 11-12. *The built control box (view 1)*

Figure 11-13. *The built control box (view 2)*

The second view of the internals of the control box shows the connector mounts in more detail. The 14-way military connector is at left, then comes the DC jack for power, then the DIN connector used to connect the near sensor (sensor 1).

Figure 11-14. *Detail showing the piezo mount*

This photo shows details of how the piezo speaker is mounted. Two nuts and bolts through the side of the box hold it captive by its edges. It needs to be able to flex in the middle to make the maximum volume of sound.

Figure 11-15. *The control box, installed*

This photo shows the control box installed high up, close to ceiling level.

The DIN plug at left is bringing in the signals from the near sensor. The DC power plug is top left –coming in from the understair location shown earlier. The 14-way mil connector at top center provides connections to the light holder assembly and–via that–to the far sensor.

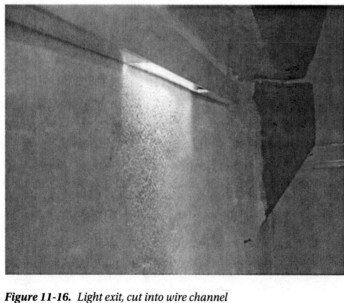

Figure 11-16. *Light exit, cut into wire channel*

Close up on one of the light exits that are cut in the underside in the wire channel. These have to be approximately the same length as the light emitting portion of the LED strips used.

Figure 11-17 shows the lights all on, having just faded up in sequence–triggered by my approach.

Figure 11-17. The finished effect

I might even get rid of that pendant light now!

Waterfall Lights Mark II

It's always the way that, a while after something is made, you start second-guessing the design, the approach, the details–everything! In this case I haven't torn it out and started again (yet) because the original works well and fills the need nicely. However, although the four-LED string version is very pretty, it's not the waterfall I originally envisaged. So, I couldn't help wondering how easy it would be to do the project a different way . . . so I have done a design for a Mark II version that uses more LEDs in smaller groups. It's just a design, but here it is!

Mark II Electronics

As you may remember, the reason that the first version ended up with four LED strips, rather than the six or eight I had originally envisaged, was that the ATmega328 (and in fact all of that series of AVRs), when used with the Arduino software, only offers four PWM outputs with rock-solid reliability. There are two others, but their PWM outputs are subject to contention with timer functions of the Arduino software which results in unreliable turn-offs and consequent possible timing problems. I also experimented with the softPWM library that is available from

```
http://code.google.com/p/rogue-code/wiki/SoftPWMLibraryDocumentation
```

That library allows you to use up to 16 pins as PWM outputs. However, although the library works fine with just a small main loop, when I added my code, I ran into problems. After a lot of head scratching and Googling, I was forced to the conclusion that something my code was doing was occasionally sabotaging the library code, making it do very sudden or jerky fades or just stopping altogether for seconds at a time. Just running the demo version alone was fine, but when I added my code, something to do with the timer functions I need to use was causing problems. It's likely that someone with a deeper knowledge of the Arduino software than myself could resolve this, but I ran out of time and patience.

In the first version, I also needed to use a driver chip to drive the LED strips since the AVR cannot do this directly.

For the MKII version design I briefly considered using a chip called the M5450–which is a 34 output LED driver that has a serial input. The problem was that the M5450 does not do PWM, which I really wanted to keep in the picture. However, I clearly had to abandon the idea of using PWM direct from the AVR.

Then, a chip called the TLC5940 caught my eye. This chip (from Texas Instruments) offers the following facilities:

- 16 outputs–all offering PWM at 4096 different levels (much finer control than the 256 levels offered by the Arduino PWM).

- One common input sets the output current limit for all 16 outputs. This prevents outputs going over-current if there is a fault condition and protects the chip against damage.

- Each of the 16 outputs can (in theory) supply up to 120 milliamps–though it's not clear whether you could use all outputs at that full amperage for very long without the chip shutting down due to an over-temperature error.

- The data specifying the brightness value for the 16 outputs is sent via a serial data transfer from the MCU to the TLC5940 using just four wires. Data can be sent at 30 MHz, which I think means that you could change the intensity of all 16 outputs around 150,000 times per second if your MCU could feed them that fast. Easily fast enough for a little bit of gentle fading in and out anyway.

- Various extra features such as slightly staggered LED turn-on times to minimize current inrush problems for the power supply, a facility to detect failed LEDs, a thermal error flag, and so on.

- Texas seems to have designed this chip with large-scale uses in mind. If you were building up a large matrix of LEDs as pixels in a picture or graphics display (such as you might see in a stadium or public mall) you would probably be very concerned about even quite small differences in the brightness of individual LEDs within your display. Using PWM techniques does tend to heighten such differences. So, if you're trying to build up a picture on a LED matrix and you can't precisely control each pixel, then you will have problems. Therefore, the other major functional block of the TLC5940 is a dot correction EEPROM which allows you to make and store a PWM correction factor for each output so that you can exactly match the output to the individual LED that is connected to it. In our application this whole area is of little interest to us, since we are using the LEDs as lighting, not as picture elements: so, we leave that block of functionality disabled. Be aware that if you did want to use this side of the chip, you would need a +22V "programming voltage" to be able to reprogram the intensity correction EEPROM.

- The ability to cascade devices. If 16 outputs is not enough, you connect two or more TLC5940s in series and you can add sets of 16 lights, so start with 16 then go to 32, 48, 64–or whatever.

This one chip could solve the PWM problem with the first design and also eliminate the need to use the ULN2803A that was required for the first version. If you're thinking of getting one of these to try out on a breadboard, make sure you order the TLC5940NT–where the NT denotes the DIP package: The device is also available in a couple of surface-mount packagings which you won't be able to use on the breadboard.

Full details of the TLC5940 can of course be seen in its data sheet; go grab a copy from

www.ti.com/lit/ds/symlink/tlc5940.pdf

However, be warned, it's not the most approachable piece of technical documentation you're ever going to read! In fact, lucky for us, that doesn't matter. Alex Leone has created an Arduino library to take most of the pain out of driving the TLC5940 for us. See details and download information at

```
http://code.google.com/p/tlc5940arduino/
http://alex.kathack.com/codes/tlc5940arduino/html_r014/
```

When using this library, you connect your AVR to the TLC5940 using the pins that the library requires, or you can try using other pins if you prefer. The file `tlc_config.h` is where you can make those changes. See the "files" tab on the second of the web sites mentioned previously. The library comes with numerous example programs. Using this library you can cascade up to 16 chips, giving a possible total of 256 individual LEDs or clusters of LEDs. If you're prepared to go in for a little LED multiplexing, then you can use TLC5940s to control an enormous number of LEDs.

The installation documentation tells you to install the library into the libraries subfolder of your Arduino sketchbook folder. However, I found that when I did that (on Windows or Linux) that I got compile errors when I tried to use even the demo programs; this was under Arduino release 0.22.

However, when I installed the library into the main installation hierarchy it all worked fine. Since the library was created in 2010, it might be that subsequent Arduino updates have created this problem, but anyway the fix for this, if you do get the problem, is to install in the library subfolder that you will find under your installation location: on Windows XP it's

```
C:\Program Files\Arduino-xxx
```

where xxx is the Arduino version number. Under the installation location you will find a folder called `libraries` which is where you should install the TLC library, in its own subfolder. On Vista and Windows 7 you will need to have administrator privileges to do this installation. It's not a problem on Windows XP or earlier.

On Linux and on Mac OS X you'll find the base directory for Arduino at

```
/usr/share/Arduino
```

Under the installation location, you will find a directory called `library` and you should install the TLC library there under its own subdirectory. On Linux or Mac machines you will need to use the `sudo` command or login as the superuser to acquire the privileges required to do this installation.

If your Arduino installation is, for some reason, nonstandard and you can't find the Arduino software set, a simple trick is to look at the properties of the clickable link that you usually use to run Arduino. Those properties should show you where the software was installed.

The downside of having to install the library under the installation folder is that, when you upgrade your Arduino software, if the old version is removed, you will also lose any custom libraries you have installed in this way. Therefore, keep copies of downloaded libraries somewhere safe, so that you can reinstate them after future upgrades if need be.

So, an MKII design using the TLC5940 would have a lot of possibilities. It would be possible (although an absolute wiring nightmare) to use a large number of individual LEDs and to have them fade one at a time. Or, we could use 5050 series RGB LED strips, and use multiple TLC5940s to drive them in various different sexy ways. The temptation to go overboard is very great. If we were we creating a disco light show or something of that kind, those would be very good options, but with our feet firmly on the ground we have to repeat the calming mantra "Passageway Lights" over and over again.

Take-Two Circuit Diagram

In the end, I decided to stay with a relatively simple scheme of up to 16 single-color LED strips, with the ability in the software to use as many or as few of the 16 as required. Figure 11-18 shows the circuit diagram.

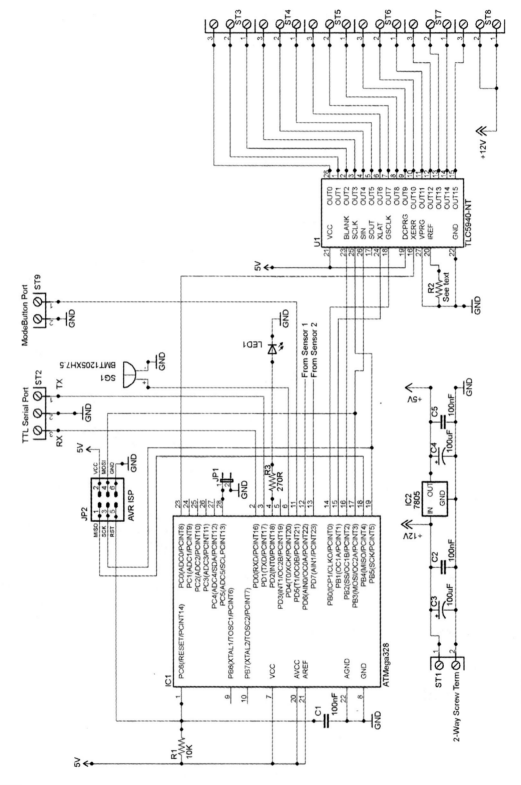

Figure 11-18. Mark 2a passage lights circuit diagram

In this circuit diagram (intended to be built up as a stand-alone project, not a test rig project) the default pins, as specified in the TLC5490 library, drive the device. Most of the other peripherals from the previous iteration (the tone sounder, the mode switch, the sensors) connect via the same pins as before: the exception is the jumper, which now connects via Arduino's pin A5 (pin 28). Note also that the XERR pin of the TLC5940 is connected to A0 of the AVR (pin 23) this gives you the possibility of checking every now and again as to whether the 5940 has detected any LED errors.

The 5940's outputs are extended out to miniature screw connectors. You would connect each set of LED strips with its positive lead to one of the +12V leads and its other to whatever output of the 5940 you needed.

R2 on this diagram is connected to the IREF pin of the TLC5940. This pin is used to set the maximum current output that can be drawn from each of the output pins. You connect the pin to ground through a resistor and the current it pulls is used to determine the current limit the chip will apply to each of the outputs. The value of the resistor is determined by the following formula:

$$R = (1.24 / Imax) \times 31.5$$

For example, if you want the max current to be 80 milliamps (0.080 amps) this becomes

$$(1.24 / 0.080) \times 31.5 = 488.25$$

So, in such a case you would probably use the nearest preferred resistor value, which is 470 Ohms.

The TLC5940NT needs a constant frequency square wave into its Grayscale Clock (GSCLK) input on pin 18. This signal is used as the master reference clock for all of the chip's PWM operations. In the default hardware configuration, instanced by the TLC5940 library, the AVR's pin 5 (Arduino pin D3) is set to give out a constant PWM pulse (at about 500 Hz) to provide this, and that arrangement will work well. However, rather than sticking with that, I perversely decided to extend out the AVR's 8 MHz clock, just to see if would work–and it does!

The AVR ATMEGA328 has a feature whereby its system clock can be extended out to pin 14 (Arduino digital pin 8). When used in this mode, the AVR calls this pin CKOUT; if you program the CKOUT fuse, whatever clock the AVR is using is enabled to be output on the CKOUT pin. This applies whether you are using the internal 8 MHz clock (as we are) or an external crystal–as detailed in Chapter 3. This CKOUT feature allows you to use the same clock frequency for all devices in your project. In this case it's the TLC5940.

To extend out the AVR's internal clock, we use AVRDude (see Chapter 3 for extensive details and examples of using this useful program) to reprogram the fuse bit. So, how do we use AVRDude to program the AVR chip to activate CKOUT? Well, as we saw in Chapter 3, the format of the FLB is

FuseName	CKDIV8	CKOUT	SUT1	SUT0	CKSEL3	CKSEL2	CKSEL1	CKSEL0
Bit #	7	6	5	4	3	2	1	0

So, in this context, bit 6 is the one of interest. We start by using AVRDude to find out the current value of the fuse. Assuming that the fuse is at its default state, we will need to invert it to turn on CKOUT.

■ **Tip** In the following command sequence you will have to "plug in" your own comms port (e.g., COM2 or /dev/ttyACM0). You will have to change the DESTination to CON for Windows or - (meaning standard output) for Unix. If you are not using an ATmega328p chip but some other AVR variant (e.g., an ATmega328), you will have to change that value too. See the section "AVRDude" in Chapter 3 for lots more details on these areas.

Begin by opening a command (terminal) window on the desktop machine to which your AVR and programmer are connected.

Now, make sure AVRDude can "see" your AVR chip

```
avrdude -p m328p -c avrisp2 -P {YOUR_COM_PORT}.
```

This should make AVRDude print out the signature bytes of your AVR and make it verify the fuses. Next, make AVRDude show you the current lower fuse byte value

```
avrdude -p m328p -c avrisp2 -P {YOUR COM PORT} -U lfuse:r:DEST:h.
```

This will show you–in hexadecimal format–the current value of the lower fuse byte. You can decode it using the bit layout diagram shown previously; or, if you prefer, you can use the online fusecalc site at

```
www.engbedded.com/fusecalc
```

to do it for you. On that site you enter your AVR part number, or use the nearest one to it, if you can't find the precise one (e.g., if you have an ATmega168-P just use ATmega168). Then, enter the value returned by AVRDude into the LFUSE box near the bottom of the calculator and you will see the tick boxes change to the settings represented by the code you just entered. Change the value of CKOUT using the tick box and you will then see the new value you need to program.

Remember that a "programmed" (active) bit in an AVR fuse is read by AVRDude as 0 and an unprogrammed (inactive) bit will read as a 1. This is the opposite way round to most logic systems. So, suppose that AVRDude returned the value xE2 (assuming you unprogrammed CKDIV8–bit 7–earlier in the book to get your MCU running at 8 MHz) you would just need to invert bit 6 and make that into xA2. In other words:

Bit #	7	6	5	4	3	2	1	0
Bin	1	1	1	0	0	0	1	0
HEX	E				2			

Becomes

Bit #	7	6	5	4	3	2	1	0
Bin	1	0	1	0	0	0	1	0
HEX	A				2			

We program the required value into the fuses, using the command

```
avrdude -p m328p -c avrisp2 -P {YOUR COM PORT} -U lfuse:w:0xA2:m.
```

And that's it! You should have a steady square wave clock coming out of what is now the CKOUT pin of your MCU. This technique is useful over and over again in designing MCU projects because it saves you having to provide separate circuitry for clocks to other devices–which usually means adding extra devices onto an already crowded board.

As of this writing the MKII project is just a proof of concept on a breadboard, and it seems to work okay there just using individual LEDs as proxies for LED strips, though for some reason that I don't understand I did have to reduce the IREF resistor lower than the equation suggested to get a good brightness. I've done a rough and ready conversion of the software for the MKII which is available through the book's web site (www.apress.com/9781430244462).

As a final word, the diagram in Figure 11-19 shows how you connect up two TLC5940s in a chain to give yourself more than 16 outputs. This is not a full waterfall lights diagram; it just shows you how to chain up your TLCs! Don't forget that, to use a circuit like this with two TLC5940s, you will need to edit the file tlc_config.h to change the value of NUM_TLCS. As stated earlier, you'll find that file in the same folder as the other TLC5940 library components.

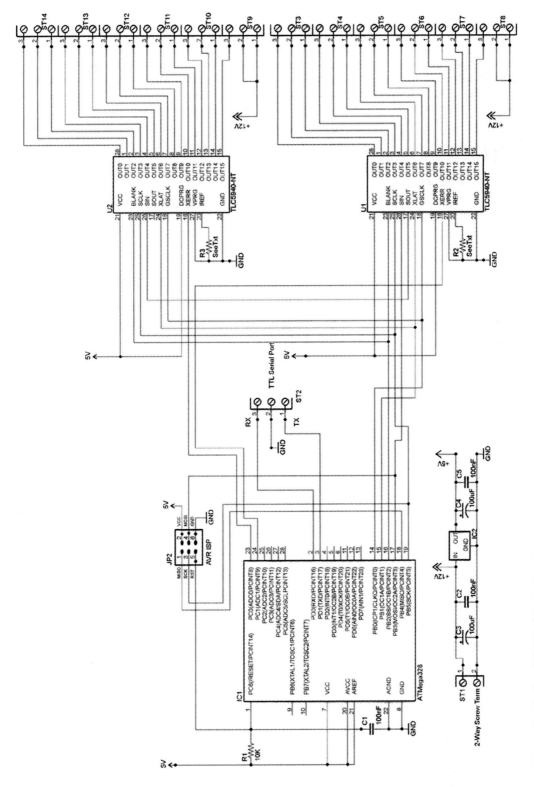

Figure 11-19. Dual TLC5940 Basic Circuit

Summary

In this chapter we have looked in detail at how to build a useful home lighting project–one with several novel features. We have looked at some different options for how to make it and some possible alternative electronic approaches. We've also seen how an MCU subsystem can gain the ability to respond to external commands. In this way, something that might once have been simply a standalone item, could in fact–with the proper infrastructure provided–participate in a wider, more coheseive whole-home control system.

Coming Up Next

Project 5: Moving to Mesmerize.

CHAPTER 12

■ ■ ■

Moving to Mesmerize

In this chapter we'll look at three small projects and some associated ideas and techniques. Each project involves actual or virtual movement. Each of these projects is–while simple in itself–intended to provide some interest and provoke other ideas, or just provide a little simple fun for you or whoever you feel like sharing it with.

Duck Shooter Game

Duck Shooter is a classic game that you've probably played at the fairground or arcade. In those real-world versions of the game, hinged cartoon duck targets go around on a chain and you have to use the provided air guns to try to hit them as they move across your line of sight. If you get all the ducks down before your time is up, you get a prize (usually quite a perfunctory one).

There have been duck shooter arcade games, pinball games, and alley games since the late 1930s. Ever since computer games were new, versions of this game have been available. For example, Sega had a version of it in 1975, various versions of the game have appeared over the years which use TTL or CMOS logic chips, and of course in more recent years there have been numerous MCU implementations and numerous Java game implementations of the same basic game. Well, you'll be glad to hear that although the format of this game follows the duck shoot format, there isn't a duck in sight. They're LEDs really, but we'll call them ducks. Okay then!

Following is a summary of the rules:

- You have an 11-slot "duck run"; each slot is represented by an LED.

- You have a button to press that represents your gun. Your gun is locked into position and can only shoot at the middle slot of the duck run, represented by LED number 6.

- At the start of each level in the game, a single duck (represented by a lit LED) progresses across the duck run from left to right. When it reaches the end, it reappears at the left and starts again.

- You must time your shot so that you hit the duck when it reaches the center slot. If you do it right, you hit the duck and its light fades out. If you miss, the duck is cloned! So now there are two ducks parading around in front of you. Miss again and there'll be three ducks–and so on. When you fire your gun, the duck run stops for a moment, so you can see what's happening.

- When you have managed to kill off all the ducks, the level ends and you move on to the next one. Each level is the same, except the duck's progress gets faster and faster and that means that you have to be more and more precise.

- If you manage to play through all the levels your reward is . . . a little light show on the duck run. It's a perfunctory prize, just like at the fairground. How true to life is that?

In hardware terms, this is quite a simple game. Eleven LEDs are connected from the +5-volt supply, via 11 270 ohm resistors to 11 AVR pins. A push button is connected to a twelfth AVR pin. And that's it really!

■ **Note**   We'll also build in a secret Easter egg feature; when the player presses the gun button for more than ten seconds, the game will show a preview of the winner's light show.

The Duck Shooter Circuit

Figure 12-1 shows the circuit diagram. You can build this on the test rig breadboard, and of course you don't need the power feed on there. You would just use the ISP breakout board that's already there to program the AVR with the software. In the diagram, I have instanced a push button with a built-in LED (S2-LED), but you don't have to use such a push button. I just used a little PCB-mounted push button on my prototype (as we shall see later). An illuminated push button is just for show really, but it would look nice!

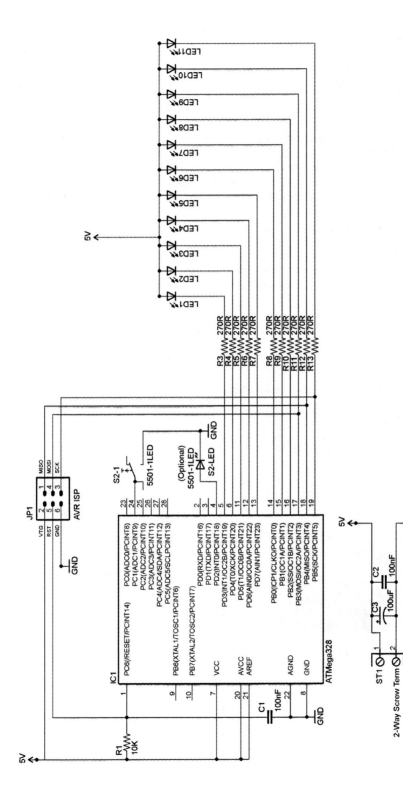

Figure 12-1. Duck Shooter game circuit diagram

I'm going to use this project to show how to transfer a design from a breadboard to something more permanent. It's not an overly complex design, but it is complex enough to show you how to make the transfer from breadboard to solder board.

Making Duck Shooter into a Keeper

All electronics enthusiasts have their own favorite way of producing a "keeper" project (i.e., one they want to keep, not just a breadboard version that they subsequently break up). Some favor making a printed circuit board (or using services allied to open source packages like Fritzing or Eagle to get a PCB produced for them); some favor a strip board on which they solder their components and cut away sections of copper strip to isolate them from one another; some people like using protoboards, where they solder their components into individual holes and then solder on wires from point to point; some people use various kinds of wire-wrap schemes. For a selection of different solder boards see the following link:

www.verotl.com/prototyping-products

My own favorite for simpler keeper projects is tri-pad solder strip board. This simplifies the tedious business of cutting off copper connections between components because, on a tripad board there are only ever three holes connected to any one connection point–thus the name. For an example product, see

- www.maplin.co.uk (UK) (stock number JP52G).

I haven't found a U.S. source of this product, though I'm sure there must be one, but you could use various protoboards.

- www.mouser.com (stock number 574-45P80-1).

- www.sparkfun.com (stock number PRT-08619).

Figure 12-2 shows a close-up of a tripad board.

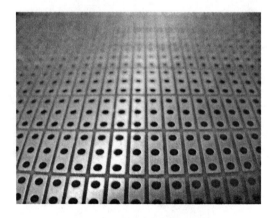

Figure 12-2. *Close-up of a tripad board*

As you can see, the solder pads are arranged in groups of three pads (thus the name), so you just need to choose your component positions such that they bridge across tripad islands and then you can make other connections from there. There is no tedious track cutting required–as when you use continuous solder strip boards–but you can still get a useful number of components on quite a small board space. The holes are 0.1" (2.54 mm) apart and for the Duck Shooter game we need a board that is 33 holes by 38 holes (give or take one or two either way). This makes the board dimensions about 3.5" x 3.75" (850 mm x 952 mm).

Building Duck Shooter

Figure 12-3 shows a piece of tripad board cut to size and with some mounting holes drilled through it, one near each corner. Drill carefully and slowly and hold the board steady; it's very easy to break off a corner if the drill catches because you go too fast. Been there, done that!

Figure 12-3. *Tripad board cut to size for Duck Shooter game*

I'm a fan of IC (integrated circuit) sockets; some people don't like them, but I've found that they save a lot of hassle if in the future you need to change a chip out. Yes, after some period of time (usually years) they can cause connection problems due to contact oxidization; however, such problems are easily fixed by reseating the chip in its socket. Also, using sockets means that you don't have to expose your chips to soldering heat, since you solder the socket into place and plug the chip in later on. So, I almost always use sockets–as you can see from the picture of the completed topside of the Duck Shooter board in Figure 12-4.

As the photo shows, the LEDs are arranged across the board at three-hole intervals. The button is at the opposite end of the board. The MCU is in the middle, and ISP jack is close to it. The power connector is at the top of the board above the LEDS. Before installing any wiring jumpers or resistors on the board, I used a Sharpie pen to make a bold line from the button to the target center LED, indicating the line of fire.

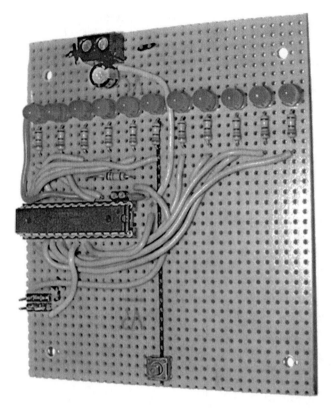

Figure 12-4. *Duck Shooter project board topside*

It's not strictly required (and it's not on the circuit diagram) but since I had an old IC socket, I cut a couple of pin sections from it to install a socket arrangement for pins 2 and 3 (serial RX and TX, respectively) in case I needed them. The software for this game does output some game metrics to the serial port, which might be of interest to someone . . . sometime! Figure 12-5 shows the serial port and the ISP plug for programming the MCU *in situ*.

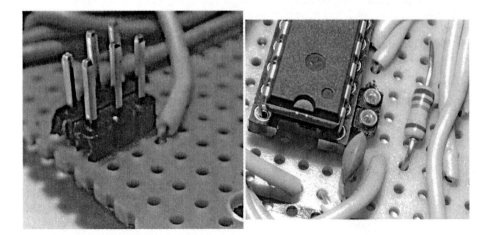

Figure 12-5. *ISP -plug and serial port add-on wire socket*

Most of the wires for the ISP plug (and a few other wires) are actually routed under the board as you can perhaps tell from the photo in Figure 12-6. For details about the ISP connector, refer to the "About In-System Programming" section of Chapter 2, specifically Figure 2-9.

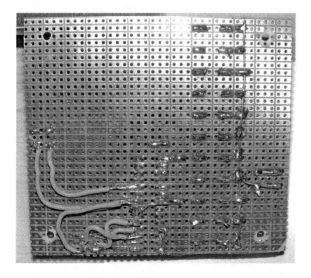

Figure 12-6. *Duck Shooter board underside*

You may just be able to see in Figure 12-6 the line of stiff wire that goes from left to right along the + side of all the LEDs. This carries the +5V feed to the LEDs.

If you've never made a board like this before it can seem quite a daunting task. However, the reality is that as long as you have the right tools for the job and some patience, it's not hard. It's just a question of methodically working through it and not rushing it. Your fine-tip soldering iron, your helping-hands gripper, and your magnifying glass should all help make it easier and even enjoyable. Use the solid wire–similar to the breadboard jumper wire–which, by now, you should be used to using. Avoid using stranded wire, which tends to "feather" at the ends and make hard-to-spot short circuits between components.

Following are some tips and points to watch out for:

- If you are unfamiliar with soldering, find one of the many tutorials on the Internet before you begin. The golden rule (as you will see in any of those tutorials) is "heat the job, not the solder." In other words, if you're soldering the pin of an LED, heat up the pin and then apply the solder to the pin: don't heat the solder and let the melted solder fall onto the pin! The latter method will make what is known as a "dry joint" which–in a digital circuit–may initially work but will soon fail. Heat the job, not the solder. Did I say that before? Good! It's very important.

- Be safety aware: if you have some safety glasses that give you good visibility, use them. Never, ever, flick solder around. Hot solder burns, and burns and burns. It burns holes in carpets, furniture, and, given half a chance, *you*. Don't give it *any* chance. Use a soldering iron with a proper holder or holster.

- Inhale as little solder smoke as possible. If you have a desk fan around, run it on low to waft the smoke away from you toward an open window if at all possible. If the room has an extractor fan, use it. Don't solder in a confined space. In any case, find a way to avoid breathing in any significant amount of solder smoke.

- Be methodical. Work from the circuit diagram (or a photo copy of it) and as you install each component or wire, cross it off on the diagram. Use a pencil so that you can erase any mistakes you make.

- Don't solder one point for too long. Even things like resistors and capacitors can be damaged if exposed to the heat of a soldering iron for too long. ICs, transistors, LEDs, and other semiconductor devices are very easily heat damaged, so don't hold the soldering iron tip on their leads for more than two or three seconds.

- Where two adjacent pins need to be connected, don't bother putting a wire between them, heat *both* pins and flood that little area with solder until they are joined together by a solder blob.

- Keep the soldering iron tip reasonably clean. Use a piece of kitchen paper towel which has been dampened with a little water to wipe the tip with if it gets messy. After cleaning, melt a little solder onto the tip to keep it coated. Many soldering stations (usually consisting of the iron itself and a holder or holster) will come with a cloth or special sponge that you can moisten with a little water. You then use this dampened surface for cleaning the soldering tip.

- When you have finished (or think you have–there's always one more thing to do!) go around the board with a watchmakers' fine-blade screwdriver or perhaps a craft knife and carefully run it between adjacent pins that are not meant to be connected to make sure there are no minute solder bridges shorting them together.

- When you connect your power source, make sure you have a fuse in the + lead. See the "A +5-Volt Regulated Supply" section in Chapter 2 for information on how to do this if you are in any doubt. The Duck Shooter game uses no more than 1 amp, so a fuse at that value should be sensitive enough. If you're using a bench supply that has a current limiter, make sure the current limiter is set on low for the first power-up of any new board.

If you are truly daunted by the prospect of building this as your first soldering project, try an easier "get started" project to cut your teeth on. A good project for this might be one of the 555 timer chip circuits shown in Chapter 3. That might give you the confidence to progress to this one. Like most things, it does get easier, the more you do it!

As the circuit diagram shows, the Duck Shooter game is intended to run from a +5V supply. However, you could also run it from 3 x AA batteries (giving about 4.5V) if you wanted to. The LEDs won't be quite as bright, but the difference is very small.

Going Further

You may want to build your version into a project box of some kind, or even build it into something else. A friend suggested it might be fun to build it into the arm of a chair in a TV room. I guess it would give you something to do during those interminable commercial breaks! If you wanted to box the project, you would need to raise up the LEDs above the rest of the circuit, either by leaving their legs longer than I have done on my prototype or perhaps by using bits of socket strips (like the one I added on for the serial port) to raise up the level of the LEDs. For a compact version of the game you could use bar graph LEDs such as

- www.sparkfun.com (sku: com-09935) (United States).

- www.maplin.co.uk (stock number BT65V) (UK).

The problem is, those only come in ten-LED groups (you can also get eight-way groups if you shop around), and so you'd have to rearrange the game somehow.

If you wanted to go nuts on the game you could dispense with the idea of driving the LEDs from the AVR directly. You could use a smaller AVR and one or more TLC5940 chips (see Chapter 11) to drive a much larger number of LEDs which you could arrange in various shapes (circles, circuits, etc.). Many developments of the basic game presented here are possible.

Duck Shooter Software

The Duck Shooter game software is quite big and so is not reproduced in full in the book itself, but you can download it via the book's web site (www.apress.com/9781430244462). The following is a code walk, function by function:

Function Name	Commentary
Declarations	The declarations section consists of numerous #define directives to define constants for the program. Notable are the declarations for LOW_LED and HIGH_LED which define the lowest and highest numbered Arduino port pins used for the required 11 LEDs. You can change these if you want, but the program assumes throughout that the LED pins are in a contiguous block.
	Also worthy of note is the SPEED_STEP variable which controls the amount of speed increase that happens between each level of the game. If you make this value larger, the higher levels of the game won't be quite so fast.
	Note that the circuit diagram and the code (via GUN_BUTTON_LED) provide for the possibility of a button with an integral LED. If you don't use such a thing and prefer to just use a standard, unlit push button as I did, then it doesn't matter, but the provision exists.
	Finally for this section, note the Debug definition. If you declare this as true then the program will output extra information to the serial channel (which you don't have to use–there is no serial input required for this project, so the serial channel is completely optional) and the embedded Easter egg is enabled. This latter feature means you can see the "winner's" light show by holding down the button for more than ten seconds.
	An important feature of my implementation of this game is the way the animation is done. An in-memory representation of the state of each LED is held in a 16-bit variable called ducks, in which the lower 11 bits each correspond to one of the LEDs. Functions that want to alter the state of the LEDs alter bits in ducks rather than directly writing to the LEDs. Each time through the main loop of the program, the state of the duck animation is advanced by one place, based on the content of ducks. In this way, only one function touches the hardware in the main loop. However, many other functions–those that run when the main game is not active–such as the showSpeedLevel function and the winner's light show, do directly output to the LED pins because the normal game animation is suspended while those things are running anyway.

(continued)

Function Name	Commentary
setup()	The setup() function contains a useful map that relates LEDs to pins and bits within the ducks variable.
	The gun button input and LED pins are defined and initialized. We're using what Arduino calls input pin A1 for our button input, but we're using it as a digital pin–not analog at all. We enable a pull-up on this port pin so we don't need an external pull-up resistor. Next, the LED pins are all initialized to be outputs. Finally we reset the ducks to their default value, which is one LED on and the rest off. We show the speed level and then we initialize the serial channel.
loop()	In the main loop, we read the button to see if it's pressed. If it is pressed
	• We start the clock, so that when it has been released we will know how long it was pressed for.
	• We advance the state of the gun LED flashing (if it's in use)
	• We invert the state of the firing line LED, updating the ducks variable (described above) in the light of whether the user missed or hit a duck. If the user hit a duck then the target LED fades out (the duck dies!) if he or she missed, then the firing line LED fades up into life (an extra duck is born).
	If the user did hit a duck and we faded it out, we check to see whether that was the last duck. If it was, then the level is over with and we do the things we need to do to bring on the next level of the game.
	We wait for the button to be released and see how long it was pressed for. If it was pressed for more than ten seconds, we do the hidden Easter egg feature.
	If the button was pressed normally (i.e., not to get the cheat) or it was not pressed at all, then we're still playing and we call the animLeds() function which is described later.
showSpeedLevel()	Speed level and game level are the same thing. This function (intended to be used to introduce a new game level) flashes the LEDs a few times (using direct LED access) and then puts all the LEDs on, and then pares them down to the point where they show the new game level (i.e., four LEDS on for level 4). After a short wait, all LEDs go off and the game resumes at the new level.
turnAllLedsOn(dly) turnAllLedsOff(dly)	These two functions turn all the LEDs on or off in sequence at the speed indicated in their argument dly.

(continued)

Function Name	Commentary
flashAlternates(dly, altCycles, varyTiming)	This function flashes the two groups of LED on either side of the firing line alternately. It does the specified number of cycles, with dly setting the speed and with a random element if indicated in the varyTiming Boolean variable. This function is used as part of the winner's light show display.
setGunButtonLedState(newState)	Sets the gun button's LED state. Used when there is an appropriate device in use.
doGblFlash()	Inverts the state of the gun button's LED, if in use.
animLeds(dValue)	Advances the state of the LED's animation by one tick. Incorporates a delay – dValue. This value is used to cause the animation function to block for a short time, thus limiting how often it can be called. This function is where the contents of the ducks variable are made real by being written out to the hardware.
weHaveAWinner()	Does the winner's light show.
resetDucks()	Initializes the ducks variable that holds all the duck states. One duck is on; the rest are off.
doFadeOutLed(pinNum)	Using software PWM, this fades out the indicated LED. If the LED pinNum is sent as zero, then we fade out all the LEDs.
doEndTogetherLeds (iterations, stepTime)	This function is used by the winner's light show. It starts a single LED from each end and they progress to the middle where they meet and disappear. Iterations tell how many times to run it, and stepTime controls the speed.

And that's it for the Duck Shooter game. I hope you enjoy building and playing it.

MCU Shadow Puppets

The second of our simple projects in this chapter is somewhat grandiosely called an animation projector–but it's really just a simple MCU controller version of a shadow puppet. The idea is that a single strong light source in a darkened room can, when interrupted by a shape, cause that shape to appear enlarged on a screen or an opposite wall. If the shape moves across the light source, then you get the illusion of a large moving object on the wall opposite the apparatus. We've all played with this idea at some time or another.

In this project we set up a single bright light source (a high-intensity LED light) and we build a simple motorized movement mechanism using a servo motor and a few household bits and pieces to move a shape around in front of the light. In a darkened or low-lighted room it's very effective. We give the MCU the ability to control the light source and to move the shape and we can even allow the MCU to be commanded via the serial port, which would make it easier for this little project to form part of something larger, such as a coordinated display or an art installation using many such mechanisms, synchronized by a central controller.

Building the Shadow Puppets

To build this quickie project I used some bits of scrap wood, a few self-tapping screws, a strip of 1/4" (about 6 mm) plastic that I cut out of an old storage box that was out for recycling, some stiff wire, a rubber band, and a couple of hooks with self-tapping screws. I used a servo motor and 3W high-intensity LED. I only intended this as a proof of concept, not a "keeper" project.

First the servo motor is mounted on a frame made of scrap bits of wood, as you can see in Figure 12-7 (and later on in Figure 12-10). Then, I drilled a pilot hole in one end of the frame and screwed one of the hooks into it. These don't have to be hooks; they could be long wood screws. Next, I drilled a hole in each end of the plastic strip and fixed the rubber band through one end: the other end of the rubber band goes around the hook.

Figure 12-7. *MCU shadow puppet*

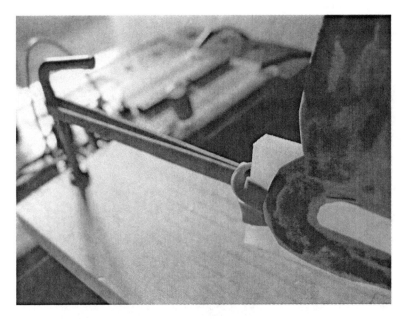

Figure 12-8. Rubber band and end anchor hook

At the other end of the plastic strip, I used a piece of stiff solderable wire to link the plastic strip to the motor horn, which has a self-tapping screw (supplied with the motor accessories kit). I soldered the wire ends together to keep them from coming undone.

Figure 12-9. Motor end linkage

As it is pulled back and forth, the plastic strip (to which we will fix a silhouette) wants to twist axially. To stop this, I fitted a second hook into the frame to hold the plastic strip roughly vertical (see Figure 12-9). The photo in Figure 12-10 shows the whole thing.

Figure 12-10. *Shadow puppet assembly complete*

Finally I used transparent tape to stick a silhouette to the plastic strip: since I can't draw to save my life, my wife kindly drew two sample silhouettes for me on 120 GSM paper. I had planned to mount these on cardboard once I had cut them out, but that proved unnecessary, the thick paper worked fine. In case you too are artistically challenged, I include these silhouettes (see Figure 12-11).

Figure 12-11. *Sample silhouettes by Wendy Trevennor*

The LED needs to be separate from the main frame so that its distance and height relative to the moving silhouette can be varied according to situation. So, I used some flat-head screws to fix it onto a couple of pieces of scrap stick wood that I made up into an L shape as shown in Figure 12-12.

Figure 12-12. *LED shining on the silhouette*

When the whole thing is put together, with the room darkened and the software running (see Figure 12-13), the effect is really excellent.

Figure 12-13. *Big cat, little cat: the project running*

As you can see from the final picture in Figure 12-13, the silhouette size obtainable in a semidarkened room is quite impressive–it certainly impressed our real cat, which ran out of the room in a hurry. Of course, this is just a 3W LED; if you used a higher-power LED you could get an even better effect. I was so impressed by the results of this quickie project that I plan to build a more permanent version. I will use a 5- or 7-watt LED for the permanent version. The mechanism will use a reversible winding motor to get longer travel, and I will use a proper metal spring return instead of the rubber band.

The Shadow Puppet Circuit

The circuit diagram for this project is very simple. As ever, you can build it on the test bed rig we built in Chapter 2 which makes many items on the circuit diagram (Figure 12-14) unnecessary. If you plan to build your own version of this as a keeper project, you'll need to build as per the circuit diagram.

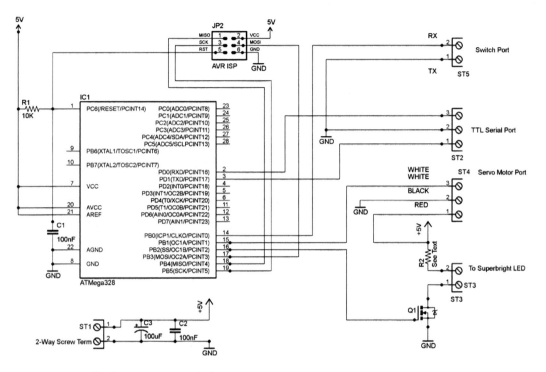

Figure 12-14. *Shadow puppets circuit diagram*

Referring to the circuit diagram you can see that this project only requires +5V, so it's easy to build it up on the test bed rig. If you wanted to use it independently, you'd need a +5V supply at about 1 amp–depending on which LED and motor you use. Because this project involves a motor (which can pull big startup currents for a brief instant) you will need to make sure the power supply rails have a good reservoir capacitor. You'll need at least a 100 uF capacitor across your +5V rail, 200 uF would be better! Without this, the motor might spike the power rail sufficiently enough to cause the MCU to crash or hang up. 100 uF proved sufficient for the motor I used, but if you, using a different motor, experience problems, try a larger value smoothing capacitor (or multiple 100 uF capacitors).

In this project, only three items are hung off the MCU: the switch, the servo motor, and the high-intensity LED.

The switch port (screw terminal 5, ST5) allows the connection of a push button to step the software through its different modes (see the "Shadow Puppets Software" section below). The ISP connector is the same as in the Duck Shooter project described earlier in this chapter.

The motor (attached via ST4) is a servo motor, as we have seen before in Chapter 3 and other places. This takes a direct logic connection from Arduino digital pin 9 (AVR pin 15). The servo motor is directly connected to the +5V supply lines and its control lead is connected to Arduino digital pin 9. We drive this in PWM mode in the software for this project.

There is a driver transistor for the high-power LED, and this hangs off Arduino digital pin 10 (AVR pin 16). Since the 3W LED that I used requires far more current than the AVR can directly supply to it, we have to use a driver transistor. I used a VNP10N6 MOSFET, which is a logic-level compatible MOSFET that includes a snubber diode. This device can sink up to 10 amps of current, so sinking 330 ma for our 3W high-intensity LED (or even a much more powerful one, should you choose to go down that route) is well within its capabilities. You could just as easily use some other logic-compatible MOSFET (e.g., an IRL540) in its place.

The MOSFET used here does not need a heatsink; it barely gets warm to the touch even after the LED has been on for half an hour. However, if you're using different components, remember to check for heat issues. The VNP10N6 MOSFET comes in a TO220 package, and the pinout (see diagram below) is a pretty standard one.

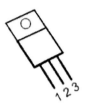

However, don't assume that *all* MOSFETs are connected like this, because although most of them are, there will be exceptions and if you make the wrong connections, you can all too easily damage your MOSFET and probably other components too. Always check the data sheet for your device to make sure you have the pinout right. For the VNP10N6 (and the IRL540), if you lay the component on its steel back, the three leads from it are as follows, from left to right:

- Terminal 1 is the input (gate).

- Terminal 2 is the drain (connect to the load): the metal tab is also connected to this terminal to aid in heatsinking.

- Terminal 3 is the source (connected to ground in this application).

The MOSFET connects to the screw terminals for the LED.

The serial port, although not used in the software as it stands, is extended out to ST2 so that it could be used with a TTL level serial port to receive commands if you wanted to extend the project for use in some larger scheme–as previously discussed.

The ISP connector is the same as in the Duck Shooter project described earlier in this chapter.

Shadow Puppets Software

The listing for the software for the shadow puppet project is quite short and reproduced in full here. There is nothing very complex about this software and I have commented it quite freely. The only thing that bears a little explanation is the program mode variable thisMode. Although it's an integer, in fact, we only care about the lowest weight two bits. Bit zero, if set, tells the program to power on the LED. Bit one, if set, tells the program to advance the motor position once each time through the main loop and to reset it when it has done a full sweep of the desired range. The following truth table summarizes the arrangement.

Bit 1	Bit 0	State selected
0	0	Motor and LED off
0	1	LED on. Motor off
1	0	LED off, motor on.
1	1	Both on.

```
/*

A sketch to control the simple shadow puppet rig
detailed in chapter 16 of "Practical AVR Microcontrollers".
The program runs in one of four modes:

00 = LED off, Motor Off
01 = LED on, Motor Off
02 = LED off, Motor On
03 = LED On, Motor On

When enabled, the motor sweeps back and forth to draw the
puppet across the light shone by the LED. This casts a moving
shadow on whatever surface the light hits (opposite wall etc).
*/

#define SWITCH_PIN 8
#define MOTOR_PIN 9
#define LED_PIN 10

#include <Servo.h>

Servo myMotor; // The servo motor
int theAngle=0; // Remembered angle of the motor.
int thisMode =0; // Program's current mode.

void setup()
{
  myMotor.attach(MOTOR_PIN); // Setup the motor control pin
  pinMode(LED_PIN,OUTPUT); // Make the LED control pin an o/p
  pinMode(SWITCH_PIN,INPUT); // Make the switch pin an input.
  digitalWrite(SWITCH_PIN,HIGH); // Enable the pull up.

  digitalWrite(LED_PIN,LOW); // Ensure the LED starts Off
  myMotor.write(0); // Ensure the motor starts at home pos.

  Serial.begin(9600); // Init serial - minimal use.
}

void loop()
{
  // Is the switch pressed?
  if (digitalRead(SWITCH_PIN) == LOW)
  {
  do
    {
      delay(5); // Wait for switch to be released
    }
    while (digitalRead(SWITCH_PIN) == LOW);

    // Switch was released.
    delay (5); // debounce delay
```

```
      thisMode++; // Increment the program mode
      if (thisMode >= 4) // If it maxes out, reset to zero
      {
        thisMode =0;
      }
      Serial.print("Software Mode Now = "); // Say the mode
      Serial.println(thisMode,DEC);
    }

// If bit zero of thisMode is set, then the LED is on.
  if (thisMode & 1)
  {
    digitalWrite(LED_PIN,HIGH);
  }
  else
  {
    digitalWrite(LED_PIN,LOW);
  }

// If bit one of thisMode is set, then advance the motor angle.
  if (thisMode & 2)
  {
    theAngle+=3;
    if (theAngle >=150) // Are we at end of desired travel for mtr?
    {
      theAngle = 0;   // We are: reset the motor back to home pos
    }
    myMotor.write(theAngle);
  }

  delay(75);
  if (theAngle==0) // If we just reset the motor, give it time to get home.
  {
    delay(1500);
  }

}
```

As previously alluded to, you could easily extend this program to receive input via the serial channel to take commands or set the mode. Look at the software for the "WordDune" project (see Chapter 10) for an example of serial channel functions of this type.

The Moiré Wheel

Before the era of animated graphics and CGI, the moiré wheel was a beloved staple of sci-fi films and TV show set designers. This wheel creates a pretty simple but very striking effect. You print a fine mesh pattern on two transparent surfaces. You shine a bright light behind them, hold one still and slowly move the other one back and forth across the moiré pattern point. The intersection points of the lines form a morphing grid pattern. When the eye views this pattern, it resolves the result into forming and deforming shapes which come and go with a pleasing fluidity.

If you want a taste of this effect you can get it quite easily. It's only enough to give you the right idea–not as good as the finished effect, but it gives you a preview without much effort!

You'll need some thin (60 gsm or less) printer paper. Use a graphics package or the "draw" facility of your word processor to make a page containing a couple of oblong boxes on a single page. Specify no outline and set the fill pattern to be a hatched, as Figure 12-15 shows:

Figure 12-15. *An example hatched pattern that could be used on your Moire wheel*

As long as both boxes have the same lined pattern, it doesn't matter whether the lines are diagonal (as in my example), vertical, or horizontal.

Print the page containing the boxes, using the best print quality available to you. If your printer is not reproducing the lines very well, try using a fill pattern where the lines are a bit bolder and not as close together. You can still get the same effect with less dense patterns; it's just less intense.

Now, cut the page in half with scissors. Find a bright light (e.g., the LED we used in the last project, or just a regular 100W house lightbulb should do). Hold the page halves one on top of the other, right in front of the light.

Hold one of the pages steady while you slowly rotate the other one. As long as enough light is getting through the paper (you'll need thinner paper or brighter light if not) you should at some point see the waves formed by the changing intersections. This gives you a rough idea of what the real thing will look like! So much for the art side of the project! Now, how do we make it?

You'll need the following things:

- A couple of transparent discs, made of fairly rigid plastic. I'd suggest using discs of between 3" and 5" (76-127 mm) across, but the size and type of these are up to you. They must be the same size and must be transparent (or almost transparent) plastic. A few possible sources:

  - Raid the recycling. Quite a lot of consumer goods and foods are packed in semirigid transparent plastic boxes or trays. You may find something you can cut discs from in that line.

  - Your local artist's shop will sell various thicknesses of clear plastic. Go for a thickness that's not floppy, but which is still transparent and easily cut to shape with normal household scissors.

  - DVD or CD recordable "cake box" packs. Most of these come with a "guard disc" at top or bottom (sometimes both) of the disc stack. These are DVD-sized discs, but they are uncoated and therefore almost transparent. You may already have some of these around, but if not, think of someone you know who burns a lot of discs (perhaps at work) and see if he or she would save some guard discs for you. They almost certainly throw them out in large numbers anyway.

  - Your local Home Depot, DIY store, or garden center may have some clear plastic sheet that you could use. These kinds of materials are often used for greenhouses, or secondary glazing for outhouse windows.

■ **Note** Don't forget, your disc will need to have a center hole. If it doesn't already have one, you'll need to make a center hole of at least 1/4" (about 6 mm) to allow the center spindle through.

- Some spray-on acrylic varnish. This goes by various names and is used to seal a surface, much like a brush applies varnish. Own-brand products tend to be a cheaper than branded ones and work just as well. You need a spray can; brush-on products won't work in this application. I used a product called triple thick by Krylon.

- Some inkjet (or laser) decal waterslide paper. This is sold under various names and brands. Most office supply outlets will have it, and you can buy it online from Amazon and eBay among many others. Just search for "waterslide decal inkjet" and you'll find lots of vendors. We'll look at how to use this stuff in just a while.

- A +5V servo motor–just like the one we used earlier for the shadow puppets.

- A long thin bolt that can screw into the center hole on the motor shaft. It needs to be a couple of inches long ideally. This bolt is needed to couple the drive shaft of the motor to the uppermost of your plastic discs. You will also need some way to secure your plastic disc to the center bolt. In my prototype I used two of the supplied horns that came with the servo motor. Using a nut, I was able to secure the disc to the center bolt (see Figure 12-19).

Figure 12-16 shows the general arrangement.

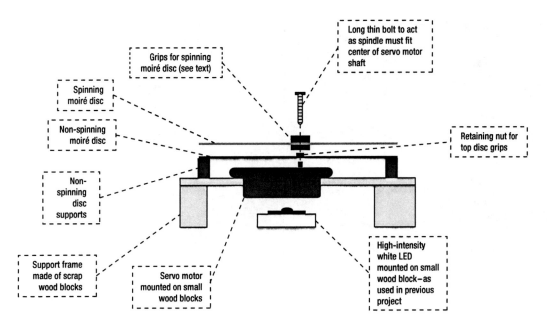

Figure 12-16. *Moiré wheel rig*

Waterslide Decals

If you have already used waterslide decals in the past and you're comfortable with using then, please feel free to skip this section. Waterslide paper lets you print transparent designs (photos, logos, moiré patterns, or whatever you want) onto a film that you can detach from its backing and affix to any plastic, metal, or glass surface. You can use it for decorating surfaces such as windows, plastic lunchboxes, or whatever else you might want.

My favorite use for waterslide paper is making light boxes. If you put a waterslide photo on a piece of thin white Plexiglas or Lexan and backlight it with a white or colored LED string you can get a lovely effect–a smaller version of the light boxes you see in stores and that light up advertising displays (see photo in Figure 12-17). If you have the skills, you could make a grid of these backlit boxes and have your own backlit photo gallery! You could use an AVR board and ULN2803 chip combination (see waterfall lights project in Chapter 11) to fade these up at down at will.

Sadly, I have found that it's only possible to use waterslide film with comparatively small photos (maximum 5" square is my recommendation) because it can crease and tear at larger sizes. I did once do an 8" x 10" but it was far from perfect and took several tries.

Another use I have found is making low-cost 5" touch panels. This method is limited in scope but quite a lot cheaper than using a LCD screen. In my version, the "press buttons" are on a backlit slide (similar to the one in Figure 12-17) and you overlay the image with a cheap four- or five-wire touch screen. Your software then uses touch coordinates to figure out which of the graphical buttons is being tapped. Of course, this approach is only good for applications where one set of permanent buttons is needed. It's no good for multilevel menu systems. Also, if you want to vary the button layout, you have to remake the backlit image. However, if used in appropriate situations, it makes a vivid and good-looking touch panel, at quite low cost as compared to the LCD approach.

So, how do we use this stuff? Waterslide paper arrives as what looks like standard sheets of photo paper. However, if you look closely you will see that it's actually a piece of paper with a film bonded to one side of it. The idea is that you print your design onto the film (shiny) side of it, using your normal printer (in color or monochrome). I usually try to do two or three designs at once. The waterslide paper is not cheap and so it makes sense to batch up your usages of it. You'll also find that you will spoil some of your designs and have to try again, especially at first.

Figure 12-17. *Example of using waterslide on a backlit light box*

Having printed your designs, you then roughly cut up the paper into pieces, each of which will contain a design you want to transfer.

Next, comes a very important step: spray at least three (preferably four or five) thin coats of acrylic varnish on. This coat seals the printed surface to protect it against moisture (as you know, inkjet print is easily washed away by moisture). Allow each coat to dry (it takes about 20-30 minutes) before applying the next. Make sure you keep count of how many coats you have put on.

■ **Caution**   Many of these kinds of products give off nasty fumes; be sure to work in a *well-ventilated* area! Open a window or turn on an extractor fan if there is one.

You'll need a "wet area" such as a sink or drainer to do the next bit. When the last coat of acrylic varnish is dry, prepare a bowl of clean water and get your target surface (in the moiré wheel project, it will be your plastic discs) close to the water bowl ready to have the film applied to them. It can help to dampen the target surface with clean water beforehand.

Place the waterslide paper into the bowl of water (cover it with water). It will immediately try to roll up around itself. Try to prevent it from rolling up, or if it rolls up before you can stop it, gently unroll it back to a flat shape, while it's still in the water. After you have done this, it should be happy to stay reasonably flat. If the ink is starting to come off the paper at this stage then, you didn't apply enough coats of acrylic varnish and you'll probably have to start over! After 30-50 seconds it should become easy to slide the film off the backing paper. Slowly and carefully lift it away from the backing paper. As quickly as you can, transfer the film onto the target surface. If you dampened the target surface you should, at first, be able to slide the film into position (thus the name) but only for a very short time. Apply the film to the target surface as smoothly as you can. Start from the center and using a smooth cloth or a plastic sponge in a wiping motion, gently smooth out any air bubbles that get trapped or creases that may form. It's pretty easy to tear the film at this stage, so be gentle. Be prepared to mess up and have to start again a few times before you get the knack.

When you have the film applied successfully, leave it to dry for an hour or two. Then, trim off any excess film from the edges of the target surface. Hey, presto! You have a light-transparent surface with your own design on it. Yes, you *can* use this technique for full sheets of waterslide paper, but don't expect it to be easy: this technique is most useful when the designs concerned are no more than about half a normal printed page.

Building the Moiré Wheel Project

By now you should have applied your moiré patterns to both discs using the techniques described in the previous section and trimmed off the excess (don't forget to open up the center hole of the disc). The next step is to secure the top disc to the spindle (see Figure 12-16). I used a 0.1" (M2.5) bolt that was about 1" (25 mm) long. This bolt screws very nicely into the center of the servo motor.

I found that I could use two of the horns (one on top of the disc and one underneath it) that came with the servo motor along with a retaining nut underneath, to grip the disc firmly and secure it to the spindle (see Figures 12-18 through 12-20). However, you will have to take a view of what suits your needs when you have the materials and parts at hand. Some large metal washers with small center holes would do the job too.

The bottom disc does not move; it simply needs to be held to position at the required height. If, like me, you're only building a temporary version of this project, you just need to hold it steady at roughly the right height. I found some metal spacers that were approximately the right height. If you can't find anything suitable you could try using something like blocks of blu-tack. You need to position the fixed (lower) disc so that it is close to, but not touching, the moving (upper) disc. If the discs are too far apart, the moiré effect will be lessened. The fixed disc needs to allow the spindle to rotate freely, but the disc must not touch the spindle, so its center hole should be quite a lot larger than the spindle.

The underlight can be provided either by a LED string or by the high-intensity LED that we used in the shadow puppet project.

Finally, Figures 12-18 through 12-20 show the prototype rig.

This first photo show a close-up of one of the uncoated CD discs I used. This view of the disc is after the waterslide film carrying the mesh pattern has been applied to it but before trimming.

Figure 12-18. *Close-up of uncoated disc*

This is a side view of the entire rig. You can see the upper disc is held onto the spindle by the horns borrowed from the servo motor kit.

If I were building a permanent version of this project I think I would try to build it into a cylindrical enclosure with a reflector at the bottom in order to minimize light loss and make sure that the wheels get maximum light through them.

Figure 12-19. *Side View of the Moire Wheel Rig*

A closer view of the two discs with the light shining through them from underneath.

Figure 12-20. *A view of the discs*

Looking through the two discs with the mesh patterns at the start of the moiré zone.

Figure 12-21. *Looking through the two discs*

The circuit diagram we need for this project is exactly the same as we used for the shadow puppet project in Figure 12-14. The software is different.

Moiré Wheel Software

The software for this project only has to do one thing–slowly and smoothly move the servo motor back and forth in the "moiré zone." Once you have built up the project you will see that you get the most pleasing effects (the moiré zone) within a comparatively small area of movement. You'll need to find this zone by experiment since it will depend on what line pattern you used and the relative mounting positions of your discs. You can, if you prefer, just let the servo motor sweep up and down its full arc of travel (the software starts from this assumption) and you will be sure to see a moiré effect at some point during each sweep.

If you do want to tune into the moiré zone, you'll need to hook up the project's TTL serial channel to your desktop. As you will recall, the Arduino servo motor library abstracts the angle of the motor for us. So all we have to do is set start and end values in the software. This allows us to quite precisely control the sweep of the turning moiré wheel.

The moiré wheel software reacts to the following commands received at the serial channel:

- S–Increase the motor's sweep start point.
- s–Decrease the motor's sweep start point.
- E–Increase the motor's sweep end point.
- e–Decrease the motor's sweep end point.
- L–Toggle the state of the LED (on/off).
- M–toggle the state of the motor (stop/start)
- A–show the current state report. Shows sweep start and end points, current angle (useful when you are trying to judge moiré zone boundaries), and LED and motor on/off states.

The adjustment commands enforce bounds checking to make sure the start and end points don't collide and that the start point doesn't go below zero or the end point above MAX_ANGLE. If you were building a permanent version of this project, a worthwhile addition to the code would be to write the moiré zone values into EEPROM so that they are not lost at power off and can be remembered for the next session.

Generally I found that fairly short (50 ms) delays between motor steps give the best results. I also tried it with a more general light source, an LED string. It made the moiré effect appear over a slightly larger area but didn't really enhance it. I found that the moiré zone on my prototype was within a range of about 25 degrees of travel.

Obviously that is highly specific and will vary according to the line density you use for your patterns, the spacing of the discs, and so on, but it gives you a guide at least.

The software is quite simple but rather too large to reproduce here. You can download it from the book's web site (www.apress.com/9781430244462). Following is a summary code walk:

Function Name	Commentary
Declarations	The declarations section consists of numerous #define directives to define constants for the program. These constants include the version number and assigning numbers to the pins that control the motor and the LED. The Boolean values for the LED and Motor state as well as the variable that holds the current angle of the motor position and several other variables are also declared.
setup()	In the setup() function the various I/O pins are assigned and initialized and the serial channel begun. The motor is set to its home position at 0 degrees rotation, and the program version string is printed to the serial channel.
loop()	In the main loop, the variable that contains the motor angle is incremented or decremented according to whether the motor is traveling clockwise or anticlockwise. • The program does checks to make sure that the start position is never set to be the same or more than the end position and that the current angle is never more that the absolute maximum angle of which the motor is capable (MAX_ANGLE) or less than zero, which in the context of a servo motor, makes no sense. If the user has set the end points to be different to the absolute end points then these set the points at which the direction of travel will reverse. • If one or other end of travel (either user set soft end points or absolute values) has been reached, then direction reverses. Having calculated the new angle, the program writes it out to the PWM pin controlling the servo motor. Finally the loop() calls the serialInput() function.
serialInput()	This function checks for input from the user via the TTL level serial channel. If anything has been received, it is fetched and parsed and actioned accordingly. Unrecognized inputs are discarded and ignored.
report()	This function outputs the current state of the application's variables. It shows the state of the LED, the motor (on or off), the current angle of the motor, and the current user set start and end points.

Summary

In this chapter we have looked at three fairly different ways of using AVR controlled movement (actual or simulated). As discussed at the outset of the book, the ways in which you can use a microcontroller to create and control movement are effectively unlimited. None of the ideas or techniques presented in this chapter are in the least bit trailblazing or earth shattering; they are just intended as examples of the kind of things that, when used in combination with other ideas of the same type, can cumulatively add up to something special.

Coming Up Next

The final chapter: Smart Home?

■ ■ ■

CHAPTER 13

Smart Home Enablers

The future almost never turns out how we think it will. The much parodied "home of the future" concepts of yesteryear all had a central controlling computer at their core. Like a spider at the center of an electronic web, this computer called all the shots when it came to controlling the automated functions within the home. It was this behemoth that controlled every aspect of the automated serving of the dog's dinner or drawing those famous motorized curtains when night fell.

In early versions of the concept, it was a basement-filling box with numerous flashing lights and hundreds of chattering relays inside it. It did, of course, have a teletype that slowly chunkered out its proclamations to the humans that notionally controlled it. Yes, home automation was the future. No doubt about it!

In later versions of the vision, the control entity became an additional desktop machine that sat alongside the existing one (or was locked away in a closet, presumably building up the heat that caused its own demise!).

In more recent times, the whole concept has undergone a rebranding. Most people working in this field now tend to use the term "Smart Home." I think that, in part, this new term was taken up enthusiastically because for many people the older term "home automation" carried the baggage of years of failed promise. However, it's also in recognition of that fact that, since the advent of cheap microprocessors and more especially MCUs, it's now possible to place numerous points of "intelligence" around the home. A central entity *may* still exist in some versions of the concept, but its role is now much more as a coordinator and facilities provider than as a direct controller.

Is Your Home Smart?

The term "Smart Home" is an imprecise one and is thus open to much abuse. Look around the modern home, look around YOUR home, is it smart? Do you find these things?

- A kettle that turns itself off when the water inside it boils.

- A heating controller that comes on at a preset time and goes off at a preset time, which you can vary by day of the week.

- A cable or satellite TV box that you can program to automatically record the shows and movies that you like—and maybe even suggest additional shows that might appeal to you.

- A motion-triggered light for that dark stairway.

- A telephone answering device.

- An oven, washing machine, or dishwasher with a timer that you can preset to come on and go off at times you preselect.

- A doorbell device that can play any one of 20 preset tunes that you can select.

- Remotely controlled power sockets that you can activate with a small remote.

- A wireless network that allows you to hop onto the Internet on any one of a dozen different kinds of devices from anywhere in your home.

- A computer with a library of music, video, and family photos on it.

You probably do find many of these items—and other things besides. So is yours a Smart Home already? Twenty-five years ago, people would have probably said that, yes, these things did indeed add up to a Smart Home! But look again at the list above. Most of these things have embedded in them islands of intelligence or automation, but do they talk to one another? Do they make one another aware of what they are doing? Probably not. This goes to the core of why the Smart Home dream has failed to deliver its full potential. In short, it's a common or garden communication problem!

A challenge! Look around and try to buy the following example products off the shelf:

- A home heating system controller that can connect to your wireless network and be commanded from your Home Theatre PC or by you from your desk at work via the Internet.

- A music player for your car that you can fill up with music or speech content wirelessly from your home music library via Wi-Fi.

- A doorbell that "knows" there is nobody home and therefore plays randomly spaced barking dog sounds if the doorbell is rung.

Yes, all of these things can be done and, yes, for serious money you *can* even buy some of them from high-end specialist vendors! However, due to their high prices, they are just techno-toys for well-heeled tech enthusiasts. For the Smart Home concept to actually succeed on a large scale, something fundamental has to change to allow the whole thing to go commodity. That thing can be summed up in one word: standards.

Very few of the available Smart Home components can talk directly to one another, and no major manufacturers of household goods has been persuaded of the merit of building in support for one of the putative standards (for example, X.10, which is the closest thing to a predominant standard, especially in the US) for their mainstream products. With almost all household goods now having one or more MCUs at their heart, you would think that it would be pretty easy to make almost any household device talk TCP/IP in some way, but no, seems like there's no demand for it.

Well, that's demonstrably not true. The enthusiastic adoption over the last 25 years of the kind of devices listed above conclusively proves that we really *do* want intelligent devices doing things for us in our homes. But we want the kind of set-and-forget simplicity that we have become accustomed to from computers and computer networks. Thus Smart Home products would have to abandon proprietary approaches in hardware and do other things such as perhaps adopting standard object models (see Chapter 6). In other words, the Smart Home industry needs to backtrack and learn from the IT industry, which realized many years ago that if you make your hardware and software interoperate as seamlessly as possible, pretty much everybody wins. The idea that the connected, automated, or Smart Home is going to become commonplace while there is no universal plug and play compatibility between any intelligent device that you might care to buy is delusional.

In a very selfish sense, the fact that you can't buy cooperating Smart Home components at your local corner store is good news for the readers of this book! It means that the MCU enthusiast holds trump cards in his or her hand when it comes to Smart Home making. You have the ability to make your own smart devices and you probably have the knowledge to engineer interfaces to allow at least some of those stubbornly isolationist smart devices referred to above to interoperate with one another. This chapter explores this area in a little bit of detail. Of course, there are whole books on the subject of home automation and the Smart Home, so in just this one section of this one book we can only skim the surface by looking at a few techniques to make communication easier, but let's make a start!

Hacking is the name of the game when it comes to compensating for the lack of Smart Home equipment standards. All consumer products have a user interface of some sort; if you can find out how that user interface works, then you can use your MCU to pretend to be a real user. Let's start with a prime example: a remote controlled power socket.

Socket Cracking

It's very easy now to buy power sockets that you can switch on and off with a supplied remote control. How these look obviously varies from country to country since power outlet formats vary so much. Most DIY stores stock these products in some format and of course you can also get them from the usual electronics outlets.

- www.homedepot.com (US), search for product number 100654961 (indoor remote kit)

- www.maplin.co.uk (UK), stock code N79KA (3-pack remote control sockets)

These products send a coded signal from a handset to one or more power socket extensions to tell them to switch on or off. Usually you can buy these in single, three, or sometimes sets of five.

For your purposes, the main limitation of these things is that they only let you control the socket on/off state via the supplied remote control. There is (of course) no other interface; you can't command it from your Wi-Fi network or from the USB port of your PC or anything as useful as that!

So, how would you go about incorporating these sorts of products in your Smart Home setup? Say you wanted to be able to command one of these devices from a desktop computer via a USB port; how might you do that? There are two ways: a mainly software way and a mainly hardware way.

The software way consists of hooking up an appropriate type of electronic "ear" (sensor) to your AVR to allow it to capture the signal sent for each keypress on the remote. You then use software to record these signals into a small digital library. You can then replay the required keypress on the appropriate radio frequency when you want to simulate a keypress[1]. This approach works in much the same way as if you were recording each of the tones from a telephone keypad and then playing them back in the required order into the phone's microphone to make a phone call. There are various Arduino libraries (e.g., the Home Easy library) to help you go down this route, plus numerous online and print publication articles about how to go about capturing keypresses, etc.

You'll find that the kind of remote controls of interest in this context operate around the 315MHz or 433MHz bands depending on where in the world you are located. The remote control for your product should have a label on it showing exactly what frequency band it uses.

The software approach can be a good one. There's almost no hardware cost involved and you don't need to break open the original remote control hardware to make it work. The downside is that it won't work with some more advanced products because they use an encryption algorithm to ensure that their signals are unique each time. That means that recording what they "say" during one session won't do you any good because what they say during the next session will be different and what you have captured will be stale and not work. With these kinds of products, you must "train" senders and receivers to recognize one another right after their first power up. If the products you are using don't need any training, then you're probably okay to go the software route!

The hardware approach is actually very simple but it will invalidate your warranty on the product! Just to be clear, I'm *not* kidding; making the modification to be described here will definitely invalidate *any* warranty you may have on the product. So, work carefully and use anti-static precautions when handling the electronic parts.

All you need to do is take apart your remote control and use the contacts of a small relay that your software will pulse to make the relay contacts bridge the same contacts that the buttons on the remote control use. You'll need to use a driver to enable your MCU to drive the relay. You could use a 2803a chip (as you used in various other projects) to activate your relay. Don't forget to use the snubber diodes inside the 2803a to deal with the back-EMF. If you need to refresh your memory about the 2803a and snubber diodes, take a look back at Figure 4-21 in Chapter 4.

Often there's just one little recessed screw to allow you to disassemble the remote control. But sometimes the hardest part is getting the remote control apart! Some of these products clip-fit together; you'll find a tiny slot where you can insert a very small screwdriver to prise the top and bottom of the case apart. Other times there is a small but continuous groove all the way around the product; if you get a small flat blade screwdriver and carefully run it around the groove, pressing down fairly hard, you will release some little tabs inside it that hold the two halves of the product shell together. Careful how you do this; keep your fingers well out of the way!

---

[1]If your interest is more in the area of hacking TV-style IR remotes, have a look at Ken Shiriff's excellent Arduino IR Library at www.arcfn.com/2009/08/multi-protocol-infrared-remote-library.html.

Other times the manufacturers hide the fixing screw under a label. If you suspect this is how your remote control is made, get the handle end of your screwdriver and rub it firmly around the label face. Then, hold the label up to a bright light and you should be able to see the indent of the screwhole. Pierce the label at that point and you should be able to disassemble.

Once you have your remote control apart, you should easily be able to see how the buttons, when pressed, bridge the sets of contacts. It's up to you to decide how many buttons you want to extend out of the remote, but it's usually a very simple job to add wires to the contact points and bring them out to the contacts of a small relay that your MCU can control. The resulting solution may not be especially elegant, but it will allow your MCU to easily control main devices in a very safe way. Usually you can hide away the wired-up remote control.

On the Radio: The Un-wired Home

As stated earlier, we can't address the massive subject of the Smart Home in a few pages of one book, but one area that seems worth spending some pages exploring—and looking at just one pragmatic solution—is the crucial area of communications.

One particular barrier to Smart Home communication is wiring. Unless you're lucky enough to be closely involved with planning, building, or completely gutting and renovating your home, running a cable to the location of each and every little device that you may want to participate in your Smart Home is quite an undertaking!

Just thinking about the AVR level of Smart Home making: you'd need to have everything from a smart bell push for the front door to a smart door sensor, temperature sensors, motion sensors, light sensors, smart locks, entry keypads, lighting controllers... the list is a potentially very long one, even before you start adding your higher-end multimedia terminals, digital music and video streaming, and so on. Are you really going to run a CAT5 or CAT6 cable for each one of these things?

There are, of course, many alternatives to running wires to each and every little AVR powered device around your Smart Home.

- Wi-Fi—802.11b/g: This is superficially attractive because you are quite likely to have a Wi-Fi network in your home already, so what could be neater than having your Smart Home devices tap into it? Logistically true, but financially flawed. Look at price of a Wi-Fi module that works with (for example) an Arduino. You'll be doing well if you can find one for less than $40 US, and it won't even be a complete solution; you'll need to add some extra stuff to make it actually work with your AVR. Add the cost of your AVR (or an Arduino, if you go that route). Multiply that by the number you will require and... well, the numbers don't look attractive.

- There are many products available now that let you make Ethernet network connections through the mains wiring of your house; this is often called powerline networking. These products work really well in most situations (though they are not legal to use in all countries as yet, so do check the local legalities). But again, explore the cost-per node: add up the cost of a mains network interface and the Ethernet module you will need to allow your MCU to be an Ethernet end node. Multiply the cost per node by the number of Smart Home peripherals you think you might need and see if your eyes don't water! By my reckoning you're looking at about $60 per node, minimum, at the time of writing!

- Zigbee is another wireless networking standard that is much vaunted by the Smart Home movement, but again, unless product prices fall (another case of a minimum $50 per viable node at the time of writing), this is not really not going to find its way into high-volume consumer products any time soon.

- There are other alternatives such as Bluetooth, which is more viable financially, coming in at about half the price of the solutions above. However, anything using a Bluetooth solution has to go through the overhead (and delay) of pairing at start-up and handling connection drops and so on.

- There are other basic ways to do certain kinds of wireless connections and these are far lower cost. We'll take a look at one of these options in the "Low-Cost Wireless Communication" section later in this chapter.

Wiring Up

So, clearly the wireless route has the potential to be fairly high cost. However, you may think that is a price worth paying in order to save having to run (and live with) all that wiring. Returning to the subject of wiring, where exactly is the problem?

Many Smart Home setups feature a radial wiring plan. In other words, there is some central point to which each and every cable goes back (see Figure 13-1). This central point is often a wiring shelf in a closet or (in a large home) a utility room containing a wiring hub in a floor standing cabinet. The nodes of the network derive their power from the nearest mains outlet.

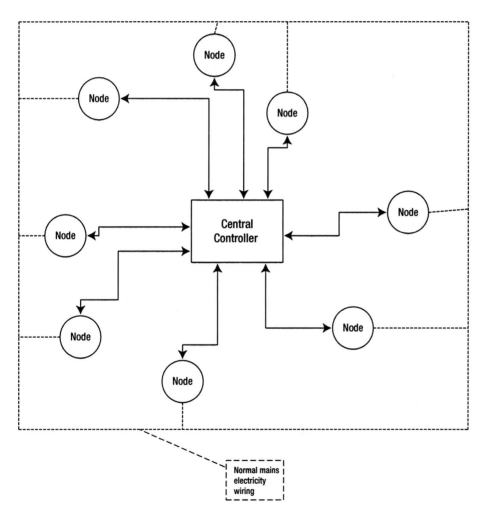

Figure 13-1. *Smart Home radial connection—central control*

Nodes can be anything from a desktop computer to a door sensor. This radial wiring approach goes back to the original notion of having a single controlling entity at a single point in the Smart Home. As outlined earlier, it goes all the way back to the days when the cost of the controlling central computer was the biggest price ticket item in the whole enterprise, back to the days when the control computer was the single most unique and complex item in the whole setup.

However, thanks in large measure to the MCU, the radial wiring approach now has competition; as described earlier in this chapter, the intelligence in a modern setup can be much more distributed. In this alternative model, there doesn't need to be a central point. There is simply a network connection linking all points in some way. It may be a simple daisy chain, as in Figure 13-2. In this model, the central controller has been simplified to a resource server. For example, it may simply issue network addresses or it may offer hard drive storage for nodes to send logging data to.

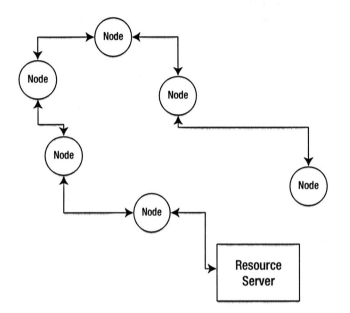

Figure 13-2. *Smart Home daisy chain wiring*

A more mixed scheme, as shown in Figure 13-3, might also be used. This is no longer a daisy chain; it is a fairly random arrangement with the only requirement being that all nodes on the network can "hear" one another in some way. In this model of operation, nodes can have the ability to generate events and to consume events and autonomously act upon them (again, see the discussion in Chapter 6).

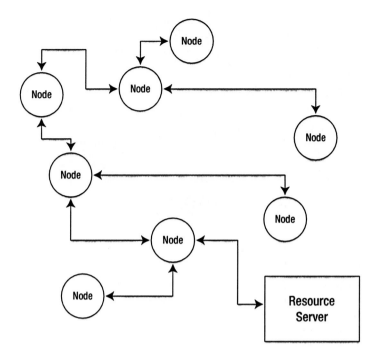

Figure 13-3. *Smart Home—mixed topology*

Back to Basics

Going back to basics, what you need is, in many cases, incredibly simple. Thinking back to Chapter 6, you saw that, with proper and tight design of your communications, messages can be very compact. For example, in the SHOM (Smart Home Object Model) imagineered there[2], the 5-byte sequence shown in the following table conveys all the information that is required for a sensor node to communicate its state:

Byte #	Means
1	1 = Fittings
2	5 = Windows
3	1 = Sensors
4	8 = Window number 8 (rear, ground floor, kitchen)
5	2 = Event code (might mean has gone from closed state to open state)

For conveying something so small, some of the connection methods listed above (and their associated costs) somehow seem like using the proverbial sledgehammer to crack a nut! Of course, as you saw in "Digitally Speaking" you'd have to add some kind of jacket around the basic 5-byte packet plus a header and some checksum protection. Even so, the whole message in this example would be unlikely to be more than 15 bytes long.

---

[2]Please remember that SHOM is not any kind of standard; it's just something I invented to show how a slim protocol can be developed for use within a closed environment.

In fact, in a network like the one in Figure 13-3, many of the nodes will be very trivial ones, such as a window sensor, a light level detector, a doorbell button, a phone ring detector, etc. These kinds of nodes are very easily implemented using a very cheap, low-end AVR; it doesn't have to offer a lot of I/O lines and it doesn't need a lot of memory. Each one only needs to do the following things:

- Interface with a sensing or switching element (for example, the window open sensor).

- Have the ability to be programmed with an ID. Going back to the SHOM example, it needs to know that it is a node of type Fittings\Windows\Sensor, it is sensing the open/closed state of window number 8, and the event code to generate for any given sequence of sensor inputs.

- It needs to be given some kind of interface to allow it to participate in the local network.

All except the last item on this list can easily be met by using a low-end 8-pin AVR costing just a couple of dollars, but what about that last item?

Low-Cost Wireless Communication

If you want to embrace the idea of having a Smart Home in which you can embed intelligence everywhere at an affordable price, you need to think pragmatically. There are low-cost wireless products that you can use; they can be bought (from Asian vendors) for as little as $5 for a transmitter module *and* a receiver module. These are usually sold as "xxMHz receiver transmitter modules" by various electronics sites (where xx is usually 433 in much of Europe and 315 or 434 in North America).

- www.sparkfun.com/products/10534 (US) Transmitter

- www.sparkfun.com/products/10532 (US) Receiver

- www.techsupplies.co.uk (UK) (search for RFA001 and related items)

Many companies seem to make these. Two typical ones that I have used are shown in Figure 13-4. The transmitter module is on the right and it has the following three pins:

Figure 13-4. *Low-cost short range radio modules*

- +Vcc (typically between 4.5 and 9 Volts)

- Ground

- TXdata (a logic-compatible input)

The receiver is on the left and it has four pins, though only three are actually used. These carry

- +Vcc

- Ground

- RXdata (a logic-compatible output)

Both modules easily plug into a breadboard (though you may need to add some header pins).

Make sure that the modules you buy have logic level (TTL/CMOS) compatible inputs and outputs and can operate on +5Volts. Most such products seem to meet these requirements, but do check before buying. The modules require the addition of an antenna (see bullet point, below).

The essential idea is that you connect the serial port pins (transmit and receive) of the AVR to the radio modules and, using a port speed of 2400 baud (as opposed to the more usual 9600), you can exchange data across the resulting link. There are some important things to be aware of when using these modules:

- The modules MUST use a wavelength (e.g., 433MHz) that is license exempt in your geography. Your vendor can advise. *Do not* import modules from another country and assume they will be okay; license-exempt frequencies vary from place to place.

- The communication they provide is usable over only very short distances inside a home. About 20 feet (approx. 6 meters) seems to be an optimum (see below) using just a wire antenna. If you are willing to use a more elaborate antenna, you will get a far greater range but at more cost and trouble.

- They are in no sense intelligent. They do no packetization of the data to be sent; neither do they offer guaranteed delivery of that data or *any* error checking.

- They are not secure. Anyone sitting outside your home with sufficiently sensitive listening equipment could listen in to the traffic passing between these modules.

Looking at the kinds of applications you have in mind, the second and third items on this list are not necessarily big problems. If you can install a small number of wired hubs around the home (hidden in ceiling voids, crawl spaces, closets, etc.), those can act as signal relays. Then you only require short distance transmission to the nearest hub node. Because they only communicate occasionally, many wireless nodes can talk to a single hub. As for these being very dumb devices, you're using an AVR in each end node and the intelligence can be built into the software of that.

As for the final item on the list, it's true that anybody with a malicious intent and the right knowledge could start commanding your Smart Home to do some wacky stuff! So you do need to be aware of this when deciding when to use this approach and when to use more expensive ones. You'll look at this in more detail in a short while.

Security is always an issue, and sadly, most wireless security protocols seem to get cracked (a quick Google search can verify this), so you should never assume that you can attain total security in wireless communications of any kind. Later in this chapter you'll look at some more detailed cases for deciding whether to use low-cost wireless or not.

Smart Home Using a Mixed Network

What would a Smart Home network built using a mix of short range radio modules and wired hubs look like? It might look something like the diagram in Figure 13-5, in which you might still have your resource server (though it's not mandatory) and a handful of wired hub nodes. Each wired node acts as a highly localized area hub, located near a cluster of wireless nodes. If the diagram brings to your mind a picture of many desktop-grade machines scattered around the home, jammed into closets, hidden under beds, or perched precariously on top of bookshelves, forget it! It's more likely that

- The hub nodes would be something like an Arduino in a box, equipped with an Ethernet CAT6 (or perhaps the compatible, but older CAT5) interface and with a low-cost radio transmitter and receiver attached to its serial port. Alternatively, it might be a naked AVR (see Chapter 3!) board of your own devising.

- The wireless nodes would be controlled by a very low-end AVR chip with a low cost radio module attached, built into something no larger than the size of a couple of matchboxes. Possibly it would be battery powered or it might just need to plug into a USB power adaptor to any nearby mains power socket.

- The resource server could be an old desktop machine or laptop.

The wired network might be a completely separate one from the one you use for your desktop machines, or it might be the same one. If it were separate, the resource server could be set to route traffic between the two LANs.

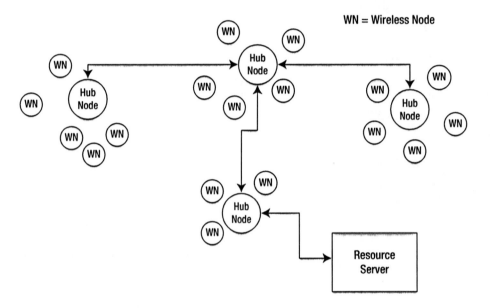

Figure 13-5. *Mixed network, wired and wireless*

The possibility (make that, probability!) that some of the data that these kinds of nodes send will be lost, or could be heard by a third party, is a deciding factor in whether you use a wireless or wired node[3].

---

[3]In passing, it's worth noting that even unencrypted traffic on a wired LAN *can* be listened to outside of your home by someone with sufficiently sensitive equipment—though such equipment is said to be very expensive.

The following are some examples of where datapath reliability or security is important and where it is not:

- Case 1: A movement sensor that is intended to trigger some lights might be connected over a short-distance radio link. If a person enters the room, the sensor is triggered and the node to which the sensor is attached broadcasts a message on the network, indicating that this movement trigger has been activated. Another node that is monitoring for such event notifications is supposed to turn the light on, but it never "sees" the movement sensor event because the network is busy. The person who triggered the light and has gotten used to the lights turning on when she enters the room simply does what we all do in such circumstances, she waves her arms around. This time the system works and the lights come on; no big deal, just so long as it doesn't happen every time.

- Case 2: A flame sensor is connected over a short-distance wireless link. The flame sensor senses a flame: a log has spilled out of the open fire and onto a carpet. The node to which the sensor is connected sends out a message that is supposed to raise the alarm, but the data packet it sends never makes it. A sprinkler system controller is listening for flame sensor triggers but never sees the alarm. Bad news!

- Case 3: A door entry system that allows a code to be entered on a keypad and then sends the entered code to a superior system via radio; it receives back an "Open" or "Don't Open" response.

So, in the first case, you don't really care if data is lost because the consequences are pretty trivial—just a minor temporary annoyance. However, in the second case, you do care a *lot* and that node should never have been made wireless! Case 3 should never be wireless because a listener could easily intercept the keycode they need to be able to get through the door.

In summary, if it's just a matter of somebody knowing when your door opens or closes, do you care? If they start commanding your feature lights to go on and off, well, it's pretty easy to disable that feature until they get tired of the game. However, for other things, this low-cost approach is not sensible to use and you will have to use a more expensive setup. Yes, this kind of wireless connection has limitations, but it is a very useful and low-cost way to avoiding running wires around your home for a significant number of purposes, especially for simple sensors or lighting control.

Taking the earlier project of the waterfall lights (the passageway lighting system) as an example, if you added a wireless sender module to that, it could send out a log of its activations and status. If you added a send-and-receive module, it could receive commands to switch on and receive updates, for example to the length of time it stayed on, based on an analysis of sensor log data collected over a period of time. If you had a house security controller, the waterfall light could receive "nobody home mode" messages that would make it ignore any sensor activations that might be made by the dog or cat wandering around.

In short, if the less critical elements of a Smart Home setup could be implemented with a cheap and easy way to allow it to contribute information into a Smart Home network, then many things would change! This approach is very much in line with initiatives like VSCP (Very Simple Control Protocol), which aim to allow cheap and simple Smart Home implementations by simplifying and commoditizing the design and topology involved.

A Simple HomeHelp Protocol

As outlined in the previous section, the low-cost radio modules do not have any embedded intelligence—none at all! They simply act as a data pipe, a radio version of a cable, except not so reliable! As you saw, data can fail to make it from one end of the pipe to the other or can be garbled en-route.

In order to be sure that you receive correct data, you need to invent a protocol that performs a number of functions:

- It allows the receiving node to distinguish between random radio noise and actual data.

- It provides a description of the data being sent.

- It provides a mechanism to provide a reasonable amount of assurance that the data that has been received is the same as the data that was sent.

- It identifies the sender and intended recipient so that, in your mixed network where all the nodes can "hear" what each another are saying, they can tell whether a data packet is something they need to pick up and look at or not.

- It provides an extensible packet scheme that can be upgraded in future while still retaining backwards compatibility if that should prove to be necessary, so that network nodes which have not been upgraded can still operate using the previous version of the protocol.

The protocol to be presented here is a simple one, but one that provides all of the functions that were listed above. It is a connectionless protocol, which means it only allows single messages to be passed from one radio equipped node to another one. There is no concept of a reply to a message and no handshaking, which means that nothing in the protocol allows the sender to know if the receiver has got the sent message or not. In networking terms, this is "best endeavor" communication—no guaranteed delivery and no failure notifications.

The HomeHelp protocol, version 1, packet layout is shown in the following table (all values in decimal unless otherwise noted):

Area Name	Byte Number	Type	Binary Values	Details
HomeHelp Packet Header	1-6	Bytes	5-4-3-2-1-0	A simple binary countdown forming a lead-in to the packet. Seeing this sequence allows a receiver to know that a packet is coming, since it is highly unlikely to occur randomly in a noise pattern.
	7	Byte	1 to 255	A byte value indicating the version number of the packet that follows. This will, at the moment, contain the value 1, since there is only one version of this protocol. If there is ever a second issue of the protocol, this byte would allow a receiving node to know which version spec to use in processing the rest of the packet.
	8-9	Unsigned int (16 bits)	0-65535	"To Node:" A 16-bit unsigned integer indicating to which local node this packet is addressed. This is sent low byte first. Special values:
				0 = Broadcast, all nodes should take notice1 to 31 (0x1F) = Reserve values, do not use
				31-65535 = Can be used as node numbers
HomeHelp Packet Header	10-11	Unsigned int (16 bits)	0-65535	"From Node:" A 16-bit unsigned integer indicating to which local node sent this packet. This is sent low byte first. Special values:
				0 = Sender is a master node1 to 31 (0x1F) = Reserve values, do not use
				31-65535 = Normal node numbers
	12-13	Unsigned int (16 bits)	0-65535	Payload packet size (PPS): This is a 16-bit value indicating how many bytes are in the payload that comes next. Low byte is sent first.

(continued)

Area Name	Byte Number	Type	Binary Values	Details
Payload	14-n	Bytes	--	The payload itself. This can be whatever you want, just a byte stream of n-14 bytes.
Checksum	$n+1$	Unsigned int (16 bits)	0-65535	This is a checksum of the payload. It uses the checksum computation scheme outlined in Chapter 6 in which each byte in the payload is added together to make a 16-bit checksum, but the result is limited to 16 bits by discarding any arithmetic carry. This value is sent low byte first.

Obviously, in this scheme, you can put whatever you like in the payload section.

An important function of the software implementing the receiver end of this protocol is a timeout. If the channel starts delivering a packet but loses connection halfway through, it's important that the receiving software knows when to give up and abort reception; otherwise it would be stuck waiting for the rest of the packet forever and the software would stall.

Using a Low-Cost Smart Home Wireless Node

In this project, you are going to build a simple door sensor. It will send a HomeHelp format wireless data packet whenever the door state changes. This will be sent to a simple receiving module, which will then display the status in a terminal window. Since the main point here is to show how to use the short-range wireless modules, the receiver is not going to be a hub node and the payload will be a single byte, not a fully qualified SHOM sequence.

In a real implementation, you would most likely want to use an 8-pin AVR (such as maybe an ATtiny85 chip) for the door sensor project, but you've been using the ATmega328 through this book, so let's stick with that. You could, of course, rig up many sensors to this one controller, but you'll use only one sensor in this example project.

Figure 13-6 shows a block diagram of the project. In summary,

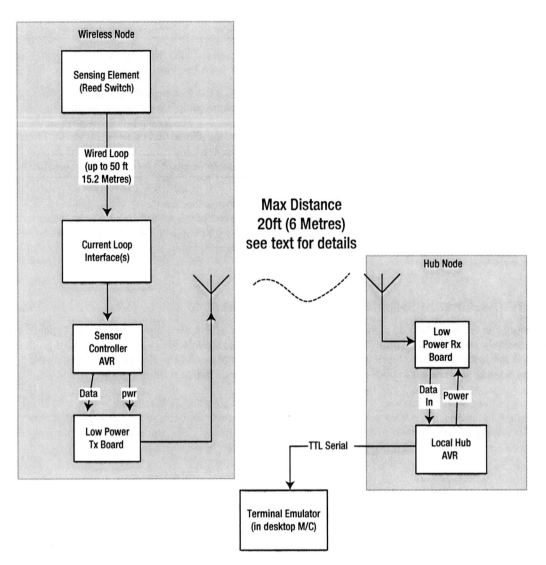

Figure 13-6. *Wireless door opening monitor*

- A door sensor is connected via a current loop isolator to a sensor controller AVR. The current loop interface allows you to have as long a cable run as you need to the door sensor; however, if you are able to locate the circuitry within a short distance from the sensor, you may be able to dispense with the current loop interface and just wire the sensor direct to an AVR input pin, thus saving the cost of the opto-coupler chip.

- The software constantly polls the state of the sensor. When a change of state is detected, it formulates an appropriate message and sends it out via the low power transmitter. Although the message is jacketed inside a HomeHelp format packet, the core of this message is very simple; it's just a single byte that takes one of the following values:

  - 01 = Started up (message sent after power on).

  - 02 = Going away (sent if controller is commanded to power off or reboot).

- 03 = The door was closed and is now open.

- 04 = The door was open and is now closed.

- 05 = The door is open (sent periodically to confirm a door left open).

- The low power transmitter used in this circuit actually requires so little power that it can be powered from an AVR output pin! This allows the transmitter to be powered off by the MCU between transmissions. This reduced power supply requirement (if you used a low-power MCU such as an ATmega328-up) might make the project a candidate for battery operation, which for this kind of usage might be very handy!

- The message travels across the air to the receiver (RX) board. I have played around with several different products and ways of doing the antenna for them. I would say that, using just a wire antenna inside a home, you should regard 20 feet (about 6 meters) as the maximum distance over which you will get reasonably reliable transfer. Obviously, using more expensive sorts of antenna (and perhaps even with different makes of board) will get you different results.

- When the local hub AVR has received the message from the sensor node, it examines the contents. If the received message is valid, it decodes the meaning and puts out a message via its TTL serial channel to a terminal window running on a desktop machine.

Using just a piece of wire as the antenna, I have had communication between sender and receiver at a distance of about 40 indoor feet, but it's very variable; some days it didn't work at all. Over a distance of 20 feet, reliability is (with the setups I have tried) very good, and actually 20 feet is quite a long distance inside a home; in an average sized home it would get you from one room into the next. Usually, you would locate your hub receivers at strategic places out of sight. Such locations might include

- Up above the ceiling or in an attic space.

- In in-between floors space.

- In a crawl space.

- In a closet or under shelving.

- Under or behind a chair or couch.

- Hidden inside some piece of household equipment such as a clock.

As long as there is no radio block (such as a steel door or masonry containing lots of flint) between transmitter and receiver, you should not have a problem. You can get a lot more range albeit (at a cost that may work out to be several times more than the cost of the module!) by using a custom made antenna; however, I used a length of breadboard jumper wire, which did the job at almost zero cost.

I found that the length of the wire makes a big difference to the performance of the link. There seems to be an optimum length, so a little experimentation with different antenna wire lengths is worth the time it takes. I found that a wire between 7-9 inches (about 180mm-230mm) worked best, but I'm sure it's highly product- and situation-specific.

Door Sensor Circuit Diagram

The circuit diagram in Figure 13-7 shows the circuit diagram for the wireless sender. You could build this as a temporary project on the test bed rig (as shown here, with the ISP port as usual) or as a separate small solder board inside a box if you want it as a permanent facility.

The MCU used is an ATmega328 (as noted earlier, you might want to use a smaller and cheaper AVR, such as an 8-pin ATmega85 in a real deployment). In this implementation,

- Pin 4 (Arduino digital in 2) is used to supply power to the radio transmitter module when needed (and only then).

- Pin 3 (Arduino TX) supplies the serial data stream to be sent over the radio transmitter module.

- Pin 15 (Arduino digital pin 9) is configured as an input to sense the state of the door switch. In the configuration shown, if the door switch is closed (i.e., the magnet is close to the sensor), then the pin will read as LOW.

- Other pins are used in the normal way for ISP programming.

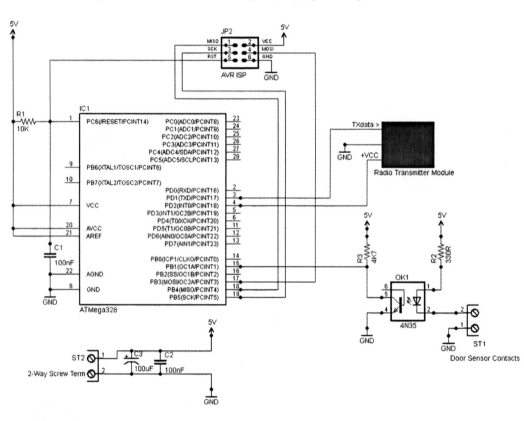

Figure 13-7. *Door sensor wireless node circuit diagram*

The door sensor is interfaced to the MCU via an opto-coupler, which you are using as the current loop interface (see Chapter 4, Figure 4-37 for more details). R3 is strictly redundant as you could use the internal pull-up resistor in the MCU, but you can use both if you so desire.

The power supply requirement for this project is +5Volts at a peak of 200ma; the average consumption on my prototype is only about 28ma.

Door Sensor Sender Software

The software for the door sensor project is pretty straightforward. Let's do the code walk:

Function Name and Args	Commentary
Global section	Declares all the constants, such as making the baud rate 2400, which pins to use, and the meanings of the single byte payload that the software will send.
setup() args: none	Initializes the serial channel and sets the required pin modes. Then uses sendPkt() sent out a packet with the "Started" value in it to let the receiver know it is alive.
loop() args: none	The loop function reads the door sensor state. If it's active (door open), it uses sendPkt() to send a notification. Then it waits for the door sensor to return to the inactive state; when it does, it uses sendPkt() to send out a notification of that event. It would be nice to have the function send out a packet every now and again if the door remains open for too long, since under the right circumstances it might be useful for some function higher up the pecking order (such as a security application) to know that the door remains open. Recognizing that the door has been open for longer than it should be could also be implemented higher up the chain, but that would make it possible for false alarms to be generated if the doorOpen event packet made it through, but the subsequent doorClosed packet did not.
	The function also contains various delays to allow for switch debounce times. However, these are probably not required since the packet send delays probably amount to a long enough time between detecting the first switch closure and contact bouncing ending.
	Finally, the main loop pauses for half a second before starting again.
sendPkt() args: byte payloadByte	The sendPkt() function sends a HomeHelp format packet out with the door event code as the payload. The code to be sent is supplied by the function's caller. Note that the sendPkt() function switches the radio transmitter on before it starts to send and off when it has completed. In both cases, it waits a short while to allow the transmitter to stabilize (at power up) and to complete sending (at power down).
	Since you're only, in this instance, sending a single byte value over the link, the only byte that is used to calculate the checksum is that value! Therefore, the payload byte and the checksum are, in this unique case, always the same!

Door Sensor Receiver Software

The door sensor receiver is essentially (in the terms of the mixed network topology that was previously discussed) pretending to be a hub. All it really does is receive the packet from the door sensor sender, make sure the HomeHelp jacket looks okay, and call out the value of the payload as a string to a software serial port, as in these examples:

```
Received "Started up" from node 51
Received "Door was closed, is now open" from node 51
Received "Door was open, is now closed" from node 51
```

The receiver has to use a software serial port since the hardware port is used for the radio channel.

Door Sensor Summary

The door sensor sender is a simple project, mainly intended to show how to use low-cost radio modules to bring down the cost of your Smart Home installation. Using this approach allows you to install sensors and nodes wherever you like without having the mess and hassle of installing and trying to conceal long wiring runs.

The project is an example of a node that only outputs sensor data, but what about the reverse case? What about a node that only receives data?

Remotely Commandable Light Stand

The door sensor is an example of Smart Home device that only sends data into the Smart Home network. In this, the final example Smart Home project, you will look at a receive-only example.

This project is essentially a demonstration of using Smart Home techniques to command this class of device; only a very small part of its full potential is exploited here. I'm sure that readers will see endless additional possibilities!

We're quite used to having remote control over things. We have remote control of our TVs, car alarm, DVD player, and so on. In this sample Smart Home project, you're going to give yourself remote control of a special light project: a light stand or shelf!

It turns out that if you shine light through the edge of a thick piece of transparent acrylic plastic, most of the light will, if the edges have been smoothed and polished properly, travel through the material and come out of the edges opposite. This gives a really gorgeous effect, lighting up a shelf or a stand for something special. If the light used is a multi-color LED strip, then, by varying the intensity of each LED (using PWM) you can create light in any color you want, including white when all LEDs are at equal intensity. So, in this project, you can use the short-distance radio link (as detailed in the previous project) to remotely command the Smart Home node that controls the LED strip.

Let's start with some basics: an RGB LED strip. Example products include

- www.sparkfun.com/products/10261 (United States and elsewhere)

- www.maplin.co.uk (UK; search for N48JX)

These are essentially flexible PCBs with tri-color, surface-mount LED devices fixed at regular intervals along their length. Each device actually contains three LEDS: red, green, and blue. The PCB provides a separate bus connection for the negative connections of all the reds, all the greens, and all the blue connections; there is also a +V lead that connects to all LED devices. The examples listed above use +12Volts, but I believe there may also be +5V products around if you look for them.

The strips have "cut points" marked along their length (see Figure 13-8), which present solder pads for attaching your connections (as shown in Figure 13-9).

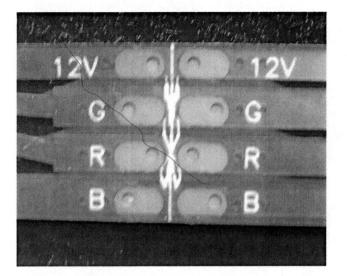

Figure 13-8. *LED strip showing cut point*

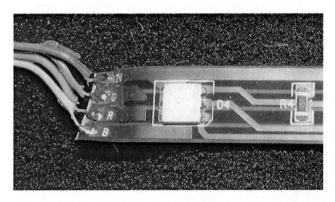

Figure 13-9. *LED strip cut and wires soldered on*

Your first decision is to decide how many lengths you want to use. I used three, which, since there are three LEDs per length, gave me nine tri-color LEDs in my setup. You could use more or less; the current consumption of the LEDs in these types of product is not huge (check your product details for specifics) so using more is fine. Having decided how many LED lengths you want to use, you should now be able to decide the sizing for your slab of plastic!

I bought my plastic shelf from an EBay vendor (there are many) who also offers a cutting and polishing service. It is made of 10mm (about 0.4") thick transparent plastic. I chose this thickness to match the width of the LED strip to make it easy to mount the LED strip along the edge of the stand. I want to use it as a stand for a miniature MP3 jukebox; you'll see how this goes together a little later. I had the vendor cut the shape I wanted and polish all the edges. This was not especially cheap (about $35) but the result was excellent, as you can see in Figure 13-10.

Figure 13-10. *Light stand*

Next, I got a plastic angle from the home improvement store (with an L-shape profile), cut it to length, and used some standard general purpose adhesive to fix it onto the plastic stand, such that it provides a channel to drop the LED strip into. The photo in Figure 13-11 shows this detail.

Figure 13-11. *LED strip channel*

Then, I soldered my four wires, making them about 3 feet long (2.7m) to the LED strip. Most of these LED strips come with a sticky back that allows you to stick the strip onto something. Thinking ahead, though, I imagined how hard it would be to remove this if the LED strip ever failed or if I wanted to swap it out for a different type. So, instead of using the sticky back, I put some 1″ black insulating tape along the underside of the LED channel to hold the strip in place in its channel. And that was it; the light stand ready to go, as shown in Figure 13-12.

Figure 13-12. *Light stand with LED strip in place and cable attached*

Light Stand Electronics

For speed and ease of debug, I built the light stand control electronics on the test bed rig, as built in Chapter 2. However, the project worked out so well that I think I shall be building a version on a solder board and boxing it up properly to make a permanent job of it!

The electronics are pretty simple. It's another two-chip project with just the ATmega328 AVR chip and a 2803 driver. However, it does requires the split rail power supply, capable of giving +12Volts for the LEDs and +5Volts for the AVR.

On the LED string product I was using, each colored LED (e.g., the red LED inside just one of the surface mounted devices) consumed a maximum of 7 milliamps. As mentioned previously, I used nine RGB devices along my LED strip. So the current requirements, in my case, were

- 9 x 7 milliamps for the red LEDs = 63 milliamps

- 9 x 7 milliamps for the green LEDs = 63 milliamps

- 9 x 7 milliamps for the blue LEDs = 63 milliamps

Thus the current requirement for the +12volt supply was, in my case, less than 200 milliamps, and the amount of current to sink for each set of colored LEDs was very easily within the capability of a 2803 chip. The full circuit diagram for the project is shown in Figure 13-13.

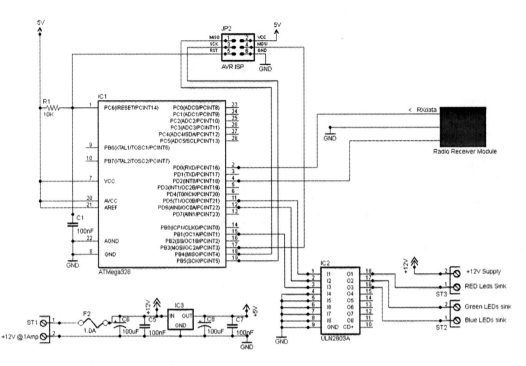

Figure 13-13. *Light stand project circuit diagram*

As you can see from the diagram, there's not an awful lot to it. The radio receiver module connects to the AVR's serial receive line. Pins 11, 12, and 15 (Arduino digital pins 5, 6, and 9, respectively) connect to the 2803A driver chip in which the first three drivers are used to sink current from the red, green, and blue LED elements, respectively. The remaining drivers in the chip are unused and their inputs grounded. The AVR's pin 4 (Arduino digital pin 2) is used to supply the minimal amount of power required by the receiver module. This allows the AVR to disable the receiver if necessary.

The RGB LED strip connects via a set of screw connectors; in a permanent version of this project you could use a small 4-way connector (see the Waterfall Lights project sensor connector for a suitable example).

Light Stand: RGB Values Sender

The software and hardware for the light stand is almost exactly the same as what you used for the door sensor. There are just three differences:

- In the hardware for this project, there is no door sensor interface.

- In the software,

  - Rather than having to wait for the door sensor to go active, the loop() function just sends a HomeHelp format packet containing a 4-byte payload consisting of a command code (which is always zero) and three randomly chosen RGB values. Such a packet is sent about every 10 seconds.

  - The checksum value is no longer a repeat of the payload; it is now properly calculated, based on the values sent in the payload.

The sender circuit diagram is shown in Figure 13-14.

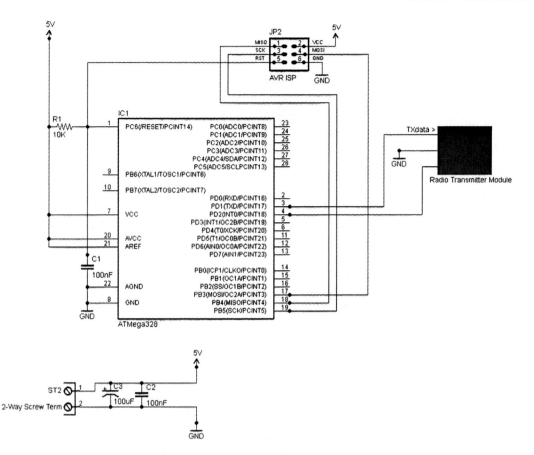

Figure 13-14. Radio sender for the light stand project

Aside from these differences, the hardware and software for the light stand sender are the same as those used for the door sensor sender. The payload sending order is shown in the following table:

Payload Byte #	Byte Usage
1	Command code. Currently, the only command that the receiver recognizes is zero, meaning that the remaining three bytes contain RGB values. Many more ideas are possible (see below).
2	Red value (8-bit byte): This is a PWM intensity value for the red LEDs.
3	Green value (8-bit byte): This is a PWM intensity value for the green LEDs.
4	Blue value (8-bit byte): This is a PWM intensity value for the blue LEDs.

Clearly, you could do a lot more with this. For example, you could implement anything up to 254 additional command codes for the receiver to action. Such commands might be

- Do fade up or down at some specified speed.
- Do random colors locally.
- Flash the LEDs at various speeds.

- Do a local sequence to gradually step through all possible colors over a period of n minutes.

- Do color chaser.

- Set LEDs to one of n preset colors (stored in the MCU's EEPROM).

- Do a light show.

All kinds of possibilities exist, and as always with MCUs, they are yours just for the working out!

Light Stand Software: Receiver

The software for the light stand is quite long, but in fact only consists of three functions! Let's do the code walk:

setup()	The usual setup function contents; it declares the pin numbers being used as PWM to sink the LED lines for red, green, and blue. Also declares the memory construct that holds the current values for RGB. Initializes the serial channel via which the software listens for commands coming in via the low cost short range radio. It initializes the PWM values so that the LEDs are all off. Then it declares the radio receiver pin and applies power to the receiver board.
loop()	Probably the simplest loop() function yet! It calls the getPacket() function. If the function returns a correctly received packet, the values it contained are written out to the LED PWM control pins to set the required red, green, and blue levels.
getPacket() args: timeoutMS	This function is the big one here. It receives and verifies a packet from the radio network in the format described in the "A Simple HomeHelp Protocol" section earlier in this chapter. It waits for a packet to turn up, but only for timeoutMS. If a packet is received (or begins to be received) during that window, it receives it, verifies the checksum, and if all is well, it returns success and passes back the payload in the global text buffer. If no packet is received before the timeout is reached or the packet is received in error, it returns a failure and the buffer contents will be invalid.

The code for this project is a good illustration of one of the principal things MCU chips have changed. The processor in this project will spend most of the time just whizzing around the loop() and getPacket() functions waiting for something to do! Even 20 years ago, this would be almost a crime because CPUs were a comparatively expensive resource that you had to make best possible productive use of. Back then, if you were making a project like this, you'd probably look for other things the unit could do so as not to waste any processing time.

However, MCUs (and indeed microprocessors) changed things by making processing power very, very cheap by comparison to what it had been; so now it's okay to only use a small part the available processing power productively[4]. You can have a separate processor for each little function within a system, almost the mirror image to the old-time home automation idea that you started off this chapter with (i.e., the monster computer in the basement)!

---

[4]Many might argue that it's bad computer science but at least now it's not compounded by being financial folly, too!

The Light Stand in Action

The photo sequence of Figure 13-15 through Figure 13-17 gives an idea of the finished result.

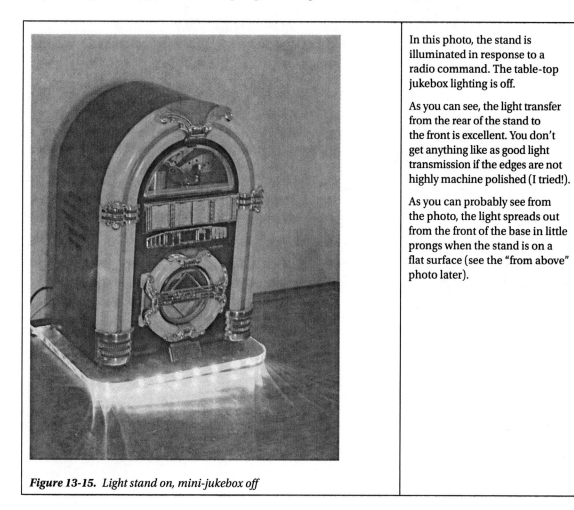

In this photo, the stand is illuminated in response to a radio command. The table-top jukebox lighting is off.

As you can see, the light transfer from the rear of the stand to the front is excellent. You don't get anything like as good light transmission if the edges are not highly machine polished (I tried!).

As you can probably see from the photo, the light spreads out from the front of the base in little prongs when the stand is on a flat surface (see the "from above" photo later).

Figure 13-15. Light stand on, mini-jukebox off

In this photo, the MP3 jukebox lights are also on, completing the effect.

If the light stand controller software was enhanced to include a set of fading and flashing effects, it would be possible to add additional items to the simple protocol to activate these via the radio command channel. This is left as a project for the reader!

The project makes an ideal addition to the décor in a themed room such as a TV or media room, a bedroom, or media library.

Figure 13-16. *Stand and jukebox on*

In the final view (from above), you can see the light prongs radiating out. In a darkened room, these reach out quite a long way.

Figure 13-17. Light effect seen from above

Summary

In this chapter, you have taken a necessarily brief look at the concept of the Smart Home and some of the history behind it. You've looked at some ideas that, for the technically-able Smart Home maker at least, can break the communications log-jam that I personally believe holds back the Smart Home from going truly mainstream.

You've looked at how to use a mixture of low-cost, easily available technologies to join up the islands of intelligence within a Smart Home infrastructure. Of course, all you have seen here is a set of individual ideas and small projects, not a detailed implementation. Nevertheless, I hope that this brief foray into this area has provided you with enough inspiration to get going on some of your own ideas!

Coming Up Next

The appendices and the end of the book!

■ ■ ■

Common Components

This brief primer appendix offers a look at the basic components that you will need to know something about if you plan to do many electronic or MCU projects. Here we look at a selection of simple components that crop up time and again and form the basic building blocks of all electronic circuitry.

Resistors

A resistor, as its name implies, is a component that, to varying degrees, resists the flow of electrical current.

When I was new to electronics, it always seemed a little odd to me that resistors were needed. After all, I reasoned, the purpose of most electronic devices is to originate or amplify electrical signals, why would you want a component to reduce them down again? I soon learned that not all electronic components operate at the same signal levels and so resistors are needed to match signal levels between devices of different capabilities and types. Resistors are also used to regulate the flow of current to levels that components can handle. For example, we use resistors to ensure that a device such as an LED (which we'll look at later) does not demand more current than it can handle, thus endangering itself, and whatever electronics it is connected to.

Resistance is measured in ohms, since it was Georg Ohm who, in 1827, first accurately described the relationships between voltage, resistance, and current. The "ohms" rating of a resistor determines how much resistance it will offer to the flow of electricity through it.

Ohm's law gives us multiple mathematical methods to calculate the characteristics of a circuit. The main method of interest in the context of this discussion states that the current (in amps) flowing through a circuit is found by dividing the voltage by the number of ohms of the resistance in that circuit (where I is the current, V is the voltage, and R is the resistance).

$I = V/R$

For example, suppose we have a simple circuit comprised of a +12V battery with a 10 ohm resistor connected across it.

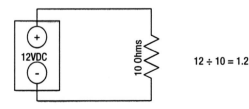

$$12 \div 10 = 1.2$$

By using this ohms equation, we can tell that 1.2 amps flows in such a circuit (don't try this at home. The resistor would get rather warm!). To take another example, if we have a +5V circuit, with a 270 ohms resistor across it we divide 5 by 270 to get 0.018 - which is 18 milliamps.[1]

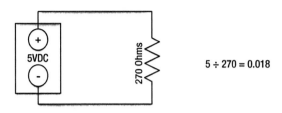

$$5 \div 270 = 0.018$$

Resistor Specifications

When specifying resistors there are three parameters of interest:

- The resistance offered: This is specified in
  - Ohms if it's less than 1,000 ohms.
  - Kilohms if it's less than 1 million Ohms.
  - Megohms if it's 1 million Ohms or more.
- The following examples show the notation and abbreviations generally used for resistor values in parts lists and circuit diagrams:
  - 270R = 270 ohms
  - 680R = 680 ohms
  - 1K2 = 1,200 ohms (1.2K Ohms)
  - 5K6 = 5,600 ohms (5.6K ohms)
  - 18K2 = 18,200 ohms (18.2K ohms)
  - 1M = 1,000,000 ohms (1.0M ohms)
  - 10M5 = 10,500,000 ohms (10.5M ohms)
- The second specifier for the resistor is the accuracy rating. This is referred to as the "Tolerance" and it tells you how close to the supposed value the resistance will be; it's specified in percentages. So, a 100 ohm resistor with a 10% tolerance may actually have a resistance anywhere between 90 and 110 ohms. I always try to use resistors with a tolerance of 1%, but in most cases 5% tolerance devices are actually okay. Higher-wattage resistors tend to come with higher tolerance values.
- The third parameter for specifying a resistor is the wattage. This relates to the amount of power the resistor can dissipate. For most logic electronics work, devices around the 0.5 watts specification are perfectly okay, and are nice and small. Where you are working with motors, relays, and other more power-hungry components, you may need to use higher

---

[1]Tech Tip   You can get Google to do technical conversions for you. For example, enter the query "What is 0.018 amps in milliamps" and you will get the correct answer: "0.018 amperes = 18 milliamperes".

wattages, up to 10 watts or even more. These are physically much larger devices. Project parts lists often specify the wattage required for each resistor.

- To calculate the wattage (Power) required for any particular situation you should use the formula P = (V times I): This means power = voltage times amperage. To reuse an earlier example: We know that our 270 ohms resistor, connected across a 5-volt power source, consumes 0.018 amps (18 milliamps): so, we can calculate how many watts the resistor will dissipate using P = (V times I), thus: 5 x 0.018 = 0.09 - which is 90 milliwatts. So, in this case, a 0.5W (500 milliwatts) resistor or even a 0.25 (250 milliwatts) resistor would easily cope.

A very few larger resistors have their values printed on them in words ("27K 10 Watts," for example). However, most use a system of color-coded rings to show their values. This is because of the difficulty of printing text on something so small. There seems little point in reproducing a chart of color codes in black and white here. However, there are many such charts online you can look at in full color. For example, see

- http://en.wikipedia.org/wiki/Resistor_colour_codes.

- www.digikey.com/web%20export/mkt/general/mkt/resistor-color-chart.jpg.

Resistor Types and Packagings

For the purposes of this book we will be using conventional resistors, but there are also even smaller resistors available as surface mount devices (SMDs). However, these can't be used on breadboards and are difficult (though not impossible) for the hobbyist to use–thus we avoid them in this book.

There are various kinds of other resistors. One prime example is the variable resistor, which is called the potentiometer (usually shortened to "pot"). On analog audio and visual gear the volume control or the brightness control was a potentiometer. A potentiometer is a variable resistor and it has a resistance value in ohms, just the same as a normal resistor. It has three terminals, and Figure A-1 shows the circuit symbol:

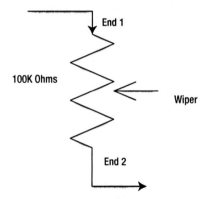

Figure A-1. *Potentiometer connections*

If you only connect the terminals marked "End 1" and "End 2" into your circuit, the pot behaves exactly like a normal resistor–that is, this 100KOhm pot could be used to replace a 100K resistor.

The third terminal, however ("the wiper"), slides up and down the resistance as the pot knob is turned: when it is exactly centered (as shown in the diagram) the resistance between the wiper and each end will be exactly half of the rated resistance. If the setup is as depicted in the diagram, you would see 50K ohms between the wiper and End 1, and the same between the wiper and End 2.

If the pot is physically turned as far as it can go in on direction, then the resistance between the wiper and one of the ends will be zero ohms and between the wiper and the other end will be 100K ohms (which end will depend on which way it is turned). Thus, the potentiometer gives you the possibility of setting any resistance value you like between zero and whatever the pot value is (in this case we can get anything between 0 and 100K ohms).

One usage for pots is, as previously mentioned, as a volume control in an analogue audio system. Figure A-2 shows how this works.

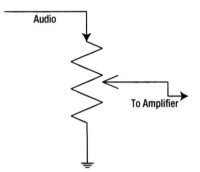

Figure A-2. *A potentiometer used as an audio volume control*

Coming in from the left we have an audio signal, perhaps from an MP3 or a CD player. To the right we exit to the input of an amplifier. The more of the audio signal that gets through to the amp, the louder the sound is going to be heard on the speakers that the amplifier (not shown) will be driving.

The fixed resistor part of the pot is connected at one end to the audio source and at the other end to ground. This means that there will be a gradually decreasing amount of signal available as the pot's wiper slides down toward the ground end of it until, when the wiper is at the bottom end of its travel, there will be no signal at all. But, as the wiper travels up toward the top, it gets less and less ground and more and more audio signal, until at the top end of its travel it's getting 100% audio signal and no ground: by that time the speakers are probably throbbing with sweet, sweet music!

Variable resistance is useful in a great many circuits for such purposes as dimming lights, setting voltage levels to an optimum, and, of course, for audio level control.

Capacitors

Resistors resist electricity flow, but capacitors store electricity. It's handy (but not entirely accurate) to think of a capacitor as being like a battery, albeit one that only holds a very small amount of charge. A capacitor has two "plates" separated by a substance called a dialectric. The two plates can be at different electrical charges. Many things have been used to make dialectric substances. For example, wads of tightly packed paper used to be widely used in large capacitors in the past! Polyester, Mylar, Tantalum, and various other man-made materials are mostly used now.

The capacitor stores static electricity, in somewhat the same way that your pesky nylon shirt or blouse does: the one that means you get a static shock when you touch something metal like a doorknob or a household appliance. The capacitor, like the garment, absorbs an electrical charge on its internal surfaces, and this charge builds up gradually. Like your shocking clothing, a capacitor can also discharge suddenly and violently if you give it a path to ground, so be careful when handling larger capacitors; they can shock and can hold a charge for days or even weeks. Fortunately, we'll mostly be handling smaller capacitors in the kinds of things we do in this book and these are not likely to bother you.

The capacitor's ability to soak up small amounts of power is used in many ways in electronics. One of the most common usages, in digital electronics, is to provide smoothing–as in the diagram in Figure A-3. In this application the capacitor's bottom plate is connected to 0V (ground). Its top plate is connected to the +5V power supply for whatever project this is part of: when power is present, the capacitor charges within a second or two up to almost the full +5 volts. If there is any momentary fluctuation in the power supply (e.g., due to a few milliseconds disruption in the mains supply) the rest of the circuit keeps going on power from the capacitor, which keeps the +5V rail going by giving up some of its charge. Unless we were to use physically huge capacitors (which we seldom do in MCU-land) this system only protects against very short power supply issues, but since minor mains power supply fluctuations are a fact of electronics life, the arrangement just described greatly improves the stability of the power supply and consequently the reliability of the project.

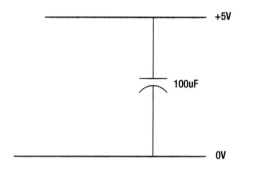

Figure A-3. *Smoothing capacitor*

In smaller electronics projects you will mostly find that two kinds of smoothing capacitors are used for the power rails, one with a small value and one with a larger value. This is calculated to smooth out minor power fluctuations at both low and high frequencies. In projects that do not use any serious electricity guzzlers (motors, relays, solenoids, large lamps, etc.) and where the leads from the PSU to the board are short, I have often got away without using smoothing capacitors: modern regulated power supplies are so good that circuit stability has not been an issue. However, where there are larger devices in the circuit it is *definitely* essential to have smoothing on the power rails of your circuit: without it you are likely to find that when your MCU commands a motor to turn or a solenoid to clunk, the whole circuit will restart because the power rails "blip" and cause a reset.

It's important to realize that although a capacitor shares superficial characteristics with a battery, it only holds enough charge to keep the circuit going for a very short time, usually just a few milliseconds. It's there to smooth the power supply's minor fluctuations, not to replace the power supply if it fails. A capacitor that could do the job of even a small AA battery would be something like 300 times the size and still not perform as well!

Measuring Capacitance

The German Ewald Georg von Kleist is said to have discovered capacitance in 1745. However, Pieter van Musschenbroek of Leiden (Leyden) in Holland was simultaneously working on his invention of the Leyden Jar (on which there is, of course, a Wikipedia page) during 1745-1746. Unfortunately for both of these gentlemen, it was later decided that capacitance should be measured in "farads" in honor of Michael Faraday (1791-1867) for his later pioneering work in the uses of electricity.

In fact, one farad is an awful lot of capacitance and a capacitor offering that much capacity is very large, far bigger than a battery. Fortunately, in electronics we rarely need capacitances anything like as large as one farad, so, we mostly use capacitors that are measured in millionths of farads, the name for which is "microfarads." This is formally written using a symbol called "mu" or "micro" and it looks like this "μ". However, the mu symbol is not found on general-purpose computer keyboards[2] and so very often the lower case "u" symbol is used instead. Thus, the following all mean the same thing:

- 100 uf (using the lower case "u")

- 100 μf (using mu)

- 100 microfarads

But, often we need even less capacitance than one microfarad. In such cases we have to go down to nanofarads and picofarads. These quantities break down as follows:

- One farad—the basic unit of capacitance.

- 1,000 millifarads = one farad (millifarads are never used in electronics).

- 1,000 microfarads = one millifarad (with 1,000,000 microfarads to the farad).

- 1,000 nanofarads = One microfarad (with 1,000,000,000 nanofarads to the farad).

- 1,000 picofarads = One nanofarad (with 1,000,000,000,000 picofarads to the farad).

Unfortunately, different capacitor manufacturers have chosen to label their products in different ways, and there are many competing labeling standards used. For example, you will find that some manufacturers sell a "0.1 μF" capacitor, while others sell a "100 nF" capacitor—both products would have the same value, just expressed in a different way; it's the same idea as $1.2 being the same amount of money as 1,200 cents. We'll look in more detail at capacitor labeling a bit later on in this section.

Time for a Capacitance

The other way that we often use capacitors is as timing components. It takes a finite amount of time for a capacitor to charge up to its full potential, and we can slow it down even more if we use a resistor and capacitor in series combination: we can then use this time delay in various ways. This kind of circuit is called an RC network, as in Figure A-4.

---

[2]In MS Word you can get a mu symbol by holding down the ALT key and typing 230 on the number pad then releasing ALT. On a Mac, hold down the Option key and press m to get a μ character. Option and Z will get the Ω character.

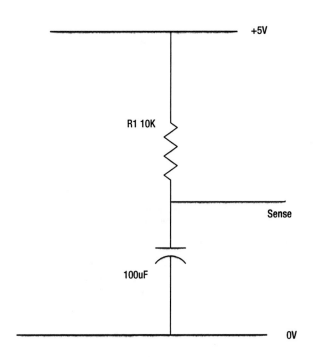

+5V

R1 10K

Sense

100uF

0V

Figure A-4. *An RC network*

In this circuit, a resistor stops the capacitor from charging up as quickly as it wants to, and the sense wire goes off into some electronics (not shown) for some purpose—see below. When the +5V supply first starts up, the capacitor's bottom plate of course remains at 0V because it is grounded to 0V. However, the capacitor's top plate gradually charges towards something close to +5Volts, through the resistor.

The "rise time" of the voltage at the "sense" point will be a lot slower than the power supply rise time. This means that any electronic devices connected to it will be "on power" *before* the capacitor is fully charged. If the "sense" lead shown in the diagram is connected to the active-low reset input of the MCU chip, you now have what is known as a "power on Reset" circuit. The MCU powers up, but for a brief time, until the capacitor charges up, its reset input will be held LOW, thus ensuring it is properly reset before operation begins and whilst the power supply stabilizes. This being electronics, all of this happens very quickly—within a few milliseconds at most. You may notice that we use an RC network on the AVR test bed that we built in Chapter 2. This is to ensure that the MCU there is properly reset at power on.

Without a "power on reset" circuit like the one just described, "intelligent" devices such as MCUs, microprocessors, complex graphics processor chips, and many others would not initialize properly and would start doing all kinds of random things because different parts of the chip begin in unsynchronized ways. Thus, holding the reset pin active for a short while after power-up gets all the pieces at the "Start line" at the same moment, ready to start working together as they should. So, although the RC network is a simple thing, it's an essential part of even the most complex circuits.

RC networks are used in all kinds of ways in electronics: for example, the venerable, but still very popular, 555 timer chip uses an RC network to provide its time delays. Many kinds of RC networks can be built: there is, of course, a Wikipedia page on this subject with lots of examples and information about calculating rise times and the shape of rise time curves. In the case of our preceding example, the exact point at which the "sense" line turns from logic LOW to logic HIGH depends equally as much on the characteristics of the device to which it is attached as to the RC rise time.

Another way that RC networks are used is in audio. The same basic idea of a resistor and capacitor in series is used, but if the resistor is made variable (like a tone control or volume control) the charge/discharge time of the capacitor can be varied, which means that the circuit will nullify audio signals at or above a certain frequency. One or many RC networks will be found at the heart of all predigital tone controls and graphic equalizers in audio gear. So as you can see, RC networks have a huge number of applications—our use for them in power-on-reset is just one of many.

All capacitors have a maximum working voltage. You can't put a capacitor rated for use at 16 volts DC into a circuit that operates at 30 volts; if you do, bad and probably smoky things will happen! On the other hand, you can put a 30 volt capacitor into a 16 volt circuit with no problem. Although it may be physically bigger than you would wish, it will still work properly. Since capacitor specs and limits usually drift as they age, it's best to allow some voltage leeway when selecting them. As a rule of thumb, allow something around 40% or so: in other words, if your circuit operates at 12 volts, select a 16V capacitor. If your circuit operates at 5 volts, use a capacitor rated for 7 volts or more.

WARNING! SAFETY NOTE: CAPACITOR FAILURE MODES

An overstressed capacitor will not fail gracefully! Generally, when a capacitor is used at too high a voltage or if you connect a polarized capacitor the wrong way around, it will burst like a popped balloon soon after power is applied to the circuit it's in. When it pops, it will likely shoot out very hot and acidic dialectric substance and bits of capacitor body in all directions. This can be very harmful and can cause injury to skin or eyes.

If you always use the right capacitor for the job, and always double-check that capacitors are connected the right way round, you should never experience this problem.

But, please, be very careful if you think there is even the slightest possibility of this happening; wear safety gloves and glasses and keep as far away from the circuit in question as you can when you power it on.

This also applies if you are trying to rescue old equipment (such as power supplies) that contains large, old capacitors. Such devices can—especially if they have been stored in a damp place—get seriously out of spec and pop when you apply power to them for the first time in many years. You should always, as a first step before power on, replace any large capacitors in an old device. I have seen an old capacitor from a pinball machine PSU explode and I can tell you from first-hand experience that it's not nice!

Capacitor Shapes and Sizes

So far, we have looked at capacitors with a positive and a negative plate. These are called electrolytic capacitors. However, capacitors in the smaller range of values (usually this means less than one microfarad) are not "polarized"—you can connect them either way around and they will work just fine.

Capacitors come in an embarrassingly large range of styles and with a confusing array of markings. We can only look at the major kinds in a short introduction like this. Wikipedia has a fuller survey of the less common types. The photo in Figure A-5 shows a handful of capacitors.

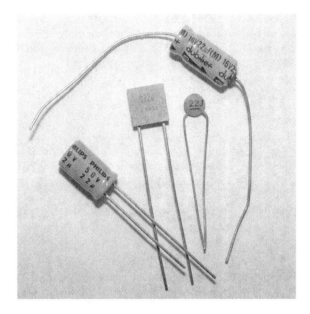

Figure A-5. *Common capacitor types*

As you can see, these vary quite a lot by size, pin spacing, and pin orientation. To begin with, when the pins come out of each end of the capacitor, we say it is an "axial" connected capacitor. When the pins come out of just one side, it's called a "radial" connection. As you can see, in the photo we have only one axial capacitor; the rest are radial. But these capacitors vary in many other ways too. Let's look at each of one separately and work through the different characteristics.

In the photo in Figure A-6 we see our axial capacitor again. From reading its markings we can tell that this is a 22 µf device with a working voltage of 16 volts. Having a value greater than one microfarad, this is a polarized capacitor and it has a positive and negative end. You may just be able to see that on the side of the body, it has a large arrow that is pointing to the negative end. Also, although you can't see it in this picture, you will find that most polarized capacitors have a black insulating disc around the positive end wire exit, and the negative end is usually connected to the metal body of the capacitor inside the plastic enclosing sleeve that we can mainly see here.

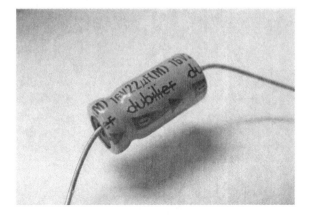

Figure A-6. *Axial, polarized capacitor*

In Figure A-7, we see the next capacitor. This is a radial device, with both pins coming out of the same side; again, you may just be able to read the markings on it. These show it to be another 22 µF device, but this one is rated to work up to 50 volts. This one has a black stripe down one side to indicate which side is the negative lead. On a radial capacitor it's easy to spot the positive lead anyway; it's always longer than the negative lead.

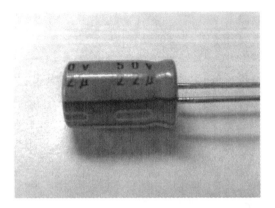

Figure A-7. *Radial, polarized capacitor*

Figure A-8 shows a nonpolarized capacitor. The markings on this one are different. The important bits on this label are "474" and "K" and "50."

Figure A-8. *Nonpolarized capacitor*

In this style of marking, the three-digit value code (474 in this case) indicates the capacitance value. The last of the three digits indicates how many trailing zeroes need to be added to the first two digits to get the picofarads value. So, this capacitor is a 470,000 (four, seven and four zeroes) picofarad capacitor. Since, as we saw above, there are 1,000,000 picofarads per microfarad, that means that this is a 0.47 µF capacitor (since 470,000 divided by one million = 0.47).

The "K" is a tolerance code: like a resistor, this specifies how close to the marked value the capacitor is likely to be. Tolerance codes may indicate percentages or absolute pF values. For example a tolerance code indicating 20% means that the capacitance may be 20% more *or* 20% less than the marked value. Tolerance codes are as follows:

Code Letter	Percentage or Amount of Tolerance
B	± 0.1 pF
C	± 0.25 pF
D	± 0.5 pF
F	± 1%
G	± 2%
J	± 5%
K	± 10%
M	± 20%
Z	+80%, –20%

Finally, the "50" on this capacitor indicates that it operates at a maximum 50 volts.

These markings vary a little from manufacturer to manufacturer. If you are in doubt about the exact value of a capacitor, try to contact its maker. If (as is often the case) you can't find out who made it, it's better *not* to use the device; buy a new one whose value you *are* sure of. It's cheaper to buy a new device than to cause damage to whatever you are building and to have to replace more expensive parts.

The final capacitor in our motley collection is a ceramic disc type (see photo in Figure A-9). We use lots of these; they are usually brownish red in color and use the same numbering scheme as previously described. This one is a 22 pF capacitor, with a 5% plus or minus tolerance. In common with many ceramic disc types this one is not marked as to the maximum voltage it can be subjected to. In the absence of any such indicator I would always assume a maximum of 16 volts for a disc ceramic. However, it is possible to get ceramic disc capacitors that will work up to 1,000 volts—though high-voltage devices are *always* marked as such.

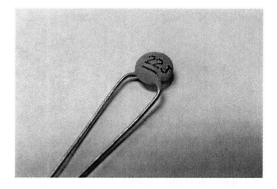

Figure A-9. *Ceramic disc capacitor*

Finally, on the subject of capacitors, remember it is possible to get variable capacitors that you can set to different values within a range for experimentation purposes. Variable capacitors tend not to be used much in digital electronics, being more useful for analogue circuits in radio and audio applications.

Light-Emitting Diodes

Light-emitting diodes show up in most kinds of electrical products now. LEDs are in many ways the glamorous superstars of the component world. You'll find LEDs on the front panel of your washing machine, on your TV, in your car, on your audio gear, in your home phone, as decorative lighting in your home or business, and just about everywhere you look. Let's take a quick look at what they are and how you use them for your own circuits.

A diode is a semiconductor device that amounts to a one-way street for electricity. It will allow power to flow in one direction but not in the other. Consider the two circuits in Figure A-10.

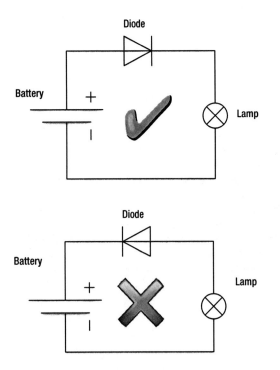

Figure A-10. *Diode circuits; one will work . . .*

The diode permits current to flow in the direction indicated by the arrowhead of its symbol. So in the top circuit the lamp will light because the diode is allowing current to flow from the battery's positive to negative terminal. In the second circuit, however, the diode blocks the flow and the lamp will not light.

The two terminals of the diode are called the anode (positive) and cathode (negative) terminals. The pointed end of the diode symbol's arrowhead points toward the cathode—the negative end, and away from the anode end. On an actual diode, a ring around the component body marks the cathode end.

So diodes are useful where you want to ensure that current can only flow in one direction; for example, they are often used as a safeguard to prevent battery connections to a circuit from being made the wrong way round.

An LED works in exactly the same way as a normal diode, except that when it is allowing current through, it lights up. Our next photo (Figure A-11) shows an LED. When you come to buy LEDs you will find they are available in many different colors and in quite a few different sizes. Sizes, which refer to the lens part of the component (shown at the left in this photo), are usually expressed in millimeters. Common sizes are 3 mm, 5mm, and 10 mm. As a very general rule (to which there are many exceptions) the larger the lens the brighter the light.

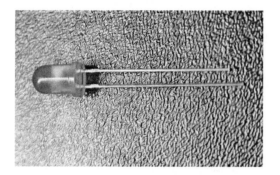

Figure A-11. *A single LED*

You will notice that one of the LED's connecting leads is longer than the other. The longer lead is always the anode (positive) one. Figure A-12 is the circuit diagram symbol for an LED.

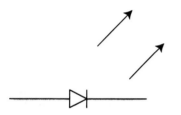

Figure A-12. *LED circuit symbol*

This shows the anode at left and the cathode terminal at right. The diagonal arrows differentiate an LED from a normal diode, which doesn't emit light at all.

You can't just connect an LED across a battery and have it light up because LEDs have limits as to how much current they can take. If you connect an LED across a battery with no current limiting resistor, it will burn out in a very short time. Most LEDs need between 10 and 20 milliamps to light up. However, some LEDs can take more current; you need to check the specs for the LEDs you buy, but if you can't find out the maximum then 20 ma is a safe bet. So, to safely connect an LED and have it light up, we would build a circuit like the one shown in Figure A-13.

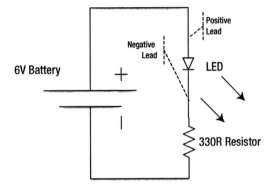

Figure A-13. *Basic LED lighting circuit*

In this circuit we connect the LED to conduct power from the battery and we use a 300 ohm resistor to limit the current through it to about 18 ma (Ohm's law again! The equation is 6 volts ÷ 330 = 0.018). If you want to satisfy yourself that the LED won't work the other way around, it's okay to try it. Just don't try it without the resistor unless you like burned fingers—or worse.

The basic LED is a start point; there are *many* other kinds of LEDs, including strings of LEDs in one color, strings and strips of LEDs that feature LEDs in multiple colors, and multicolor LED strings that have a red, green, and blue LED behind a single lens. This allows you to vary the amount of power going to each one, thereby enabling you to mix up your own custom colors. Then, there are high-intensity LEDs which provide a very bright light for use in applications like torches and spotlights. We use many of these kinds of LEDs in the projects section of this book.

LEDs generally give out useful amounts of light and—when you use them in multiples—give an equivalent amount of light to a conventional filament lamp, but LEDs give out a lot less heat. They are thus more power efficient, which is why—in a world of ever increasing energy prices–they do seem to be gradually displacing many other kinds of less efficient lights. LED light is very directional, which means that unless you use a diffuser, it has a different quality to what you get from older types of lamps. Some people find this directional light pleasing; some people don't.

■ ■ ■

A Digital Electronics Primer

Microcontroller units (MCUs) are great big blocks of digital electronic circuitry, but they still obey the basics of digital electronics. I'd like for us to take a short walk through these basics in this appendix. As we go through this, we'll also be using a "breadboard"—which I explain in Appendix C.

This appendix aims to provide a basic introduction to digital electronics. It doesn't cover the whole subject (which is vast), and it won't make you into an instant expert on the subject. However, it should cover enough of the groundwork for you to understand the material presented throughout this book.

The Highs and the Lows

Like all circuits, digital devices have inputs, via which signals enter the circuit, and outputs, via which signals leave the circuit. In an analog circuit, the signal coming into the circuit can vary right across the allowed voltage range, and the output from it can also be at any allowable level. In other words, the inputs and outputs from an analog circuit can vary continuously; they can be at any voltage allowed for that circuit.

For example, if the inputs to an analog circuit (such as an audio amplifier) are designed to accept inputs of between zero and 2 volts, then the input signal can be at any level (0.1 volts, 1.1 volts 1.8 volts, 1.99 volts, etc.) between those two voltages. Each tiny change of input voltage results in a slightly different output from the circuit. Digital circuitry is very different.

Digital circuits are designed to accept only two levels of input. These are "LOW" and "HIGH." Many, but by no means all, digital circuits use a power supply voltage of 5 volts DC. In such circuits anything above about 3 volts is interpreted by the circuit as HIGH, and anything below about 1.8 volts is interpreted as LOW. Similarly, the outputs from digital circuits are designed to put out a HIGH or a LOW level and never anything in between. This is why digital circuits are incredibly reliable; they don't have to be designed with the finesse that it takes to respond to very small changes of signal, the signals they process are always very definite, HIGHs or LOWs (also known as ones and zeroes).

Because it works in this somewhat brutal fashion, digital circuitry is comparatively simple, meaning you can get lots of it on a single chip. It also means that it fails in different ways. If you think back to predigital TV, if you were getting interference it would just distort or cloud the picture. On a bad digital TV signal, you lose chunks of the picture, or a few seconds of picture disappears, completely. Similarly, if you think about copying your files to a CD or a floppy disc, it either works or it doesn't. If you can remember trying to copy tapes, it would usually work, but the copy would be degraded to some degree. These are the kind of differences you get between digital and analog circuitry and processes.

I Count—In Denary?

Now, the behavior of digital electronics is, of course, ideal for use in circuits that use binary data. Binary numbers consist of only ones and zeroes and so can be stored, manipulated, and transmitted via digital circuits very easily. Let's briefly review how binary works.

It comes as a shock, perhaps, to realize that the number system you have used all through your life is only one of many possible systems. The denary system is the one we use to represent values in everyday life, and it deals in powers of ten. By adding zeroes to the right of a number (e.g., by turning 10 into 100), we multiply it by ten.

In the denary number system we use ten different symbols (0 to 9) and we arrange them in columns to show their "weight" in the represented value. The leftmost digit has the greatest weight, and the rightmost digit has the least. For example, the number 2390 in denary means (reading from right to left):

```
0 times 1 +
9 times 10 +
3 times 100 +
2 times 1000
```

So each column has a "weight" in our denary system, and each column's weight is ten times that of the column to the right of it.

When representing values in the binary system, we use only two symbols (0 and 1) and the "weight" of a column is twice the value of the column to the right of it. So, in binary the column weights, reading from right to left are 1, 2, 4, 8, 16, 32, 64, and so on. For example, the binary number 1110 means (reading from right to left again):

```
0 times 1 +
1 times 2 +
1 times 4 +
1 times 8
```

If you work that one out, it means that the binary number 1110 is actually representing the value 14.

With only 0 and 1 to represent, binary and digital electronic circuits are a match made in heaven! Of course, this was no accident: digital circuits were specifically designed to handle binary data and to do arithmetic operations in binary.

The problem is that we humans don't find it easy to deal in just ones and zeroes or HIGHs and LOWs. We like and demand subtlety and nuance; our preferred world is analog. Imagine a picture of a rich red sunset featuring a thousand subtle shades of color. Now, imagine that same scene rendered into just pure black and pure white: Yuk! So, to interface the binary world of computers with our real analog world, we need some special interfaces.

Hybrid circuits called A/D convertors and their mirror image, D/A convertors, allow the interchange of signals between digital and analog.

An A/D (analog to digital) convertor can continuously sample the voltage of an analog signal and represent it—moment to moment–to digital circuitry as a continuous stream of binary values that can be stored in the memory of a computer (e.g., your AVR microcontroller), so that it can be manipulated in some way.

Similarly, a D/A (digital to analog) convertor can be used to convert a succession of binary values (e.g., a file containing digitally sampled music) back into an analog signal suitable for feeding into an amplifier. Very fast A-to-D and D-to-A convertors are the whole basis for digital audio and video recording and playback. Without them there would be no digital TV or MP3 players. Your iPod or iRiver MP3 player has at least two such convertors in it—probably more.

However complex the information you are providing, whatever the source of the information (a camera, a DVD, a microphone, a scanner, a GPS system . . .) to the basic levels of your computer, it's all just ones and zeroes; there may be trillions of them, but they're all just binary data.

In this book you'll see how binary data are acquired (via A/D circuits which are built in to the AVR chip we're using) and you'll see how binary data are sent back out into the outside world as analog data (again, using built-in AVR chip features).

Deciding, Logically

I've done some explaining about specific digital electronics within the main part of this book. However, it's probably a good idea to look at one very specific digital electronic concept here, so that you hit the ground running when you encounter it later. That concept is "gates" (no, nothing to do with Bill at Microsoft, before you ask).

A great deal of digital electronics is composed of a structure called gates. A gate—as its name implies—is really just a device for letting through (open) or blocking (closed) a digital signal, based on certain conditions.

In the real world we make very simple decisions based on conditions. For example, if it's sunny AND my car is dirty, I will go out and wash my car. A digital circuit called an "AND gate" could be used to make this decision for us—as illustrated in the diagram.

Suppose we build a "sunshine detector," which gives a digital HIGH output when the sun is shining brightly. Also, we build a "car dirty" reflectivity sensor which also gives a digital HIGH when it detects that the car needs washing.

The characteristic of the AND gate is that its output will only go HIGH when *all* its inputs are HIGH. Thus, when both our sensors are sending High, then the output of the AND gate also goes HIGH, and the "wash car" light comes on.

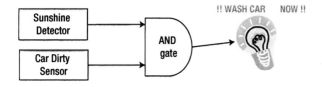

The AND gate in this simple example has only two inputs, but in real circuits, a gate can have as many inputs as required. However many inputs are provided on an AND gate, the same rule applies: the output only goes HIGH when *all* inputs (input 1 AND input 2 AND input 3 AND input 4 . . . you get the idea) are HIGH.

Let's look at another example use for an AND gate. Suppose we have a digital music stream (just a huge long stream of ones and zeroes, remember) and we want to make sure that it only plays out loud at night and remains silent during daylight hours. We connect the digital music stream to one input of our AND gate. We make a light detector which outputs a LOW signal during daylight hours and a HIGH signal when night falls. We connect this detector to the other input of our AND gate.

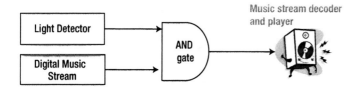

Now, during daylight the digital music stream will not make it through the AND gate to the music decoder and player; the AND gate blocks it because one of its inputs is always LOW. When darkness comes, and the light sensor output goes HIGH, the AND gate will start letting through the music stream: with the light sensor input always HIGH, the output of the AND gate will exactly follow the ones and zeroes of the music stream input.

Of course, this idea could be extended in various ways. For example, we could use a three input AND gate, with the extra input used for a "person detector" (to ensure the music only plays out loud when there is someone in the room to hear it).

There are also NAND gates (Negative AND gates) whose outputs go low only when *all* the inputs are high.

As these AND gate examples illustrate, gates are used to make simple rudimentary decisions, and gate chips are used in exactly these kinds of ways in consumer goods and in industrial devices and systems. However, the real power of gates is that they can make such decisions many tens of millions times per second. When thousands of gates are interconnected in complex ways, the result can be the processor in your desktop machine, or the processor core of your AVR microcontroller chip.

General Gates

There are five basic kinds of logic gates, and they each make a decision based on different rules. Table B-1 summarizes these (H = HIGH and L = LOW).

Table B-1. *Main Types of Logic Gates?*

GATE TYPE	PROPERTIES	EXAMPLE USE
AND	Output = H if ALL inputs are H	See previous examples.
NAND	Output = L if ALL inputs are H	Switch intruder alarm off if "activate" key switch is sending HIGH (meaning disarmed) AND code keypad is sending HIGH (indicating correct PIN code entered).
OR	Output = H if ANY of inputs are H	Switch on light if it's dark OR it's after 8 PM.
NOR	Output = L if *any* input is HIGH	Switch off light if daylight detector sending H *or* current time is before 8 PM.
XOR	Output = L if all inputs are at same logic level	Switch on fuel supply pump if air pressure detector and fuel pressure detector are both indicating same status.

The palette of logic functions summarized previously means that it's possible to construct interconnected combinations of gates to meet any conceivable requirement for electronic decision making. You can make very complex circuits from strings of gates connected in ways that take signals from various sources (other logic circuits, digital sensor, etc.) within a piece of equipment. Having said this, it's now a lot more common for electronic decision making to be done in software running on MCUs. The days when almost all hardware used lots of gates in "combinational logic" have passed; however, the technique is still widely used for certain kinds of functions. You will still find it useful to have a basic understanding of how gates can be used.

In order to be able to make use of the decision-making power provided by gates (or MCUs), sensory inputs (people detectors, light detectors, etc.) must all be designed to provide a binary–HIGH or LOW–signal suitable for feeding into digital circuits. The interfacing of the real world to digital processors (in our case, the AVR) is what a substantial part of this book is all about.

The function of logic gates is usually expressed in truth tables. These show the output of each type of gate for any possible set of input conditions. The following truth tables instance a two-input gate, with the inputs called A and B. Alongside each truth table you can see the electrical circuit symbol used for the gate, as used in the circuit diagrams in this book.

AND Gate

The output goes HIGH only if all inputs are also HIGH. The logical symbol for the AND gate is shown adjacent to the table.

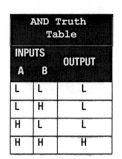

AND Truth Table		
INPUTS		OUTPUT
A	B	
L	L	L
L	H	L
H	L	L
H	H	H

Figure B-1. *AND truth table*

NAND Gate

For the NAND gate, the output goes LOW only if both inputs are HIGH. The circuit symbol for a NAND gate is shown adjacent to the table.

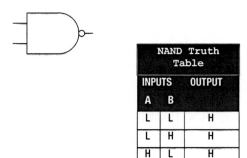

NAND Truth Table		
INPUTS		OUTPUT
A	B	
L	L	H
L	H	H
H	L	H
H	H	L

Figure B-2. *NAND truth table*

OR Gate

For the OR gate the output goes HIGH if either or both of the inputs are HIGH. The circuit symbol for the OR gate is shown adjacent to the table.

OR Truth Table		
INPUTS		OUTPUT
A	B	
L	L	L
L	H	H
H	L	H
H	H	H

Figure B-3. *OR truth table*

NOR Gate

For the NOR gate, the output goes HIGH only if both inputs are LOW. The circuit symbol for a NOR gate is shown adjacent to the table.

NOR Truth Table		
INPUTS		OUTPUT
A	B	
L	L	H
L	H	L
H	L	L
H	H	L

Figure B-4. *NOR truth table*

XOR Gate

For the XOR gate, the output goes HIGH if the inputs differ and LOW when inputs are the same. The circuit symbol for an XOR gate is shown adjacent to the table.

XOR Truth Table		
INPUTS		OUTPUT
A	B	
L	L	L
L	H	H
H	L	H
H	H	L

Figure B-5. *XOR truth table*

Understanding the Specifications of Gates

Following are some general points about gates:

- Although, so far, we have used the terms "HIGH" and "LOW" to indicate voltage levels, they are equally often indicated by "1" and "0" (indicating HIGH and LOW, respectively). Both methods indicate the same thing in a different way. You may also occasionally hear logical levels referred to as true and false.

- Although the truth tables in the preceding sections show only two inputs, bear in mind that real gate devices can have many inputs. No matter how many inputs a gate has, the same rules apply.

To give just one multi-input gate example, the following symbol indicates a 4 input AND gate, and following that is its truth table (in this table we use "0" and "1" instead of LOW and HIGH).

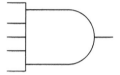

Four-Input AND Gate Truth Table				
INPUTS				OUTPUT
A	B	C	D	
0	0	0	0	0
0	0	0	1	0
0	0	1	0	0
0	0	1	1	0
0	1	0	0	0
0	1	0	1	0
0	1	1	0	0
0	1	1	1	0
1	0	0	0	0
1	0	0	1	0
1	0	1	0	0
1	0	1	1	0
1	1	0	0	0
1	1	0	1	0
1	1	1	0	0
1	1	1	1	1

Figure B-6. *Four-input AND gate truth table*

This multi-input gate obeys the same AND gate rule as the smaller two input gates: its output only goes HIGH ("1") when *all* its inputs are HIGH.

To show how gates are used in combination, let's extend one of our AND gate examples—this time we will use the real circuit symbols.

As you may recall our original setup looked as follows:

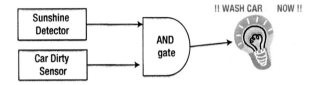

However, at certain times of the year where I live we can get sunshine at 6 AM in the morning, and I probably would not thank this circuit for bleeping or flashing a car wash reminder to me at such an hour. So, let's extend this example by adding a new gating factor, a special time detector circuit that only outputs LOW between the hours of 9 AM and 6 PM—and outputs HIGH through the evening and nighttime. In this version we add a NOR gate and we replace our original AND gate with a NAND gate.

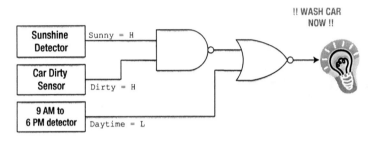

In this diagram, I've added labels to the interconnections to help you visualize the logic levels on each one.

When the sunshine and the car dirty sensors are both sending HIGH into the inputs of the NAND gate, the gate's output, which is connected to one input of the NOR gate, will go LOW (see Figure B-2).

When the daytime detector is detecting that we are in the daytime, it sends LOW to the other input of the NOR gate. As we saw previously in Figure B-4, its output goes HIGH, only when all its inputs are LOW. So, the effect of this circuit is that when my car is dirty, and the weather is sunny, and it's daytime, the "Wash Car Now" light will come on.

Of course, if we could arrange for the daytime sensor to output HIGH during the daytime and LOW at nights, then we could implement this whole scheme with just a single three-input AND gate. However, doing it as just illustrated gives you a small taste of how gates can be used in endless combinations to implement decisions based on multiple inputs.

An additional point to note is that in other circuit configurations, the sensors or detectors might be used in a different way. For example, another kind of gating circuit might react when the "Car Dirty Sensor" is outputting LOW and the daytime detector output is HIGH. Such a circuit might, for example, initiate the printout of a "Certificate of car cleanliness" as a reward for having a clean car in the nighttime!

Real Live Gates

To end this brief primer on digital electronics, let's step outside the world of truth tables, theoretical diagrams, and fancy schemes for getting my car washed. Let's look at how we wire up a real gate circuit. You don't have to build this example if you don't want to; it's really just so that if (like me) you learn better by doing, you can cement your understanding of how we do gates in the real world.

The 7400 range of integrated circuits (commonly called TTL chips, for Transistor-Transistor-Logic) were originally designed in the 1960s. They provided basic logic functions (gates, counters, registers) that proved so useful that they are still being sold and designed into commercial equipment today.

Today's versions of the 7400 series use much less power than the originals, but they still offer the same functions and connections as their predecessors. We will use just one of these chips, the 74LS08, in this visual example of using gates. We could also have used the 74HC08, the 74 AC08, the 74 F08, or one of the other many variants of the 7408.

The 74LS08 (a low power equivalent of the original 7408 chip) is a 14-pin device that contains four two-input AND gates. The diagram in Figure B-7 shows the pin connections of the DIP (Dual Inline Package) packaging of this device.[1]

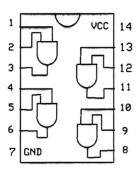

Figure B-7. *Pinout for a 74LS08 Quad AND gate chip*

The indent at the top of the package indicates the top end of it. On some versions of the product, a small indent is placed over a pin, to indicate which is pin 1. On integrated circuits using DIP packages you will always find that the pins number as shown here, down one side starting from pin 1, then up the other to the highest numbered pin.

As you can see from Figure B-7, the four gates inside the 74LS08 are all independent of one another, though of course, by linking pins together, you can use them in combination if you need to.

Pins 14 and 7 bring the power supply—the +5 V (called VCC in TTL-Land) and ground connections–onto the chip.

I built a very simple circuit using a 74LS08 on a breadboard (see Figure B-8) using the following steps:

---

[1]Be aware that the 74LS08 (in common with most other chips) is also available in other packages too. However, hobbyists usually prefer to use DIP packaged devices because the far smaller surface mount (SMT) packages are normally too small for the hobbyist to use easily, being mainly intended for use in precision automated electronic manufacturing systems.

Figure B-8. *A TTL chip in the breadboard*

1. First, I connected the +5 V rail of the breadboard to pin 14 of the device, and then connected ground to pin 7:

2. Then, I connected an LED and a series resistor (which, as we previously saw in Appendix A) is needed to prevent the LED from drawing too much current from the chip) to pin 3, the output of the first gate in the package. The LED was just a standard 8 mm red LED, such as the kind you can buy from your electronics supplier (see picture of Figure B-9). The resistor was a 330 ohm 0.25 watt resistor, which again should be easy to get from any electronics outlet.

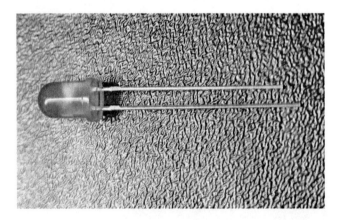

Figure B-9. *A single LED – the longer of the two wires is the positive lead*

3. One side of the resistor connects to pin 3, which is the output of the first gate of the chip. The other side of the resistor connects to the longer pin of the LED (which is the positive, or anode). The shorter LED pin (the negative, or cathode) connects to the breadboard's ground plane. See Figure B-10 for these connections.

4. Now, the LED will light up if the output from the AND gate is HIGH and go out if it is LOW.

At this stage, the inputs to the gate were not connected to anything, yet, when I powered up the circuit, the LED lit up (see Figure B-10)!

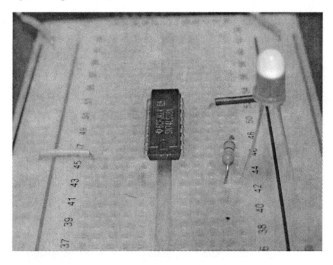

Figure B-10. *LED lit up by AND gate output – even though no inputs are connected!*

Why did that happen, when there were no connections to the inputs of the AND gate? Well, it is a characteristic of TTL logic circuits that an unused input will always count as HIGH, so since there are no connections to the gate inputs yet, they both count as HIGH and the output therefore also goes HIGH.

It's widely regarded as bad practice to leave logic chip inputs disconnected in finished circuits. Unconnected inputs can be subject to interference and noise when left floating, and this often causes problems with circuits. Normally, unused inputs should "tied HIGH," meaning they should all be connected to VCC through a single 1K ohm resistor.

While experimenting, you usually don't need to worry too much about this issue, but when you finalize a project you need to do your "tie-HIGHs" to ensure reliability.

To complete this practical visualization of how a gate works, let's set the inputs to various combinations and see what makes the gate output get HIGH, and thus turn the LED on.

Let's start with both inputs of the gate—pins 1 and 2–tied to LOW (ground). The LED is off (see Figure B-11).

Figure B-11. *Grounded inputs to AND gate turn LED off*

Then, with just one input tied to HIGH (VCC) and the other still grounded, the LED is still off (Figure B-12).

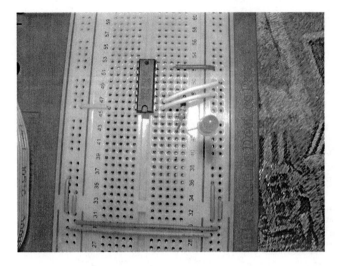

Figure B-12. *One AND gate input LOW, the other HIGH. Output LED is off*

Finally, we tie both inputs to HIGH (VCC). Now, the LED is on (Figure B-13)! The output from the gate is HIGH because input pin 1 is HIGH *and* input pin 2 is HIGH.

Figure B-13. *With both AND gate inputs tied HIGH, the LED finally comes on!*

If you check against the truth table in Figure B-13 you can see that these combinations match the expected behavior of the AND gate.

Playing around with gates on a breadboard is a great way to learn visually how they work and it can be quite fun too. So, do try out your own ideas for wiring up the four different gates in the chip in different ways until you get a good feel for how it works.

APPENDIX C

■ ■ ■

Breadboards

There are lots of reasons to build electronic and computer circuits; but only some of them involve building a circuit to keep forever. In many cases (such as building as a learning exercise, or just seeing if an idea works without any real application for it) you may just want to get it working and then tear it down and reuse the pieces for something new.

If you build your circuits by soldering all the components together, you expose the components concerned to quite a lot of heat and you will have to cut the component leads to size. Electronic components are not meant to stand up to repeated soldering; if you solder them more than a couple of times, it's quite likely that they will be heat damaged and could stop working properly. The second problem with the soldering approach is that if (or more likely, when) you want to make even minor changes to the circuit you may find that it's a difficult thing to do.

So, for circuits which are yet to be finalized it's usually better to use a product called a breadboard. A breadboard is a plastic board containing lots and lots of tiny sockets, each of which is just big enough to take a piece of solid 23–26 AWG wire, or the leg of a component such as integrated circuit, like your AVR chip, or the leads of a capacitor or a resistor or an LED.

Figure C-1 shows a close-up of the end of a breadboard. In this picture, we can see that there are ten *rows* of holes (running from bottom right to top left of the picture) and these are labeled A through J. In case you are unclear about the distinction, the preceding line drawing illustrates the general idea of columns and rows.

Figure C-1. Breadboard columns and rows

The columns that are visible in Figure C-1 are numbered from 1 to 7 (though, as you shall see, this is only a small part of this breadboard). The important thing to know about the breadboard is that the holes in each numbered column (but *not* the holes in each lettered row) are connected together on the underside of the board.

Here's the same photo again (see Figure C-2), but this time I have overlaid lines on the columns to show which holes are connected together.

Figure C-2. *Interconnected column holes*

As you can see there are five holes in each connected column strip. The gulley separating the two sides of the board is coincidentally the same width as a small integrated circuit (well, okay, it's not actually a coincidence) as we shall see shortly.

The photo in Figure C-3 shows this complete breadboard.

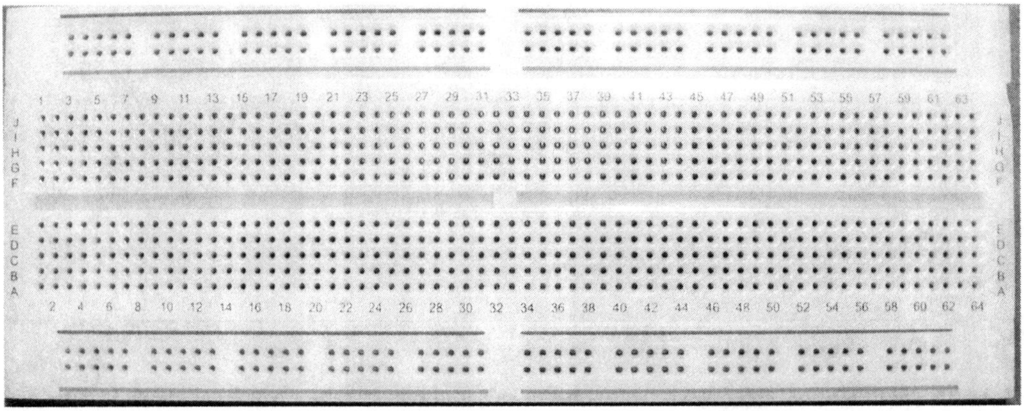

Figure C-3. *Complete 64 × 10 breadboard*

As you can probably see, this breadboard actually has 64 columns and 10 rows. Thus it would be sold as a 10 × 64 breadboard–or sometimes a 640-hole breadboard. This is a pretty standard layout for a breadboard, but there are also many variations that give you more or less space. You may notice some extra rows of holes running from left to right in the photo. These are the power rails. Figure C-4 shows the same photo again, but this time I have overlaid arrowed lines, indicating which sets of power rail holes are connected to one another.

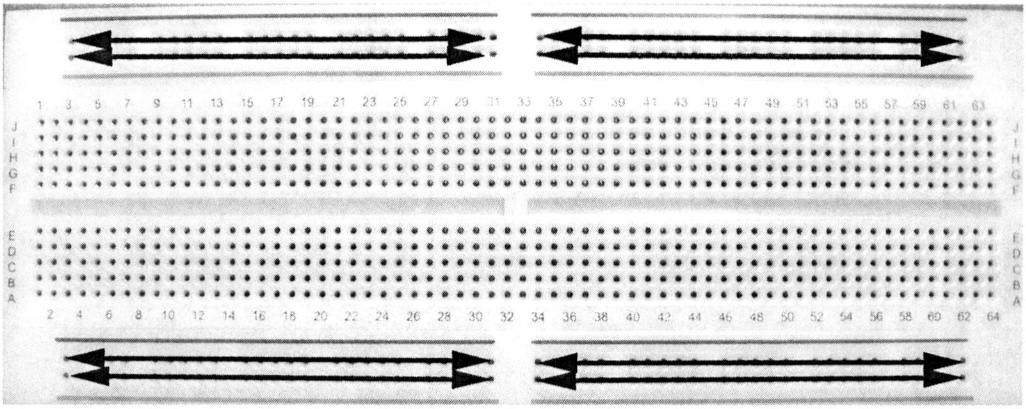

Figure C-4. *Breadboard power rails highlighted*

The idea is that you feed power on from your power supply source (see Chapter 2) at one end of the breadboard, and power is then available to tap into at any point along the breadboard top and bottom. You usually need to put a joining jumper in between columns 31 and 34 on each of the four power rails in order to make power available all the way along the board. You also often need to link the two sides (top and bottom power rails). We won't go into details on that, because in Chapter 2 you'll see details and photos of this being done.

Okay, so now that you know which breadboard holes are connected to which, let's see how we use this layout.

The next photo (in Figure C-5) shows an integrated circuit (chip) plugged into the breadboard at column 46. Notice how the chip bridges the middle gully so that the pins make connection with both sides of the breadboard.

Figure C-5. *74LS08 chip at breadboard column 46*

Let's just add some jumpers to this chip to give it power (see Figure C-6).

Figure C-6. *Chip with power jumpers in place*

This chip needs a ground connection to pin 7 and a +5V connection to pin 14. If you're unsure how the pins number, refer to Appendix B where I describe the pinout for this chip. As you can see in Figure C-6, the chip is now connected (at top right) to the ground rail and at the top left to the +5 volts rail. This is done using some jumper wires. You can get jumper wire sets from your favorite electronics supplies outlet–Chapter 2 mentions some example products. You can also make your own jumpers if you want to; you should use 23AWG solid (not stranded) insulated wire.

Now, refer to the next photo in Figure C-7. In this picture, we have the power jumpers installed, but you can also see that there are now some additional jumpers installed. A jumper has been used to link together two of the pins (pins 3 and 4) and another jumper is used to link together two pins, one on either side of the chip (pins 1 and 11, since you ask!) and yet another jumper ties pin 5 to the positive power rail (this is a tie-high, since we are permanently connecting the pin to a logic HIGH level).

Figure C-7. *Chip with power and signal jumpers installed*

At this stage you don't need to worry about what these pins do, or why they are being linked together: the only thing to you need to understand is how putting these jumper wires onto the breadboard makes connections between pins of the chip, and from the pins of the chip to the power rails.

Now, suppose we want to bring more components into the picture? Suppose we wanted to add another chip and connect a resistor between a pin on our existing chip and the new one: How would we do that? Figure C-8 shows one way to do it. The newly added chip has its power connections, as the first one did. It has a link jumper between its pin 4 and pin 5. The resistor (which luckily has quite long leads at each end) easily reaches from the original chip's pin 2 to the new chip's pin 6.

Figure C-8. *Two chips and a resistor*

But, what would we do if the chips were further apart, or if the resistor's leads were shorter? In such a case we could use the arrangement shown in Figure C-9. In this iteration, we have made use of a spare column of sockets (column 44) to make an intermediate connection to a jumper, and the other end of the jumper reaches across to the new chip's pin 6.

Figure C-9. *Connecting the resistor via unused breadboard column 44*

Using the holes of unused columns to make interconnections is a very common requirement when using breadboards, so you'll need to understand this technique.

I hope that, even from this quick look at breadboards, you can see how easy they are to use and can appreciate how much easier they can make prototyping or perfecting your electronics creations. Of course, in these simple examples we have only made a few connections and (for the sake of clarity) used very neat jumpers. When you get into making real circuits you will often (though not always) need to use more jumpers and you'll get used to the jumpers being a little messier. However, messy or not, using a breadboard is far simpler and faster than using solder board methods of prototyping, though of course when you have a working circuit you will often want to make a permanent version on a solder board.

We've looked at the most basic style of breadboard, but there are a great many others. For example, when your circuit ideas got more extensive (which, trust me, they will!) you may find that you can't accommodate everything you need on one breadboard. In that case, you can get modular breadboards which securely clip together to expand to whatever size you want. Your preferred electronics supplier should be able to provide you with something suitable, but take a look at the following examples:

- `www.sparkfun.com/products/137` (United States)
- `www.maplin.co.uk/ad-101-breadboard-5199` (UK)

and you can also get much larger single breadboards if you look around on the Internet.

There *are* alternatives to prototyping on breadboards: If you're interested in those, check out the Wikipedia pages on "wire wrapping" and "electronic circuit simulation." The former uses wire wrapping posts to do roughly the same job that we just saw on a breadboard. Simulations let you virtually model your circuits in a desktop computer using purely software–which for more complex circuits is a more viable method of initially assessing what works and what doesn't–though there is a learning curve involved. There are entry-level simulation packages you can get for free to try out: QUCS is one such you can get from the SourceForge site at `http://sourceforge.net/projects/qucs/`.

■ ■ ■

Serial Communications

This appendix provides an overview of the serial data transmission techniques you may need to understand when creating an in-depth design and implementing your AVR projects. This is by no means an exhaustive survey of the subject, which is huge, but it should give you the information that you need in understanding the serial data communication methods used in this book's projects.

Data communication over long distances has always had to be a serial process, but at one time it looked like serial transmission would be consigned to history for very short distance transfer purposes. However, as machines got faster and faster and the amount of data to be moved around got ever bigger, some physical limits came into play which could not be overcome in any practical way, other than by reembracing (and to some extent, reinventing) serial data transfer. But, before we unpack those statements, let's look at some basics.

Data Transfer Basics

In this section we begin by reviewing the binary number system and the basics of how information is stored inside a computer. About now, the question may pop into your mind as to why it's necessary to review all this material in a section that's supposed to be about serial data transmission.

I believe that, as you can infer from the name, serial transmission involves taking bytes of data apart, serially sending them down some kind of communications medium, and then correctly putting them back together at the receiving end of the transaction. That being the case, knowing a little about bits and bytes is a great help in gaining a clear understanding of this subject and, of course, of digital electronics in general. Feel free to skip the next section if you're already okay with binary, bytes, and bits.

Binary Me!

It might come as a shock to realize that the number system you have spent your whole life (up to now) using is only one of many possible number systems! In our "real world" we use the "denary" number system. Like denary, binary is simply a system of counting.

Denary uses the symbols "0" to "9" (ten symbols, thus the name) to form representations of numbers. The position of each symbol in any given number indicates whether the symbol represents thousands, hundreds, tens, or units. For example, in denary, the sequence of symbols "900" means no units, no tens and nine hundreds. So, in denary, each column is worth ten times as much as the one to the right of it, and the rightmost column is worth exactly what it says (i.e., "008" represents eight).

Binary works in the same way, except that it only uses the symbols "1" and "0," and each column represents a power of two. The rightmost column is worth one, and each successive column going left is worth two times as much. So, in a binary number, reading from right to left, columns are worth 1, 2, 4, 8, 16, 32, and so on, rather than a power of ten. So, for example, in binary–which, remember, only uses the symbols "0" and "1"–the symbol sequence "110" reading from right to left means no 1 s, one 2, and one 4–the denary equivalent of which is six (2 + 4).

Digital electronic circuits were developed specifically to handle binary. In a digital circuit a signal is said to be in only one of the two following states:

- One: (also called "logic HIGH," or True).

- Zero: (also called "logic LOW," or False).

And in reality, these are the only signals that the digital circuits inside your digital devices really understand how to process and store: they *appear* to understand numbers and letters and colors and images and music and sound and video only because mountains of software (itself composed of binary codes) does endlessly clever interpretations of the binary data that the electronics are really dealing in. However, these digital circuits process binary data really, really fast!

The Byter Bit

Computers store binary numbers in bits and bytes. A byte is made up of eight bits of data. Each "bit" (short for "Binary digIT") can be set to a "1" or a "0." Within an eight-bit byte, each bit has a worth (also called a "weight") which, if it is set to "1," contributes to the overall value of the byte.

The rightmost bit in an eight-bit byte has a weight (a worth) of 1. The weight of each of the other bits is twice that of its right-hand neighbor. The following table illustrates this.

Byte contents	Value of highlighted bit
00000001	1
00000010	2
00000100	4
00001000	8
00010000	16
00100000	32
01000000	64
10000000	128

In other words, if there is a "1" at the indicated position in the byte, then the weight of that bit is contributed to the value that the byte represents–as in the following examples:

Byte contents	Value of the byte	Because . . .
00000011	3	$1+2=3$
10000010	130	$2+128=130$
00001111	15	$1+2+4+8=15$
00000000	0	None of the bits contain a 1
01000001	65	$1+64=65$
11111111	255	$1+2+4+8+16+32+64+128=255$

To be able to identify bits within a byte, the bits are given numbers, starting from the right, as in the following example which represents the value 64, because bit 6 is "set" but all the others are "clear":

Binary Value	0	1	0	0	0	0	0	0
Bit Numbers	Bit 7	Bit 6	Bit 5	Bit 4	Bit 3	Bit 2	Bit 1	Bit 0

Because it has the lowest weight, the rightmost bit (bit 0) in the byte is referred to as the "least significant" bit, and the leftmost bit (bit 7) as the "most significant" bit.

Using the bit number and a calculator capable of doing exponentiation (raising one number to the power of another) you can easily calculate the value of any bit in a binary number. For example, if you set Windows Calculator to its scientific view, you'll see a button marked x^y (see calculator picture): if you wanted to calculate the value of bit 6 (2 raised to the power of 6) in the preceding table you would press 2 then "x^y" then 6 then "=" to get the answer, 64.

In fact, inside many computers, bytes are often combined to form bigger groups such as Words (2 bytes) and LongWords (4 bytes) and QuadWords (8 bytes). Grouping them together in these bigger units allows the representation of far larger numbers. For example, the Word (which, remember, is 2 bytes grouped together):

10000000 00000000

represents a value of 32,768 because only bit 15 is set and 2 ^ 15 = 32768. Another example: The Word:

10000000 00000001

represents a value of 32769 because bits 15 and bit zero are set and 2 ^ 0 = 1 and 2 ^ 15 = 32,768.

There's a lot more to know about how numbers are actually represented inside a computer, but there are very useful Wikipedia pages on that whole subject (start with the "Integer (Computer Science)" article if you want a deep dive into that area). You'll probably be relieved to know that, for the purposes of this discussion on serial transmission, we'll focus only on eight-bit byte values; we won't need to go into anything more complex than that!

The Trouble with Parallel

Given that we know that data are stored inside eight-bit bytes, it would seem sensible to move whole bytes around at a time. For example, suppose we wanted to connect two nearby devices together so that we could transfer data between them.

Intuitively, it would seem sensible to connect an eight-way cable between them and blast byte after byte over the eight connecting wires of a parallel cable, as depicted in Figure D-1. This would be fast and pretty simple to do. Many printers used to be interfaced to computers using pretty much this parallel data arrangement, and it is still used in specialized circumstances.

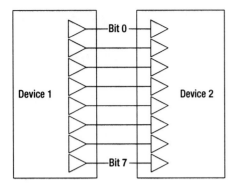

Figure D-1. *Parallel data transfer over eight-way cable*

However, parallel data transfer schemes suffer from some distinct disadvantages.

- Suppose our two devices are microcontroller chips. Using this scheme means that we have to dedicate eight of our precious I/O pins on each chip, just to this single purpose.

- Circuit board layouts are complicated by having to accommodate eight PCB wires to the PCB edge. There also have to be eight-way connectors at each end of the connection, and suitable connectors can be quite large by modern standards. Both factors add expense and complexity.

- If the eight-way cable is any longer than a couple of feet (60 cm) and the data rate across the cable is above the 20 MHz range, data transfer can begin to get unreliable due to:

  - Crosstalk between the wires in the cable. Crosstalk is a phenomenon in which the electromagnetic energy from one wire is induced onto one or more adjacent wires in the cable, thus changing or obscuring the signal that the adjacent wire is supposed to be carrying.

  - Signal "skew," in which signals rise, stabilize and fall at slightly different rates at the receiving end, due to minute differences in the capacitance of each wire in the cable. This can sometimes result in the receiver reading a logic high as a logic low, or vice versa. This effect is hard to engineer out of an arrangement where the data pulse lengths on the cable are, at a data rate of 20 Mbytes/second, less than 50 nanoseconds (that is 0.00000005 seconds) long.

- Very high-grade cables, additional checking electronics, and alternative cable insulating and screening arrangements have all been used to mitigate these problems. The problem is that such fixes can result in unacceptable increases in the size, complexity or cost of products (often, all three).

Tear It Down, Ship It Out!

The alternative to parallel data transfer between devices is serial transfer. There are very many schemes for implementing serial data transfer: this explanation concentrates only on the ones that are most applicable to AVR project work.

The first method is asynchronous serial transfer. In this method, there is only one wire required to send data because, to send one byte of data, the sender places each bit of the byte on the wire, in a prearranged order, for a predetermined amount of time after transmission begins. The most commonly known asynchronous serial device is the serial port on your desktop machine (if it has one; they are becoming rare now), but most AVR microcontroller chips have a serial port, and some have more than one (or can be configured to provide more than one).

If required, you can connect the serial ports of two AVR microcontroller chips together, as shown in Figure D-2.

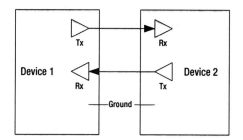

Figure D-2. *Send and receive paths between devices*

In this arrangement, the transmit (TX) wire of each device is connected to the receive (RX) of the other and they share a common ground connection. When used in this way, the signaling voltages used are normal logic levels, that is, between 0V and +5V (see Appendix B). Both serial ports have to be set to operate at the same speed, so that when one is sending data, the other one can receive it correctly.

In the AVR context, a serial port is a chunk of electronics inside the AVR that our software can control, read from, or write to. We usually use the SERIAL object in the Arduino Programming environment to access it. The serial port hardware inside AVR performs all the timing and synchronization tasks about to be described.[1] This means that our project software and hardware designs don't usually need to be concerned with the minutiae of managing serial transfer. However, we do need to understand the underlying technology so that if things go wrong, we can understand error conditions that might arise and rectify them more easily.

Let's now look in detail at how this asynchronous transmission method actually works.

Asynchronous Data Transmission

Asynchronous transmission relies on the sending and receiving serial ports running at exactly the same rate. In the case of AVR microcontrollers, we can set the data rate to one of the standard rates (in this example we use "9600 baud") by using the following Arduino Programming line:

```
Serial.Begin(9600);
```

The port at the receiver has to be set to the same speed, or no valid data transfer will occur; if they are set to different speeds, only gibberish will be received at the far end (if anything at all).

---

[1]There are also free software libraries for use with the Arduino Programming environment that allow normal I/O pins to be used as additional serial ports. This would in theory allow your AVR to have multiple serial ports implemented in a mix of hardware and software. See the Arduino library downloads page for details on libraries, and the Arduino help page on the "SERIAL" object for more details on multiple serial port usage.

What exactly is the baud rate? It defines the number of bits per second that will be sent and received over the serial connection. To put it another way, it allows the participating devices to know precisely how long the transmission of each bit of data (the "bit-slot") will be.

At 9600 bits per second, each bit-slot will be:

```
1 Second ÷ 9600 = 104.16 microseconds
```

As long as both the sender and receiver devices know the precise moment when transmission begins, they can both use their highly accurate internal timers to advance transmission or reception of the data at the same instant (the end of each bit-slot time), until all the data bits have been processed.

Figure D-3 provides a general illustration of what happens during the transmission of a single byte from the TX of one AVR (device 1) to the RX of the other (device 2). In this example we will be sending a byte containing the value 70 (0100 0110 in binary) between the two microcontrollers.

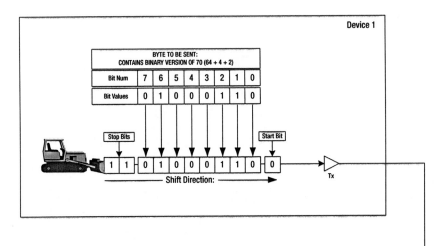
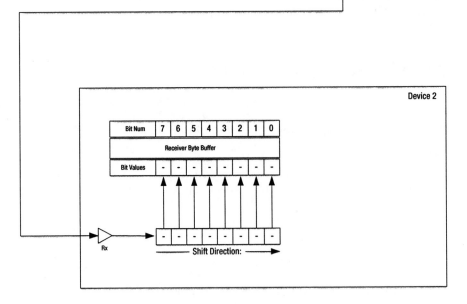

Figure D-3. *Asynch serial transmission illustration*

In summary:

- We have a byte containing a binary value of 0100 0110 to send from device 1 to device 2.

- The byte contents are copied into a transmitter buffer, which also contains space for some extra bits, a start and two stop bits (see Figure D-4, below).

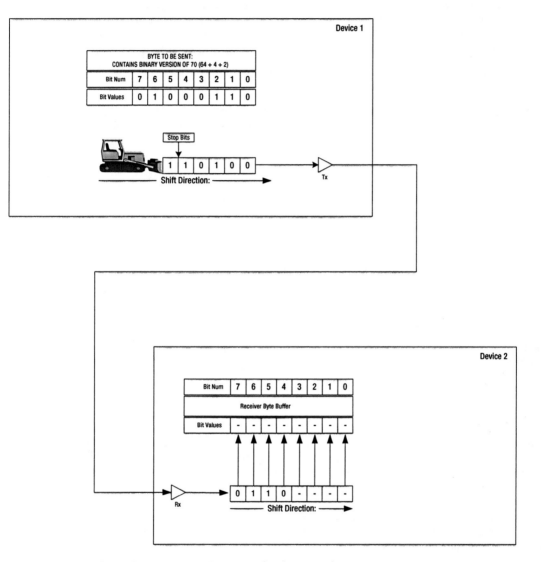

Figure D-4. *Asynch serial transmission illustration (halfway done)*

- The transmission begins (and each device's bit-slot timing clock begins) from the moment the start bit is placed on the TX line. The TX line is normally held at a logic HIGH. This is called its "marking" state. When the start bit is placed on the TX line, both devices start their bit-slot timers–and are thus in synchronism. It's a bit like a starting pistol that both devices can hear being fired!

- At the end of the slot-time for the start bit, the sending device moves bit zero of the actual byte to be sent onto the TX line. About halfway through this bit-slot time, device 2 reads the state of the TX line and places the value (in this case it will be a 0, because that's the value of the least significant bit in the byte we're sending) into a received data register.

- At the end of the bit-slot time for the least significant bit, the sender places the next bit on the TX line, the receiver reads its value halfway through that bit-slot, and so it goes on.

- Figure D-4 shows how things will look after four bits of the payload have been sent in this fashion. As you can see, although the receiver read the start bit, it has not saved it anywhere. However, bits 0 to 3 of the payload byte have been shifted into the receiver's RX line buffer and bit 4 is now in transfer.

- The steps detailed previously repeat, until all eight bits of the payload byte have been transferred.

- After the most significant bit (bit 7) of the byte has been sent, the sender sends a further two bits, these are called the "Stop bits" (see section below) and they are always ones. The receiver reads these two bits and makes sure they are indeed both received as ones (HIGH). If, for any reason, either stop bit is not received as a one, then the receiver declares a "framing error" and the received byte should be discarded as corrupted.

- When the entire byte has been received, and the receiver has validated the required stop bits, it transfers the received byte into its receiver buffer, at which point it becomes available to the kind of programs we will be using in the projects in this book, via the Serial.Read facility provided by the Arduino software.

Stop Bits

The stop bits serve two purposes. They allow the receiver to do a sanity check on the received data. Since these must be ones, if they arrive as zeroes, something is obviously wrong! The other purpose is that where multiple bytes are being sent one after the other (which is much more generally the case than our single byte send example) they represent a return of the TX line to its "marking" state, ready for the next start bit to trigger a new byte transmission.[2] Since sender and receiver restart their bit-slot timings at reception of each new start bit, they are resynchronized very frequently, ensuring that their bit timings do not drift from one another to any fatal degree.

If you have ever had to set up serial ports on a desktop machine you will know that the number of stop bits is usually a configurable parameter; it can be either one or two. Microcontroller systems and desktop machines almost always configure two stop bits.

---

[2]The duration of the final stop bit must be at least one and a half times the bit-slot length, but it can be as long as the transmitter wants. The receiver, however, must be ready for another start bit within one and a half times the bit-slot length, in case the transmitter wants to proceed straight into the next byte's start bit.

Word Length

In our example, we showed the transfer of an eight-bit byte. It is possible to configure serial channels to transfer only seven-bit values. This is still useful if all you want to do is send or receive the letters and characters in American Standard Code for Information Interchange (ASCII), which is a seven-bit character set (just put "ASCII" into a search engine to see a list of character codes it supports).

Parity Checking and Error Detection

When only seven-bit values are being sent over a serial link, the eighth bit can be used for an additional error checking mechanism called parity checking. Parity checking comes in two flavors: even and odd parity. For even parity, the parity bit is set to a 1 if the number of 1 s in the transmitted byte (which does not include the parity bit) is odd. This is called even parity because if there are an odd number of bits set to 1 in the data byte, the parity bit being set brings the tally of 1 s to an even number.

If you use odd parity, the opposite happens. The parity bit is set only if there is an even number of 1 s in the sent byte–and, of course, setting the parity bit to a 1 makes the total number of 1 s odd. The idea is that if any one of the bits arrives at the receiver in error, the parity bit setting is unlikely to match the parity flag value and the receiver can know that the received data is likely to be wrong.

Parity checking is only a very basic method of error checking; it only takes the inversion of any two bits in the sent byte to make everything seem okay at the receiving end. Furthermore, by using the eighth bit of the byte for a parity flag, you lose one-eighth of the potential throughput of your serial channel.

In MCU-land, seven-bit usage of serial ports is almost unheard of because we need our serial channels to transfer full eight-bit bytes, so we set our serial channels to eight bits, with no parity. Error checking, if it's done at all, is usually done at a higher level, using checksums within packets of data. See Chapter 6 for more details in these general areas.

Protocol Overhead

It's worth noting that–in our example–we transferred 8 bits of actual payload data, but with the start bit and the two stop bits, what actually went over the wire was 11 bits. The collective name for the necessary extra bits is protocol overhead.

In the case where we are sending one start bit, 8 data bits, and two stop bits, the protocol overhead is 3 bits out of every 11–or about 27 %. This means that at a baud rate of 9600 you cannot, in fact, send 9600 bits of actual per second.[3] If you need to use a serial port for transferring significant amounts of data, it's worth remembering to factor in the protocol overhead to any throughput predictions or assumptions you may make–or else you may end up scratching your head about the perceived under-performance of your serial link!

■ **Important Note**   Don't *ever* connect your AVR chip's serial port pins directly to your desktop computer's serial port. You will very likely fry your AVR chip and it's likely that you will damage your desktop machine.

Okay, So Tell Me About RS-232 and RS-485

The serial ports we have looked at, so far, have been dealing only in the voltage levels that logic chips such as AVRs use. In such circuits a HIGH (or a "1") is represented by about +5V, and a LOW by anything under

---

[3]Due to various factors, such as interrupt latency, buffering delays, and many other issues, it's never possible to attain the full data transfer rate that the baud rate might seem to indicate. I always derate by at least 40% to be realistic. That is, at 9600 I would expect a microcontroller serial port carrying out continuous activity to shift, perhaps, 5KB/second.

about +1.8V: Using these voltages for serial communication between chips on a circuit board, or between two circuit boards separated by a distance or just a few inches, works very well and errors are rare.

However, very often there is a need for a longer separation between sender and receiver—for example, when two AVRs must talk to one another between rooms or between buildings. It turns out that our logic level signals don't work too well for longer cable lengths. For various reasons the error rates in the transmitted data rise markedly when cable runs get longer than four to five feet: in a very noisy electrical environment, usually when close to machines or appliances that use a lot of power, or powerful radio devices, data transmission errors may happen, even on short runs.

The need to connect serially connected devices to one another over long distances is not a new one. It's been a requirement since the 1960s. Indeed, the serial data transmission method that we looked at in the preceding section was originally worked out to allow typewritery machines called teletypes (you sometimes see them in very old movies) to talk to early computers. Of course, being entirely mechanical, they seldom worked at any baud rate faster than 110, but I digress!

By the early 1960s, the need to link serially connected devices that were not co-located spawned a new standard called RS-232. The key thing about RS-232 is that the signals from the logic circuits are transformed into higher voltages for transit along the transmission line, and then back again to logic level signals at the receiving end. This improves noise immunity and allows serial transmission between sender and receiver devices that are not adjacent to one another.

Specifically, in RS-232 transmission,

- A logic one (HIGH) travels over the interconnecting cable as a negative voltage: this voltage can be anywhere between –3V and –15V. Most usually, it is set to around –12V but not always.

- A logic zero (LOW) travels over the interconnecting cable as a positive voltage: this voltage can be anywhere between, yes you guessed it, +3 and +15V. Again, +12V is most usually used.

Having these much bigger voltage swings on the cable gives the signals more immunity against noise from electromagnetic interference and also protects better against voltage loss down a long cable run. The nine-pin D-connector serial ports found on older desktop machines, and some older printers, all used RS-232 signaling—which is why you should never directly connect the serial pins of your AVR chip to such a port.

Even today, in applications where only small amounts of data need to be transferred, RS-232 (or its successor RS-423, which although it works similarly, uses much smaller connectors) is still in widespread use. For example, medical, retail, military, and transport equipment still uses RS-232 or RS-423 as its interface, because it offers better noise immunity than more modern alternatives such as USB or Firewire (though, of course, those are far faster interconnects). In MCU-land, RS-232 also still has its uses, as you'll see from some of the examples in this book.

RS-232, then, is intended to facilitate asynchronous serial communication from point to point by converting the logic voltages into higher, more noise immune, signals and then back to logic signals again at the receiving end.

Another standard, much used in automation systems of various kinds, is RS-485 which is intended to be used in a multidrop environment. In other words, RS-485 connections are not point to point; you can daisy-chain RS-485-connected devices together on one shared circuit. Unlike RS-232, RS-485 uses terminating resistors at each end of the shared cable run to promote noise immunity.

Logic level serial ports simply connect to RS-485 driver chips, which do the required voltage level shifting, and turn the signals back to logical levels at the receiving end. Serial port handling on an RS-485 network is a little more complex, though, because serial transmission is over a shared pathway, the RS-485 bus. When two devices try to talk at the same time on that bus, data will be lost. This means that—unless data loss is not a problem for the application—the software driving the serial ports has to be able to implement methods to ensure data delivery, such as a resending capability and an acknowledgements scheme for received packets.

We won't need to use RS-485 in this book, but many other AVR projects do use it. RS-485 is gradually being replaced by newer technologies—such as CAN (Controller Area Networks)—but it remains in wide use in such places as automated factories, automated warehouses, and TV and radio studios as well as in military equipment of various kinds.

Are There Other Types of Serial Data Interface?

There are many other serial data interconnects and interfaces. USB, for example, carries serial data (though it uses a different protocol from the one we examined earlier), as does Firewire. Then there's SATA . . .

If you look inside a computer made before about 2002, you will find that the hard drives and optical drives are connected to the motherboard via flat, wide, ribbon cables. These will be ATA (which stands for AT Attachment), though it's now often called PATA–for Parallel ATA) cables. ATA used a 16-bit parallel data transfer method, similar to the one we discussed previously in this appendix, with all the attendant problems that brings.

When it became apparent that the storage devices in commodity IT kit needed faster interconnects, it proved problematic to make faster versions of ATA at a price point that the industry and consumers were willing to bear; enter SATA.

SATA (Serial ATA) is based on ATA, but uses serial data transmission to move data between storage devices (mainly hard drives, but also DVD-ROMS or Blu-Ray drives) and computer motherboards. SATA is intended only for short-haul serial connections: it imposes a one meter (39 inches) maximum cable length.

Although SATA is a serial interface standard, it operates completely differently to the serial interfaces we looked at previously. Being primarily intended as a storage interconnect, SATA is a lot faster too. As of this writing there have been three SATA standards, SATA 1.0 through SATA 3.0. These are all backward compatible and all use the same physical connectors: in other words, a SATA 3.0 port will still recognize and connect to a SATA 1.0 hard drive.

These three levels of SATA connections offer raw data transfer rates as follows (notice these are Bytes, not Bits, per second, multiply by ten to see the bit rates):

- SATA 1.0: 150MB per second.

- SATA 2.0: 300MB per second.

- SATA 3.0: 600MB per second.

As with all raw transfer rates, these are absolute maximum figures that can never be truly attained in a real system. However, SATA is far faster than the older IDE, ATA, and PATA standards that it replaced because it overcame the problems of parallel data interfaces by reinventing serial data transmission for the modern era.

SATA, USB, and Firewire together rescued the idea of serial data transfer, a technique which, at one point, seemed to have had its day. Sadly, since we do not use spinning storage devices in this book, we do not use SATA for any of the projects.

Index

■ **B**

C

D

■ U, V

■ W, X, Y, Z

CPSIA information can be obtained
at www.ICGtesting.com
Printed in the USA
LVOW09s0751100318
569384LV00015B/143/P